Regional Hegemons

Regional Hegemons

Threat Perception and Strategic Response

EDITED BY

David J. Myers

Routledge
Taylor & Francis Group
LONDON AND NEW YORK

First published 1991 by Westview Press

Published 2019 by Routledge
52 Vanderbilt Avenue, New York, NY 10017
2 Park Square, Milton Park, Abingdon, Oxon OX14 4RN

Routledge is an imprint of the Taylor & Francis Group, an informa business

Library of Congress Cataloging-in-Publication Data
Regional hegemons : threat perception and strategic response / edited by David J. Myers.
p. cm.
Includes bibliographical references and index.
ISBN 0-8133-8155-X
1. Regionalism (International organization). 2. Developing countries—National security. 3. Iraq-Kuwait Crisis, 1990–
I. Myers, David J.
JX1979.R3918 1991
327.1'14—dc20 **91-6736**
CIP

ISBN 13: 978-0-367-28546-3 (hbk)
ISBN 13: 978-0-367-30092-0 (pbk)

Contents

Contents

Preface

The bitter U.S. experience in Vietnam and the pain inflicted on the Soviet Union by its Afghanistan adventure have caused Washington and Moscow to rethink the costs and benefits of unilateral military intervention on behalf of threatened clients, especially in the third world. Also, as the Cold War winds down, the crusading spirit that has driven superpower competition since the end of World War II appears increasingly anachronistic. Expenditures by the superpowers in pursuit of military superiority, or even to ensure parity, are now criticized for the security they do not provide or for detracting from economic growth. The latter criticism has grown in importance as the U.S. economy has confronted new challenges from Japan and Germany and as the Soviet economy struggles to avoid collapse. Thus when Saddam Hussein's August 1990 invasion of Kuwait challenged the political and economic status quo in the oil-rich Middle East, neither the United States nor the Soviet Union responded unilaterally. Cooperatively they crafted an international consensus to confront the challenge.

The Persian Gulf Crisis of 1991 was perhaps the most dramatic of many recent events underscoring the need to move beyond preoccupation with bipolarity and superpower competition. The relative decline in U.S. and Soviet power since the middle 1970s has mandated an examination of alternative international relations paradigms. In this context an important pioneering effort was the volume edited by Rodney W. Jones and Steven A. Hildreth, *Emerging Powers: Defense and Security in the Third World.*[1] Jones and Hildreth analyzed the new importance of states whose interests had been overridden or submerged in the bipolar international order; their concerns led me to organize a panel on "Threat Perception and Strategic Response of the Regional Powers" for the 1988 annual conference of the Northeast Political Science Association at Providence, Rhode Island.

This volume is an outgrowth of that panel. It begins with the premise that the late twentieth-century decline in capability (most notably that of the United States and the Soviet Union) to project power simultaneously into several major geopolitical arenas has permitted governments desirous of special local influence to pursue long-suppressed aspirations. The volume's focus is on a distinctive kind of regional international system, one possessing a powerful state with aspirations of regional hegemony. Discussion and analysis probe how such states perceive threats to their regional aspirations and respond to them. Significant differences emerge in how perceptions crystallize and how responses are chosen; they appear to depend, in large measure, on whether the aspirants are superpowers, pariahs or upwardly mobile third-world states.

There are three parts to this study. The first, an overview chapter, pulls together the most important thinking about threat perception and strategic response. The second, the volume's core, revolves around seven regional international systems in which a powerful state seeks special influence. These are: the Caribbean Basin (United States); Southern Africa (South Africa); the Middle East (Israel); South Asia (India); Southeast Asia (China); South America (Brazil); and West Africa (Nigeria). The concluding chapter integrates into a broad, interactive model the overview and insights from examination of the seven hegemon-centered, regional international systems. In so doing it identifies and analyzes the critical structures and processes common to aspiring regional hegemon threat perception and strategic response. Also discussed are the most important differences between superpower aspirants, pariah aspirants and third-world aspiring hegemons. This analysis contributes toward revitalization of an orientation that is especially helpful for understanding international structure and processes as bipolarity dissolves.

Edited volumes demand close and sustained cooperation between editor and contributors. This study was no exception; individual chapter authors commented generously in ways that improved the integrating framework. Any shortcomings that remain, however, are the responsibility of the editor. Special thanks are due to Dean David Palermo of the Penn State University College of Liberal Arts Research Office and the Department of Political Science. Their funding, of assistance for content analysis, travel, and manuscript preparation, made this volume possible. Carol Spotts is to be commended for her care in preparing the manuscript. I also would like to acknowledge the editorial assistance of Hillary Pops and the encouragement of acquisitions editor Peter Kracht, both of Westview Press. Finally, I owe much to my wife, Cynthia Theresa Myers. Her support and interest in the project speeded it to completion, and it is to her that I dedicate this volume.

David J. Myers

Notes

1. Westport, CT: Greenwood/Praeger, 1986.

1

Threat Perception and Strategic Response of the Regional Hegemons: A Conceptual Overview

David J. Myers

The global character of World War II focused international politics on issues that transcended local balances of power. There was some recognition that regional issues and perspectives remained important, but they were viewed as second-order problems. During the 1970s, however, limited wars and low-intensity conflicts revealed unanticipated limits on the exercise of superpower influence. Neither Washington nor Moscow seemed capable of simultaneously dominating more than a few regional or subordinate state systems. As of July 1990, at the Houston economic summit, the situation had changed so dramatically that an aid to President George Bush bluntly proclaimed "The age of the superpowers is obviously over."[1] While perhaps premature, this outburst confirmed that regional power balances had become newly important for understanding international politics and making effective foreign policy. However, the trend away from a tight bipolar world has been evident for some time. A growing body of work already discusses and analyzes subordinate state system politics in the most important regional geopolitical arenas.[2]

Regional geopolitical systems crystallize when over time the actions of states suggest that their foreign policy elites (and those of most external powers) perceive that a system does indeed exist. Role theorists would term this agreement on one of many international positions (or series of international prescriptions) and assign each nation a corresponding status in relation to it.[3] During the 1960s, some widely recognized regional international systems became battlegrounds in the global competition between the United States and the Soviet Union to gain allies and control natural resources. Most notable were the Middle East and Southeast Asia. Others served as secure preserves facilitating the global projection of superpower influence. In this latter context, the Caribbean Basin and Eastern Europe immediately come to mind.

Third World nationalism has complicated the exercise of economic and political influence by the superpowers. Also, continuing military stalemate between the United States and the Soviet Union has constrained each in its attempt to influence by military means. When armed force has been employed, domestic constraints interacted with international limitations to complicate its effective use. Washington and Moscow have seen the costs of using force so escalate that, in the long run, military solutions appear cost effective in only a few circumstances. The most obvious confirmations of military deployment's negative cost-benefit ratio have been the courses of United States involvement in Vietnam and Soviet intervention in Afghanistan.

Decline in superpower capability to project effective power uniformly around the planet has permitted influential regional states to pursue long-suppressed hegemonic aspirations within local geopolitical arenas. Policy makers for these regional or "aspiring" regional hegemons face new opportunities and problems. Among the most important is that of crafting mutually acceptable relationships with the still-influential superpowers. Some aspiring hegemons have sought to exclude the superpowers entirely; they perceive any intrusion of superpower influence into their sphere of influence as threatening. Other aspiring hegemons have entered into alliances with one or the other superpower in order to consolidate regional hegemony, or to prevent a rival state from so doing.

For one variant of the subordinate state system, the most obvious examples being Eastern Europe and the Caribbean Basin between 1948 and 1989, special regional influence is exercised by a superpower. Here no local state is able by itself to challenge the superpower/hegemon. In both, however, the resident superpower/hegemon (the United States in the former and the Soviet Union in the latter) found itself concerned that the rival superpower would exploit intraregional tensions in order to make the exercise of special influence consume resources which otherwise could be used in the wider superpower competition. Any important initiative by the Soviet Union toward the Caribbean Basin or by the United States toward Eastern Europe, therefore, was viewed by the other superpower/hegemon not only as a threat to its regional hegemony, but also to its position in the global balance of power. Even given these global concerns, the role of the superpowers as regional hegemons (between 1948 and 1989) within the Caribbean Basin and Eastern Europe appeared conceptually distinct from that of global superpower. Inside of the aforementioned regions, the United States and the Soviet Union enjoyed many of the prerogatives to which an India aspires in South Asia or a Brazil in South America.

This volume focuses on how powerful states desirous of special influence within a subordinate state system respond toward threats to their hegemonic positions or aspirations. Threat, when discussed by international relations theorists, usually is given one of two meanings. The first views threat as a "communication or an undertaking by one actor to impose sanctions on another." This meaning fits the traditional international politics definition of threat as a "declaration of or an intention to inflict punishment, injury, death or loss upon in retaliation for, or conditionally upon, some action or course." In the second meaning, threat is considered simply a perception of danger. Cohen defines this second alternative as "an anticipation on the part of an observer, the decision maker, of impending harm—usually of a military, strategic or economic kind—to the state."[4] These two meanings also can be grasped by taking into account, as does Klas Knorr, that threats either may be "actual," that is inferred from more or less definite signals or intent, or potential, that is, inferred from some state of the environment or the mere capability of an opponent.[5]

Distinguishing conceptually between these two kinds of threats is basic. *To divide perception/anticipation of danger from potential threat comes close to differentiating between long-range threat perception and crisis threat perception.* In focusing on perception of threat to position or influence within a hegemon or aspiring hegemon's geopolitical sphere of influence, concern here is with long range threat perception. We will look at anticipations by the observer/decision makers of the regional or aspiring hegemons of an impending harm—usually of a military-strategic, political or economic kind, to their state.

The contributions of role theory is highly relevant for this purpose. Role theorists seek to explain perceived threats in terms of policy makers' conceptions of the roles which their state is capable of playing. They would point out that aspiring regional hegemons experiencing a threat to their regional position would conceptualize events and behavior as somehow jeopardizing their capability to act out regional leadership roles.[6]

Analyzing perceptions of potential threats to regional hegemons or aspiring regional hegemons, and their strategic responses to those threats, involves exploring the following research questions: (1) What are the major elements and operational characteristics of the most important regional state systems? (2) Under what circumstances do states perceive the existence of a potential threat to their interests from sources inside of the regional system in which they exercise or aspire to exercise hegemony?, (3) When do states perceive threats to their hegemonic interests from sources outside of the region?, and (4) How do aspiring hegemons respond to these threat perceptions?

This introduction identifies the common concerns and potentially important differences which the threat perception literature discusses. Use of the terms "common concerns" and "potentially important differences," rather than the more elegant "theoretical framework," implies that analysts have yet to elaborate on an integrated theory of when and why regional hegemons perceive threats to their positions and aspirations; also lacking is a theory of strategic response to those threats. Subsequent chapters will examine the components of threat perception and the patterns of strategic response in the most important subordinate state systems having an aspiring regional hegemon. A concluding chapter profiles similarities and differences in the politics of hegemonic aspirations. However, two obvious aspiring hegemon-centered regions, the North Atlantic and Eastern Europe are omitted. Their status as primary and adjacent arenas of superpower conflict has given the exercise of hegemonic influence within them a cast that is significantly different from politics in other hegemon-centered regional systems. While the waning of the cold war is setting in motion an evolution that may make subordinate state system politics in the North Atlantic and Eastern Europe less unique, these changes have yet to crystallize.

To repeat the purpose of this volume is twofold. It looks to advance middle range theorizing about hegemon-centered subordinate state systems. It also seeks to clarify and analyze regional international relations for policy makers in ways that provide helpful and non obvious insights.

Elements and Operational Characteristics of Regional State Systems

Some consensus exists about which elements comprise the global international system. States, nationalities, international organizations and transnational corporations are the most important, commonly accepted units of analysis. In contrast, given the many alternatives, potential definitions and groupings, even determining the identity of subordinate or regional systems is difficult and complex. This study begins by identifying the components and most prominent examples of regional or subordinate international systems which contain either a hegemon or an influential state with aspirations to create a special sphere of influence. Four important kinds of actors are found in hegemon-oriented regional systems: (1) the hegemon or aspiring hegemon, (2) bargainers, (3) peripheral dependents, and (4) external challengers. Each merits further exploration.

Regional hegemons are states which possess power sufficient to dominate a subordinate state system. Holsti's exploration of role theory suggests that states aspiring to special regional influence possess a strong self-conception as a regional leader or protector and command multi-dimensional power.[7] Three dimensions of power appear especially relevant: the material, the military and the motivational. Power sufficient to dominate is, of course, relative. A state "weak" in terms of the power exercised by a Venezuela or Belgium would be capable theoretically of dominating a regional system if all other members were third world microstates. However, the intrusive potential of states possessing sufficient power to be categorized as a "primary power" or "secondary power" probably makes the concept of regional hegemony meaningless unless the state aspiring to its exercise ranks at least as a "middle power."[8] Also, should most states in a regional system be "middle" or "secondary" powers, only a "primary" or "superpower"—for example, the United States in the North Atlantic—realistically could aspire to exercise hegemony. The most obvious examples of subordinate state systems with hegemons, as suggested earlier, are the United States in the Circum-Caribbean and the Soviet Union in Eastern Europe.[9] On the other hand, many third world or "southern" states pursue hegemonic aspirations within geopolitical arenas located in Asia, Africa, South America and the Middle East.

A second central actor in hegemonic or proto-hegemonic regional systems are states possessing sufficient power to bargain effectively with the hegemon or aspiring hegemon. Such states will be referred to as "bargainers." To draw upon the language of role theory, a bargainer appears to approximate the role conception of active independent, independent, and to a lesser extent that of balancer.[10] An important marking trait of all bargainers, therefore, is their capability—within the relevant subordinate state system—to make the costs of exercising influence significant for the aspiring hegemon when it seeks to impose its will in the face of bargainer state opposition. At a minimum, bargainers possess the capability to refract material, military, and motivational power projected from the hegemon or aspiring hegemon of its region.[11]

Regional systems also include "peripheral dependents." Peripheral dependents, unlike bargainers, possess little capability to refract power projected by their region's hegemon or aspiring hegemon. They also lack the national attributes to act out such bargainer state roles as active independent and balancer; thus they are left to pursue self-conceptions such as regional collaborator.[12] Peripheral dependents are sometimes microstates; they are often linguistically, culturally or religiously distinct from others in the region.

Finally, all subordinate state systems are influenced by power projected from external challengers. Role theorists portray external challengers as part of "alter" (as opposed to ego), while describing the preferences of external challengers (as to ego's behavior) as "role prescriptions."[13] For those regions in which they are unable to exercise or aspire to hegemony, the superpowers are the most obvious external challengers. Superpower influence, as evidenced by the Soviet Union's alliance with Cuba, may permeate even into geopolitical arenas within which the rival superpower aspires to hegemony.

Aspiring regional hegemons (for example, India in South Asia and China in Southeast Asia), pursue a broad range of strategies to discourage the superpowers from projecting power into their special regional preserves. Playing one superpower's fears off against those of the other is common. On the other hand, regional hegemons occasionally attempt to inject superpower influence into the region over which they seek special influence. This occurs when the aspiring hegemon calculates that a superpower's presence will strengthen its position in relation to the regional system's "bargainer" states. Israel's use of the United States in the Middle East, and Syrian cooperation with the Soviet Union, are obvious examples of this strategy.

In the developing world, aspiring regional hegemons sometimes seek to improve their capabilities by drawing upon resources or technology transferred from a "bargainer" belonging to a subordinate system composed of industrialized states. Industrial and technological sophistication allows an industrialized state of the second or third magnitude within its own region to exert a strong influence upon the local balance of power inside of African, Middle Eastern, South American, and to a lesser extent Asian regional systems.[14] Thus the global structure of usable power, and the interrelatedness of economic activity, places serious limitations on the aspirations of any developing state seeking to dominate a major subordinate geopolitical arena.

Nine regions contain states with realistic possibilities of exercising local hegemony. They are profiled in Table 1.1. Differences in the levels of power prevailing within each of these geopolitical arenas, as suggested earlier, constrain or facilitate the ability of the superpowers—and external secondary and middle powers—to exercise influence within the nine. As the twenty-first century approaches, these differences will lead to increasing autonomy for the more powerful, especially if nuclear stalemate, distrust of government and relative economic decline continue to undermine the ability of the United States and the Soviet Union to project power globally.

The nine regional systems of Table 1.1 share several central operational characteristics. First, is the presumption by member states, and generally

TABLE 1.1 Aspiring Regional Hegemons and Subordinate State Systems

Subordinate State System	Hegemon or Aspiring Hegemon	Bargainer	Peripheral Dependents	External Challenger
North Atlantic	United States	United Kingdom France W. Germany* Italy Spain Canada Turkey	Belgium Denmark Greece Iceland Luxemburg Netherlands Norway Portugal Sweden Switzerland	U.S.S.R.
Circum-Caribbean	United States	Colombia Cuba Guatemala Mexico Venezuela	Antilles Belize Costa Rica Grenada Guyana Dominican Republic El Salvador Haiti Honduras Jamaica Nicaragua Panama Suriname Trinidad	U.S.S.R. W. Germany* France Britain

(Continues)

TABLE 1.1 (Continued)

Subordinate State System	Hegemon or Aspiring Hegemon	Bargainer	Peripheral Dependents	External Challenger
Eastern Europe	U.S.S.R.	Poland E. Germany* Hungary Bulgaria Romania Yugoslavia	Albania	U.S.A. China W. Germany* France
Middle East	Israel	Egypt Jordan Iraq Lebanon Libya Iran Syria Saudi Arabia	P.L.O.	U.S.A. U.S.S.R. Iran Turkey
Southern Africa	South Africa	Angola Madagascar Mozambique Zambia Zimbabwe	Botswana Lesotho Namibia Swaziland	U.S.A. U.S.S.R. Cuba Britain Zaire
South Asia	India	Bangladesh Burma Pakistan Sri Lanka	Bhutan Nepal	China U.S.A. U.S.S.R.

TABLE 1.1 (Continued)

Subordinate State System	Hegemon or Aspiring Hegemon	Bargainer	Peripheral Dependents	External Challenger
Southeast Asia	China	Burma Indonesia Malasia Philippines Taiwan Vietnam	Cambodia Hong Kong Laos Macao Singapore	Japan U.S.A. U.S.S.R. Britain
South America	Brazil	Argentina Colombia Chile Ecuador Peru Venezuela	Bolivia Cayenne Guyana Malvinas Paraguay Suriname Uruguay	U.S.A. U.S.S.R. Britain W. Germany* France Japan
West Africa	Nigeria	Cameroon Ghana Ivory Coast	Benin Chad Niger Togo	France Libya South Africa

*prior to the reunification of 1990

recognized by other international actors, that together states within a region possess enough in common to warrant treatment as a discernible regional system. Second is the capacity as a subordinate state system to refract power projected: (1) from either superpower, (2) from any alliance of non-member states or, (3) from an international organization. Third, there must be some degree of geographical propinquity among states within the region.[15] Finally, some additional characteristics may not be shared by all nine regional systems. For the North Atlantic and Eastern Europe, as suggested earlier, they are significantly central to justify exclusion from this volume. For the remaining seven, characteristics will be identified and analyzed.

Concerning the first operational characteristic, a regional system can be said to exist when governments perceive that a grouping of states displays a significantly higher level of cohesion among members, in comparison with that prevailing between members and non-members. Cohesion encompasses a socio-cultural, an economic and a politico-organizational dimension. On occasion, special circumstances may dictate that for short periods a member state of a regional system will have especially intensive interaction with a non-member state along one or more of the above dimensions. Should this intense interaction overshadow relationships with other members of the regional system for a prolonged period, it would be legitimate to ask whether or not the state in question had forfeited membership in the subordinate state system to which it initially belonged.

In order to attain international significance, regional systems must be able to refract power projected by external actors from the larger global environment. Underlying the notion of refraction is an assumption that members of the regional system, linked by a feeling of community or distinctiveness, will react to intrasystemic and intersystemic stimuli primarily in terms of their position within the regional system; in other words, with a view to the effects of their response on their interest and position within that system.[16]

Finally, high levels of intraregional cohesion and configurative capability to refract power projected from the global international system seem in fact to be spatially concentrated.[17] While the necessity of this third operational characteristic may be open to challenge, there is no example of a successful hegemonic or proto-hegemonic subordinate state system coalescing without some generally contiguous territorial identification area. The British Commonwealth of Nations was the most notable example of an unsuccessful attempt to construct a hegemonic subordinate state system along dimensions which excluded the regional territorial identification condition. This shortcoming was one of several important reasons why the Commonwealth failed to preserve an international political sphere over which Great Britain could exercise meaningful hegemony.

Perceptions by Hegemons and Aspiring Hegemons of Threats to Their Interests: Inside the Regional State System

Theory views two kinds of factors internal to the regional state system as determining how hegemons perceive threats to their sphere of influence aspirations. First are intervening predispositions. Intervening predispositions cause decision makers to become more or less sensitive to information about threats and potential threats.[18] Intervening predispositions include: the predetermined expectations and mind set of decision makers in the hegemon or aspiring hegemon; the "lessons" of the hegemon or aspiring hegemon's past experience with other states in the region; the perceptions of elites and masses in the regional hegemon or aspiring hegemon concerning the present state of affairs in the region; and the structures, procedures, and purposes of the foreign and national security policy making bureaucracies in the regional hegemon or aspiring hegemon. Second, threat perception is influenced when foreign and national security policy makers receive information that threatening situations are continuing, or dissipating, or crystallizing. Threatening situations can be military, political, or economic in character; they also may contain elements of all three.

Predispositions That Intervene in Intraregional Threat Perception

The predetermined expectations and mind set of policy makers in aspiring regional hegemons may raise or lower receptivity toward threatening information. Predetermined expectations and mind set encompasses a broad range of phenomenon. In this context, three factors merit special consideration: the pariah state role perception, the impact of early sociopolitical experiences upon policy makers, and personality.

States such as Israel and South Africa appear as pariahs to their neighbors.[19] Arabs have challenged Israel's right to exist since she emerged as an independent entity in 1947. Blacks in Southern Africa view South Africa's racist policies as so odious that they invalidate any claim that the Pretoria government might advance as a legitimate repository of political authority. Therefore, ruling elites in Israel and South Africa seek military hegemony within their respective regions in order to survive. Pariah status positively predisposes them toward threatening information originating within the subordinate state system of which they are a part.

The socio-economic origins and path to power of the elite in a regional hegemon or aspiring hegemon also predisposes toward acceptance or denigration of information about threats from neighboring states.[20] Acceptance or magnification is most likely when the ruling elite's ideology and world view are at odds with those whose intentions are being assessed. On the other hand, threatening information originating in bargainer states whose rulers possess socio-economic backgrounds and world views similar to those of the information receiving elites will be downplayed, at least initially.

In revolutionary societies, political elites from the historic ruling class normally have been displaced. If the ruling class in neighboring states enjoyed a camaraderie with their ousted counterparts, they will tend to view the new regime's rulers as enemies. Consequently, policy makers in traditionalist regional hegemons or aspiring hegemons will perceive efforts by new elites to protect their revolution as undermining the ability of traditionalist policy makers to project power throughout their historic sphere of influence. Traditional elites within a hegemon also may view neighboring revolutions as threatening their own domestic power position. Fear reinforces their hostile predisposition toward the revolutionaries. However, if the state experiencing revolution is the regional hegemon, and if other states in the region continue under the domination of their historic ruling class, revolutionary policy makers in the regional hegemon appear similarly predisposed to view the activities of their traditionalist neighbors as threatening. However, not surprisingly, the magnitude of the threat perceived by hegemons and aspiring hegemons from bargainer states is less than what a bargainer state feels in relation to the hegemon.[21]

Finally, emotional and personality factors predispose policy makers to take seriously or dismiss threats. The predisposing consequences of emotional and personality factors are most usefully analyzed on a case by case basis.[22] Individuals with an inclination to vacillate, for example, will be likely to underestimate threats if threat recognition would demand bold action. On the other hand, policy makers with authoritarian personalities tend to be intolerant of elites in neighboring states who even tangentially threaten their state's position or aspirations. In an essay on foreign policy role orientations, Margaret Herman develops an even more exhaustive account of these linkages. She sets forth the central relationships between the personality traits of leaders and policy role orientations. Six traits (nationalism, efficacy, need for power, need for affiliation, conceptual complexity and distrust) are related in varying degrees to six role orientations (expansionist, active independent, influential, mediator-integrator, opportunist, and developmental).[23]

The past experiences of a hegemon or aspiring hegemon with other states in its region also predispose policy makers either to downplay or overestimate threatening information.[24] In this context, the first important consideration involves whether one state ever has employed armed force against the other. If the hegemon and a neighbor went to war in the past, armed confrontation in the future will be perceived by policy planners in both as more likely than if relations had always been peaceful. Second, throughout the developing world there are situations in which relations between states sharing largely vacant border areas have been almost non-existent. Toward such a neighbor, an aspiring hegemon appears predisposed not to act in an alarmist manner. Finally, some studies suggest that experience, interacting with calculations concerning the probability of maximizing the most favorable outcome (exchange theory), determine how nations choose between alternative role conceptions.[25] They imply that predispositions towards recognizing regional threats vary according to past experiences insofar as the consequences of adopting some regional roles are ranked against the consequences of adopting others.

Perceptions by the hegemon's foreign and national defense policy makers concerning the present state of affairs within the region also raises or lowers responsiveness to threats originating inside of the subordinate state system. Here four situations seem especially significant. First, overt declarations of hostility are obvious and difficult to ignore.[26] Leaders in a hegemon or aspiring hegemon will be highly sensitive to threats or potential threats emanating from bargainer states which have declared themselves openly antagonistic to the hegemon's strategic position, policies, and aspirations. In estimating the magnitude of threat implicit in this antagonism, however, hegemon policy makers take into account the hostile state's capabilities. A hegemon or aspiring hegemon obviously will consider enmity from neighboring states possessing greater power capabilities to be more threatening. Relevant power capabilities in this context, as suggested earlier, are military, economic and political.

An important qualifying condition in this context is the inclination of challenger and peripheral dependent states to form alliances with powerful external states. The incorporation of external states by bargainers and peripheral dependents is normally viewed by the aspiring hegemon as undercutting its capability to exert special regional influence. Also, perceptions that balances or trends in the sphere of actual or desired influence are shifting unfavorably add to the anxiety of aspiring hegemon policy makers.[27] It increases their predisposition to give credence to intraregional threats when danger is emanating from a state perceived as gaining in relation to the aspiring hegemon along an important dimension of power.

The final group of factors predisposing an aspiring hegemon to view threats from within its sphere of influence as important or unimportant relate to the structure, standard operating procedures, and purposes of its foreign and national security policy making bureaucracies. Analysis of structure suggests that decision processes that depend on achieving a consensus from decentralized bureaucracies tend to underestimate threats. This is the consequence of inputs from numerous rival institutions creating an inertia that predisposes against decisive action; it was described in "Model II" of *Essence of Decision*, Graham Allison's analysis of the 1962 Cuban missile crisis.[28]

Analyzing how the purposes of bureaucracies influence threat perception predispositions involves looking at the resources which bureaucracies can bring to bear when responding to threats.[29] The armed forces, for example, will be predisposed toward taking the lead when threats appear amenable to military solutions which lie within their capabilities. While armed force has the advantage of being subject to rapid employment, it has the disadvantage, especially for democracies, of inviting mass demonstrations against authority unless there is a broad consensus that the application of military force is justified. Consequently, military planners tend to magnify threats to the state. Diplomats, on the other hand, possess negotiating skills. Their inclination is to define threat in a manner that makes it amenable to negotiations. This often requires underplaying its potential for damage to the position of the hegemon within the region. Similarly, bureaucracies with economic capabilities will frame threats so as to orient policy makers toward employing economic instruments such as foreign aid and trade agreements. Finally, other special interests which are given an opportunity to participate in foreign and national security policy making also will be predisposed to define, magnify and downplay threats in a manner which does not adversely affect their narrow interests.

Receipt of Information That Threatening Situations Are Continuing, Dissipating or Crystallizing

To this point, we have explored how predispositions shape threat perception in the filtering of the threat containing information received by policy makers. The nature of the threat revealed in the information being processed through predispositional filters also determines the magnitude of seriousness assigned to the threat.[30] Therefore, a hegemon's perception of threat from inside the regional system is the outcome of a two stage process in which a regional bargainer state or states emit threatening information. This information then passes through the predispositional filters of the regional hegemon's policy makers, after which it may be recognized as a threat. Threats are perceived as primarily military, political or economic, and evoke varying degrees of concern.

Military threats present the clearest dangers. They require planning for the contingency that armed forces from within the region may be employed to challenge the exercise of special influence. Political threats are more ambiguous. The sense of danger associated with political threats usually is less intense; among policy makers there is often disagreement about the extent to which any specific political threat should be considered a matter of urgent concern. Finally, two world wars in the twentieth century demonstrated that capability to project influence is tied closely to a state's industrial base, its command of technology, and its access to strategic resources. Threats that are primarily economic increasingly appear capable of diminishing ability to exercise subordinate state system influence.

Four specific situations or developments within a subordinate state system lend themselves toward being interpreted by the hegemon as having militarily threatening overtones; (1) territorial disputes, (2) creation of a domestic arms industry, (3) acquisition of additional weapons by bargainer states, and (4) new deployments of military forces by a bargainer state.[31] Most obviously, claims on territory which a hegemon or aspiring hegemon has incorporated into its homeland, and which a neighboring state believes rightfully belongs to it, fall into the first category. As long as a hegemon's national security planners view a state with which it has a territorial dispute as possessing significant military capability, the hegemon will feel militarily threatened. In this situation the hegemon's policy makers will attach great significance to matters which, in the absence of conflicting territorial claims, might be viewed as only marginally threatening. Also, territorial disputes make states highly sensitive to any shift in the intraregional military balance. If the state perceived to have improved its position in such a shift were one which harbored a territorial grievance against the hegemon, the hegemon's sense of threat would be magnified.

The upgrading of a neighboring state's arms production capabilities is the second condition that may increase perceptions of military threat on the part of a hegemon or aspiring hegemon. Should the weapons produced carry with them the potential to reduce a hegemon's military advantage over its neighbor, threat perception by the hegemon of the producer state will be particularly intense. As suggested above, threat perception rises exponentially if nuclear weapons are involved. The willingness of a producing state to supply others in the region with arms is the third military factor which may crystallize threat perceptions.

If the intent of supplying the arms is interpreted by a hegemon as a reduction in its influence within the subordinate state system, the supplier state will be viewed as actively hostile. Countermeasures will be attempted even if the deployed arms do not directly threaten the hegemon's home territory.

An important determinant of whether domestic arms production in bargainer states will be perceived as threatening by a regional hegemon derives from the preconceptions of hegemon policy makers about how responsibly elites in the bargainer state have behaved in the past, and whether they will be useful and reliable allies for whatever the hegemon may have in mind beyond the region. If an arms industry is developed or upgraded by bargainer state elites in whom hegemon policy makers have confidence, and whom they view as probable allies in the larger international arena, it is unlikely their arms industry will be considered threatening.

A related strategy by which bargainer states can increase their military capabilities relative to those of the hegemon or aspiring hegemon is to purchase sophisticated arms from an industrially advanced state.[32] One important drawback to this strategy, however, is that states supplying arms often attempt to condition sales upon some desired modification in the international or domestic policies of the recipient state.

If, in the eyes of the hegemon, the external power supplying arms to a bargainer state is hostile, perceptions of threat associated with arms acquisition will be magnified. United States concerns with Soviet arms in Cuba is perhaps the most obvious example of how arms transfer from a hostile intrusive power can magnify a hegemon's threat perceptions. On the other hand, if the external state selling weapons is viewed as friendly by the aspiring hegemon, threat perceptions deriving from the transfer of arms to a bargainer state will be diminished.

Finally, a hegemon's perceptions of threat may intensify when neighboring states deploy their military forces. Deployment takes place most commonly in war games or maneuvers. While maneuvers are necessary to test military readiness, they may also be planned to intimidate or deter another bargainer state within the region. If the bargainer state deploying its forces possesses significant military power in comparison with that of the hegemon, even though the hegemon is not the object of the war game or deployment, its policy makers tend to perceive them as threatening. A hegemon's concern would intensify should one bargainer state actually intervene militarily in another; intervention would appear as a breakdown of the hegemon-sanctioned regional order. It might also be viewed by the hegemonic power as an attempt by the bargainer to increase its capability to frustrate hegemon policy within the region. Only the threat of a direct military attack upon the hegemon itself would be of greater concern than an unfolding of the aforementioned scenario.[33]

Political threats to a hegemon or aspiring hegemon also may become matters of great concern. Obviously they are less immediately dangerous than direct military threats. Four political conditions or developments within the subordinate state system are commonly perceived as threatening by hegemons:[34] (1) a sharp increase of political instability in a neighboring state, (2) a change in the ideological orientation of a neighboring state to one which is hostile toward the elites and/or hegemonic position of the regional hegemon, (3) accumulation of evidence within the hegemon itself that an ideology hostile to the governing elite is attracting support, and (4) the crystallization of an alliance between a neighboring bargainer and a powerful state from outside of the region. These political threats will be explored in the regional chapters.

The defense of hegemon economic interests within the subordinate state system is critical.[35] Any relative increase in the economic capabilities of a bargainer state, especially if the bargainer's production competes with that of the hegemon, will be viewed as potentially threatening. Neighboring states usually constitute important markets for goods produced by the hegemon, and their loss may lead to increased domestic unemployment. Historically, rising unemployment has been a primary source of political instability. A politically unstable hegemon forfeits much of its capability to project power beyond its borders. In addition, any shrinkage in economic capability relative to neighboring states reduces the capacity of the hegemon or aspiring hegemon to impose its preferences within the region.

Sustained advances in a bargainer's economy may be perceived as threatening because expansion is viewed as evidence of growing technological sophistication. Sophisticated technology is the foundation of modern military power, and its mastery by a bargainer state forces the regional hegemon to rethink its strategy of regional domination.[36] From a different perspective, illegal migration into the aspiring hegemon by the poor and unskilled of neighboring states may undermine economic stability inside of the aspiring hegemon. The government is forced to direct scarce resources into managing the flow of immigrants. Illegal immigrants compete for jobs with the aspiring hegemon's least skilled workers[37]; and, the new arrivals may become a political force acting against the hegemon's efforts to influence the neighboring states in which the immigration originated.

The process analyzed above has a great deal in common with how threats from the more encompassing international environment are perceived. Nevertheless, there are important differences. Attention now shifts to the process of threat perception crystallization that occurs external to the subordinate state system.

Perceptions by Hegemons and Aspiring Hegemons of Threats to Their Hegemony: The Larger International System

The high cost to the superpowers of intervening directly and simultaneously in more than one subordinate state system, as noted earlier, is a necessary condition for the exercise of regional hegemony by states in Asia, Africa and South America. However, should either superpower concentrate on any regional geopolitical arena, each remains capable of bringing greater military power to bear than any aspiring regional hegemon. In addition, industrial states with medium sized populations—Germany, Britain, France, Italy and Japan—can project power, under specific conditions, into third world subordinate state systems sufficient to undercut the local aspiring hegemon.[38] Consequently, aspiring hegemons in these regions are highly sensitive to threats from the larger international environment. At the height of the Cold War this was also true for the Soviet Union in regard to Eastern Europe and the United States in the North Atlantic and the Caribbean Basin.

As with potential threats originating inside the regional state system, two factors determine how a state perceives external threats to its hegemonic designs. Again, they are intervening predispositions and the receipt of information that threatening situations are intensifying, remaining constant or dissipating.

Intervening Predispositions and the Perception of Threats Arising in the Larger International System

The categories of intervening predispositions are essentially the same for external threats as for ones internal to a subordinate state system. To review, these include: the mind set of a hegemon's national security policy makers; the lessons they learned in dealings with external states and forces; hegemon policy makers' perceptions concerning the capabilities and inclination of forces in the larger international arena to intervene inside the region; and, the structures, procedures and purposes of a hegemon's foreign and national security policy making bureaucracies. Turning to the first, again it is helpful to focus on the pariah state syndrome, the impact of early socio-political experiences, and personality.

Hegemons seen as pariahs by their neighbors will, to an important degree, be perceived similarly by the larger international community.[39] Thus pariah states with hegemonic aspirations become apprehensive over cooperative arrangements involving outside states and bargainer states within their desired sphere of influence. When agreements with an external state strengthen a neighbor's military or political capabilities, they will be seen as especially threatening. Also, the pariah hegemon often interprets new tensions between itself and an external state as evidence that the antagonist is interested in allying itself with a hostile neighboring bargainer state. On the other hand, pariah states often attempt to increase capability in relation to their neighbors by seeking out cooperative arrangements with friendly and powerful states in the larger international system.

In external assessments, as in those internal to the subordinate state system, the socio-economic origins and path to power of a hegemon's elite predisposes it toward perceiving or not perceiving a development as threatening. New revolutionary regimes initially tend to view states ruled by ideologically compatible elites as supportive of their efforts to achieve or exercise regional hegemony.[40] States within which their defeated rivals' ideology continues to legitimate the political order are perceived as hostile. Turning to the impact of impact of emotions and personality on threat perception from the larger international arena, these also do not appear to be appreciably different from what was discussed in relation to intrasystem dynamics. In contrast, the impact of past experiences with states outside of the region merits special attention. It is helpful in this context to separate those regional systems in which the aspiring hegemon is a superpower from ones in which it is not.

Washington and Moscow, as suggested earlier, have identified Eastern Europe, the North Atlantic and the Caribbean Basin as spheres of special interest. Because of their global reach, the superpowers can use allies in the larger international system to assist in the exercise of regional hegemony. When international rivalry between Washington and Moscow was at its height, each was predisposed to interpret the erosion of influence in these special regions, especially the former two, as the consequence of conspiracy by the other.[41] This predisposition denigrated information that regional problems derived from long-standing, internal antagonisms. In other words, suspicions based on post World War II rivalry colored threat perceptions in Washington and Moscow when it came to interpreting new trends and developments in Eastern Europe and the North Atlantic. This additional atypicality is another reason for not examining these regions in this context.

The other regional state systems identified in this essay once were controlled by colonial powers. While South America broke the chains of Spanish and Portuguese domination more than one hundred and sixty years ago, the Europeans retreated from Africa and Asia only after 1945. Throughout the former African and Asian colonies, vestiges of

European imperial cultures, as well as European economic and political institutions, remain. Elites in the states which replaced the colonial empires presently are torn between the need to strengthen ties with their former masters, in order to acquire industrial technology, and fears that once again they may lose control over their destinies. Controlling one's destiny has been interpreted by the most influential of the new states to include an exercise of special prerogatives in geopolitical regions adjacent to their national heartland.

Love-hate feelings toward the industrial states, evoked by the aforementioned needs/fears conflict underlie orientations which often result in inconsistencies when interpreting threatening information from the larger international system. For example, an aspiring hegemon may invite an advanced industrial power to transfer technology in order to strengthen its capability to project power within its subordinate state system; however, at the same time the transfer increases dependency. Initially dependency may be overlooked because of euphoria derived from the acquisition of new capabilities. Once the limitations imposed by increased dependency begin to manifest themselves, they appear highly threatening.[42]

Aspiring regional hegemons which have become unexpectedly dependent may see their new condition as more than offsetting the advantages gained through technology transfer. Especially if dependency circumscribes capability for regional power projection, the aspiring hegemon's elites may turn antagonistic and bitter toward the "offending" industrial states. This circumscription and related fears predispose aspiring hegemons throughout the third world toward magnification of threat potential when assessing the dangers of economic penetration by institutions based in the industrial states.

The third intervening predisposition again involves the aspiring hegemon's perceptions of forces whose reach is global. In former colonial areas, conflicting territorial claims involving vestiges of the imperial power's empire may facilitate potentially threatening intrusions of outside force.[43] An aspiring regional hegemon may be directly involved—the case of India in regard to Goa; or conflict may break out between a bargainer state and a former imperial power—the case of Argentina and Britain in the April 1982 Falkland Islands conflict. Because most vestiges of empire have been transferred to local states, this kind of threat will be of declining importance during the 1990s.

Finally, as in the case of threats originating inside of a subordinate state system, interpretations of danger from the larger international arena will be influenced by predispositions derived from the procedures and purposes of the foreign and national security policy making bureaucracies. Again, analysis must take into account the resources which each bureaucracy commands when responding to threats. Here it is enlightening to expand on earlier comments about the predisposition of military planners to magnify threats to the state. In Africa, Asia and South America, with the possible exception of China, the aspiring hegemons have yet to develop integrated nuclear weapons and weapons delivery systems. Consequently, they lack the capability to deter by military means either superpower—or even a medium nuclear power, such as Britain or France—should a confrontation develop that involves an interest which the third world hegemon defines as critical.

Information from the Global Arena Which Hegemons Perceive as Threatening to Their Aspirations or Position Within the Regional State System

Threatening information from the larger international system can be predominately military, political or economic. Militarily, the creation by an outside power of forces, especially nuclear ones, targeted on a region usually is perceived as a threat by the aspiring hegemon and its local allies. Actual military deployment into the region appears even more alarming. Two modes of deployment are common: maneuvers as a show of force and combat operations against a subordinate state system member. However, pariah state perceptions may be different. Outcast status sometimes forces the pariah to seek out militarily powerful allies in the larger international system and encourage them to project power into the region. This choice would be intended to deter hostile neighbors.

Political events originating in the larger international system often appear as threatening to a regional power's hegemonic aspirations. First, special significance is assigned to the appearance of political instability in states which border on the region over which hegemony is desired. Instability along the regional frontier has the potential of spilling over into the hegemon's realm, forcing it to expend resources in influence preserving stabilization operations. Also, efforts by outsiders to integrate bargainers into a transnational organization over which the hegemon has marginal influence normally is viewed as an unwelcome reduction in regional influence by hegemon policy makers. Finally, powerful states tend to oppose the intrusion of global collective security institutions into the geopolitical arenas over which they aspire to special influence. Article 52 of the United Nations charter reflects this opposition. Imposed by the great powers, it affirms the need for regional international organizations to act as institutions of first resort in resolving local threats to the peace.[44]

Economic messages are the final category of information from the larger international system which crystallize perceptions of threat to sphere of influence designs. While third world states no longer worry about the possibility that the United States or a European nation might employ military force to collect debts, loans by the industrialized to the developing countries remain an important fact of international life. Indebtedness reduces the capability of Asian, African and Latin American states to influence their neighbors. Therefore, policy makers in these countries treat as threatening economic decisions in the industrialized countries that weaken their ability to project power, especially in the subordinate state system to which they belong. For aspiring third world hegemons, this is especially true if industrial country demands constrict economic growth and raise unemployment.

Information about technological advances may also be perceived as threatening. National security elites appear especially predisposed to believe that somehow new technology has either direct or indirect military applications.[45] Even if this turns out not to be the case, new technologies often present those possessing them with economic advantages which strengthen their competitive international position. Also, when a state desires military capabilities to influence events beyond its borders, certain critical industries must be nurtured, even if they are not competitive. Critical military-related industries include metals, shipbuilding, aviation, electronics, computers and automobiles. Hegemons and aspiring hegemons will treat as threatening evidence that their capability in any of the above is eroding.

At this point, the synthesizing capabilities of role theory facilitate a useful summary. Aspiring regional hegemons (or, nations placing a high value on leadership and security roles within a regional "position") perceive and weigh threats as prescribed by two factors: predispositions to regional threats (including determinant components in role conception development, such as leadership, personality traits and past experiences); and, the types of threats (military, political or economic). Concurrently, aspiring hegemons are situated internationally (or in a "position" or "status" external to the regional subsystem). Threat perception in the external realm operates analogously to threat perception within the regional system. Thus, aspiring hegemons must balance at least two threat perception systems (or, two "positions" or "role prescription systems") when choosing a strategic response. Strategic responses to these systems of threat perception comprise the final focus of this introduction.

Strategic Responses by States Toward Challenges to Their Hegemonic Aspirations

The concern of this study, to repeat, is on threats to hegemonic influence and aspirations; it does not deal with all international challenges faced by regional hegemons. When the hegemon is also a superpower, it is especially important to distinguish efforts to exercise regional dominance from those which are intended primarily to pursue broader global interests. It is obvious, however, that as a component of global strategy, each superpower may seek to undermine its rival within the subordinate state system over which it exercises hegemony.

Strategic responses to threats against regional hegemony are long term. Some options for dealing with immediate threats, surrender and attack, for example, are not relevant in the strategic context. Policy makers dealing with medium or long term threats to regional hegemony generally consider four options or strategic responses. They are: accommodating, deterrence through defense or allying, state strengthening, and counterthreat. These can be pursued individually or in concert.[46]

Accommodation

This response is defined as those acts of one-sided concession that are taken by a hegemon or aspiring hegemon to preserve some measure of influence over a regional state system in order to avoid making increased provisions for deterrence by defense or to win clients inside of the region. Accommodation can be seen, from a role perspective, as the hegemon's choice of its international, as opposed to regional, "position" or "status." Concessions to preserve some measure of regional influence would seem the likely response of aspiring hegemons in Asia, Africa or South America, especially when their regional systems become the focus of superpower competition.

Deterrence Through Defense and Allying

The response of deterrence through defense is well documented. It involves reconfiguring available resources, often those which are predominantly military, in order to deal more effectively with perceived threats. In contrast to the role choices involved in accommodation, the deterrence option pursues regional, as opposed to international, role conceptions. In this context, as has been noted previously, concern is with threats to hegemonic aspirations within subordinate state systems.

Allying, in contrast to defense through deterrence, involves a hegemon in cooperative relationships with other states. Its great advantage is that it allows the hegemon to protect its position while expending less of its own wealth and energy than if the response were unilateral. Also, in some cases, the alliance seeking hegemon is not strong enough by itself to neutralize the threat to which it is responding. Whether an allying response is one among several available options, or the only realistic choice, its selection mandates acceptance by the hegemon of a fundamental constraint: the interests of the state being courted. If the courted bargainer state possesses sufficient power to make a major difference in the hegemon's ability to manage a threat, and should it be part of a regional system over which the aspiring hegemon seeks hegemony, the aspiring hegemon will be forced to modify or disguise its intentions. Until the immediate threat subsides, the aspiring hegemon must treat its new ally as a partner rather than a client.

For aspiring hegemons in South America, Africa, the Middle East and Asia, the United States and the Soviet Union—despite their overwhelming military power—are not allies of first choice. As suggested earlier, fears of imperialism and claims about the universal desirability of Soviet and American life styles reduce the attractiveness of allying with either superpower. The two pariah hegemons, however, appear more willing than other aspiring regional powers to enter into such an alliance. They view the protection that the United States and the Soviet Union can provide as more than offsetting the risks that universalistic ideologies might set in motion unwelcome domestic changes.

State Strengthening

State strengthening, a long term response, is pursued when danger appears to be intensifying, or when a threatening situation seems likely to persist into the indefinite future. Like deterrence, state strengthening is a choice to emphasize domestic over international role conceptions. State strengthening may be attempted along three dimensions; political, economic and military. The most common political manifestation of state strengthening involves the suppression or neutralization of political opponents by the government. It is often accompanied by state centralization. Officials justify stifling dissent on the grounds that unity is necessary for the state to protect itself. The suppression-destruction response is most easily implemented in states lacking a tradition of tolerance, especially when the threat to hegemonic aspiration can be presented credibly as a threat to core national values. Opponents of the official line thus appear as subversives whose suppression is justified in the national interest. Because of advances in information management, it is now possible to implement a suppression-neutralization response more efficiently than at any time since the modern state emerged.[47]

It has become a truism during the twentieth century that a state's ability to defend its international interests is highly correlated with the relative sophistication of its economic and technological infrastructure. Military inferiority related to technological backwardness causes aspiring hegemons in South America, Africa and Asia to be highly sensitive to the economic dimensions of state strengthening. Technology transfer and industrialization have been the preferred economic state strengthening responses. The use of tariffs to protect local markets also is common. In addition, government has made credits available to local entrepreneurs interested in developing strategic industries or itself established state corporations for this purpose.[48] State corporations have even searched internationally for the strategic minerals on which an aspiring hegemon's heavy industry depended. Finally, dispersing strategic industry and relocating population also reflect economic considerations; however, they are even more manifestations of state strengthening's military dimension.

The strategic nuclear capabilities of the superpowers, while best understood as a manifestation of global competition, also have important consequences for regional international relations. Since the late 1970s, especially throughout Asia, South America and Africa, aspirations for local hegemony by important regional states had an increased impact on international affairs because of the strategic military parity prevailing between the Soviet Union and the United States. As either superpower could inflict unacceptable damage on the other, their strategic nuclear weapons were viewed as unusable. Local military superiority took on new importance as a facilitator of power projection within subordinate systems. The acquisition of conventional arms received a high priority. However, technologically advanced weaponry was increasingly expensive and difficult to obtain. This gave rise to the final state strengthening military response, development of a conventional arms manufacturing capability.[49]

Counterthreats

These can be either positive or negative. Positive counterthreats intimidate; they are promises of actions that will sanction the state from which danger is perceived. Positive counterthreats include warnings that military forces may be deployed, that an arms race may be initiated, that other potentially counterthreatening state capabilities will be increased, and that hostile alliances may be pursued. Negative counterthreats, on the other hand, communicate that the threatened hegemon will not follow policies nor act in ways which the state perceived as the source of the threat desires or values. Negative counterthreats would include warnings that technology might not be transferred, that export purchases might be suspended, or that valued treaties between the two states might be terminated. The role approach allows one to conceive of counterthreats as attempts to recreate one's "position" or "status" by offering "alter" the chance to revise its prescriptions, normally by creating a hypothetical (or imaginary) position.

Thus, the goal of counterthreats is to alter threatening behavior without actually having to carry out the counterthreat.[50] Bluff is a critical component of the counterthreat response. However, unless policy makers in the state against which counterthreats are directed believe that there is a significant probability that they will be sanctioned, the counterthreat response has little impact on threatening behavior. Linkages between threat perceptions and counterthreats, especially in the context of analyzing perceptions of long term threats, have been largely ignored by social scientists. Subsequent chapters will look at these linkages, as well at those between other kinds of responses which aspiring hegemons perceive as threatening to their subordinate state system aspirations. To summarize, the thrust of this volume discusses and analyzes the dynamics set in motion by the threat perceptions and strategic responses of those seeking to preserve or attain regional spheres of influence.

Notes

1. *New York Times,* July 12, 1990.

2. See the highly suggestive "Preface" and "Introduction" of Louis J. Cantori and Steven L. Spiegel, *The International Politics of Regions* (Englewood Cliffs, N.J.: Prentice Hall, Inc., 1970). Also, Joseph S. Nye, ed., *International Regionalism* (Boston: Little, Brown and Company, 1968); Bruce Russett, *International Regions and the International System: A Study in Political Ecology* (Chicago: Rand McNally and Company, 1967); Jaynti Prasad Garg, *Regionalism in International Politics* (Delhi, India; Research Association, n.d.); Leonard Binder, "The Middle East Subordinate International System," *World Politics,* Vol. XI (April 1958), pp. 408–429; Kal Kaiser, "The Interaction of Regional Subsystems: Some Preliminary Notes on Recurrent Patterns and the Role of Superpowers," *World Politics,* Vol. XXI (October 1968), pp. 84–104; "International Relations and Asian Studies: The Subordinate State System of Asia," *World Politics,* Vol. XV (January 1963), pp. 212–235; Larry W. Bowman, "The Subordinate State System of Southern Africa," *International Studies Quarterly,* Vol. XII (September 1968), pp. 231–262; and William Zimmerman, "Hierarchical Regional Systems and the Politics of System Boundaries," *International Organization,* Vol. XXVI (1972), pp. 18–36.

3. K. J. Holsti, "Toward a Theory of Foreign Policy: Making the Case for Role Analysis," in Steven Walker, ed., *Role Theory and Foreign Policy Analysis* (Durham: Duke University Press, 1987), pp. 8, 11.

4. Raymond Cohen, *Threat Perception in International Crisis* (Seattle: University of Washington Press, 1979), p. 4.

5. Klaus Knorr, "Threat Perception" in Klaus Knorr, ed., *Historical Dimensions of National Security* (Lawrence, KA: University of Kansas Press, 1976), p. 78.

6. The entire volume of Walker, ed., *Role Theory,* is an account of the resurgence of role theory in foreign policy analysis. Holsti, "Toward a Theory of Foreign Policy: Making the Case for Role Analysis," p. 21, describes seventeen role conceptions, including those of regional leader and regional protector; also, pp. 85–86 elucidate the process by which nations balance competing role conceptions

(e.g. regional roles, as opposed to roles as a faithful ally to a superpower) with the use of exchange theory.

7. Holsti, in Walker, ed., *Role Theory,* p. 21; and in the same volume, Naomi Bailin Wish, "National Attributes as Sources of National Role Conceptions: A Capability-Motivation Model," pp. 95–96.

8. According to Steven Spiegel, during the 1970s, the international hierarchy was broken down into a number of levels. In addition to the two superpowers, there were six secondary or "major" powers: Japan, the United Kingdom, France, China and the Federal Republic of Germany. Brazil, India and fifteen other states placed in the third level as middle powers. Steven Spiegel, *Dominance and Diversity: The International Hierarchy* (Boston: Little, Brown & Co., 1972), pp. 93–94.

9. Zimmerman, in "Hierarchical Regional Systems and the Politics of System Boundaries," Jan Triska, ed., *Dominant Powers and Subordinate States: The United States in Latin America and the Soviet Union in Eastern Europe* (Durham, N.C.: Duke University Press, 1986) pp. 18–19.

10. See the analysis of "level of power" in Louis J. Cantori and Steven Spiegel, "The International Politics of Regions," *Polity,* Vol. 2, No. 4 (1970), pp. 397–425.

11. Holsti, in Walker, ed., *Role Theory,* pp. 21, 25, 27.

12. Wolf Grabendorff, "Interstate Conflict Behavior and Regional Potential for Conflict in Latin America," *Journal of Interamerican Studies and World Affairs,* Vol. 24, No. 3 (August 1982), pp. 285–287.

13. See Holsti, in Walker, ed., *Role Theory* p. 23, for a description of the "regional collaborator" role conception; see also Wish, in that volume, pp. 94–103, for an elaboration of the relationship between national resources and role conceptions.

14. For a useful account in the area of minerals see Heraldo Muñoz, "Strategic Dependency: Relations Between Core Powers and Mineral Exporting Periphery Countries," in Charles Kegley and Pat McGowen, eds., *The Political Economy of Foreign Policy Behavior* (Beverley Hills, CA: Sage Publications, 1982), pp. 191–214.

15. Cf. Kay Boals, "The Concept 'Subordinate International System:' A Critique," in Richard A. Falk and Saul H. Medlovitz, eds., *Regional Politics and World Order* (San Francisco: W.H. Freedman and Co., 1973), pp. 399–411.

16. Ibid., p. 406.

17. Roger D. Masters, "A Multi-bloc Model of the International System," *American Political Science Review,* Vol. 55, No. 4 (December 1961), pp. 783–784.

18. Cohen, *Threat Perception,* pp. 6–7.

19. Robert Harkavy, "The Pariah State Syndrome," *Orbis,* Vol. 21, No. 3, pp. 623–649.

20. For an informative illustration see Ronald Reagan and Alexander Haig, "Soviet Ambitions and Soviet Immorality," in Marvin E. Gettlemlan, et al., *El Salvador: Central America in the New Cold War* (New York: Grove Press, 1981), pp. 6–9.

21. See Arthur Krok's comments on Eisenhower's reaction to the Franco-British invasion of the Suez Canal in 1956. *Memoirs: Sixty Years on the Firing Line* (New York: Funk and Wagnalls, 1968), pp. 291–293.

22. Knorr, ed., *Historical Dimensions,* pp. 113–114.

23. Cohen, *Threat Perception,* pp. 128–132, analyzes the impact of Chamberlain's view of World War I as a conditioning factor in his estimation of the German threat during the late 1930s.

24. Margaret G. Herman, "Foreign Policy Role Orientations and the Quality of Foreign Policy Decisions," in Walker, ed., pp. 124, 125.

25. Walker, ed., *Role Theory,* pp. 85, 86.

26. Reagan and Haig, *Soviet Ambitions,* pp. 7–8; and Cohen, *Threat Perception,* p. 9.

27. See the discussion of Chinese perception of growing Japanese threat in Knorr, ed., *Historical Dimension,* pp. 107–108.

28. Graham Allison, *Essence of Decision* (Boston: Little, Brown & Company, 1971).

29. Knorr, ed., *Historical Dimension,* p. 115.

30. Cohen, *Threat Perception,* p. 9.

31. See the discussion of "Structure of Relations" in Cantori and Spiegel, *The International Politics of Regions,* (Englewood Cliffs, N.J.: Prentice Hall, Inc. 1970), pp. 17–20.

32. For example, David Carleton and Carlo Schaerf, *The Arms Race in the 1980s* (New York: St. Martins Press, 1982).

33. Allen S. Whiting, *China Crosses the Yalu* (Stanford: Stanford University Press, 1968).

34. Confirmation of the importance of these political conditions can be found in the "Core Sector: Readings" section of Cantori and Spiegel, *The International Politics,* pp. 69–149.

35. Joan Spero, *The Politics of International Economic Relations* (New York: St. Martins Press, 1981), pp. 37–73; Robert D. Hormats, "Soviet–West European Natural Gas Pipeline," *Current Policy, U.S. Department of State* (October 14, 1981), pp. 1–5 and E. Kanovsky, "Arab Economic Unity," *The Middle East Journal,* Vol. XXI (Spring 1967).

36. Michael Adas, *Machines as the Measure of Men: Science, Technology and Ideologies of Western Dominance* (Ithaca, N.Y.: Cornell University Press, 1989); and Gail Bridget, "The Arsenal of Inferiority: Halting the De-Industrialization of American Defense," *Armed Forces Journal International* (February 1981), pp. 198–228.

37. "Illegal Aliens and the U.S. Mexico Interface" in Kenneth F. Johnson, *Mexican Democracy: A Critical View* (New York: Praeger Special Studies, 1978), pp. 198–228.

38. For example, see Herbert Goldhammer, *The Foreign Powers in Latin America* (Princeton: Princeton University Press, 1972).

39. Robert S. Jaster, "South Africa," in Jed C. Snyder and Samuel F. Wells, Jr., eds., *Limiting Nuclear Proliferation* (Ballinger: Cambridge, MA, 1985), pp. 146–180.

40. "Epilogue: The Impact of the Sino-Soviet Dispute," in Zbigniew K. Brzezinski, ed., *The Soviet Bloc: Unity and Conflict* (New York: Praeger, 1960), pp. 409–444.

41. cf. William Zimmerman, "Hierarchical Regional Systems and the Politics of System Boundaries," and Roger D. Hanson, *Power, Purpose and Proportion: U.S. Foreign Policy and the Third World Agenda 1982,* (New York: Praeger, 1982), pp. 32–36.

42. G.K. Helleiner, "International Technology Issues: Southern Needs and Northern Responses" in Jairam Ramesh and Charles Weiss, Jr., eds., *Mobilizing Technology for World Development* (New York: Praeger, 1979), pp. 84–97.

43. Bernard Gwertzman, "The Falkland Stakes Are High for Washington Too," *New York Times* (April 18, 1982), Section 4, p. 1.

44. Inis Claude, Jr., "The OAS, the UN and the United States," *International Conciliation,* No. 547 (March 1964), pp. 3–67.

45. Richard D. Delaver, "Stabilizing Our Industrial Base," Defense 81 (December 1981), pp. 25–32.

46. Peter Karsten, "Responses to Threat Perception: Accommodation as Special Case" in Knorr, ed., *Historical Dimensions,* p. 120.

47. Cf. Hadley Cantril, *Soviet Leaders and Mastery over Men* (New Brunswick, N.J.: Rutgers University Press, 1960); and Kenneth Jowitt, "An Organizational Approach to the Study of Political Culture in Marxist-Leninist Systems," *American Political Science Review,* Vol. LXVIII (September 1974), pp. 1171–1191.

48. Kenneth Paul Erickson, "State Entrepreneurship, Energy Policy, and the Political Order in Brazil," in Thomas Bruneau and Philippe Faucher, eds., *Authoritarian Capitalism* (Boulder: Westview Press, 1981), pp. 141–178.

49. Lewis A. Frank, *The Arms Trade in International Relations* (New York: Praeger, 1980).

50. R. Harrison Wagner, "Deterrence and Bargaining," *Journal of Conflict Resolution,* Vol. 26 (June 1982), pp. 329–357.

2

The United States and the Caribbean Basin

G. Pope Atkins

The boundary of the Caribbean Basin in international politics has been perceived by both local and external states to surround the islands of the Caribbean Sea and those nearby in the Atlantic Ocean, the entire Central American isthmus, and the north coast of South America extending to the Atlantic Ocean. The term "Circum-Caribbean" is better descriptive and analytic terminology for this international political-geographic subregion, but the expression "Caribbean Basin" is used in this essay because U.S. policy makers have employed it as their preferred term.

This chapter analyzes U.S. threat perceptions in the Caribbean Basin and the strategic responses to those threats as the United States sought to play the role of regional hegemon. While the region has continuously been the object of great power rivalry, pressure, intervention, and domination, throughout the twentieth century the U.S. presence has been one of the clearest cases of hegemony in the international political system. That hegemony, however, has not been total, constant, or simple, and has had numerous challenges to its assertion. The chapter explores the decisional and perceptual bases for U.S. policies over time; particular attention is paid to the Central American crisis in the decade dating from the Nicaraguan Revolution of 1979, and the subsequent attempt on the part of U.S. decision makers to reorient policies toward the Caribbean in terms of the post-Cold War world and a new set of nontraditional security issues. The aspirations and strategies of certain challengers, bargainers, and dependents are evaluated, including the degree to which they seem to have conformed or not to U.S. perceptions.

Table 2.1 profiles the Caribbean Basin Subordinate State System.

Table 2.1 The Caribbean Basin Subordinate State System

Political Entity	Population (millions) (1990)	Area (sq. km) (thousands)	GDP (US$/billions) (1990)*	Regional Type
United States	250.4	9,372.6	5,233.3*	Hegemon
Soviet Union	290.9	22,402.2	2,659.5*	Hostile External Challenge
Colombia	33.1	1,138.9	35.4*	Regional Challengers
Mexico	87.8	1,932.6	187.0	(Contadora Group)
Panama	2.4	77.1	3.9	
Venezuela	19.7	912.1	52.0	
Cuba	10.6	114.5	20.9	Hostile Local Challenger
Nicaragua	3.7	130.0	1.7	Hostile Local Challenger
W. Germany	62.1	248.6	945.7	European Challenger
France	56.3	547.1	819.6	European Challenger
Netherlands	14.9	40.8	205.9	European Challenger
Spain	39.3	504.8	398.7*	European Challenger
United Kingdom	57.4	240.0	818.0	European Challenger

*GNP

(Continues)

SOURCE: U.S. Central Intelligence Agency, The World Factbook-1990 (Washington, DC: CR WF 90001, 1990).

TABLE 2.1 (Continued)

New States**	Regional Dependents (Sovereign)
Antigua & Barbuda	
Bahamas	"Old States"*
Barbados	Costa Rica
Belize	Dominican Republic
Dominica	El Salvador
Grenada	Guatemala
Guyana	Haiti
Jamaica	Honduras
St. Kitts-Nevis	
St. Lucia	
St. Vincent	Regional Dependents (Nonsovereign)
Suriname	
Trinidad & Tobago	France
	(Overseas Departments)
Netherlands	French Guiana
(Coequal Commonwealth	Guadeloupe
Netherlands Antilles	Martinique
United States	United Kingdom
Commonwealth	(Colonies/Associated States)
Puerto Rico	Anguilla
	Cayman Islands
(Federal Territory)	Montserrat
Virgin Islands	Turks & Caicos

*All but Haiti are Spanish American. Costa Rica, El Salvador, Guatemala, and Honduras have also been Local Challenges (Arias Peace Plan).

**All but Suriname (former Dutch Guiana) comprise the Commonwealth Caribbean Countries (former British colonies).

U.S. Policy Considerations

Threat Perceptions

The concept of threat perceptions is useful as a starting point in describing U.S. orientations toward the Caribbean Basin. U.S. policy, from the earliest days of inter-American relations in the early nineteenth century to the late 1980s, was preoccupied with two major interrelated objectives: the United States saw foreign intrusions and political instability in the Caribbean nations as inimical to its strategic, political, economic, military, and ideological interests (as specifically defined at different times). Consequently, U.S. policy actions first and foremost attempted to prevent and exclude, as far as possible, nonhemispheric influence and control in the Caribbean. From the early nineteenth century into the 1980s, the U.S. leaders feared that part of the Caribbean Basin might serve as a military base of operations against what came to be called its "southern flank." They also feared that hostile political-ideological threats might take such forms as European recolonization, monarchism, fascism, or communism, and competed against the economic influence of other external industrial states. The goal of domestic and international stability in the Caribbean was most often a corollary to the desire to exclude foreign influence, in that the maintenance of stability was presumed to be necessary to reduce foreign intervention in the area. U.S. perceptions of the level of outside threats determined the intensity of its activities in the area. The lack of foreign threats even muted concern about instability, with the United States sometimes choosing the policy option of doing little if anything. The United States usually justified other objectives and more specific goals by linking them to long-term concerns with "foreigners" and instability.

In the late 1980s, as the international political system entered a post-Cold War era, certain global, Latin American regional, and U.S. domestic trends converged to force a fundamental historic change in U.S. orientations toward the Caribbean region. It will be argued later in this essay that U.S. policy makers have discarded the 180-year-old paradigm of strategic denial[1] based on threat perceptions of outsiders and are searching for a new framework to deal with a set of nontraditional security issues emanating from Latin America—the obvious but not exclusive list of categories includes economic questions of the external debt and foreign trade, the illicit traffic in narcotics, dilemmas of immigration and refugee policies, problems of democracy and human rights, and degradation of the environment.

National Roles

The idea of national roles further assists us in understanding U.S. behavior in the Caribbean Basin. The literature on national role analysis, following the early lead of K.J. Holsti,[2] focuses on the general types of decisions, rules, norms, guidelines, standards, commitments, and international functions that decision makers translate into various kinds of actions to be taken when confronted with external challenges. National roles refer to policy makers' views of what the nation-state should do in international relations, based on their perceptions of both the outside world and of their own societies. Role conceptions are the policy makers' definitions of the kinds of commitments and actions considered appropriate in terms of national values within different international contexts. They in effect define national purposes and provide tactical and instrumental guidelines, regarding not only threats from enemies but the nature of other states with whom they interact. Holsti posits some typical national roles that are suggestive of U.S. perceptions of its functions in the Caribbean Basin. They include, for example, the roles of regional defender-leader-policeman protecting other states in a defined area, of mediator assisting in international conflict resolution, and of "protector of the faith" (urging, in this instance, anti-communism and democratic development).

In many ways, it should be noted, U.S. national role conceptions toward the Caribbean reflect traditional sphere of influence calculations in balance of power theory. Only in the Caribbean Basin in its Latin American policies did the United States develop a continuing strategic view. Furthermore, in conjunction with these national role choices, a strain of paternalism ran throughout U.S. policy. It involved the assumption that Caribbean nations were incapable of handling their own affairs, as well as an unwillingness to relinquish the thrust for predominance (the "hegemonic presumption").

Role theory is related to tendencies regarding alignments, as decision makers evaluate the state's place in the international system and choose methods for coping with the external world. Aspects of military alliance and economic and political coalition are taken up below. It should be noted as a general matter that the United States has never been isolationist toward the Caribbean Basin. U.S. isolationism from independence until the end of the nineteenth century, and again in the twentieth century during the period between the two world wars, was relevant primarily to Europe and then in the special sense of political noninvolvement or "nonentanglement." The United States, in fact, was highly active in the Caribbean Basin, including in the nineteenth century prior to its rise to great power status.

Role conceptions ultimately translate into the kinds of actions policy makers decide to take when confronted with various geographic and issue challenges. A state's choice of instruments and tactics may be classified in terms of the degree of multilateralism versus bilateralism and of activism versus passivity. The more active a state, the more likely it is to initiate actions in international relations or to resist initiatives taken by others. An important aspect of activism is how willing decision makers are to use coercion—to intervene in the domestic affairs of other states (through diplomatic, economic, or paramilitary means) or to use armed force to resolve conflicts. U.S. actions in the Caribbean during the 20th century have ranged from imperialism and intervention during the first three decades, to the Good Neighbor Policy of nonintervention and consultation in the 1930s and World War II, a post-war period in which the region was largely ignored, intense interest after the Cuban Revolution of 1959 with the Alliance for Progress and developmentalist policies that ended with a massive military intervention in the Dominican Republic, another decade of neglect beginning in 1968, then a decade of intense activity following the Nicaraguan Revolution of 1979 with a mix of unilateralism, intervention, and a form of developmentalism, and, from the late 1980s into the 1990s, the low-resource attempt to cooperate with Latin America in a series of severe problems. In its Latin American policies, the United States has intervened militarily only in Mexico and the Caribbean Basin, and has never landed its troops for such purposes in South America beyond the Caribbean. The last U.S. military intervention in Mexico was in 1914; the latest in the Caribbean Basin were in Grenada in 1983 and Panama in 1989.

The Internal Political Process

The related concepts of threat perception and national roles are essentially an extension of the "rational actor model" that emphasizes strategic analysis, the requirements for ideal diplomacy, and rational policy formulation and execution. This model must be tempered with the realities of the U.S. domestic political system in order to provide a balanced conception of U.S. policy making in the Caribbean Basin. That is, we must also apply certain aspects of a "political process" model, which subsumes such elements as the constitutional balance, the interaction of government and non-government actors, bureaucratic and organizational politics, and ideologies, perceptions, and idiosyncracies of decision makers. This involves particular reference to the familiar questions of policy conflict and fragmentation versus coordination, accommodation, and bipartisanship.

Policy Evolution

Historically, the United States has been the most active in Caribbean affairs when nonhemispheric states seemed most threatening. Conversely, during periods when threats seemed to be low or nonexistent, the United States became less connected with security goals, sometimes neglecting the region. While national role conceptions remained relatively constant, changes in U.S. policies over time coincided with Caribbean subsystem changes as measured by the redistribution of international power and influence.[3] Domestic political processes had a variable influence over time; they were especially consequential from the late 1970s into the 1990s.

The Caribbean Basin Subsystem and U.S. Policy to 1979

The nineteenth century roughly marked the first era of the Caribbean Basin subsystem. It evolved from the prior Latin American colonial period, from the late fifteenth to the early nineteenth centuries, when colonialism bound the entire Caribbean Basin to European powers. Spanish control of the Caribbean, unlike other parts of the Spanish-American empire, was eroded by other European challengers who acquired territories. Throughout the nineteenth century, the newly independent Spanish American states and Haiti were pawns in European great power rivalry, with close attention on the part of the United States. A significant portion of the region, especially in the Eastern Caribbean, remained in colonial status under Spanish, British, Dutch, French, or Danish rule.

The emergence of new Caribbean states in the nineteenth century stimulated rivalry among the external powers to gain regional influence or control. The United States was relatively weak in relation to the European states; Great Britain was the dominant (but not unchallenged) external actor and held the primary power position in the Caribbean Basin. Nevertheless, the United States early-on made statements laying the historical foundations for traditional policies of strategic denial. In 1811, Great Britain, allied with Spain in Europe and on the verge of war with the United States, threatened to seize Spanish Florida and use it as a military base. In response, the U.S. Congress adopted the No-Transfer Resolution asserting, among other things, that the United States "cannot without serious inquietude see any part of the said territory pass into the hands of any foreign Power." Soon thereafter France, in the name of the Holy Alliance, indicated it would assist Spain in recovering its lost American colonies. This led President James Monroe, in 1823, to enunciate what was later called his doctrine, warning Europe to keep "hands off" the western hemisphere.

Britain discouraged many other power excursions into the area until the turn of the century—it was, in fact, responsible for deterring French actions in 1823—but it was not entirely successful. Central America was of special importance as a potential or actual site of a transisthmian canal, which both Britain and the United States wanted to build and control. The rivalry led Britain to sign the Clayton-Bulwer Treaty with the United States in 1850 in which they agreed that neither would construct or exclusively control a canal. With British and U.S. power neutralized in Central America, a private French company gained a concession from Colombia and began construction of the Panama canal; the project went bankrupt and was abandoned in 1887. In the 1860s Spain briefly reoccupied the Dominican Republic at the latter's request, but was soon forced to depart.

After the turn of the twentieth century, the Caribbean Basin was generally a U.S. sphere of influence. The United States continued to rise in power and Europe to decline, with European capabilities and interests reduced by the effects of two world wars and the interbellum economic depression. The principal exceptions to total U.S. hegemony were the territorial holdings of the United Kingdom, France, the Netherlands, and (until 1917) Denmark; and the Soviet alignment with Cuba after 1960. Nevertheless, U.S. power and influence were the primary realities in Caribbean international politics.

During the first three decades of the twentieth century, the United States presumed hegemony in the Caribbean Basin. The U.S. war with Spain in 1898 forced the end of the Spanish American empire and signalled U.S. emergence as a great power. The United Kingdom retired from competition to dominate the area but kept its territorial holdings and commercial interests; other European states clung to their small colonies, except for Denmark, which sold its Virgin Islands to the United States in 1917. Washington assumed a new role of international policeman in the Caribbean Basin and converted most of the area into a bilateral trade area. President Theodore Roosevelt assisted Panamanian revolutionaries to gain national independence from Colombia in 1902 and then attained canal rights from and a dominant position in the new state. U.S. construction of the Panama Canal was undertaken and the waterway opened to traffic in 1914. Unilateral U.S. interventions were designed to preempt similar European actions and to enforce stability in the environs of the new Panama Canal, considered vital to U.S. strategic interests. By the 1920s, as a result of U.S. assertiveness in the Caribbean and European exhaustion in the wake of World War I, all real and imagined extrahemispheric threats to the primary U.S. position had disappeared.

The period from 1929 to the end of World War II contrasted sharply with the previous period in that U.S. intervention was first reduced and then, after 1933 under the Good Neighbor Policy, formally renounced in multilateral inter-American treaties. The change came at a time when no serious outside threats to U.S. hegemony existed. With the subsequent rise of Fascist governments in Europe and their increased activities in Latin America, and the threat and then outbreak of European war, the United States agreed to multilateral security policies with all Latin American states in the context of the Inter-American System. The United States, however, did not reduce its view of the Caribbean as a vital strategic region or of the primary military and commercial significance of the Panama Canal.

After World War II, the Caribbean Basin did not figure prominently in the cold war criteria that were fundamental to U.S. global policies. The United States had replaced all foreign powers, except for their small and burdensome colonies; the long U.S. effort to insulate the Caribbean into a sphere of influence seemed complete. The United States, overwhelmingly powerful in the area and secure in its hegemonic position, perceived little threat from communism. The United States was the region's largest trading partner and capital investor and monopolized military relations. The again-war-exhausted Europeans and the Soviet Union did not view the Caribbean among their important interests and offered virtually no challenge to U.S. dominance. Consequently, the entire region assumed a low priority in U.S. calculations. Infrequent perceived threats were dealt with individually, such as covert support of the overthrow of a leftist government in Guatemala in 1954.

U.S. perceptions changed again after the Cuban Revolution of 1959. The United States temporarily assigned a prominent position to Latin America in its global policies after Fidel Castro's rise to power and subsequent alignment with the Soviet Union. The new policy emphasis had special implications for the Caribbean Basin. With the region no longer isolated in the Cold War, U.S. and Latin American interests converged in what came to be called the Alliance for Progress. From late 1959 to the mid-1960s, the United States temporarily defined the concept of security to include national development, coinciding with the Caribbean states' primary economic interests. The United States also pursued coercive strategies, including the sponsoring of an unsuccessful exile-invasion of Cuba in 1961, mobilizing multilateral agreements in the Inter-American System to impose sanctions on Cuba in 1962 and 1964, and ordering a military intervention in the Dominican Republic in 1965 aimed at preventing "another Cuba." In the meantime, the U.S.-

Soviet confrontation in the Cuban missile crisis of October 1962 was viewed by the antagonists in terms of global balances of power. In any event, the 1965 intervention in the Dominican Republic signalled the effective end to the Alliance for Progress and to convergence of U.S. and local Caribbean states' security-economic interests.

For the decade beginning in 1968 the United States chose policies that again placed a low priority on the Caribbean. The Soviet-Cuban threat seemed to recede; an informal agreement had been reached between the United States and the Soviet Union in the wake of the missile crisis that the latter would not place its nuclear weapons in the hemisphere in exchange for the former's pledge not to intervene militarily in Cuba. The United States abandoned developmentalist policies; levels of funding for foreign assistance programs, both economic and military, declined sharply and direct arms sales were severely limited. Certain bilateral relationships were important, such as negotiations with Panama over new canal treaties, as were the human rights policies pursued after 1976—U.S. sanctions related to human rights abuses were applied against the military junta in El Salvador, the Somoza regime in Nicaragua, and the Lucas Garcia dictatorship in Guatemala. U.S. trade and investment were still dominant, even without the security concerns. The external states continued to have low levels of political interest in the area, except for the Soviet relationship with Cuba.

The Course of U.S. Policies, 1979–1988

Passive U.S. orientations in the Caribbean Basin dramatically changed to assertiveness after the Nicaraguan Revolution of 1979. Upon taking office in 1977, President Jimmy Carter had discounted the Soviet threat and rested foreign policy on the commitment to human rights. After the Sandinista-led revolution overthrew Somoza in 1979, however, President Carter accused the Soviet Union and Cuba of increased activities in Central America—relations with Cuba had already deteriorated because of its expanded African adventures in concert with the Soviet Union. Policy toward Nicaragua gave way to antagonism on the grounds that the government was shipping Soviet-provided arms to leftist guerrillas in El Salvador. Military transfers were resumed to the Salvadoran government despite the lack of substantive reforms.[4]

President Ronald Reagan, inaugurated in 1981, was determined to increase the U.S. presence in the Caribbean and recapture its influence.[5] Central America became the front line in a new global cold war. The new administration charged Nicaragua with transshipping communist-source arms to Salvadoran insurgents, and Cuba of providing Soviet financed arms and advisors to Central American guerrilla groups. It threatened to "go to the source" (with obvious reference to Cuba) to stop the arms flow. Pressures were brought to bear on Nicaragua, aid extended to El Salvador, and various overtures made to other Central American countries. The United States sought military victory against leftist forces rather than meaningful negotiations. The U.S. invasion of Grenada in late 1983 led to speculation that it would be followed by military intervention in Nicaragua, where the United States had held nearby naval and military maneuvers, armed and financed anti-Sandinista guerrillas (called the Contras), and mined its harbors.[6] These actions were taken in the name of the Reagan Doctrine, a pledge announced early in the Reagan presidency to reverse Soviet expansion in league with its "proxies" in strategically important areas of the Third World.[7]

U.S. policies were incrementally broadened in response to domestic and international criticism as well as the administration's growing recognition of the complexity of the problems addressed, although the thrust of policy, and much of the rhetoric, remained the same. The Caribbean Basin Initiative (CBI) was proposed and eventually implemented, framed in terms of the Soviet-Cuban threat but recognizing poverty as a source of instability and providing for trade preferences and economic aid to friendly governments. The administration put increasing pressure on the Salvadoran government to follow a reformist course and hold elections, and sought to legitimize governments in Guatemala and Honduras with elections and improved human rights records. In July 1983, President Reagan appointed the National Bipartisan Commission on Central America, headed by former Secretary of State Henry Kissinger, to recommend long-term strategy and short-term tactics in order to broaden congressional and public support for its efforts.

The Reagan administration evolved a geopolitical strategic view of the Caribbean Basin centered on Central America.[8] The Kissinger Commission report, issued in January 1984, reinforced the administration's assumptions and policies (although with some qualifications and extensions).[9] The key assumption was that the global balance of power could be shifted by the advance of Soviet and Cuban power in Central America. Their argument stressed the strategic and commercial importance of the Caribbean Basin to the United States, and that the security and well-being of countries there were necessary for the protection of vital U.S. interests. These interests were threatened by Soviet-Cuban expansionism, in particular Soviet backed and Cuban-managed support for violent revolution aimed at establishing Cuban-style Marxist-Leninist dictatorships allied with the Soviet Union. The "domino-theory" was advanced, arguing that the Soviet Union, already enjoying a permanent presence in the Caribbean through its Cuban surrogate, was acting to reinforce and expand this penetration to Nicaragua and El Salvador; from there communism would spread to the other small Central American countries and then threaten the major bordering states of Mexico, Colombia, and Venezuela—Mexico was the "big domino."

Certain implications, the argument continued, evolved from this calculation of U.S. interests and Soviet-Cuban motives: (1) Vital Caribbean sea lanes, already threatened by Cuba's geographic position, would be more vulnerable with additional Soviet surrogates; these shipping lanes, as well as unimpeded passage through the Panama Canal, must be protected. (2) Communist military expansion in the region would not only threaten sea lines of communication and the Panama Canal but allow the placement of hostile forces and weapons capable of striking deep within the United States and in Latin American states; such a situation would force significant alteration in the U.S. forward deployment strategy requiring that resources be diverted from other areas or that new ones be created. (3) Communist takeovers in Central America would send a new tidal wave of refugees to the U.S. shores; if the region's economic problems were not resolved in the meantime, a vast increase in illegal immigration to the United States would be inevitable. (4) U.S. credibility was at stake; the Kissinger report asserted that "the triumph of hostile forces in what the Soviet Union calls the 'strategic rear' of the United States would be read as a sign of U.S. impotence."

The conclusion was that the United States was required to act to prevent the political and economic collapse of the region with a multifaceted policy: provide threatened countries with military assistance so that they might effectively combat leftist guerrillas; extend economic aid and facilitate trade to bolster their economies; and press them to improve their records of democracy and human rights as a matter of their own legitimacy and as an alternative to the Marxist option. Policies generally sought a military victory over insurgents and a rectification of the sources of instability that were taken advantage of by hostile outsiders. U.S. commitments to negotiated regional settlements or internal power-sharing arrangements with leftist governments or movements were not encouraged.

Reagan Calculations Evaluated

U.S. actions in the Caribbean Basin were based on geopolitical, power, and developmental perceptions. The dominant conceptual bases, paradoxically, were drawn from a combination of strategic calculations of the region dating from the early twentieth century and experiences far removed from the Caribbean. The Reagan administration's approach, and that of President Carter in the latter half of his tenure, in considerable part conformed to traditional U.S. calculations. That is, they emphasized concern with nonhemispheric intrusions, including the penetration of hostile ideologies, and linked those concerns with Latin American political instability. While the Reagan administration amended its initial contention that Soviet-Cuban agitation was almost solely responsible for insurgency and acknowledged internal problems as sources of dissatisfaction, policy remained rooted in anti-communism. In the U.S. view, whatever the sources of instability might be, the Soviet Union and Cuba were determined not only to take advantage of the opportunities offered but to extend them as much as possible. The Kissinger report was also preoccupied with the Soviet-Cuban threat, even while stressing internal problems. We are left with the conviction that if it were not for the Soviet-Cuban connection with Central American insurgency, or the fear that successful insurgencies would inevitably take on a Soviet orientation, the Reagan presidency would have felt no such urgency about Central America.

While policies to a considerable degree were extensions of tradition, they also drew from rationales reminiscent of prior Vietnam policies. Arguments invoked for actions in Central America—global power balances, drawing the line against communist expansion, domino-like threats to contiguous countries, a crisis for U.S. credibility—evoked memories of the justifications for actions in Southeast Asia. A problem with these rationales was their tendency toward abstraction, positing unproven and unprovable imperatives for deeper involvement. The credibility argument, for example, was the ultimate kind of justification that could be used to counter any objections to any policy. Yet it was self-imposed, since the United States had unilaterally declared Central American conflict to be a test of U.S. resolve. Furthermore, it did not specify with whom credibility was at stake or in what sense. The Soviet Union and Cuba did not respond to assertive policies as the United States expected. Some Europeans and Latin Americans agreed with the Reagan-Kissinger formulation of the credibility concern but, by and large, most of them advised the United States to negotiate and compromise, not up the costs and risks. Finally, also reminiscent of U.S. thinking on Vietnam, the heavy emphasis placed on recapturing the U.S. hegemonic position in Central America encouraged the view that, since the United States had overwhelming power in its own "back yard," the primary requirement was to summon the political will to assert that power in order to protect vital interests.

Challenges to U.S. Hegemony

Internal Challengers: U.S. Domestic Politics

The conflictual and fragmented nature of U.S. foreign policy making, especially during the 1979–1988 decade, constituted an internal challenge to U.S. hegemony in the Caribbean.[10] The Reagan administration's actions in Central America received less than enthusiastic support at home and the issues were difficult to manage with congress. Members of both political parties, and the public opinion to which they were sensitive, expressed skepticism about the administration's view of the threat and reluctance to support strong measures. They disputed facts of the case and interpretations of events. Some critics saw the administration's geopolitical-strategic rational as a mere cover for simplistic anti-communism. Many feared "another Vietnam"— shared by certain key military (especially U.S. Army) leaders—in which the United States would become mired in an unwinable Central American war unsupported by the American people. This domestic opposition probably reduced the possibility of direct U.S. military intervention in Central America. Legislative prohibitions and congressional controls in human rights continued, with prior prohibition of arms transfers to Guatemala remaining in effect and monitoring and reporting requirements imposed with regard to El Salvador. The president had difficulty getting support of his own party in congress for aid to the contras. Republicans (including Senator Barry Goldwater of Arizona, the president's political mentor) joined Democrats in denouncing the U.S. mining of Nicaraguan harbors and the subsequent awkward and losing U.S. position in the World Court. Sharp differences arose within the administration among high level political appointees ("pragmatists" versus "ideologues") that cut across bureaucratic politics. The Kissinger Commission, a politically disparate group appointed to enhance bipartisanship, not only failed to inspire congressional and public unity but was itself divided over human rights conditions on military aid to El Salvador, covert support for the Nicaraguan contras, and other basic issues. Disagreements occurred not only between the executive and legislative branches, but within the administration itself, as various agencies and individuals competed for influence. Requirements for providing aid to the contras was among the most divisive issues.

The "Iran-contra scandal," which became public in late 1986 and was the subject of extensive and highly publicized congressional hearings in 1987, was particularly debilitating.[11] The National Security Council (NSC) staff took an unprecedented role in foreign policy execution as some of its members, led by Marine Lieutenant Colonel Oliver North, devised and executed a secret plan to divert funds from the sale of weapons to Iran to the counter-revolutionary forces (the contras) fighting the Sandinista government in Nicaragua; the contras themselves were largely a U.S. creation. This activity took place outside the established foreign policy channels, apparently in league with CIA Director William Casey, with the knowledge of two national security advisers to the president (retired Marine Lieutenant Colonel Robert McFarlane and Rear Admiral John Poindexter), with at least some knowledge of President Reagan, and with the operational help of a network of hired private individuals (including a number of retired military officers, some of general rank). It was designed essentially to bypass congressional legislation regarding funding of the contras. That legislation, which underwent changes over time, dated from 1982; a key provision was the "Boland Amendment," which stipulated, among other things, that no funds would be provided for the purpose of overthrowing the Nicaraguan government. The secret plan was also intended to avoid the knowledge of key executive department figures, notably Secretary of State George Shultz and Chairman of the Joint Chiefs of Staff Admiral William Crowe. The Iran-contra scandal dramatically increased the distrust between the President and Congress, including not only many Democrats but a number of Republicans as well, and sharply decreased the president's personal authority in the policy process.

Hostile Challengers: Soviet Union, Cuba and Nicaragua

The Soviet Union paid little attention to the Caribbean area after World War II, apparently calculating that internal conditions of the small countries, the U.S. great power presence, and its own low priorities in the region and capability disadvantages made the chances of successful revolutionary movements unlikely and its own serious attention not worth the effort.[12] In about 1960, with its attachment to Cuba, the Soviets decided to breach the tacit agreement with the United States that neither superpower would physically intrude in the other's sphere of influence. The decision was taken cautiously, however, after the Castro government had demonstrated its permanence and independence from the United States. Less cautious was the Soviet decision to place its missiles in Cuba in 1962; but, after resolution of the crisis, the Soviet Union appeared to adopt a revised version of the unwritten "sphere-of-influence" agreement.[13] While it did not give up its Cuban connection, it restrained Cuba's ambitions to export revolution and, in 1975, shifted the burden of the military relationship with Cuba to joint African ventures. The Nicaraguan revolution of 1979 seemed to take the Soviet Union by surprise, just as revolutionary events in Cuba had done twenty years before. The Soviets again proceeded cautiously until, seeing increased consolidation of the revolution under Sandinista control, they decided to take advantage of the Nicaraguan opportunity.

A number of considerations challenged U.S. interpretations of the expansionist purposes of the Soviet Union, the surrogate roles of Cuba and Nicaragua, and the kinds of U.S. policies to which the Soviet Union and its aligned partners would respond. The Reagan administration-

Kissinger commission analysis about the sources of Soviet behavior, with its exclusionary emphasis on ideology and expansionism, was incomplete. It seems plausible to argue that maximum Soviet objectives in Central America were to weaken U.S. influence and increase its own as much as possible, but within the limits of modest political and financial cost and risk; and that the Soviet Union saw Central America as a target of opportunity, not of deep strategic value, and as a vulnerable investment. The Nicaraguan revolution of 1979 gave heightened possibilities for Soviet influence in Central America, but anything more than incrementally increased support for Nicaragua or probing in Central America was constrained by a variety of factors. Among them were external problems in Afghanistan and Poland and with China and the Middle East; internal economic and leadership concerns; the Cuban analogy of the high level of financial cost that went with commitment to the survival of a regime in the Caribbean Basin; and realization of Central America's distance in terms of both geography and interests and the capability advantages enjoyed by the United States.

Yet the Soviet Union did not respond to assertive U.S. actions in Central America by reducing the level of confrontation. This defied the U.S. assumption that the Soviet Union clearly understood power politics and would respond to strong counterpressures to its expansionist probing, an article of faith since containment in Europe and applied to drawing the line in Central America. This would indicate that Soviet policies in Central America were in part a function of more general relations with the United States. The decline of those relations after 1979 helps explain the lack of Soviet response to forceful U.S. actions in Central America. That is, in the Soviet view, meddling in Central America was appropriate as long as "detente" and "peaceful coexistence" were already eroded. Soviet actions were probably even more related to their domestic issues and to situations in Eastern Europe and elsewhere close to home. Especially important were the Soviet economy and evolving new leadership. In the meantime, the Soviets found advantage in the relatively low investment combined with a waiting game and the possibility that U.S. policy errors might serve Soviet goals.[14] They could hope for a deterioration of the U.S. position in El Salvador, or even an invasion of Nicaragua, with the attendant high costs for the United States in either instance. The conclusion is that the Soviet Union did not have deep strategic interest in Central America beyond contributing to U.S. problems in the area and was not pursuing a high priority forward policy.

The question of Cuban and Nicaraguan positions and actions, including their relationships with the Soviet Union, was also more complex than the articulated official U.S. perceptions suggested. Viewing Cubans and

Nicaraguans simply as Soviet surrogates, proxies, or puppets inadequately explained their behavior.

Cuba was dependent on the Soviet Union for its security and economic survival; but the relationship also had important elements of interdependence, and Cuba was able to maintain a degree of independence.[15] They had disagreed in the past over revolutionary tactics. In the 1960s, Cuba insisted on attempting to export its version of armed revolution, while the Soviet Union counseled caution and more attention to political relations. They later had different sympathies in the Grenadan internecine strife just prior to the U.S. invasion; during the U.S. action, Cuban-Soviet relations were as difficult as those between the United Kingdom and the United States. In addition, Cuba clashed with the Soviet Union over its involvement in Africa. In Central America, the stakes were higher for Cuba than for the Soviet Union. It was closer to home and of sharp interest to a powerful and hostile United States. Cuba cared more about the survival of the Nicaraguan revolution, which was similar in origins and outlook and reduced Cuba's regional isolation. In sum, Cuba's freedom of action was limited but it was able to manipulate the relationship with the Soviet Union to its advantage because of the Soviet commitment to the survival of the Castro regime.

Nicaragua had its own interests to consider, the most fundamental of which involved external threats to the very survival of the regime.[16] The Soviets assisted the Sandinistas with military and economic aid; but they did not make the same firm and extensive commitment to the Nicaragua that it had to Cuba, indicated by considerably lower levels of economic help than desired by the Sandinista government. The Soviet Union might even have welcomed a U.S. invasion with all the attendant difficulties for the United States at home and abroad. Nicaragua, unlike Cuba, had limited leverage with the Soviet Union and important Sandinista elements recognized the tenuous nature of its support.

This interpretation of Soviet-Cuban-Nicaraguan behavior casts a different light on U.S. fears about military threats. It suggests that serious limitations existed for the projection of their military power in the region. I agree with Jerome Slater's analysis that Caribbean shipping lanes and the Panama Canal were not remotely threatened; that Soviet military bases serving a conventional military invasion in the region was a fantasy (it would have been met with an overwhelming, probably combined United States-Latin American response); and, with regard to nuclear weapons and bases, the Soviet Union already had the capacity to destroy the United States with missiles launched from submarines and its own territory. The most plausible use of Cuban and Nicaraguan military forces were to defend against a U.S. or U.S.-proxy attack.[17] This conclusion does not address the more urgent U.S. concern with external support for insurgent guerrillas, especially in El Salvador.

Regional Challengers: Contadora and Esquipulus

One of the most striking new conditions of Caribbean Basin international politics was the concerted assertiveness of local Latin American states. In January 1983 the presidents of Mexico, Venezuela, Colombia, and Panama organized the Contadora Group (named for the island off Panama where they first met) to challenge the United States with a formula for the negotiated settlement of Central American conflict. Six South American states later joined in a Contadora Support Group. The Latin Americans continued to resist U.S. leadership in the Inter-American System; it was no longer available to legitimize U.S. actions. In fact, the irrelevance of the Inter-American System to the Central American crisis partially explains why the Latin American states rallied around the Contadora Group as a substitute multilateral forum.

The Contadora Group sought peaceful negotiated outcomes in Central America.[18] In time all five Central American states agreed to a set of twenty-one "principles" attempting to facilitate discussions between the United States and Nicaragua and, in El Salvador, between the government and insurgents. The principles included, among other things, limiting arms flows, prohibiting all foreign bases, withdrawing external advisers (including Salvadoran guerrillas and Nicaraguan contras). The United States indicated verbal encouragement but in fact gave no substantive support. The Kissinger report proposed a "comprehensive regional settlement" but refused to accept any regime that might serve as a "crucial stepping stone for Cuban and Soviet efforts to promote armed insurgency in Latin America." With direct reference to the Latin American initiative, the report said: "The United States cannot use the Contadora process as a substitute for its own policy."

Members of the Contadora Group had special interests in Central America and were anxious for a peaceful settlement for both external and internal reasons. They felt threatened by nearby isthmian conflict but did not consider themselves the ultimate "dominos" and saw the Central American situation and solution differently than did the United States. They saw insurgency as rooted in the conditions of internal life, not Soviet-Cuban inspired. Furthermore, Contadora members had important individual domestic considerations. For example, leading political parties in Venezuela had Central American connections, especially the Christian Democrats with their counterpart in El Salvador and the Accion Democratica with Social Democrats in El Salvador and Nicaragua. All of them feared Central American conflict as a possible source of their own internal political polarization, in that a clear defeat of the Central American left might lead to repressive rightist regimes that would precipitate an internal conflict adversely affecting their own domestic consensus.

Mexico was the most notable case of Latin American assertiveness. It remained a supporter of the Sandinista government (although suspicion was well founded that it was not pleased with certain Nicaraguan actions but was determined to remain independent of U.S. policy). Mexico provided hospitality for the insurgent Salvadoran political group in exile. Mexican presidents offered to mediate between the United States and Nicaragua and strongly opposed military intervention. Mexican interests to the south particularly involved contiguous Guatemala, with whom Mexico had long-standing territorial disputes and which it viewed as a source of undesirable immigration and insurgent activity that might, among other things, threaten Mexico's southern oil fields.

The Contadora Group faced a more difficult task in implementing its specific steps than in having them agreed upon. Its initiative declined with time and events. In the wake of the impasse over the Contadora initiative, President Oscar Arias of Costa Rica proposed a plan (for which he won the Nobel Peace Prize in 1984) that became the basis for an important conflict resolution effort. On August 17, 1987, the five Central American presidents of Costa Rica, Guatemala, El Salvador, Honduras, and Nicaragua met in Guatemala City to consider the Arias proposal. They signed documents titled "Procedure for the Establishment of a Firm and Lasting Peace in Central America," known informally as the "Esquipulus II Accords" for the town in Guatemala where an earlier meeting had taken place. The plan sought political reconciliation based on ceasefires, amnesties, and dialogues within each of the Central American nations, the democratization of their domestic political processes, and the cessation of civil and international hostilities and of external support of aggression against other nations.[19] The Arias peace plan was even more striking than the Contadora initiative as a local-regional challenge to U.S. hegemony. Official statements by the Central American presidents indicated a determination for the region to forge its own destiny. Until then all peace initiatives had come from outsiders; even the Contadora process led by other Latin American countries was an external effort from the point of view of Central Americans.

Regional Dependents

A large number of Caribbean Basin states were small and weak, dependent (in at least some meaning of the term) on outsiders (most often the United States) and strongly subject to their influence. They traditionally played passive roles in international politics and were subordinate to outside powers. Yet these states were not without recourse in their external relations. They had long before developed tactics reflecting their capability deficiencies toward the outside world—they played the external powers against each other, organized among themselves and joined other international organizations on several levels, and promoted the principles of sovereign equality and nonintervention, all as ways to limit great power actions. Their efforts suffered, however, from their own national rivalries and diverging interests as well as internal political and economic problems.

European Challengers

Numerous European actors were a growing challenge to U.S. hegemony in the Caribbean Basin.[20] Europeans did not view Latin America in terms of security interests, other than NATO members' contingency concern that the Gulf of Mexico and Caribbean Sea be open for movements of military forces and supplies in the event of European war. Trade and investment were of paramount importance. After the Nicaraguan revolution of 1979, Europeans took a political interest in the evolving Central American crisis and by and large dissented from the U.S. approach. Their concern had to do with the nature of commitments by the West to social change in the Third World in general. NATO governments largely ignored President Reagan's message in 1981 that their support in Central America was expected. France, West Germany, Spain, and the Socialist International (SI) joined other governments and organizations in giving aid to the new Nicaraguan government after 1979. West German cultural institutes and political party-sponsored foundations were highly active. France joined Mexico in August 1981 to issue a communique recognizing the insurgent Salvadoran FMLN/FDR as "representative political forces" (some Latin American governments criticized the action because it violated their long-standing principles regarding neutrality in civil wars and recognition of governments). Felipe Gonzalez, installed as Prime Minister of Spain, had long taken a special interest in Central American affairs and was the driving force behind the Socialist International's activities there. The SI and the Christian Democratic World Union also had Central American counterparts that influenced European governments' interest perceptions.

Europeans generally agreed that Soviet-Cuban influence should be minimized in Central America and that democratic systems with social justice and economic development be established. Their assessment of situations and choice of instruments and tactics, however, sharply diverged from the U.S. orientation. They played down the importance of East-West considerations and argued that attempts to isolate Nicaragua lost the ability to influence events there. Their own policy preferences tended to follow the Contadora line and, later, the Arias initiative—they pressed for negotiations between conflicting groups and states, warned against isolating some political movements to the point that they sought Soviet-Cuban help, and opposed unilateral coercion and direct military involvement from the outside.

The European presence did not develop to the extent anticipated during the immediate post-Nicaraguan revolutionary period, when the situation was in flux. Europeans exercised little influence on Central American events or on restraining U.S. actions. They drew back from Nicaragua, which was slow to adopt its original goals of democratic pluralism, mixed economy, and nonalignment. They were discouraged by increasing political polarization in Central America and the rigid military-mindedness of many revolutionaries. Most of all, the Grenada intervention in 1983 took the ground from under European efforts and signalled that Central American crisis had entered a new and more serious phase. Europeans nevertheless remained concerned about Central America and sympathetic to the Contadora and Arias solutions, indicated in the former instance by the meeting in September 1984 in Costa Rica of all European Community foreign ministers, the four Contadora countries, the five Central American countries, and observers from Spain and Portugal. Europeans refused to commit large sums of aid moneys, but the conference issued a formal endorsement of the Contadora proposals. Without their own primary interests in Central America, and mindful of U.S. irritation with its "meddling" in the area, European governments avoided another alliance problem with the United States.

The Post-Cold War Caribbean Subordinate State System and U.S. Policies

A U.S. orientation of strategic denial focussed on outsiders became irrelevant to Latin American policy. The explicit official acknowledgment of the end of the Cold War and events in Central America (especially the remarkable elections in Nicaragua in February 1990 that ended Sandinista rule) confirmed that the Soviet Union was no longer an expansionist threat. This was evidenced by the Bush administration's defense of its military intervention in Panama in December 1989—anti-communism and the threat of Soviet expansion were never mentioned as part of the justification for the coercive actions. This was the first time since World War II that a U.S. intervention had not been justified in terms of the communist threat and a landmark in terms of 180 years of U.S. policies of strategic denial.

The dramatic new U.S. policy conclusion, however, was the culmination of other factors that had already been transforming U.S.-Caribbean relations.[21] The momentous changes in East West relations that influenced

U.S.–Latin American relations in the late 1980s were the most obvious impetus to the end of strategic denial, but they occurred in an already-changing context of the steady rise of nontraditional security issues, the intensification of fragmentation in U.S. policy making, and the growing autonomy of local Latin American states in opposition to U.S. policies. These factors combined to force a reevaluation of policies even before the Bush administration was inaugurated.

It may be argued that the traditional U.S. security assumptions revolving around military and ideological threat perceptions were anachronistic when they were revived in the 1980s and were at least partially responsible for the failed policies in Central America and the difficulties in reorienting policy thinking. In the first place, they tended to exaggerate the threat of communist adventurism and Soviet expansionism, as analyzed above. Furthermore, strategic denial was an ineffective basis for policy when dealing with drug trafficking, illegal migration, international debt, trade questions, and democracy and human rights, all of which were clearly evident as crucial problems in the early 1980s and had little to do with excluding extra-hemispheric rivals from Latin America.

A significant element in the failure of Reagan's Central American policies was conflict and fragmentation in the U.S. foreign policy process. President Bush was required to compromise policy goals, making them less ideological and rigid, in order to achieve bipartisanship in Washington with respect to Central America. A bipartisan accord was reached between congressional leaders and the president. On March 24, 1989, President Bush and Secretary of State Baker, along with House Speaker James Wright, Senate Majority Leader George Mitchell, Senate Minority Leader Robert Dole, House Majority Leader Thomas Foley, and House Minority Leader Robert Michel, signed the Bipartisan Accord on Central America.[22] Aimed at promoting peace, security, and continued democratization in Central America, the policy agreement in effect repudiated several fundamental aspects of the Reagan approach: President Bush agreed to support the Arias peace plan, exclude the idea of overthrowing the Sandinistas, and deny military support to the contras. When Nicaraguans voted the Sandinistas out of office in February 1990, certain aspects of the agreement became moot.

Structure and Strategic Responses

The Hegemonic Structure

There is nothing new about great power geopolitical conflict in the Circum-Caribbean. In this respect, international politics have not changed for centuries; only the actors have shifted. There is nothing new about outside challenges to U.S. predominance in the Caribbean in the twentieth century. Even with the reassertion of U.S. power beginning in 1979 and intensified after 1981, many U.S. efforts were frustrated. The United States retained primary external influence but its policies were challenged from several quarters. The challenges came not only from the Soviet Union and its regional partners but from important dissenting Latin American states and an array of European states and organizations as well.

One of the most striking new conditions of the hegemonic structure was the rise to power of regional states, most notably Mexico, Colombia, and Venezuela, in the Contadora Group. Europeans, including NATO allies, the Socialist International, the Christian Democratic World Union, trade unions, and others, increased their political attention toward the Caribbean Basin and opposed the United States. The hostile challengers displayed shifting positions, including strong Soviet interest in Central America, the tactical reversals of the Soviet Union and Cuba from their respective approaches to revolutionary movements, and the determination of the revolutionary government in Nicaragua. In this regard, inasmuch as Cuba and Nicaragua were independent as well as surrogate actors, they were part of the larger group of regional challengers to the United States. Finally, the fragmented nature of the U.S. foreign policy process eluded bipartisan consensus and the ability of the U.S. government to speak with one voice.

Limitations on U.S. capabilities should not be overstated. The United States clearly retained considerable influence. The area remained a bilateral trading zone. Some local governments and many political groups expected and desired U.S. leadership. The effectiveness of Latin American opposition was suspect. European and other external roles did not develop to the degree that they and others anticipated. Yet the assertion of U.S. power did not achieve many of the goals sought and, in this sense, revealed limitations on U.S. influence. The efforts of President Reagan, like those of President Carter before, did not solve the fundamental problems dealt with. If the Reagan administration expected an early or easy victory over communism in Central America, it was disappointed; the civil war in El Salvador remained a stalemate, the Sandinistas continued their stubborn resistance, and the Soviet Union and its aligned partners were not deterred by assertive U.S. policies.

Limitations on U.S. policies stemmed in large part from the intractability of the problems addressed. On one level, policy dealt with the most basic aspects of individual political cultures. On another level, Washington made the Caribbean Basin, especially Central America, an integral part of global confrontational politics. In a sense, the U.S. predicament was a case of over-ambition, of taking on problems that, by their very nature, either could not be resolved by outsiders and/or could not be accommodated quickly, easily, or cheaply.

Strategic Response

For the purposes of this volume, four strategic responses on the part of hegemons or aspiring hegemons were identified. The first, *accommodation,* was defined as "one-sided concessions undertaken to preserve some measure of influence over a state system in order to avoid increased provisions for deterrence or to win clients inside the region." The United States accommodated the actions of outside challengers during the nineteenth century when its position of weakness gave it little other choice. For example, a treaty compromise was reached with Great Britain in 1850 when both parties agreed not to proceed unilaterally with a transisthmian canal, which the British probably would not have allowed the United States to do anyway. As a further example, the United States, while it was engaged in civil war, accepted Spanish recolonization of the Dominican Republic in the 1860s.

During the twentieth century, after its rise to great power status and primacy in the Caribbean Basin, the United States was willing to make accommodations, but this was not the preferred response and came only with compelling demands of outsiders or when faced with a powerful fait accomplis. The Roosevelt Corollary of 1905 and the following interventions in its name were a form of accommodation with Europe, inasmuch as it recognized acceptance of European grievances that threatened their intervention as justified under international law; but the United States then preempted them with its own interventions in order to master the situation. The United States relatively easily accepted the territorial intrusion of European powers in the form of small but not insignificant dependencies. For one thing, their ownership was settled during the Latin American colonial era so that the United States had little basis for opposing existing colonies, and the nature of evolving status arrangements between the colonies and the metropolis did not invite U.S. opposition. Furthermore, the continued presence of European colonial powers did not seriously challenged the U.S. position as the local great power—in fact, in some ways, it was a friendly presence that relieved the United States of a more extended police role.

The most dramatic example of superpower accommodation on the part of the United States was the arrangement with the Soviet Union in the aftermath of the missile crisis of 1962 and acceptance of the Soviet-Cuban connection thereafter. The informal agreement, however, was not one-sided. Acknowledgment of respective spheres of influence and offering quid pro quo (the Soviet pledge not to introduce nuclear weapons into the hemisphere again and U.S. agreement not to invade Cuba) conformed to geopolitical aspects of traditional balance of power thinking. Furthermore, this accommodation was reluctant and sometimes tentative, being challenged by important domestic politicians and even administrations. Strong pressures continued to be applied against Cuba; President Carter tried but abandoned policies of accommodation and the Reagan administration entertained no such plans. President Reagan was even more adamant in his opposition to the Sandinista regime in Nicaragua; while administration officials sometimes sharply debated among themselves the proper approach to Nicaragua, no evidence suggests that anyone was arguing for acceptance of a marxist regime in Central America ("another Cuba").

Accommodating local states was another matter, especially in terms of tolerance toward authoritarianism and extension of various forms of aid when they were perceived as having salutary "anti-foreign" and stabilizing consequences. Such U.S. accommodations were from the position of the strongest subregional actor. U.S. willingness to extend broad-ranging forms and significant amounts of aid under the Alliance for Progress represented a kind of accommodation. From 1959 to the mid-1960s the temporary U.S. definition of its concept of security to include national development coincided with Caribbean states' primary economic interests. Changes in the Reagan administration policies in terms of bilateral aid and under the Caribbean Basin Initiative resembled the earlier Alliance for Progress. Accommodation, however, had its limits, not to include negotiated regional settlements or power-sharing with the left in response to the demands of major local powers and several of the smaller affected states (the Contadora and Arias initiatives).

The United States over the years accommodated to unsavory local regimes that contradicted U.S. value preferences in the name of security and stability. This form of accommodation was unevenly applied, however; it was caught up in the longstanding U.S. debate over the relative merits of shoring up the status quo or encouraging reform. Both Carter and Reagan shifted their position toward dictators and humans rights violators—Carter accommodating them to a degree after 1979 and Reagan coming to oppose them—with both shifts of policy being explained in security terms.

The second strategic response of hegemony is *deterrence through defense and allying*. Allying is presented in the overview chapter as involving cooperative relationships with other states; defense focuses on reconfiguring resources that are predominantly military. Both are short term responses intended to make the best use of the existing situation, and politically the allying response depends on strengths derived from diplomatic coordination to deter. The U.S. response in the Caribbean

Basin only partly followed these definitional elements. For the United States, direct commitments of its own forces were by and large short term except for some military occupations prior to the Good Neighbor era (notably in the Dominican Republic, Haiti and Nicaragua); but allying has been on a relatively long-term basis. The United States viewed the Inter-American System (IAS) beginning in 1889 as a way to organize all of Latin America under its leadership. Defense alliance was not considered until the late 1930s, when mutual security principles and procedures were developed in the context of World War II. Until then, the United States had insisted on its unilateral defense of the hemisphere under the Monroe Doctrine.

The United States after World War II successfully transformed the IAS into an anti-communist alliance. As in most interstate organizations, the IAS is based on principles of juridical equality; in fact, the United States insisted on being the senior partner in security affairs. Latin American resistance to that U.S. role led the United States, beginning under Johnson, continuing under Nixon, hesitantly under Carter, and primarily under Reagan, to approach security questions through a series of unilateral and bilateral measures rather than through regional multilateralism (Reagan clearly could not have found support for his Central American policies in the IAS). All U.S. military aid to Caribbean states, whether under multilateral or bilateral programs, was aimed at strengthening local military forces to handle insurgencies; it was also related to the goal of bringing stability to local systems. These policies also sought to avoid large or permanent U.S. force commitments that would require changes in the global deployment scheme.

State strengthening is the third hegemon response to perception of threat. U.S. efforts to increase its state capabilities were undertaken in a general global context. They had local consequences and took into consideration Washington's role in the Caribbean; however, they were not based primarily on Caribbean calculations. The major recent consideration was the Soviet presence in the Caribbean Basin, but that was approached as part of the larger East-West conflict. U.S. policies at least since World War II, in fact, were in some measure aimed at avoiding the necessity to direct more resources toward Caribbean security. Rather, the state strengthening aspect of strategic response meant helping to develop the Caribbean Basin states themselves (closely associated with the developmental aspects of local accommodations); to strengthen allies and mitigate regional disputes (through defense and allying techniques); and to weaken adversaries (through counterthreats). Such local state strengthening tried to enable threatened states better to resist hostile challengers and to create and maintain a stable environment that would not provide opportunities for them. This approach assumed that the vast U.S. relative economic and military capabilities would ensure its continued regional domination.

States with hegemonic aspirations, as analyzed throughout this volume, regularly experiment with *counterthreats.* The United States viewed the Caribbean Basin as the geographic area most affecting its core interests. Furthermore, it was the most powerful and influential power in the region for more than eight decades. Consequently, it was here that the United States had longest and most readily applied geopolitical thinking that led it to apply counterthreats with the least hesitation. The more serious the challenge from the U.S. point of view, the more likely and forceful were U.S. countermeasures.

Counterthreats, as defined in the overview chapter, promise positive or negative actions on the part of the hegemonic power that punish the state from which danger or hostility is perceived. The United States perceived danger stemming not only from outside challengers but local internal conditions of instability as well. Both invited sanctions of all kinds, to include military intervention in the Caribbean Basin. While the number of U.S. military interventions was dramatically reduced after the late 1920s, they were not abandoned as a countermeasure. The United States, however, was not entirely free in its use of intervention in the name of anti-communism. While the Reagan administration was able to invade Grenada in 1983 at relatively low cost and risk, a number of constraints (discussed throughout this chapter) impinged on similar action in other parts of the Caribbean, notably Nicaragua and El Salvador. Nevertheless, it was able to apply an extensive mix of coercive measures short of a direct U.S. combat role.

Policy Implications

U.S. officials in the 1990s are attempting to make a fundamental reorientation of U.S. policies toward Latin America, with the Caribbean Basin a continuing special focus. The traditional guiding policy framework, focused on threats that great powers outside the hemisphere might pose to U.S. security through their operations in Latin America, is no longer relevant. The historic thrust of strategic denial has given way to a whole set of nontraditional security issues alluded to above, relating to economic questions, the traffic in illicit drugs, massive migration, the problems of democracy and human rights, and degradation of the environment. Since strategic denial is no longer useful, yet important issues must be faced, U.S. officials are required to reorient their policy thinking about Latin America. Effective policy dealing with the new nontraditional security issues requires overcoming certain intellectual, material, and political hurdles—the perceptual and doctrinal baggage from the past regarding

Latin America combined with enormous domestic problems and the high-priority international challenges elsewhere.

In a sense policy in the post-Cold War era is more difficult to manage. It must create a domestic consensus, or at least arrive at an accommodation, on problems that have a less clear focus regarding external threats than the relatively easier target of communism and Soviet expansionism. In addition, the nature of the new problems means that U.S. decision makers must confront Latin Americans themselves, toward whom U.S. officials have historically taken a paternal (and sometimes disdainful) attitude. A retreat into "benign neglect" will fail; crucial problems in inter-American relations will inevitably intrude onto the U.S. foreign policy agenda.

Two general policy implications emerge from the analysis in this essay. First, domestic political cooperation and bipartisanship do not necessarily ensure policy success in the sense of achieving stated goals, but its lack contributes to its failure; that is, accommodation, bipartisanship, and coordination, given the nature of the U.S. political system, are necessary but insufficient prerequisites for effective foreign policy action. Some accommodation, which requires presidential leadership to achieve, is required in the inherently normative selection of purposes, goals, and, to a considerable degree, tactics and instruments. Second, continued paternalism—the traditional assumption that Latin America needs U.S. supervision—will seriously undercut U.S. efforts to fashion effective regional policies. We are left with some fundamental questions in this regard: How does the United States replace gross involvement and paternalism with an orientation based on mutual dependency and partnership? How does it disentangle mutual misperceptions and move from simplistic negative stereotypes to balanced images of complex reality?

Notes

1. This expression was suggested by Professor Lars Schoultz of the University of North Carolina at Chapel Hill.

2. K.J. Holsti, "National Role Conceptions in the Study of Foreign Policy," *International Studies Quarterly,* Vol. 14 (1970), pp. 232–309.

3. The narrative in this section draws on G. Pope Atkins, *Latin America in the International System,* (Boulder: Westview Press, 1989), chapters 2 and 5. See Cole Blasier, *The Hovering Giant: U.S. Responses to Revolutionary Change in Latin America,* (rev. ed. Pittsburgh: University of Pittsburgh Press, 1985); Tom J. Farer, *The Grand Strategy of the United States in Latin America,* (New Brunswick: Transaction Books, 1988), Margaret Daly Hayes, *Latin America and the U.S. National Interest,* (Boulder: Westview Press, 1984); John D. Martz, ed., *United*

States Policy in Latin America: A Quarter Century of Crisis and Challenge, 1961–1986, (Lincoln: University of Nebraska Press, 1988); Lars Schoultz, *National Security and United States Policy toward Latin America,* (Princeton: Princeton University Press, 1987); and three volumes by Lester Langley, *Struggle for the American Mediterranean: United States-European Rivalry in the Gulf-Caribbean, 1776–1904,* (Athens: University of Georgia Press, 1976); *The United States and the Caribbean, 1900–1970,* (Athens: University of Georgia Press, 1980); and *The United States and the Caribbean in the Twentieth Century,* (4th ed. Athens: University of Georgia Press, 1989).

4. For a review of the Carter Administration policies and shifting emphasis, see Richard R. Fagan, "The Carter Administration and Latin America: Business as Usual," *Foreign Affairs,* Vol. 57 (January 1979).

5. On the Reagan administration's early approach, see G. Pope Atkins, "Reorientation of United States Latin American Policies." in Jack W. Hopkins, ed., *Latin America and the Caribbean Contemporary Review,* (New York: Holmes and Meier, 1983): and Paul Sigmund, "Latin America: Change or Continuity?" *Foreign Affairs,* Vol. 60 (1982), pp. 629–657.

6. A large number of works appeared after 1979 that, when taken together addressed the salient elements in the international relations of the Caribbean Basin from a variety of analytical and political perspectives. Among the most useful are Edward Best, *U.S. Policy and Regional Security in Central America,* (New York: St. Martin's Press, 1987); Morris J. Blachman, William M. Leogrande, and Kenneth E. Sharpe, eds. *Confronting Revolution: Security through Diplomacy in Central America,* (New York: Pantheon Books, 1986); Harold Blakemore, "Central American Crisis: Challenge to U.S. Diplomacy," monograph supplement to *Conflict Studies* (1984); Anthony T. Bryan, J. Edward Greene, and Timothy M. Shaw, eds. *Peace, Development and Security in the Caribbean,* (New York: St. Martin's 1990); Bradford E. Burns, *At War with Nicaragua: The Reagan Doctrine and the Politics of Nostalgia,* (New York: Harper & Row, 1987); Peter Calvert, ed., *The Central American Security System* (New York: Cambridge University Press, 1989); H. Michael Erisman, ed., *The Caribbean Challenge: U.S. Policy in a Volatile Region,* (Boulder: Westview Press, 1982); Erisman and John D. Martz, eds. *Colossus Challenged: The Struggle for Caribbean Influence,* (Boulder: Westview Press, 1982); Lloyd S. Etheredge, *Can Governments Learn? American Foreign Policy and Central American Revolutions,* (New York: Pergamon Press, 1985; Richard Feinberg, ed., *Central America: International Dimensions of the Crisis,* (New York: Homes and Meier, 1982); John E. Findling, *Close Neighbors, Distant Friends: United States–Central American Relations,* (New York: Greenwood Press, 1987); Wolf Grabendorff, Heinrich W. Drumwiede, and Jorge Todt, *Political Change in Central America: International and External Dimensions,* (Boulder: Westview Press, 1984); Jorge Heine and Leslie Manigat, eds. *The Caribbean and World Politics: Cross Currents and Cleavages,* (New York: Holmes and Meier, 1988); Walter LaFeber, *Inevitable Revolutions: The United States in Central America,* (New York: Pergamon Press, 1984); Robert S. Leiken, ed, *Central America: Anatomy of Conflict,* (New York: Pergamon Press, 1984); Leiken, ed., *The Central American Crisis Reader,* (New York: Summit Books, 1987); Robert Pastor, *Condemned to Repetition: The United*

States and Nicaragua, (Princeton: Princeton University Press, 1987); Steven C. Ropp and James A. Morris, *Central America: Crisis and Adaptation,* (Albuquerque: University of New Mexico Press, 1986); and Thomas W. Walker, ed., *Reagan Versus the Sandinistas: The Undeclared War on Nicaragua,* (Boulder: Westview Press, 1987).

7. For an explanation and defense of the doctrine, see William R. Bode, "The Reagan Doctrine." *Strategic Review* (Winter 1986), pp. 21–29.

8. The official strategic view was expressed in the following State Department publications: in the *Current Policy,* Series—No. 352, "Strategic Situation in Central America and the Caribbean," statement by Assistant Secretary Enders (December 14, 1981); No. 364, "Democracy and Security in the Caribbean Basin." statements by Enders (February 1982): No. 370, "Caribbean Basin Initiative," speech by President Reagan before the Organization of American States (February 24, 1982); No. 424, "Areas of Challenge in the Americas," statement by Enders (September 30, 1982); No. 464, "Strategic Importance of El Salvador and Central America," address by President Reagan (March 10, 1983); No. 482, "Central America: Defending Our Vital Interests," address by President Reagan (April 27, 1983); No. 572, "U.S. Central American Policy at a Crossroads." statement by Assistant Secretary Motley (May 2, 1984); No. 576, "U.S. Interests in Central America," address to the nation by President Reagan (May 9, 1984); no. 655, "The Need for Continuity in U.S. Latin American Policy," statement by Motley (January 29, 1985); in the Gist series—"Central America: U.S. Policy" (April 1982); "U.S. Interests in the Caribbean Basin" (May 1982); and "Central America: U.S. Policy" (1983).

9. *The Report of the President's National Bipartisan Commission on Central America,* (New York: Macmillan, 1984). On subsequent policy proposals submitted to Congress, see Department of State, "Central America Democracy, Peace, and Development Initiatives," statement by Assistant Secretary Motley to House Subcommittee (March 27, 1984); and "Central America Democracy, Peace, and Development Initiative," *Gist* (March 1984).

10. For a good general overview of the U.S. political process and policy toward Latin America, see Michael J. Kryzanek, *U.S.-Latin American Relations* (2d ed. New York: Praeger, 1990). Three chapters in Leiken, *Central America* (1984) specifically addressed Central American policy issues: Viron Vaky, "Reagan's Central American Policy: An Isthmus Restores" (Chap. 11); Barry Rubin, "Reagan Administration Policymaking and Central America" (Chap. 14); and I.M. Destler, "The Elusive Consensus: Congress and Central America" (Chap. 15); also see David J. Myers, "Reagan's Central American Crusade," *Current Affairs Bulletin,* Vol. 63, No. 12 (May 1987), pp. 24–31.

11. See Johnathan Marshall et al. *The Iran-Contra Connection: Secret Teams and Covert Operations in the Reagan Era,* (Boston: South End, 1987); and U.S. Congress, Senate Select Committee on Secret Military Assistance to Iran and the Nicaraguan Opposition and House of Representatives Select Committee to Investigate Covert Arms Transfers with Iran, *Report of the Congressional Committees Investigating the Iran-Contra Affair with Supplemental, Minority, and Additional*

Views, S. Rept. No. 100–216; H.Rept. No. 100–433. Washington, D.C.: GPO, December 1987.

12. See Timothy Ashley, *The Bear in the Back Yard: Moscow's Caribbean Strategy,* (Lexington: Lexington Books, 1987); Cole Blasier, *The Giant's Rival: The USSR and Latin America,* rev. ed. (Pittsburgh: University of Pittsburgh Press, 1985); Bruce D. Larkin, ed., *Vital Interests: The Soviet Issue in U.S. Central American Policy,* (Boulder: Lynne Rienner, 1988); Nicola Miller, *Soviet Relations with Latin America, 1959–1987,* (New York: Cambridge University Press, 1989); Eusebio Mujal-Leon, ed., *The USSR and Latin America: A Developing Relationship,* (Winchester: Unwin-Hyman, 1988); Illya Prizel, *Latin America through Soviet Eyes: The Evolution of Soviet Perceptions during the Bhezhnev Era, 1964–1982,* (New York: Cambridge Press, 1990); and Augusto Varas, ed., *Soviet–Latin American Relations in the 1980s,* (Boulder: Westview Press, 1987).

13. On this subject, see Edy Kaufman, *The Superpowers and Their Spheres of Influence: The United States and the Soviet Union in Eastern Europe and Latin America,* (London: Croom Helm, 1976).

14. Blakemore, *Central American Crisis,* pp. 3, 7–8.

15. On Cuba's foreign policies and key international relations, see Philip Brenner, *From Confrontation to Negotiations: U.S. Relations with Cuba,* (Boulder: Westview Press, 1988); Jorge I. Dominguez, *To Make a World Safe for Revolution: Cuba's Foreign Policy,* (Cambridge: Harvard University Press, 1989); Dominguez and Rafael Hernandez, eds. *U.S.-Cuban Relations in the 1990s,* (Boulder: Westview Press, 1989); W. Raymond Duncan, *The Soviet Union and Cuba: Interests and Influence,* (New York: Praeger, 1985); Morris H. Morley, *Imperial State and Revolution; The United States and Cuba, 1952–1986,* (New York: Cambridge University Press, 1988); and Wayne S. Smith and Esteban Morales Dominguez, eds. *Subject to Solution: Problems in Cuban-U.S. Relations,* (Boulder: Lynne Rienner, 1988).

16. See Mary B. Vanderlaan, *Revolution and Foreign Policy in Nicaragua,* (Boulder: Westview Press, 1986); and Thomas W. Walker, *Nicaragua in Revolution,* (New York: Praeger, 1982).

17. Jerome Slater, "Dominos in Central America: Will They Fall? Does it Matter?" *International Security,* Vol. 12 (Fall 1987), pp. 105–134.

18. Bruce M. Bagley, ed., *Contadora and the Diplomacy of Peace in Central America,* (2 Vols. Boulder: Westview Press, 1989).

19. For a full analysis of the thinking underlying the Arias initiative, see Luis G. Solis-Rivera, *Peace and the Future of Central America: A Costa Rican Viewpoint,* (Washington, D.C.: Friedrich Ebert Stiftung, Washington Office, 1987).

20. On European policies toward Latin America, see Esperanza Duran, *European Interests in Latin America,* (London: Routledge and Kegan Paul for the Royal Institute on International Affairs, 1985); and Wolf Grabendorff and Riordan Roett, eds., *Latin America, Western Europe, and the U.S.: Reevaluating the Atlantic Triangle,* (New York: Praeger, 1985). On the European presence in Central America, see Wolf Grabendorff, "Western European Perceptions of the Turmoil in Central America," in Feinberg, *Central America* (1982); and Andre J. Pierre,

ed., *Third World Instability: Central America as a European-American Issue,* (New York: Council on Foreign Relations, 1985).

21. I acknowledge my debt to Professor Lars Schoultz for several of the ideas expressed in this section and the final one on policy implications.

22. U.S. Department of State, *U.S. Support for Democracy and Peace in Central America,* (Washington, D.C.: GPO, April 1989).

3

Israel: An Aspiring Hegemon

Zachary T. Irwin

In classical theory, the domination of a hegemon was portrayed as undisputed, a condition in which "alternatives are not mooted [and which] ultimately rests on agreement with a specific set of norms and values."[1] The contemporary Middle East is inimical to classical hegemony for several reasons: the character of the larger international system; the relative power of states comprising the Middle East region; and the ethnic and ideological differences that divide them.

L. Carl Brown's often quoted description of the Middle Eastern international subsystem revolves about analysis of the obstacles to regional hegemony. Brown also finds a basic continuity between the diplomacy of the Arab-Israeli conflict and the nineteenth century "Eastern Question" system. He views both eras as sharing a distinctive set of diplomatic rules, perceptions, and interactive patterns. They include "sustained efforts" at conference diplomacy, successful attempts by regional powers to disrupt developments from outside the region which go against their "perceived interests," and the "use of *fait accompli* steps consistent with technical virtuosity and zero-sum mentality, but possibly contrary to long term strategic requirements."[2] Even so unprecedented an event as the Egyptian-Israeli Peace Treaty, in Brown's view, bears the marks of "vintage Eastern Question diplomacy." It is in keeping with tradition, therefore, that despite superpower efforts to influence the Middle East (including through the imposition of a comprehensive peace), the region's states have successfully resisted external manipulation.

Alternative versions of the Middle East subsystem support Brown's judgment, but they also identify the bases for Israel's hegemonic aspirations. Mansbach, Ferguson and Lampert have described the Middle East subsystem as a "complex conglomerate" of actors confronting six overriding "superissues" in distinct periods since 1948. The superissues are "Arab-Israeli, colonial, inter-Arab, regime stability, superpower, and

Palestine areas."[3] One indication of Israel's hegemonic potential has been the coappearance of the Arab-Israeli superissue with all others, and Israel's role as a primary "initiator and target" of events in most categories during all periods since 1948.

Consideration of the territorial dimension of the subsystem illuminates Israel's position from the viewpoint of the "superissues." Yair Evron conceptualizes the Middle East as a compound of three distinct loci of conflict and alliance: The "Core Area" of Israel, Egypt, Syria, Jordan, Lebanon and Iraq; the Red Sea Area of Israel, Egypt, the Yemens, Sudan, Saudi Arabia, and Ethiopia; and, the Persian Gulf Area of Iran, Iraq, Saudi Arabia, Kuwait, and the Emirates.[4] The North Africa Area from Egypt to Morocco begs inclusion as a fourth locus of conflict. Table 3.1 profiles the Middle East Subordinate State System from these perspectives.

Israel has extended its territory within the Core, and its presence in the Red Sea by means of war (1948, 1956, and 1967), by selective strikes (Lebanon, Iraq, Tunisia), or through ties with peripheral states (Iran, Turkey, and Ethiopia). In addition, Israel has frustrated any joint challenges by manipulating the divisive Inter-Arab, Palestinian, and regime stability superissues.

Egypt remains the single regional actor capable of challenging Israel in both the Core and Red Sea subsystem loci. Evron observed in 1973 that Cairo and Jerusalem "showed interest in some kind of settlement which would enable them to continue to be the major powers in the Middle East [Core] subsystem."[5] President Sadat's dramatic trip to Israel in October 1977, shortly after issuance of the Soviet-American communique that envisioned superpower cooperation in the regional peace process, demonstrated that Evron's assessment was correct.

Of special concern to the "rejectionist" states was Jerusalem's (the Likud Government) expression of interest in replacing Hashemite Jordan with a "Palestinian government" in exchange for American recognition of West Bank annexation. Egyptian acquiescence in such an arrangement, or in an Israeli dominated Jordanian-West Bank Federation, would have guaranteed Israeli hegemony in the Core Area by neutralizing the Red Sea, and perhaps, the Persian Gulf loci.

Although no Middle East state seems likely to attain regional hegemony in the traditional sense, the regional international system is conducive to aspirations of hegemony on the part of Israel. Israel seeks to achieve a desired state of affairs along three dimensions: relations of absolute military superiority with respect to individual states within the region; relations of cooperative interdependence with or immunity from extra-regional challengers; and, a situation of dominance within the "Core Area" subsystem, and neutralization of the Red Sea and Persian Gulf states.

Table 3.1 The Middle East Regional System

State	Population (millions) (1990)	Area (sq. km) (thousands)	GDP (US$/billions) (1990)*	Regional Type
<u>Core</u>				
Egypt	54.7	1,001.5	38.3	Primary Bargainer
Israel	4.4	21.0	38.0*	Aspiring Hegemon
Jordan	3.1	91.5	5.2*	Bargainer
Leganon	3.3	10.4	2.3	Peripheral
Syria	12.4	185.1	18.5	Bargainer
Turkey	56.7	780.6	44.9	Borderline Bargainer
<u>Red Sea Area</u>				
Egypt	54.7	1,001.5	38.3	Primary Bargainer
Ethiopia	51.6	1,221.9	6.6	Peripheral
Saudi Arabia	17.1	2,149.7	73.0	Bargainer
Sudan	24.9	2,505.8	8.5	Peripheral
Yemen	7.1	195.0	5.5	Peripheral
Democratic Yemen	2.6	333.0	1.2*	Peripheral

(Continues)

Table 3.1 (Continued)

State	Population (millions) (1990)	Area (sq. km) (thousands)	GDP (US$/billions) (1990)*	Regional Type
Persian Gulf Area				
Iraq	18.7	434.9	35.0*	Bargainer
Iran	55.6	1,648.0	97.6*	Bargainer
Kuwait	2.1	17.8	20.5	Peripheral
Oman	1.4	212.0	7.8	Peripheral
Saudi Arabia	17.1	2,149.7	73.0	Bargainer
United Arab Emirates	2.2	83.6	23.3*	Peripheral
North Africa				
Algeria	25.6	2,381.7	54.1	Peripheral
Egypt	54.7	1,001.5	38.3	Primary Bargainer
Libya	4.2	1,759.5	20.0*	Peripheral
Morocco	25.6	446.6	21.9	Bargainer
Tunisia	8.1	163.6	8.7	Peripheral

*GNP

SOURCE: U.S. Central Intelligence Agency, The World Factbook-1990 (Washington, DC: CR WF 90001, 1990).

Any understanding of Israel and "aspiring hegemony" requires assessments of political and economic relations on three levels: among domestic political actors; with adversaries in the Core subregion; and, with external powers. While the following discussion can not deal with all post 1948 behavior on the three levels, the basic thrust of activity within each suggests a persistent pattern supportive of Jerusalem's hegemonic aspirations. Table 3.2 presents a schematic and selective inventory of events at the internal, regional and extraregional levels which facilitate analysis of these aspirations.

While the choice of events in Table 3.2 is highly selective, the interactive quality of the three levels is self-evident. For example, the 1976 Likud victory appears to have been a requirement for the Camp David Accords in view of Labor's earlier experience with the Rogers' Plan, and given the components of an acceptable settlement that previous governments had crafted. The Accords themselves eliminated (at least in the short run) the possibility that a Geneva Conference would be convened. Jerusalem perceived the Geneva Conference milieu as threatening to Israel's retention of the West Bank.

Neither the 1973 Arab-Israeli war, nor Israel's 1982 invasion of Lebanon, have redeemed the promise of potential territorial gains from the June War. Although Israel has retained control of the West Bank, Jerusalem, and the Golan Heights for a longer period that the state has existed without them, regional "bargainers" have refused to recognize Israeli territorial claims. The Israeli-Egyptian treaties of 1979 marked a historic reversal in acknowledging a boundary, yet the Camp David Accords were both the result of a specific power balance and a mutual response to the threat of extraregional intervention. President Sadat, as well as Prime Minister Begin, opposed a renewal of the Geneva conference implicit in the October 1977 Soviet-American communique to bring about "normal, peaceful relations" in the area.[6] The Israeli government, by vehement opposition to the threat of joint intervention, compelled President Jimmy Carter to reconsider the communique in an American-Israeli "working paper" that agreed to limit the scope of any future conference. Lacking such influence with the Soviet Union, President Sadat undermined the projected conference by his decision to negotiate directly with Israel.

Israel, as suggested earlier, has long feared that the setting of an international peace conference could become a forum for imposing territorial concessions. This reflects suspicion that the international community is hostile or indifferent to the Jewish state; it also leads to a distrust of diplomacy. Yehoshafat Harkabi offers a psychocultural explanation for this mind set in the "Bar Kokhba Syndrome" i.e., "the glorification of rebelliousness and heroism detached from responsibility

TABLE 3.2 Events Affecting Israel Along the Internal, Core and External Dimensions

Period	Internal	Core Relations	External
1948-49	Territorial consolidation	Military superiority	US-USSR support; limited UN role
1955-58	Red Sea navigation, Eliat development; water carrier project	Rise of Egyptian; pan-Arabism; disputed DMZ	Franco-British withdrawal; Soviet hostility; French alliance
1967-69	Territorial expansion; inclusion of large Arab population	Arab resistance to parietal accommodation; rise of the PLO; "war canal"	US support; Soviet conflict; Rogers Plan
1973-79	Altered strategic doctrine; Golan, West Bank consolidation; *Mapai* defeat	Camp David Accords; Arab-Egyptian alienation; PLO consolidation	Specter of "conference diplomacy"; Soviet expulsion from Egypt
1982-88	"Catastrophic" inflation; coalition government; political fragmentation and polarization; Palestinian "uprising"	Lebanese invasion and withdrawal; Syrian confrontation; PLO expulsion; fragmentation	US-Strategic accord; increased US economic dependence

for its consequences."[7] Through his extensive interviews with Israel's political elite, Michael Brecher detected a "spirit of militancy and an emphasis on military strength" as an alternative to diplomacy.[8] Brecher held the response to be a consequence of Israel's experience under the mandate regime and the War for Independence. Shlomo Aronson established that Jerusalem's bargaining behavior with the Arabs reflected an attitude of "pessimism about the real intentions of the other side and about human nature in general."[9]

Israeli perceptions of threat to its regional aspirations differ in an important respect from analysis in the overview chapter. Discussion there envisions regional hegemony in terms of dominance along several dimensions, with minimal attention to assessing the relative importance of each. The dynamics of a situation in which the military dimension is uniquely significant is not discussed. For Israel, however, regional military superiority appears as the requisite for survival. As this discussion progresses, I will analyze how Israel has responded to a broad range of perceptions about threat, military and otherwise, to its position in the Middle East. The first order of business, however, is to examine the critical threat perceptions that precede those responses. Critical threat perceptions are those that derive from Israel's understanding of: the regional military balance; the role territoriality plays in national security; the dangers posed by extraregional challenges; and the problem of water resources.

Water Denial: The Potential to Thwart National Development

The Jordan river valley ranks with the city of Jerusalem as a primordial symbol linking modern and ancient Israel. Seventy-five percent of Israel's water originates in the Jordan river and other sources in the north, including water piped to the Negev from Lake Tiberias (Kinneret). Israel viewed unrestricted use of the Jordan as necessary not only for symbolic reasons, but also for the practical question of immigration and agricultural development. Soon after independence, Prime Minister Ben Gurion stated; "Israel can have no security without immigration, and security means the settlement and peopling of the empty areas in the North and South . . . [and] the development of agriculture in all suitable areas."[10] Gaining control over Jordan river water illustrates Israel's capability to overcome obstacles posed by the Arab states and the United States to economic development.

Controversy over use of the Jordan river and Lake Tiberias originally revolved about Israeli plans to divert water from the upper Jordan at Gesher B'not Yaacov, within the Syrian-Israeli demilitarized zone. Project feasibility studies were completed during the Mandate period.[11] Israeli attempts to divert the Jordan were halted following orders from the United Nations truce supervisory officer, and the public threat of American economic sanctions. At that time, Washington promised financing for the alternative Main Plan. Israel and the Arab League Council proposed mutually exclusive alternatives to the Main Plan. Of the two, the Arab plan envisioned a smaller water allocation for Israel, but one implying *de facto* recognition of Israel as a "riparian state." Washington's envoy attempted to promote a compromise. He called upon Israel to accept the following conditions: recognition of Jordan's prior claim to water as a basis of the resettlement of 200,000 Palestinian refugees; Israeli-Jordanian use of Lake Tiberias as a regional reservoir; and, creation of a neutral supervisory agency with authority to oversee further development.

Israel rejected outright the first two principles, and gave only qualified approval to the third. Subsequently, Jerusalem gained Washington's recognition of the principle that the water it received could be used outside of the Jordan valley; in addition, allocation of water from Lake Tiberias was to be decided by a neutral supervisory board. These principles formed the basis of an unpublished Israeli-American Memorandum of Understanding, signed in the spring of 1955. The Memorandum was reflected in the Revised Unified Plan submitted to the Arab states.[12] After some encouraging discussions, the Arab League Council indefinitely tabled the Plan for "further study," in October 1955. In the wake of rejection, Israel diverted the Jordan and Lake Tiberias, combining their diversion with the Huleh Marshes Drainage Project. The unified system became the National Water Carrier to irrigate Southern Israel.

The final challenge to Israel's Water Carrier developed in 1964, following the Arab League summit. As Israel moved to complete the Carrier, Arab heads of state approved plans for a unified military command and a diversion project at the Jordan's headwaters. The Lebanese Hazbani and Syrian Banias rivers were to be diverted. Together they provided about half of the Jordan's total flow. Prime Minister Eshkol warned that Arab diversion would be considered as an "aggressive act," requiring that Israel "act to protect her vital rights."[13] The Arab scheme was a dead letter from the onset.

Over subsequent decades, the National Water Carrier was to prove of inestimable value for desert irrigation. Currently it supplies water to one half of all cultivated lands in the northern Negev, and the Jordan watershed satisfies about one-third of Israel's total water requirements. Thus, between 1949 and 1978, the Jewish state was able to add an annual average of 10,000 hectares of land to cultivation. Agricultural production, however, kept pace with industrial growth; continuing to account for about 5% of Gross National Product.[14] Between 1965 and 1977, water usage per area actually declined by 20%, making Israeli irrigation the world's most efficient. Future water needs will most likely be met by purification of brackish water and desalination. Prior to 1985, water resources did not appear as a constraint on Israel's national development. Despite the critical nature of this resource, Israel has seldom acknowledged the existence of an Arab threat to water access. Levi Eshkol's warning that Arab diversion of Jordan river water would constitute an aggressive act was a notable exception.

The United States, while becoming less involved in the politics of water during the mid-1960s, has never totally withdrawn. Thus, between 1967 and 1971 Washington secretly mediated the Israeli-Jordanian conflict over water use and Israeli military threats against the East Ghor canal in Jordan.[15] The control that military victory in 1967 gave Israel over the West Bank offered new water sources that Jerusalem was determined to exploit. By the mid-1980s, almost 40% of Israeli needs were satisfied by West Bank aquifers.[16] Exploitation of these aquifers has been accompanied by limitations on Arab rights to drill new wells; in addition, deeper Israeli wells have caused some Arab wells to run dry.

Even with new water sources, Israel is straining the region's ecology. During the summer of 1986, the director of Israel's Environmental Service called for a "crash program" to arrest deteriorating water reserves in several areas. He presented the problem as multifaceted; over pumping, polluted wells, and agricultural runoff.[17] Although shortages forced a curtailment of 15% in water use by urban customers, the larger problem is in agriculture (approximately 75% of water consumption goes for agricultural purposes). Thus Jerusalem was forced to scale down agricultural settlements in the Nitzana area bordering Egypt. The magnitude of Israel's insatiable thirst for water is revealed by the increases in consumption, roughly 500% since 1948. Annual consumption currently runs at about 1,750 mcm. It is estimated that this will rise to 2,500 mcm by the year 2000.[18] Thus the need for water alone makes the possibility that control over the West Bank could be lost a catastrophic threat to existing development.

The future of potential water sources in the West Bank and along the Israeli-Lebanese border (the Litani River basin) remains uncertain. To the north, perceptions that Israel needed additional water reserves may have played a central role in the 1982 decision to invade Lebanon. This view had considerable support in Washington. In a secret report prepared by the United States Department of State, for example, the Jewish state was portrayed as seeking new water sources by annexing territory up to the Litani River.[19] The problem of West Bank and Litani water reserves for Israeli development is a critical component of the more inclusive dimension of threat perception: territoriality.

Territoriality: A Centerpiece of Israeli Threat Perception

To exercise hegemony Israel must remain dominant within the Middle East Core, while deflecting threats from states in the Red Sea and Persian Gulf subregions. This requires an effective territorial strategy based on maintaining Israeli military superiority within the Core. In this context, an effective territorial strategy involves the "acquisition, maintenance, and defense of a territory-getting, keeping up, and maintaining a discrete physical space."[20] The origins of Israeli territoriality are intrinsic to Zionism and exist independently of the regional balance of power. Most Zionist ideals, and especially the centrality of securing and defending a homeland, are shared throughout the Israeli political spectrum.

Israel's territorial development, and accompanying perceptions of threat, have extended through four distinct phases: early rejection of enforced territorial compromises and/or the "internationalization" of territories with Arab populations; the consolidation of pre-1967 boundaries and their extension through the Red Sea subregion; territorial expansion between 1967 and 1973; and, Sinai disengagement and the neutralization of threats from Lebanon and Syria. In each phase, Israeli governments have opposed the permanent stationing of United Nations troops on acquired territory. They also have resisted successfully efforts that would have compelled the state to make territorial concessions for settlements of displaced Palestinians.

The first phase of territorial strategy concluded upon establishment of the 1948 cease fire-lines, in accord with the Rhodes Formula. Threats to Israeli territoriality once these lines firmed centered on the Bernadotte Plan. This proposed settlement would have awarded the Negev and Jerusalem to Trans-Jordan, and Western Galilee to Israel, thus creating a land bridge between Jordan and Egypt. Cairo's refusal to accept the Bernadotte Plan led to a resumption of fighting. In the wake of additional Israeli military success, Secretary of State George Marshall advanced a second plan. He envisioned "international" status for Jerusalem, Haifa and Lot (Lydda). In addition, Marshall's plan would have guaranteed the right of return to Palestinian refugees. Guaranteeing the right of Palestinian refugees to return threatened Israeli sovereignty and the Jewish state's position in the Core Area.

President Truman disavowed the approach of his Secretary of State during the 1948 presidential campaign.[21] Subsequently, both superpowers came to support Israel's demand for direct negotiations with the Arabs prior to a peace agreement. Cease-fire lines permitted Israel to retain control of the Negev and a strategic belt of land along the central section of the Jordanian Front. Thus Israel was left with substantially more territory than had been offered in the 1947 Plan of Partition. That plan envisioned both an Arab and Jewish state in Palestine. It would have left Israel in control of 5,600 square miles and divided the state between its Mediterranean littoral and the area west of Galilee to Nazareth. The cease-fire lines included an additional 2,500 square miles. Indeed, only a British ultimatum prevented Israel's penetration of the Sinai.

The 1948 war, in the words of Nadav Safran, "stamped a sense of unity and common destiny" on those who took part. Within the global Jewish community, success in creating and defending Israel provided "a redemption of Jewish history . . . following the remorse of the holocaust."[22] Victory also silenced those gradualist Zionists who would have bargained territory for the promise of Arab reconciliation.

The 1956 Suez invasion served as a transition to the second phase of activity centered on territorially based threat perception. Retaliation against terrorist *fedayeen* forces had become extremely costly. A single Israeli attack on an Arab Legion post in Jordan at Kalkilia, for example, had resulted in 18 Israelis dead and 50 wounded. Moshe Dayan recalled that this event left the Israeli public depressed because "despite the action and the casualties, terrorism was likely to continue."[23] Israeli leaders viewed participation in the 1956 Suez invasion as an opportunity to escape from this depressing situation.

Israel expected specific gains from the Sinai campaign: the destruction of *fedayeen* bases in Sinai and Gaza; access to the Straits of Tiran and the Red Sea; consolidation of the alliance with France; and, the overthrow of Egyptian President Gamel Abdul Nasser. While elimination of the Nasser government held the highest priority, Prime Minister Ben Gurion was ever alert to the possibility of territorial gain.[24] In the end, Washington's acceptance of Israel's right of access to the Red Sea was the only concrete gain of the Sinai campaign. Free access to the Red Sea would allow the Negev to emerge as a vital center of Israeli development.[25] Finally, the opening of Eilat ended Israel's exclusive dependence on Mediterranean ports.

Maintenance of the right of access to the Red Sea dominated Israeli perception of threat prior to the June 1967 War. Ambassador Eban had insisted in private talks with British Prime Minister Wilson that "Israel would not live without access to Eilat or under the threat of Egyptian encirclement."[26] This declaration was consistent with Israeli doctrine defining the conditions for preemptive strike prior to Nasser's May 23 blockade of the Straits of Tiran.[27] Subsequent successes in occupying the Sinai, the Golan Heights, and the West Bank dramatically raised

Israel's threat perception threshold. The new acquisitions afforded strategic depth and recovered what Baruch Kimmerling describes as "the major primordial symbols of Jewish identity, Old Jerusalem, Judea and Samaria."[28] From a geopolitical point of view, Israel's situation had improved dramatically. Chief of Staff Rabin observed that before the war the Egyptian border had been only 130 kilometers distant, but after the war Israel's border on the canal was 130 kilometers from Cairo and 400 kilometers from Tel Aviv. Finally, the new armistice lines increased eightfold Israel's ratio of territory to border length.[29]

Israel's victory in the June 1967 war pivoted on surprise and mobility. It confirmed the Jewish state's "iron law" of military doctrine,[30] that any war be fought on enemy territory as soon as possible. The new boundaries, however, facilitated movement away from the doctrine of preemptive planning. The Bar Lev strategy of military fortification enabled Israel to reduce military expenditures by demobilizing large numbers of troops. Here the central requirement was that active duty units be capable of holding off an enemy attacks during the time needed to mobilize reserve forces.[31] Despite some difficulties, the strategy worked in October 1973, after Egypt breached the Bar-Lev line through a surprise assault with water cannon. Israel's mobilized reserves blunted Egyptian and Syrian advances short of Israel proper. The Egyptian Third Army was cut off in the Sinai from its lines of supply. Without Soviet-American intervention, Israeli bombing of Cairo and Damascus could have forced the Arabs to sue for peace.

The dynamics of territorial defense during the 1967–1973 period redefined Israel perceptions of threat in ways that had long term importance for hegemonic aspirations. First, the termination of Soviet-Egyptian military cooperation appeared to reduce the capability of Cairo's armed forces to threaten Israel. The resulting situation offered Israel an opportunity to share power in the Core Area with an Egypt that appeared less threatening. Second. Israel refined its capability to deflect United States pressure for withdrawal from the occupied territories. Jerusalem placated Washington by endorsing the Rogers Plan B which established procedures for Egyptian-Israeli negotiations under the auspices of United Nations Ambassador Gunner Jarring. Acceptance of Plan B avoided any territorial concession without provoking a suspension of arms deliveries. An important byproduct for regional international relations of this process was the increasing role played by the United States.

Coordination between the United States and Israel lowered the Jewish state's threshold of territorially linked insecurities. United States willingness to plan jointly with Israel became evident during September 1970, when Jerusalem and Washington framed joint contingency plans to intervene directly in the Syrian-Palestinian assault against Jordan.

However, Soviet pressure on Syria, Syrian hesitation, and Jordan's air power eventually defeated the combined Palestinian-Syrian ground forces. Contingency planning never had to be put into effect. However, the episode served to underscore evolving interdependence between Israel and the United States. In return for support from Washington, Jerusalem's occupation of the West Bank respected United States interests in protecting Jordan, preserving the inter Arab balance, and in limiting Moscow's regional options.[32] Finally, the United States indefinitely deferred demands for Israel's withdrawal.

The fourth dimension of redefining territorially linked threat perception revolves about Sinai disengagement and neutralization of threats from Syria and Lebanon. It makes a clear distinction between the intentions of Egypt and Syria toward Israel. Thus, in 1974 Prime Minister Golda Meir viewed the "inhuman" Syrian leadership intending to subjugate Israel as contrasting with the possibilities she perceived for an "overall settlement" with Egypt.[33] Meir's successor, Yitzhak Rabin suggested that Henry Kissinger ask if Sadat would be willing to "conclude a separate peace and full peace agreement in exchange for most—or possibly all—of the Sinai." Rabin's request may have simply recognized the growing influence of the United States, Jerusalem's vulnerability on Washington, and the Arab diplomatic strength following the increase in petroleum prices. Yet it accompanied growing international support for buffer zones in the Sinai and Golan Heights.

United States mediation led to a series of agreements designed to lower the level of Israeli insecurity. Thus, when Israel withdrew from the ruined town of Quenetra in the Golan Heights, it was allowed to retain most of the region's strategic topography. Jerusalem also gained insertion of a United Nations Disengagement Observer Force, a Syrian commitment to prevent guerilla infiltration, and Washington's promise to condone and politically support defensive anti-guerrilla attacks throughout the Heights.[34] In the Sinai, the agreement creating a Multinational Observer Force obligated the United States to coordinate its peace efforts with Israel and to refrain from proposals Israel considered "unsatisfactory." The Camp David Treaty envisioned a further defense of Israel territoriality. Cairo and Jerusalem were to establish a framework with Jordan for resolution of the Palestinian question through "autonomy."

Establishment of the mandatory boundary (Israel retained the Gaza Strip) entailed strategic or territorial costs to Israel.[35] Almost a decade after the assassination of Anwar Sadat (in 1981), however, the gain to Israel's security remains.

Israel's perception of threat to its northern borders with Syria and Lebanon remains the most complex and dynamic problem of Israeli territoriality. Perceptions of threat along the northern frontier intensified in 1976, following Syrian intervention in the Lebanese civil war. Initially placement of Syrian military units was governed by the so-called Red Line Agreement indirectly negotiated through the United States.[36] Syria promised not deploy its forces south of the Litani river, nor would Damascus use its air force, or place ground-to-air missiles in Lebanon. In addition, Syria conceded Israel's right to continue supporting the Christian militias. Damascus, however, soon violated the Red Line agreement; missiles were placed in the Bekka Valley. This set in motion a chain of events that destabilized Israeli-Syrian relations and culminated in Israel's 1982 invasion of Lebanon.[37]

The central problem along the northern frontier was the PLO's use of Lebanese bases for raids into Israel. For example, on March 13, 1978, PLO forces infiltrated Israeli and destroyed a bus. Forty passengers died, and Jerusalem launched Operation Litani within days. In spite of inflicting considerable pain on the PLO, Operation Litani failed to prevent new attacks on Galilee from within Lebanon. By the time of the 1982 invasion, destruction of the PLO infrastructure had become Israel's highest priority.

Other developments inclined Jerusalem toward a strike into Lebanon. First, fundamental changes in relations within the Maronite Phalange between 1976 and 1981 appeared to provide an opportunity to reduce the intensity of threat from the north. As of 1981, Syria and the Phalange were engaged in a struggle for control of Zahle and East Central Lebanon. Fighting led to the rise among Maronite Christians of Bashir Jumayyid.

Within Israel, the resignations of Moshe Dayan and Ezer Weitzman from the first Likud government removed a constraint on the Prime Minister. Their replacements, Chief of Staff Raphael Eytan and Defense Minister Ariel Sharon, favored a more aggressive policy in the north. It began to be implemented following the Likud's 1981 electoral victory, with announcement that the Golan heights had been annexed. Finally, changes in Syrian and Israeli relations with the superpower increased the probability of conflict. Soviet objections to Syria's involvement in Lebanon gave way to full-fledged alliance between Moscow and Damascus in 1980.[38] President Carter's anxiety that Israeli retaliation would jeopardize his peace efforts was followed by the more ambiguous tolerance of the Reagan administration.[39]

The Lebanese invasion and the siege of Beirut created political demands within Israel that permanent security arrangements redeem the costly operation. In 1983 an Israeli-Lebanese Treaty reflected new Israeli thinking about its territorially linked security concerns in north. The treaty established a *de facto* alliance with the Maronite government and a "security zone" in southern Lebanon. The Zone extended to about five miles north of Sidon and thirty miles northeast to the Golan Heights.[40] Israel intended that the treaty bolster the Jumayyil regime against Syria, secure Northern Israel and the Golan Heights against the Syrians and Palestinians, and prevent encirclement in any future conflict with Egypt.[41]

What happened to the 1983 Israeli-Lebanese Treaty demonstrates the fragility of Israel's hegemonic aspirations. Its provisions became unenforceable following the assassination of Bashir Jumayyil. Israel subsequently withdrew from most of Lebanon. In place of the treaty, Israeli forces and a weakened Christian Militia patrolled a truncated "security zone." The Zone was limited to between ten and fifteen miles north of the Israel-Lebanon border.[42] Syrian military power remained entrenched, and Palestinian forces returned during 1986. Beyond the southern security zone, Israel and the United States currently have little influence.

The Palestinian Threat to Israeli Territoriality

Until the mid-1980s, the Palestinian threat to Israeli territoriality was limited largely to attacks on border installations by armed *fedayeen*. Israel held the neighboring Arab states responsible for these attacks. Until recently, the success of Israeli policy toward Palestinians rested on the Jewish state's ability to insulate its domestic Arab population, as well as Arabs in the occupied territories, from external threats. Here Israel's capability to identify and destroy infiltrators was critical. An important consideration in Israel's early success was the character of the terrain.[43] After 1986, however, the Palestinian threat changed; it came to pivot on internal insurrection and external diplomacy. The new equation forces discussion about a possible Palestinian state.

Creation of a Palestinian state on the West Bank and Gaza would compromise Israel's pledge to redeem Samaria and Judea. A Palestinian state would also be detrimental to Israel's position in the regional international system, becoming a pole for external involvement and reducing Israel's weight in the power balance with Jordan and Syria. Also, in contrast to the fragile Jordanian state, Palestine would be a vigorously nationalistic entity capable of advancing legitimate claims to the occupied territories. More than a million Palestinians live in these areas; neighboring Arab states host an additional two million. Only two percent of Israel's population resides in the West Bank, less than fifty thousand Israelis. This underscores another source of threat to Israel should a Palestinian state come into being; the existing spatial distribution of Israelis and Palestinians in the Core Area weakens Israeli dominance.

The Palestinian challenge to Israel currently has four dimensions: the dynamics of unity within the Palestinian movement and its linkage to Arabs in the occupied territories; the relation of the PLO to Israel and to other Arab states, particularly Jordan; Israel's response to the Palestinians aspirations, and more recently to the Palestinian uprising, the

Intifada; and, the PLO's role as negotiator in any peace conference. Attention turns to analyzing the Palestinian challenge in order to assess the overall threat that Palestinian aspirations present to Israel's regional position.

Despite the tenuous association between the PLO and Palestinians under Israeli rule, the PLO has enjoyed overwhelming support among Arabs under Israeli rule. Perhaps the last poll taken before the *Intifada* of West Bank Arabs indicated that 93.5% viewed the PLO as "sole legitimate representative" of the Palestinian people; 80% rejected United Nations resolution 242; and, 78% favored the creation of a democratic state throughout Palestine, rather than a confederation with Jordan or a separate state.[44] A new complicating factor is the uncertain impact of the *Intifada* on the allegiance of the Arab population in the West Bank and Gaza to the PLO. It is possible that a Palestinian majority now considers its representative to be *Hamas,* the movement of Islamic opposition, rather than the PLO.[45] Unlike the secular PLO, *Hamas* maintains that any Palestinian state must be based on the Koran. Without elections, it is impossible to assess their relative strength.

Ironically, as PLO's support was challenged within the occupied territories, its coherence as an organization increased. PLO independence from Syria opened the way for Jordan and Egypt to respond favorably to PLO efforts at establishing new linkages. Jordan and Egypt feared that if PLO leaders remained isolated they would become ever more radical. With little to lose, the PLO might attack their ties with the United States in hopes of destabilizing them internally.[46] Jordanian and Egyptian efforts yielded mixed but overall positive results at the 18th session of the Palestine National Conference in 1987. On the negative side, Arafat came out in favor of unification with the Popular Front for the Liberation of Palestine and the Democratic Front.[47] However, unification with these "rejectionist" Fronts appeared to have had little effect on Arafat's willingness to negotiate. Here the growing appeal among Palestinians of the Islamic *Hamas* movement had an impact. It both encouraged Arafat to behave in ways that made external powers more likely to recognize the PLO, and encouraged all Arab states to promote the PLO as the sole legitimate spokesman for Palestinian aspirations.

The PLO's suitability as a negotiating partner was further enhanced by Arafat's December 1988 statement concerning relations with Israel. The Palestine National Covenant implicitly rejected United Nations Resolutions 242 and 338, which affirmed Israel's right of security. Arafat accepted these resolutions in December 1988, proclaiming "the right of all parties concerned in the Middle East conflict to exist in peace and security." He also renounced "totally and absolutely all forms of terrorism."[48] However, Jerusalem dismissed Arafat's concession, even after he insisted that the new stance was a "strategic [goal] and not an interim tactic." The United States responded differently. Within hours of Arafat's declaration, Washington opened a "diplomatic dialogue" with the PLO.[49] Thus the United States joined the more than eighty governments recognizing the PLO, even though it represented a nation without a state. Although the "dialogue" has been suspended, the United States remains unlikely to seek a peace conference exclusive of PLO involvement.

The enhanced position of the PLO set in motion changes that complicated Israeli efforts to deal with the Palestinian question. Jordan's King Hussein publicly renounced any claim as a spokesman for Palestinians in the occupied territories. He also severed legal and administrative links with the West Bank. The action removed from the diplomatic agenda immediate consideration of a Jordanian-Palestinian confederation, the option supported by Israel's Labor Party.[50] This turn of events accentuated diplomatic pressure on Israel by removing an intermediary between Israel and the PLO; in addition, it created an incentive for the PLO to press for direct negotiations with Israel.

The status of the PLO as a negotiator has long been an issue with significant potential to threaten Israeli territoriality. He responded to the PLO with a proposal that sought to avoid a direct exchange. Prime Minister Shamir called for unsupervised elections to be held in the occupied territories.[51] This proposal was stillborn. In its place, Egypt's President Mubarak offered a ten-point program that would lead to West Bank elections.[52] Although the PLO rejected the Mubarak Offer (it failed to guarantee an independent state as the outcome of elections), Jerusalem portrayed Mubarak as maneuvering in collusion with the PLO. More to the point, Mubarak's offer divided the Israeli government. Over the heated objections of several cabinet ministers, Defense Minister Rabin journeyed to Cairo and discussed the Mubarak's Plan.[53] Subsequently, following a meeting between Prime Minister Shamir and a PLO supporter, several Likud Ministers threatened to work for the Prime Minister's removal.[54] Prime Minister Shamir's April 1989 proposal for unsupervised elections was but the culmination of an unsuccessful policy to isolate the PLO. The Palestinian uprising on the West Bank has intensified domestic Israeli disagreement and strained relations between Jerusalem and Washington. Israeli public opinion polarized between those who consider retention of the West Bank and Gaza basic to the state's survival and those who believe its Jewish and democratic character to be threatened by retention.

The costs of the West Bank uprising are staggering. As of July 1990, approximately 725 Palestinians had been killed by Israeli forces; an indefinite number waited in detention.[55] Most Palestinian police and other officials had resigned; those remaining on the job were threatened and attacked. A clandestine "National Committee of the Uprising" created and managed organizations that paralleled the Israeli occupation infrastructure. In addition, the Committee of the Uprising called effective strikes and mounted mass demonstrations. Ephrarm Sneh, an Israeli general and former West Bank administrator, commented that the "uprising will not subside because the basic reasons remain . . . the popular base is very broad. The fact that there are so many casualties increases the constituency."[56] Defense Minister Yitzak Rabin estimated the direct military cost of the uprising at $300 million as of mid 1988.[57] The price of pursuing territorial ambitions, by a wide margin, had exceeded initial Israeli calculations!

Perceptions of Threat to the Military Balance

Israeli perceptions of Arab intentions toward the Jewish state mandate a significant military cushion; nevertheless, Israeli spokesmen refuse to acknowledge the superiority of their armed forces. Recent governments have avoided public comment about the military balance. However, documents prepared before 1973 by United States military intelligence (and subsequently declassified) speak of Israel's "qualitative" superiority over combined Arab forces, independently of Arab manpower and Soviet supplied weapons.[58] The character of the arms supplied over time to Egypt and Syria by the Soviet Union is one reason for Israeli superiority. These arms appear to have been intended to preserve Israel's qualitative superiority, thus denying to the Arabs the potential to mount a decisive offense.[59] "Qualitative" Israeli superiority has not depended on armaments alone. The Arab states never have made optimal use of their combined military forces. Cooperation among Arab militaries has been the exception, confined to short periods just prior to war. Apparently the regional context of dynastic, ideological, and personal conflicts precludes a strategy of sustained cooperation. The Israeli Defense Force, in contrast, generally has been skillfully coordinated.

Israeli arms acquisition policy has displayed several consistent features; success in obtaining superior performance aircraft and battle tanks from abroad; conclusion of agreements facilitating the production of spare parts within the country; and, development of a domestic capability to produce systems suitable for Israeli combat conditions. Prior to 1962, Israel depended on a variety of European suppliers. These included Czechoslovakia (1948), France (1952–1967 and 1984), and West Germany (1959). The first major Israeli-American transfer did not occur until the autumn of 1962, with purchase of the Hawk antiaircraft missile.

The United States and Israel moved closer during the Johnson administration. In 1964, President Johnson agreed to provide Israel with the offensive A-4 Skyhawk and M-48 Patton tank.[60] Yet a year later, as recalled by Chief of Staff Rabin, the process of implementing this agreement occasioned a "cascade of terms." Israel was asked to instruct its supporting lobbies in the United States to cease objections to corresponding arms transfer to Jordan, to pledge it would not attack the Arabs preemptively, and to commit itself not to develop nuclear weapons.[61] While the final Memorandum of Understanding remains classified, the Skyhawks and Patton tanks were not delivered well after the June 1967 War.

The Nixon administration was supportive but cautious in dealing with Israel. In 1969 the Jewish state received American Phantom F-4's; they were last dramatic symbol of Washington's commitment to Israeli air supremacy before the transfer, a decade later, of the F-14 and F-16. The F-4 aircraft guaranteed Israel's ability to defend territories occupied in 1967 war. By publicly confirming Israel's "ongoing" arms relation with the United States, the Nixon administration incorporated the American congress into the transfer process as a necessary partner.[62] Between 1967 and 1973, the congress underwrote Israel's superiority through the subsidy of military credits, serial deliveries of aircraft, and electronic countermeasures (ECM), first provided during the "War of Attrition," late in 1970.

The October 1973 War tested all aspects of Israel's weapons policy; it also exposed Israel's vulnerability to manipulation by American suppliers. The threat to deny American support in order to compel a cease fire brought public recognition by Prime Minister Golda Meir of dependency on the United States.

> There is only one county to which we can turn and sometimes we have to live into it—even when we know we shouldn't. But it is the only real friend we have, and a very powerful one. We don't have to say yes to everything, but lets call things by their proper name.[63]

The 1973 cease-fire became more acceptable to Israel because of the superior performance of its Air Force. Imaginative countermeasures neutralized antiaircraft weapons in the Golan and Suez Canal areas; the Israeli-developed air-to-air *Shafrir* rocket proved highly effective, and Israel lost by far the smallest number of combat aircraft among the engaged forces.[64] In addition to their value in ground operations, Israel's air strikes acted as a deterrent against the most advanced Soviet weapons. On October 9, a Soviet "Frog" missile (surface-to-surface with a forty-mile range) landed at a kibbutz near Nazareth. Over the next two days a total of sixteen such rockets fell on Israel. The Israeli Air Force responded by inflicting massive damage on Syrian industrial and refining facilities in Damascus, Homs, and Banias.[65]

Since the October War, four dimensions of the military balance have structured Israel's threat perception: vulnerability to manipulation by the supply of American weapons, the deployment of Soviet supplied weapons by Syria in Lebanon or in Syria itself, the supply of western weapons to Middle East states outside the Core Area, and the development of Iraqi nuclear capacity. The October War confronted Israel with unprecedented vulnerability to the supply of American weapons. In response, toward the end of financing its own weapons production, Israel expanded of its weapons export program. By 1980 foreign sales reached a total of $1.2 billion, or about 21% of total foreign purchases by third world countries.[66] These sales helped to finance production of the Merkava Tank, the Mach-2 Kfir fighter bomber, and the surface to surface Jerico missile. All, excepting the Kfir's engine, were manufactured from Israeli built components.

Continuing military relations with the United States guaranteed Israel's technological superiority. The basis of this relation was established in the 1975 Disengagement Accord with Egypt. An ongoing system of threat analysis developed with the 1981 Israeli-American strategic accord. Assistant Secretary of State Robert H. Pelletreau explained the "process and procedure" of joint consultation. "We analyze the threat; we exchange views; we fight about it, and then we reach conclusions about what the Israeli force structure should look like over a number of years to maintain its qualitative edge to defeat any combination of threats that might realistically come up."[67] Mutual agreement on force structuring assisted Israel in securing United States funding for its own weapons production. During August 1986, the first Israel-produced Lavi fighter was flight tested. United States investment in the project was estimated at $2 billion.[68] On August 30, 1987, however, the Lavi project was canceled; it became the victim of Washington's skepticism over requests for additional funding, and disputes between the Israeli Defense Ministry, the IDF and the United States Treasury.[69] American officials subsequently expressed willingness to consider co-production of the F-16C.[70]

Syrian deployment of Soviet supplied weapons; for example, SA-6 missiles in Lebanon and the long-range SA-5 in Syria, underlies a second Israeli perception of military-related threat perception. Concerns date from May of 1981, following discovery of deployed SA-6 missiles along Israel's northern frontier. At that time, American envoy Philip Habib initiated negotiations to remove the missiles; they quickly became deadlocked. Defense Minister Ariel Sharon threatened a direct strike to remove the missiles.[71]

Late in November 1982 Prime Minister Shamir arrived in Washington to discuss the Lebanese situation and the "Syrian threat to the peace."[72] Tension between the two allies were high. Nevertheless, they were able to join in assessing the placement of SA-5 and mobile SS-21 missiles inside of Syria. This was the first time the Soviet Union had deployed these missiles externally, and Washington saw deployment as "a new level of escalation."[73] The SS-21 was able to reach northern Israel. The SA-5, with a range of 150 miles and an altitude of 95,000 feet, could penetrate Israeli airspace and threaten American carrier aircraft in the Mediterranean. Soon after completing these assessments, the United States urged the Soviet Union not to introduce the even more sophisticated SA-6; the request was not honored.[74] Behind Washington's efforts lay apprehension about the consequences of possible Israel air strikes against the Syrian sites at Homs and Damascus, which also housed approximately 5,000 Soviet advisors. In an effort to lower the Israeli perception of threat, the United States obtained Soviet assurance that the missiles would not be used against Israel, providing that Israel did not retaliate against Syria.

Israel has appeared reluctant to comment publicly on Syrian military policy since its withdrawal from Lebanon. This reflects Jerusalem's concern that Damascus would see any such comment as threatening action Israel chose not to take. It also suggests that Israel perceived no direct threat from Syria, owing to the stable conditions in the Golan area and Syria's inability to dominate Lebanese affairs.

The absence of a radical Israeli response to Assad, especially in light of his past provocations for a "Greater Syria," derives from several conditions. First, the sophisticated weapons on which Syria would depend in any military showdown with Israel continue under the control of Soviet advisors. Unlike Egyptian President Sadat in 1974, Syrian President Hafez al-Assad depends on Soviet forces both to deter an Israeli attack, and to constrain his own military. Second, evidence suggests that Syria remains incapable of attaining "parity" with Israel in any meaningful sense. Reports abound of fundamental Syrian problems in using sophisticated weapons and in operating an effective military chain of command.[75]

Given the tenuous basis of his Alawite regime, especially the intense hatred directed at him by the Muslim Brotherhood, the existence of the "Zionist" enemy provides a rallying point for his beleaguered government.[76]

The supply of Western weapons to Arab states underlies a third source of Israeli threat perception. Jerusalem has concerned itself with the sale of American weapons to Arab clients, regardless of whether they shared a boundary with Israel. By contrast, Jerusalem's objections to European weapons transfers to Arab states have been halfhearted and ineffective; there is grudging recognition that Israel lacks the means to influence European initiatives.

In an unusual step that challenged Reagan administration policy, the Israeli Cabinet formally opposed the AWACS E-3A transfer to Saudi Arabia. Implicitly supporting Congressional opposition to the transaction, Foreign Minister Shamir referred to Saudi "fanatical hatred of Jews and Israel."[77] He also expressed anger over Washington's coupling of the sale with a proposed Israeli-American strategic accord.[78] Since Israel's failure to prevent the Saudi weapons transfer, Israel has not attempted to mobilize its influence in Washington to prevent further transfers.

The problem of nuclear weapons in the Middle East represents a dramatic and final element of Israeli threat perception. On June 7, 1981, Jerusalem announced that it had attacked the Osirak nuclear reactor near Baghdad. Destruction of the facility with American supplied weapons constituted a probable violation of the 1952 Mutual Assistance Agreement; it also flouted informal warnings on the use of American weapons.[79] Prime Minister Begin's defense of the decision revealed his perception of equivalence between Arab capabilities and intentions. Begin claimed that Iraq intention to build as many bombs as possible. "With three, four, or five such atomic bombs, Saddam Husein, an incomparably cruel person . . . wouldn't have had the slightest hesitation to drop these bombs on concentrations of our population. . . ."[80] Begin confessed that he alone had made the decision to destroy the reactor. The attack was timed before destruction of the reactor would expose the population to escaping radiation. Eradication of Osirak eliminated a potential threat from the most likely nuclear power in the area besides Israel itself. Subsequently, no foreign state offered assistance to rebuild the Iraqi reactor, nor to transfer nuclear technology to an Arab state.

Elimination of Osirak effected the Arab balance of power, Iraq's war with Iran, and Israel's relations with the Arabs. The effect of the attack preserved Israel's potential nuclear monopoly, and it prevented development of a regional system of nuclear deterrence. Subsequent information provided by the Israeli nuclear engineer Mordechai Vanunu has confirmed Israel's long assumed nuclear capacity.[81]

Nevertheless, Iraq remains a potent and volatile threat. In April 1990, Saddam Huseyn warned, "We will make the fire [chemical weapons] eat half of Israel," should it attack Iraq a second time.[82] Although the timing of the comment is unclear, it may have been a response to the danger posed to new Iraqi efforts to attain nuclear capacity. Huseyn's reference to "dual chemical" [binary?] weapons in the Iraqi arsenal confirms the opinion of an American expert that the country possesses the "largest and possibly the most sophisticated chemical weapons in the Third World," estimated conservatively at 700 tons of annual production.[83] Israel's ability to neutralize such a treat is likely, but difficult, to establish. Iraq may have inflicted some 50,000 casualties with chemical weapons during the war with Iran. At the time of writing, the consequences of Iraq's invasion of Kuwait are unresolved. Although the event obviously enhances Israel's value as a strategic asset for the United States, Iraqi belligerence could provoke an Israeli strike, especially if Iraqi forces enter Jordan. War between Israel and Iraq mandates that combatants factor into the military equation problems associated with the of use of ballistic missiles.

Introduction into the Middle East of intermediate range missiles outside of superpower control is potentially destabilizing of the regional military balance. Israel's Jericho II has been tested at a range of 820 km, slightly more than half of its projected range of 1450 km. The Jericho II is capable of delivering a nuclear warhead throughout the Middle East. In April 1990, Israel launched an artificial satellite from a modified three-stage Jericho IIB. Estimates of the Jericho IIB suggest it is capable of delivering a payload of 2,200 pounds up to 1,500 miles or one of 1,100 pounds up to 2,200 miles.[84] Notwithstanding Israel's capability, Syrian requests for the comparable SS-23 ballistic missile from the Soviet Union have been refused. Anticipating reciprocity, the Soviet Union asked Israel to join in a ban on intermediate missiles in Asia.[85] Israel ignored the request and transferred Jericho technology to China. Washington, not to mention Moscow, was displeased. Inside of the United States, transfer strengthened the hand of interests desirous of selling the intermediate range CSS-2 to Saudi Arabia.[86] Following the sale, Washington warned Jerusalem not to attack the Saudi missiles.[87] In the absence of an effective Israeli antimissile-missile (the Israeli-American produced Arrow antimissile-missile is behind schedule because of cuts in SDI finding), sale to Saudi Arabia of the CSS-2 eroded Israeli ballistic missile superiority.[88] Finally Iraq's modified SCUD-B, the Husayn, became operational in late 1989; it possesses a range of 375 miles, well beyond the distance to Tel Aviv and Tehran.

To summarize, the ambiguity of Israel's nuclear potential satisfies certain needs of regional bargainers and selected external powers. For Israel, ambiguity allows conventional superiority to adapt itself to changing security needs without sacrificing the ultimate deterrent should conventional forces be defeated. For the United States, the ambiguity relieves pressure to weaken its security linkages with Israel and to transfer ever more sophisticated conventional weapons its Arab clients. The ambiguity serves an analogous purpose for the Soviet Union; e.g., avoiding a public discussion with Syria about Middle East nuclear parity. Finally, public recognition of an Israeli nuclear capability would present another important obstacle to Israeli aspirations for regional hegemoı It would stabilize Middle East power relations in a manner comparal to the post World II division of Europe; that is, channel behavior that "even low-level confrontations are eschewed for the incalculal destabilizing effects they might have."[89]

Threats to Israeli Hegemony: The Comprehensive Peace

Israel perceives superpower guarantees of Middle East security throu a comprehensive regional peace settlement as potentially threatening its hegemonic aspirations. Conceding security responsibility to extraı gional powers is seen as undermining the prerogatives of meaning regional hegemony. Also, a settlement accompanying outside guarante implies limitations on regional armaments. Enforcement of such lin tations, in addition to threatening Israeli military superiority, could of the guarantor a pretext for intervention. An international conference which guarantees could be crafted would also reopen negotiations ov the annexed Golan heights and Palestinian rights on the West Ban Jerusalem, finding this highly threatening, has opposed the conveniı of any comprehensive peace conference. Correspondingly, the Isra government has negotiated bilaterally for limitations on all forces mo itoring the disengagement of its military units from those of Egypt aı Syria. The treaty creating the Sinai Multinational Observer Force we so far as to obligate the United States "to coordinate its peace effoı with Israel toward the end of refraining from 'putting forth' proposa which Israel considers unsatisfactory."[90] Interpretation of this stipulati generated intense controversy.

In defusing periodic proposals for a comprehensive peace, Israel h labored to reconcile maintenance of support from Washington with steadfast refusal to negotiate the status of the occupied territories beyoı discussion of Palestinian "autonomy." The question of a Palestinian stat as indicated earlier, took on new life following presentation of the Fal Plan. Advanced by Crown Prince Fahd of Saudi Arabia, this seven poi proposal for peace in the Middle East was perceived as a threat Jerusalem. Israel was concerned over its substance and over the intere it aroused within the Reagan administration.[91] The Fahd Plan repeat Arab demands for Israeli withdrawal from the occupied territories aı the dismantling of Israeli settlements. It also envisioned the creation a Palestinian state with East Jerusalem as its capital (following a transiti regime under United Nations supervision); compensation for Palestiniaı "who do not wish to return to their homeland;" freedom of religioı practice in East Jerusalem; and, guarantees of the plan by the Unit Nations or some of its members.

The United States government viewed the Fahd Plan favorably. President Reagan considered that "implicit in the offering of the plan [is] recognition of Israel's right to exist as a nation." He held that this "hopeful indication" suggested a basis for negotiations.[92] The Likud government, intent on not alienating Washington, waffled on whether the Plan implied recognition of Israel. The extent of Jerusalem's accommodation was expressed by Moshe Arens, chairman of the Knesset Foreign Affairs and Defense Committee. Though "totally unacceptable," he acknowledged that the Plan went "a little way in the right direction, but a long way from making Saudi Arabia a partner for peace negotiations with Israel."[93] Israeli disapproval, however, went deeper; for Washington's interest in the Plan coincided with the proposed sale of AWACS aircraft to Saudi Arabia. Israeli Foreign Minister Shamir spoke more bluntly; he branded the plan a "prescription for the dismemberment of Israel."[94] In fact, congressional failure to thwart the AWACS sale appeared to pave the way for the Israeli-American Memorandum of Understanding announced late in November 1981. Aimed at the Soviet Union, this memorandum restrained the Reagan administration, at least initially, from advancing its own peace plan.

United States willingness to press for a peace settlement independently of Israel's endorsement increased dramatically following the Likud Government's "angry rejection" of President Reagan's 1982 Peace Plan. Reagan's initiative envisioned "full autonomy" for Arabs on the West Bank and Gaza, and a lose "association" of the territories with Jordan.[95] The Israeli cabinet considered Reagan's plan a "serious danger" to the country's security. Prime Minister Shamir insisted that the peace process could start only after all participants included the Golan Heights, Judea and Samaria within the boundaries of Israel. He added that "the world had better know that we will take no more serious risks."[96] The Reagan Peace Plan also aggravated a long-standing difference between the Gahal Party (in the Likud coalition) and the Mapai opposition. The opposition leader, Shimon Peres, saw Shamir as being unnecessarily rigid.

Differences between Washington and Jerusalem clarified after the Israeli elections of July 1984 produced a deadlocked parliament. With neither major party controlling the Knesset, the resulting Government of National Unity alternated the post of Prime Minister between Peres and Shamir. Peres' approach to peace initially materialized against a background of Lebanese rejection of the treaty intended to facilitate Israel's dominance in the southern portion of Lebanon. American sponsorship of the treaty, and Israel's commitment to withdraw from other parts of Lebanon, restored a high level of Israeli-American cooperation in late 1983. This led to organization of a joint committee "to coordinate military planning, maneuvers, and stockpiling of American weapons in

Israel."[97] Subsequently, between February 1985 and mid-1986, most elements viewed as necessary for a return to conference diplomacy (of the sort described earlier by L. Carl Brown) coalesced. Yet, despite United States support, a comprehensive peace conference never convened. This failure confirmed Israel's continuing capability to undermine American initiatives seen as incompatible with its interests.

The Peres Plan rested on principles that underlay an earlier Israeli consensus about the shape of an acceptable peace. These included: the absolute rejection of diplomatic involvement with the PLO; a limited role for the United Nations, beyond general endorsement of a conference; and, the exclusion of Jerusalem and the Golan Heights from negotiations.[98] However, it was doubtful by 1990 whether the earlier consensus remained; certainly, Israelis disagreed over the operational meaning of these principles. In any case, tensions within the Labor-Likud coalition government had led to its breakdown and brought Labor into opposition. In March 1990, the National Unity Government collapsed over disagreement about the terms put forward by the United States for initiating Israeli peace talks.[99] The precarious balance within the Likud government and its narrow majority highlight the serious political risks associated with negotiations. Too, the Prime Minister's position that any talks could not raise the question of East Jerusalem suggests the difficulty of finding Palestinians with authority sufficient to meet with Israel.

The United States, nevertheless, has continued to push for a comprehensive Middle East peace. In 1988, Washington proposed that all parties to the Middle East conflict (including a Jordanian-Palestinian delegation) be invited to attend a conference sponsored by the permanent members of the United Nations Security Council.[100] Based on the outcome of the conference, the future of the West Bank and Gaza would be fixed, following a three-year waiting period. Only President Mubarak of Egypt endorsed the plan without qualification.[101] Nevertheless, it gave the United States an image of involvement against the background of Palestinian violence. It also revealed that the Reagan administration was prepared to include Moscow as a partner.

Initially the Bush Administration endorsed an Israeli-Palestinian dialogue as a "first priority" in its Middle East policy.[102] Apart from the practicality of such a step preceding a peace conference, a "dialogue" may also be intended to forestall further Palestinian radicalization, owing to the pressures of the Intifada and the influence of Iraq's Saddam Huseyn on Yasir Arafat.[103] In any case, the failure of Secretary Baker and Foreign Minister Moshe Arens to agree on conditions for an Israeli-Palestinian dialogue not only precipitated the fall of the National Unity Government, but an unusually sharp American response to the new Likud government. The United States threatened to withdraw from the entire peace process, strenuously objected to plans for Soviet Jewish immigrants to settle on the West Bank, and announced its readiness to support the presence of UN observers to monitor Israel's treatment of Palestinians.[104]

Conclusion: Aspiring Hegemony Deferred

Jerusalem has been successful in deflecting diplomatic threats to impose a disadvantageous settlement to the conflict that has raged since its birth. Challenges to Israeli military superiority and to its territoriality fell short. Development of the Jordan River Basin enabled the Jewish state to irrigate the Negev and expand Eilat. The Basin also served as a "natural" boundary between Jordan and the Israeli-ruled West Bank. Through gaining United States military technology and assistance, Israel laid the basis for strategic cooperation, and with it an increased capability to manage demands for obedience to Washington's diplomatic interests. Both the military balance and the development of the Jordan as a water source were pivotal to Israel's territorial strategy. Neither the Likud nor National Unity governments had any intention of permitting autonomy negotiations to upset the course of that strategy. Prime Minister Shamir has rejected the pre-1967 boundaries because they had proved to be "a prescription for chronic instability and warfare," and because they had "ceased to have any relevance" to existing conditions.[105]

According to Shamir, the greatest danger to Israel's security, and by implication to its territoriality, consists in any attempt to create a "second Palestinian state [besides Jordan] to the west of the Jordan river . . . [it] is a prescription for anarchy, a threat to both Israel and Jordan, and a likely base for terrorist and Soviet penetration."[106] This declaration leaves no doubt concerning the central place of the Palestinian question in Israeli threat perception. Insecurity derived from this threat perception has risen dramatically when, under the mantle of Pan-Arab solidarity, Arab governments proclaimed their commitment to recover a homeland for their Palestinian "brothers." This commitment legitimated warfare against Israel in both 1967 and 1973. By contrast, threats from individual Arab states have appeared much less threatening.

For the greater part of its history, Israel's strategy of aspiring hegemony has pivoted on a combination of "defense through deterrence" and "state strengthening." Available resources were configured to deflect the most likely contingencies of Arab attack. Constant dollar defense expenditures, the most visible measure of configured resources, have remained roughly equivalent to the combined defense expenditures of Egypt, Iraq, Syria, and Jordan.[107] Israeli fixed capital investment, until 1974, exceeded that of Egypt, a state roughly ten times larger in population. As a percentage of gross domestic product (GDP), Israeli defense expenditures rose consistently in the 1960s (from six to ten percent between 1960 and 1966). They approached 24% of GDP in 1970. They peaked a decade later, at 24% of GDP; subsequently, they fell back to 24%. This confirms that as Israel seeks to deter, its economic capacity is being stretched close to its limits.

Exports have long played an important role in Israel's state strengthening response. Between 1960 and 1980, total Israeli exports increased 400%, a rate nearly double that of Egypt.[108] Here the contribution of Israel's defense industry is especially revealing. Taking 1980 as a representative year, arms and security-related exports accounted for 25% of total industrial exports.[109]

Successful deterrence permitted Israel to feel secure despite perceptions that the state was ever more threatened. However, there was concern that deterrence by itself was transforming Israel into a garrison state. The Sinai Disengagement, the Camp David Accords, and the Israeli-American Strategic Accord represented a fundamental strategic shift; allying became newly important as a complement to deterrence and state strengthening. The choice of accommodation as a strategic approach in Israeli-Egyptian relations facilitated a Middle East condominium. This condominium enabled Cairo to direct its interests to the west, against Libya; also, to the south, in cooperation with Sudan. At the same time, Egypt regained the Sinai peninsula and use of the Suez canal. Israel saw the condominium as increasing its latitude to deal with the issue of Palestinian autonomy. The Jewish state also perceived the condominium as enabling it to act on its interests in the Middle East Core Area. Most importantly, it facilitated annexation of the Golan Heights and incorporation of the West Bank.

Israel sought United States ratification of its dominance within the Core area. Tacit alliance between the two states flowing from the 1983 Israeli-Lebanese treaty confirmed a broad range of mutually agreed upon Israeli and American interests. On the other hand, by its failure to frustrate the American-Saudi arms agreement, Israel was forced to accept a not necessarily supportive United States presence in the Red Sea and Persian Gulf areas. Within the Core Area, however, Washington deferred in practice to Israel, even when objecting to Israeli policy. In other words, the United States did nothing to prevent annexation of East Jerusalem, the Golan Heights, and, until recently, expropriation of West Bank territory for settlement.

Despite Israel's domination of the Core Area, the Lebanese invasion exposed a degree of vulnerability incompatible with the exercise of hegemony. The Jewish state could neither sustain the occupation nor enforce the treaty with Lebanon. Between June 1982 and February 1984, the Israeli Defense Force suffered 4,289 causalities, including 614 killed. This is a high number of losses when compared to the 2,523 killed in the October war against two major adversaries.[110] Secret battlefield reports by Israeli officers cited stunning "ineptitude" to explain that about 20% of Israeli casualties during the invasion were the result of self-inflicted, "friendly fire." However, the government ruled out any public inquiry into the conduct of the war. Israeli vulnerability to irregular forces in Lebanon confirmed earlier experiences in the War of Attrition (1969-1970).[111]

Fallout from the Lebanese adventure reinforced negative trends in the economy present since 1974. These included increasing vulnerability to foreign energy supplies, declining economic growth rates, accelerating inflation, higher taxation, and growing trade deficits. Some specifics illustrate the magnitude of these negatives. Real economic growth averaged only 3.5 % between 1973 and 1986; a dramatic decline from the 9.2% rate prevailing between 1960 and 1972. In 1989 the growth rate fell to 0.6%.[112] Inflation was equally destructive of economic performance. At times it reached 25% monthly (equivalent to 1,260% on an annual basis). Finally, Israel's current account deficit (in 1983) reached $2,167 million in Special Drawing Rights (SDR's), an increase of 800% over 1977.[113]

Economic crisis forced Jerusalem to request special emergency aid from Washington. Key Israeli military industries; for example, those specializing in small arms and aircraft, experienced a decline in Ministry of Defense orders of more than 50% between 1983 and 1986.[114] Profits once available for research and development became "loans" to the Ministry. The accompanying increase in Jerusalem's dependency on Washington for additional military aid has reduced Israel's ability to realize what Stanley Hoffman describes as the "manipulation of interdependence," particularly in times of crisis.[115]

Jerusalem's strategy of state strengthening also has been undermined by recent increases in political dissent associated with hyperinflation and the Lebanese war. Israeli involvement in the American-Iranian arms transfer stimulated debate both about government security and export policies. Subsequently, Israel's profitable arms export program came under attack inside of the Knesset.

A consensus remains within Israel that regional military dominance must be preserved. However, Jerusalem's ability to conduct a policy of "aspiring hegemony," or even maintain coherent discussion on regional political options, has never been so uncertain. Without a unifying national vision, Israel's potential for hegemony is sharply diminished; discord undermines capability to implement the strategies of deterrence, state strengthening, and allying. Paralysis allows others to set the regional agenda. Pressures for "conference diplomacy" are likely to increase in light of trends in superpower cooperation. Thus Israel may have to defer its regional leadership aspirations indefinitely. Regardless of extraregional pressures, however, no other Middle Eastern state can equal Jerusalem's potential to exert influence within the region's Core Area. None is capable of successfully challenging Israel's right to exist.

Notes

1. Antoni Gramschi, *Prison Notebooks*, cited in Michael Mann, *The International Encyclopedia of Sociology* (New York: Continuum Publishing Co., 1984), p. 154.

2. L. Carl Brown, *Politics and the Middle East, Old Rules, Dangerous Game* (Princeton, NJ: Princeton University Press, 1984), pp. 243–244.

3. Richard Mansbach, Yale H. Ferguson and Donald E. Lampert, *The Web of World Politics, Nonstate Actors in the Global System* (Englewood Cliffs, NJ: Prentice Hall, 1976), p. 72.

4. Yair Evron, *The Middle East: Nations, Superpowers and Wars* (New York: Praeger, 1973), pp. 193–194.

5. Ibid., p. 205.

6. *The New York Times*, October 2, 1977, pp. 1, 16.

7. Yehoshafat Harkabi, *The Bar Kokhba Syndrome: Risk and Realism in International Politics*, translated by Max Ticktin and edited by David Altshuler (Chappaqua N.Y.: Rossel Books, 1983), p. 105.

8. Michael Brecher, *The Foreign Policy System of Israel: Setting, Images Processes* (New Haven CT: Yale University Press, 1972), p. 72.

9. Shlomo Aronson, *Conflict & Bargaining in the Middle East: An Israeli Perspective* (Baltimore MD: Johns Hopkins University Press, 1978), p. 351.

10. David Ben-Gurion, *Rebirth and Destiny of Israel* (New York: Philosophical Library), 1954.

11. The substance of Israel's policy described here has been adapted from Fred J. Khouri, *The Arab-Israeli Dilemma* (Syracuse, NY: Syracuse University Press), 1976, pp. 225–229 and from Michael Brecher, *Decisions in Israel's Foreign Policy* (New Haven, CT: Yale University Press, 1975), pp. 173–229.

12. Brecher, *Supra*, p. 203.

13. *The Jerusalem Post*, January 18 and 21, 1964, pp. 1 and 1.

14. *Israel: A Country Study*, edited by Richard F. Nyrop (American University, Washington, D.C., 1979), p. 191.

15. Thomas Naff and Ruth C. Matson, *Water in the Middle East: Conflict or Cooperation?* (Boulder, CO: Westview, 1984), p. 45.

16. Joe Stork, "Water and Israel's Occupation Strategy," *Merip Reports* 13 (6) July–August, 1983, p. 21.

17. *Jerusalem Post* (International Edition) June 21, 1986, and June 7, 1986, p. 9.

18. Stork, *Supra*, p. 20 and Frederick W. Frey and Thomas Naff, "Water: An Emerging Issue in the Middle East," *Annals of the American Academy of Political and Social Science*, v. 482, November 1985, p. 67.

19. *Washington Post,* September 27, 1982, p. C 14.

20. This definition is associated with individual behavior and originated as a concept of psychology. *Encyclopedia of Psychology* edited by Raymond J. Corsini (New York: John Wiley, 1984), V. III, p. 411.

21. *The New York Times,* October 29, 1948, pp. 1, 8.

22. Nadav Safran, *Israel, The Embattled Ally* (Cambridge, MA.: Harvard University Press, 1981), pp. 62–63.

23. Moshe Dayan, *Story of My Life* (London: Weidenfeld and Nicolson, 1976), p. 223.

24. Michael Brecher, *Decisions in Israel's Foreign Policy,* p. 280.

25. Shimon Peres, *David's Sling* (New York: Random House, 1970), p. 187.

26. Michael Brecher, *Decisions in Crisis-Israel, 1967 and 1973* (Berkeley, CA.: University of California Press, 1980), p. 129.

27. Y. Allon, " 'Active Defense': A Guarantee for Our Existence," *Molad,* 1 (July–August 1967), pp. 137–143, cited in Michael Brecher, *Decisions in Crisis, Israel, 1967 and 1973,* p. 99.

28. Baruch Kimmeling, "Change and Continuity in Zionist Territorial Orientations and Politics," *Comparative Politics,* 14(2), January 1982, p. 200.

29. Steven J. Rosen, "Military Geography and the Military Balance in the Arab-Israeli Conflict," *Jerusalem Papers on Peace Problems,* No. 21, 1977, pp. 12–13.

30. Michael Handel, *Israel's Political-Military Doctrine* (Cambridge, MA: Center for International Affairs, Harvard University, 1973), pp. 66–67.

31. On Israel's Twenty-fifth Anniversary, May 7, 1973, mobilization of civilian reserves in anticipation of attack had cost ten million dollars. Insight Team of the London *Sunday Times, The Yom Kippur War* (Garden City, N.J.: Doubleday, 1974), p. 69.

32. Safran, *Supra,* p. 455.

33. Yitzhak Rabin, *The Rabin Memoirs* (Boston: Little Brown, 1979), p. 254.

34. *The New York Times,* May 31, 1974, pp. 1, 8.

35. Among the liabilities resulting from the Sinai withdrawal are (1) the need to redeploy forces from the Sinai to the Nagev, (2) a loss of "strategic depth" and the requirement of improved air defense, (3) the loss of a naval base at the tip of the Sinai. *The Middle East Military Balance-1983,* edited by Mark Heller (Tel Aviv: Jaffee Center for Strategic Studies, 1983), p. 27.

36. Itamar Rabinovich, *The War for Lebanon 1970–1983* (Ithaca, NY: Cornell University Press, 1984), p. 106.

37. The account is based on Ibid., pp. 89–120, Efraim Inbar, "Israel and Lebanon 1975–1982" *Crossroads* 10 (1) Spring 1983, pp. 39–80, and David Wurmser, "Egypto-Centrism in Israel's Peace for Galilee," *SAIS Review* 4 (2) Summer-Fall 1984, pp. 65–76.

38. "Soviet-Syrian treaty of Friendship," *Survival,* 23 (1) January–February 1981, pp. 43–44.

39. Zeev Schiff, "The Green Light," *Foreign Policy,* No. 50 Spring 1983, p. 73–6.

40. *The New York Times,* May 17, 1983, pp. 1, 4.

41. David Wurmser, *Supra*, pp. 65–66.

42. *The New York Times*, September 26, 1986, p. 8.

43. Bard E. O'Neil, *Armed Struggle in Palestine: A Political-Military Analysis* (Boulder CO: Westview, 1978), p. 206.

44. *Jerusalem Post*, (International Edition), September 20, 1986, p. 9.

45. *New York Times*, September 9, 1989, p. 13.

46. *Washington Post*, March 15, 1988, pp. 1, A.18, and *New York Times*, June 11, 1988, p. 4.

47. *Jerusalem Post*, (International Edition, April 21, 1987.

48. *New York Times*, December 15, 1988, p. A19.

49. Ibid., p. A1.

50. Ibid., October 23, 1985, p. A1, 14.

51. Ibid., May 15, 1989, p. A11.

52. Ibid., September 14, 1989, p. A7.

53. Ibid., September 18, 1989, pp. A1, A8.

54. *Jerusalem Post*, July 27, 1989, p. 12.

55. *New York Times*, July 3, 1990, p. A4.

56. *New York Times*, May 15, 1988, p. A8.

57. Ibid., p. 8.

58. Joint chiefs of staff, JCS 1886/340 cited in *Declassified Documents Quarterly*, Item "B", 6(2) April–June 1980, p. 153.

59. Jon D. Glassman, *Arms for the Arabs* (Baltimore: Johns Hopkins University Press), 1975, pp. 186, 187, 188.

60. Shimon Peres, *David's Sling*, New York: Random House, 1970, p. 108.

61. Rabin, *Supra*, p. 65.

62. *The New York Times*, December 4, 1971, p. 3. By an 81–14 vote the Senate offered Israel $500 million in military credits, half of which was earmarked to cover purchase of Phantom jets. The vote coincided with the announced meeting between Meir and Nixon on December 2, 1971. *The New York Times*, November 24, 1971, pp. 1, 5.

63. Golda Meir, *My Life* (New York: G.P. Putnam's Sons, 1975, p. 441.

64. On the use of the ECM, in the October War and use of the Shafrir see London *Sunday Times* Insight Team, *The Yom Kippur War*, Garden City, NJ.: Doubleday, 1974, pp. 184–189, 201–204, 338. Of the 367 interceptors and fighter bombers in the Israeli Air force, a total of 79 were lost in the October War; Egyptian losses stood at 182 of 390 aircraft and Syrian losses at 165 of 310. *Strategic Survey 1974* (London: Institute for Strategic Studies), 1975, p. 15.

65. *Janes Weapons Systems 1982–1983*, edited by Ronald T. Pretty (London: Janes Publishing Co. 1982), p. 179.

66. *SIPRI Yearbook of World Armaments and Disarmament 1982* (Stockholm: Almgvista and Wiksell, 1983), p. 188.

67. Robert H. Pelletreau, Deputy Assistant Secretary, Bureau of Near Eastern and South Asian Affairs. House of Representatives, Foreign Assistance Legislation for Fiscal Year 1986–1987 (Washington DC: GPO, 1985), p. 117.

68. *The Washington Post*, August 6, 1986, pp. 1, 22.

69. On Conflict over The Lavai, See *The Jerusalem Post,* March 29, 1987, p. 8, July 11, 1987, p. 7.

70. *Developments in The Middle East, September 1987,* Hearing before the Subcounter on Europe and the Middle East U.S. House of Representatives, September 15, 1987. Washington GPO, 1988, p. 76–77.

71. *New York Times,* November 10, 1981, pp. 1, 3.

72. Ibid., November 28, 1981, p. 1.

73. Statement of Assistant Secretary of State, Nicholas A. Veliotes, Bureau of Near Eastern and South Asian Affairs in Committee on Foreign Affairs. House of Representatives *Developments in the Middle East, June 1983,* Washington DC.: GPO, p. 10; *The New York Times,* January 8, 1983, p. 3.

74. *The New York Times,* January 8, 1983, p. 3.

75. Scott MacLeod, "How Assad has Won," *The New York Review of Books,* 33(8) May 8, 1986, pp. 29–34.

76. Daniel Pipes, "Syria's Imperial Dream," *The New Republic,* 195 (23) June 9, 1986, pp. 13–16.

77. *New York Times,* October 6, 1981, pp. 1.

78. *The New York Times,* April 27, 1981, p. 7 and October 5, 1981, pp. 1, 7. The Israel-American Memorandum of Understanding was signed immediately following the failure of Congressional attempts to halt the AWACS sale. *The New York Times,* December 1, 1981, p. 1.

79. Committee on Foreign Affairs, House of Representatives, *Israeli Attack on Iraqi Nuclear Facilities* (Washington DC: GPO, 1981), pp. 4, 36.

80. "Prime Minister Begin, The Attack on Iraq," June 8, 1981, *Documents and Statements on Middle East Peace,* 1979–1982, p. 104.

81. *New York Times,* October 29, 1986, pp. 6, 102.

82. *New York Times,* April 3, 1990, p. A8.

83. Ibid.

84. Jane E. Nolan and Albert D. Wheelon, "Third World Ballistic Missiles," *Scientific American,* 263(2) August 1990, p. 37.

85. *Jerusalem Post,* August 1, 1987, pp. 1, 2.

86. *Washington Post,* May 23, 1988, pp. 1, 17A.

87. Ibid., March 25, 1988, pp. 1, A28.

88. "Funding Problems Dampen U.S. Support for Israeli Arrow Missile" *Aviation Week & Space Technology,* December 7, 1987. p. 32.

89. Steven J. Rosen, "A Stable System of Mutual Nuclear Deterrence in the Arab-Israeli Conflict," *American Political Science Review,* 71 (4) December 1977, p. 1379.

90. *The New York Times,* May 31, 1974, p. 8.

91. "Saudi Crown Prince Fahd on Peace, August 6, 1981" in *Documents and Statements on Middle East Peace, 1979–1982* (Washington, DC: GPO, 1983), p. 52.

92. Ibid.

93. *The New York Times,* November 12, 1981, pp. 1, 6.

94. Ibid., October 6, 1981, p. 11.

95. Ibid., September 2, 1982, p. 1.

96. Ibid., January 25, 1982, p. 6.

97. Ibid., November 30, 1983, p. 1.

98. Conor Cruise O'Brien, "Why Israel Can't Take Bold Steps for Peace," *Atlantic* 256 (4) October, 1085, pp. 45–55.

99. *The New York Times*, March 14, 1990, p. 1.

100. For details of the Shultz plan, see *Washington Post*, March 5, 1988, p. A15.

101. *The New York Times*, June 12, 1988, IV p. 3.

102. Ibid., July 9, 1990, p. 16.

103. Ibid., May 13, 1990, p. A3.

104. Ibid., May 24, 1990, p. A10.

105. Yitzhak Shamir, "Israel's Role in a changing Middle East," *Foreign Affairs*, 60 (4) Spring 1982, p. 792.

106. Ibid.

107. *SIPRI Yearbook of World Armaments on Disarmament 1969–1970 and 1982*, Stockholm: Almqvist and Wiksell; 1971 and 1983, pp. 273 and 143 respectively.

108. *World Business Cycles*, London: The *Economist*, 1982, p. 56.

109. *The New York Times*, December 7, 1986, p. 1 (Section 3).

110. *Washington Times*, August 27, 1984, p. 1.

111. Michael Brechner observes the "severity" of the war of attrition in view of the fact that more than a third of all casualties (319 killed; 1,131 injured) for a five year period after the 1967 war occurred during the final year of the war of attrition. Michael Brechner, *Decisions in Israel's Foreign Policy* (New Haven, CT: Yale University Press, 1975), p. 454.

112. *New York Times*, November 5, 1989, p. 22; *Jerusalem Post*, August 2, 1989, p. 9.

113. International Monetary Fund, *Balance of Payments Statistics*, V. 36 pt. 1, 1985, p. 299; *Washington Post*, August 25, 1984, p. 1.

114. *Supra*, note 102, p. 10.

115. Stanley Hoffman, *Primacy or World Order: American Foreign Policy since The Cold War* (New York: McGraw Hill, 1978), p. 296.

4

South Africa in Southern Africa

David E. Albright

South Africa has long possessed assets for asserting hegemony in Southern Africa, but its interest in exercising such hegemony has varied over the years. Between the late 1940s and the late 1980s, that interest—as well as South Africa's capabilities to play a hegemonic role in the region—increased steadily. Since 1989, however, the interest has waned somewhat, although South Africa still dominates Southern Africa.

These changes in South Africa's desire to act hegemonically in the region have stemmed from shifts in the Pretoria government's threat perception. Prior to 1989, South African authorities saw a growing challenge in the alterations taking place in the state system in Southern Africa. The exact nature of the challenge that they discerned reflected two other major factors: (1) The Afrikaner ethnic group that controlled the Pretoria government felt beleaguered by domestic forces racially linked with the ruling elements in the newly emerging states of the region. (2) Modifications of the state system in Southern Africa permitted additional countries from outside the region to become active there, and by no means all of these evinced friendly attitudes toward the South African government. The USSR constituted the key source of hostility, yet there were several others as well. Since 1989, in contrast, the threat that South African officials have perceived emanating from the region, from domestic forces, and from outside states like the USSR has declined. At the same time, authorities in Pretoria have displayed a heightened sense of danger from the limited economic sanctions that the United States and the European Community imposed against South Africa in 1985–86.

An earlier version of this chapter was published in *In Depth*, the journal of the Washington Institute for Values in Public Policy, Vol. 1, No. 1 (March 1991), pp. 114–215.

In attempting to deal with the challenges that it has identified, the Pretoria government since the late 1940s has employed various types of concrete response, but it has consistently opted for a multifaceted approach combining several of these. The mix, however, has altered significantly over time. Before 1989, responses relying essentially on military means gained increasing weight in it; since 1989, political accommodation has predominated in it.

This chapter will go into these matters in depth. It will begin with a look at the factors that have shaped South Africa's threat perception in the post–World War II era. Specifically, it will deal with the changes that have occurred in the state system in Southern Africa during the period; the initial impact that these shifts, in combination with conditions and developments in South Africa and the broad global arena, had; the reduced effect of such considerations after the late 1980s; and the importance since the late 1980s of the international economic sanctions against South Africa put in place by the West in the mid-1980s. Then the chapter will examine Pretoria's response to the challenges that it has discerned. Because the precise goals and character of this response have evolved over time, these will be addressed in terms of historical phases. The chapter will conclude with a brief assessment of the prospects for continuity and change in the 1990s in the country's revised attitude toward regional hegemony.

Threat Perception Prior to the Late 1980s

The South African government betrayed a mounting sense of challenge to its existence between the late 1940s and the late 1980s. To some extent, this trend stemmed from alterations in the state system of Southern Africa, but this consideration by no means accounted for either the depth of the South African authorities' feelings of insecurity or the exact nature of the threat that they perceived. Other things determined these. The primary influences were the background and perspectives of the ruling elements in Pretoria and the expanding role in the region of new outside powers that the South African government deemed essentially antagonistic toward it.

The State System of Southern Africa

Southern Africa's state system has undergone dramatic transformation since the end of World War II. This transformation has rendered the system vastly more complex than it was at the outset.

The Early Years. In the latter half of the 1940s, many of the foundations for South African dominance of the region already existed.[1] South African armed forces had conquered the former German colony of South West Africa (Namibia) during World War I, and the League of Nations had granted a mandate over the territory to South Africa in 1920. Railway lines running through South Africa linked landlocked territories like Bechuanaland (now Botswana) and Southern Rhodesia (now Zimbabwe) to South African ports, and a large share of the trade that such territories carried on with the outside world flowed along these routes. Since 1910, a customs union had been in operation between South Africa and its small neighbors, Bechuanaland, Basutoland (now Lesotho), and Swaziland. Laborers from Mozambique had worked under contract in the Transvaal coal and gold mines of South Africa since the 1890s, and during the intervening years recruits from Bechuanaland, Basutoland, Swaziland, and other territories farther north had joined them. By 1945, foreign laborers in the mines totaled roughly 160,000. These men contributed substantial income to the territories from which they came, through remittances to their families back home.

In addition, the end of the Anglo-Boer War in 1902 and especially the formation of the Union of South Africa in 1910—embracing the largely Afrikaner Transvaal and Orange Free State as well as the long-time British territories of the Cape and Natal—had opened the way for the flow of considerable investment from abroad into South Africa, and the country had experienced major economic growth, including expansion and diversification of manufacturing, over the years that followed. Its GDP, for example, nearly quadrupled between 1911 and 1950. In fact, despite the travails inflicted by the Great Depression of the late 1920s and early 1930s, the South African economy had reached the point of takeoff to self-sustained growth by the mid-1930s. World War II had facilitated such a takeoff by forcing local production of many goods that the country had imported in earlier periods. As a result of the magnitude of South Africa's economic growth, not only did the country's economic power at the time of the 1948 political takeover by the (Afrikaner) National party exceed that of other territories in the region, but this power had even made it the economic hub of the region. For instance, South Africa was beginning to supply many areas of the region with some manufactured items that they wanted to import.

Yet control of the region lay in the hands of outside powers. France maintained an imperial position on the periphery in Madagascar, and Portugal retained a hold on Mozambique and Angola on the African mainland. Great Britain, however, constituted the preeminent force. London exercised protectorates over Bechuanaland, Basutoland, and Swaziland, and direct control over Northern Rhodesia (now Zambia) and Nyasaland (now Malawi). Although Southern Rhodesia had enjoyed internal autonomy since 1923, it too fell under British jurisdiction. Even

South Africa itself remained subject to substantial British influence despite its status as an independent entity since 1934. Not only did the country belong to the British Commonwealth, but British interests still claimed just under half of its wealth, resulting in the continuing transfer abroad of most of the profits from its gold and diamond mines.[2] Furthermore, South Africa was integrated into Great Britain's defense system, with relatively little capability to function on its own militarily.[3]

Modifications of the 1950s and 1960s. This situation began to alter in the early 1950s, but it was not until the late 1960s that a new state system emerged in Southern Africa. The fundamental cause of the shift was the diminishing British role in the region. Great Britain's decline there took place in two more or less distinct stages.

First, British influence in South Africa waned. Soon after the National party won power in 1948, it launched efforts to distance South Africa from Great Britain and to reduce London's potential for interfering in South Africa's domestic and foreign affairs. Through a combination of increased taxes on British-owned firms, creation and/or expansion of public corporations, encouragement of private Afrikaner businesses, and protection of both parastatals and Afrikaner businesses from foreign competition, the Pretoria government managed to decrease British economic power within South Africa significantly in the space of a few short years.[4] In 1955, South Africa assumed sovereignty over the British naval facility at Simonstown. In negotiating the agreement, to be sure, the Pretoria government did evince great interest in continued cooperation with the British to protect Southern Africa from military threats originating elsewhere, but the terms of the agreement specified that the internal security of Southern African territories would be a matter to be handled by individual countries of the region.[5] Then in May 1961, after a government-initiated referendum of the white minority of the country, South Africa became a republic. Although the Pretoria government did intend to remain in the Commonwealth in this new status, its application to do so evoked a storm of criticism of South Africa's internal policies—especially from leaders of the Commonwealth's Asian and African members; hence, the authorities in Pretoria withdrew their application.[6]

In the second stage, Great Britain gave up its colonies throughout the region. By 1960, London had already yielded to the demands of black nationalists in parts of sub-Saharan Africa for independence. It had granted Ghana (formerly the Gold Coast) sovereignty in 1957, and it was moving to do the same in Nigeria and other West African countries. On a trip to Southern Africa in early 1960, British Prime Minister Harold Macmillan made clear that this policy would extend to Southern Africa.[7] By 1964, Zambia and Malawi had gained independence. Lesotho and Botswana acquired it in 1966, and Swaziland did the same in 1968. Although Great Britain retained legal jurisdiction in Southern Rhodesia, the unilateral declaration of independence by that colony's white minority in 1965 effectively deprived London of any real say there.

The eclipse of Great Britain as a force of consequence in Southern Africa left South Africa in a dominant position in the region. Not only did the potential bases for hegemony evident in the mid-1940s persist in the late 1960s, but others had appeared to reinforce them in the intervening years.[8] South Africa still retained de facto control of South West Africa, despite a 1966 UN resolution revoking the League of Nations mandate that had handed administration of the territory over to the Pretoria government. A major portion of the trade that landlocked countries like Botswana and Southern Rhodesia (or Rhodesia, as it now called itself) conducted with the outside world continued to move along South African railways and roads and through South African ports. The customs union linking Botswana, Lesotho, and Swaziland with South Africa remained in existence, although a renegotiation of its terms in 1969 benefited the three small states. A number of countries of the region still derived significant income from remittances home by nationals working as contract laborers in the mines of South Africa or in other sectors of the South African economy. In fact, the total of foreign workers in South African mines had risen by about 50 percent between 1945 and 1965.

By the mid-1960s, South Africa (including South West Africa) boasted a gross domestic product nearly four times that of the rest of Southern Africa combined, and the economic development that it had experienced had afforded it a growing variety of manufactured and agricultural items to offer other countries in the region as well as funds to invest in projects there. The outcome was an expanding network of trade and other forms of economic interaction between South Africa and the rest of Southern Africa. During the latter half of the 1960s, for example, trade with South Africa accounted for 80 percent of all foreign trade of the other countries of the region together, and states such as Botswana, Lesotho, and Swaziland were even obtaining critical imports of food from South Africa. By the close of the decade, Portuguese colonial authorities in Angola and Mozambique were also receiving capital from the Pretoria government and South African private interests to construct dams locally for mutually advantageous purposes.

South Africa's preeminence in the region was now striking in the military realm too. In 1970, the state's full-time armed forces of 43,800 and mobilizable forces of more than 150,000 dwarfed those of the rest of Southern Africa in toto. In addition, a roughly sixfold rise in the Pretoria government's defense allocations during the 1960s had permitted

South Africa to acquire an inventory of hardware unmatched throughout the region. Some of these items had come through imports from abroad, despite the UN Security Council's call in 1963 for a general ban on the sale of arms to the country, but a substantial share of them were being produced by South Africa itself.

No less important than the objective ground for South Africa's predominance in Southern Africa, there was relatively little inclination on the part of the other members of the regional state system to chafe at that predominance.[9] Portuguese colonial authorities, finding themselves faced with insurgencies by local nationalists in both Angola and Mozambique from the mid-1960s on, did not hesitate to cooperate with a power that they deemed sympathetic to a continued Portuguese presence in the region. After Rhodesia declared its independence unilaterally in 1965, the white-minority government there relied heavily on Pretoria for support. Given their overwhelming economic dependence on South Africa, the new states of Lesotho, Swaziland, and Botswana felt that they had no choice but to accept South African hegemony, although the Botswanan rulers in particular displayed a tendency to test South Africa to the limit. Upon winning its sovereignty, Malawi also decided that there was little sense in contesting a reality that it could not change, so it opted to enter into formal relations with Pretoria and carry on a variety of types of intercourse with South Africa. Only Zambia kept its distance from Pretoria, and even it eschewed, at least for the time being, attempts to sever its economic links with South Africa.

The Mid-1970s to the Present. Further evolution of the state system in Southern Africa took place in the latter half of the 1970s. During these years, the system went from one in which the bulk of the members of the system tolerated, if they did not always welcome, South African dominance of the region, to one in which the vast majority of them actively opposed that dominance.

The transition got under way in the mid-1970s in the wake of the April 1974 coup in Lisbon. By the end of 1975, Portuguese authorities had turned over control of Angola and Mozambique to radical black groups that had been waging guerrilla warfare against Portugal for a decade or more. Perhaps more salient, the new regimes expressed great unhappiness with South Africa's current role in Southern Africa, although the government in Mozambique did refrain from blatant provocation of the ruling elements in Pretoria because of Mozambique's extensive economic ties with South Africa.[10]

Not only did the Lancaster House agreements of December 1979 end the escalating civil war in Rhodesia between the territory's white-minority regime and insurgent black forces, but they also rendered it possible for authority there to pass into the hands of elements that would not acquiesce to the hegemony of Pretoria. The Rhodesian elections of March 1980 in actuality produced such an outcome. Robert Mugabe and his Zimbabwe African National Union (ZANU) won an outright majority in the new legislature. Although Mugabe adopted a conciliatory posture toward whites in Zimbabwe, he left no doubt about his aversion to the South African government.[11]

The symbolic capstone of the change in the state system of the region came in April 1980. A summit meeting of the Southern African Development Cooperation Conference (SADCC) in Lusaka brought together representatives of nine states—Angola, Mozambique, Zambia, Malawi, Zimbabwe, Botswana, Lesotho, Swaziland, and Tanzania. At the close of this gathering, the nine states issued a declaration that explicitly set reduction of economic dependence on South Africa as a goal for all of them, and they pledged to work closely together to achieve that objective.[12]

This revamped state system in Southern Africa remained essentially unaltered throughout the 1980s and into the 1990s. The one minor change that took place was the addition of Namibia to the list of black-ruled states in 1990. Thus, in the 1990s South Africa constitutes the regional hegemon, while all of the other nine states in the region stand opposed to it (see Table 4.1). (Although Tanzania belongs to SADCC, Tanzania is normally classified as an East African country.) It should be underscored, however, that the black-controlled states of Southern Africa, both individually and collectively, still have quite limited capacities even to bargain with South Africa, for they have not managed to diminish South Africa's preeminent position in the region much.[13]

The South African Government and Its Outlook

After 1948, the government of South Africa was solely in the hands of Afrikaners. Afrikaners trace their origins back to the arrival of Dutch, French, and German settlers in the Cape area in the seventeenth century, and they possess a distinctive language and culture.

From 1948 to 1951, the Afrikaner-based National party ruled in coalition with the small Afrikaner party, but the two bodies merged in 1951 to form the present National party. Never, it should be stressed, did the National party, in either its old or its new guise, speak for the whole of Afrikanerdom. Indeed, major political divisions that predated the National party's rise to power persisted well into the 1950s, and significant new cleavages developed at the beginning of the 1980s. Nonetheless, the party represented mainstream Afrikanerdom across the years.

The "Afrikanerness" of the South African government played a key role in forming Pretoria's attitudes toward the outside world and created

Table 4.1 The Southern African State System

Political Entity	Population (millions) (1989)	Area (sq. mi.)	GNP (US$/millions) (1987)*	Regional Type
South Africa	38.5	471,879	77.1	Hegemon
Angola	8.5	481,351	9.7 (1985)	Bargainer
Botswana	1.2	231,804	1.1	Peripheral Dependent
Lesotho	1.7	11,720	0.5	Peripheral Dependent
Malawi	8.7	45,747	1.2	Peripheral Dependent
Mozambique	14.3	309,494	1.2	Bargainer
Namibia	1.4	318,259	1.3 (1986)	Peripheral Dependent
Swaziland	0.8	6,703	0.6	Peripheral Dependent
Zambia	7.9	209,584	1.7	Bargainer
Zimbabwe	10.1	150,803	5.7	Bargainer

*In cases where 1987 figures are not available, figures for the latest years for which data exist are given.

SOURCES: Population data and the figure for Namibia's GNP come from U.S. Central Intelligence Agency, The World Factbook-1989, CPAS WF 89-001 (Washington, DC, May 1989). The statistics on area may be found in Arthur S. Banks, ed., Political Handbook of the World, 1986 (Binghamton, NY: CSA Publications for the Center for Education and Social Research of the State University of New York at Binghamton and for the Council on Foreign Relations, 1986). All figures on GNP except for Namibia are taken from U.S. Arms Control and Disarmament Agency, World Military Expenditures and Arms Transfers, 1988 (Washington, DC, June 1989).

a prism through which it assessed events beyond South Africa's borders. Thus, this "Afrikanerness" had a profound impact on the way that the South African government viewed the changes in the state system of Southern Africa after the late 1940s.

This is not to suggest, however, that the effect of Afrikanerness on the Pretoria government's perspectives was static. On the contrary, the thinking of mainline Afrikaners about how they should relate to others altered to some extent over the years, and these shifts in their thinking inevitably colored the government's outlook toward the rest of Southern Africa.

Three specific dimensions of the Afrikanerness of the South African government have direct relevance to the analysis of threat perception here. They are the general world-view of mainstream Afrikaners, the modifications across time in their judgments about the proper approach to others, and the connections that they saw between South Africa's domestic political context and the nature of the state system in Southern Africa.

Afrikaner World-View. Most Afrikaners regarded themselves as engaged in an unremitting struggle to preserve their cultural identity in the face of hostile forces. This sense of insecurity derived from the experiences of their people—or at least from Afrikaners' interpretation of that history.[14]

Although the original settlers of the Cape, Afrikaners came under British control in the early 1800s during the Napoleonic wars in Europe, and they soon found themselves transformed into a powerless minority as a result of the British colonial government's efforts to anglicize the Cape. This situation eventually led to the Great Trek. Between 1836 and 1838 alone, one-fifth of the white settlers of the Cape abandoned the colony and set off to look for a place where they could live free of British interference.

In their quest, the Afrikaner trekers encountered black African tribes that vastly outnumbered them. Nevertheless, they succeeded in fending off the military challenges that these tribes posed for them. Their most famous triumph, which present-day Afrikaners celebrate with near reverence, was over the Zulus in December 1838. By the 1850s, the Afrikaners had carved out two republics, the Transvaal and the Orange Free State, in the interior of what is now South Africa.

With the discovery of diamonds and gold in the interior later in the nineteenth century, however, the two republics became targets of British imperialism. British maneuvering for control of the republics culminated in the Boer War of 1899–1902. Although the republics managed to withstand the British onslaught for three years, they ultimately surrendered, and Afrikaners once more fell under British jurisdiction.

The terms of the surrender did promise the erstwhile republics early self-government, and by the time of the formation in 1910 of the Union of South Africa—combining the two former republics with the long-time British territories of the Cape and Natal—Afrikaner politicians played a leading role in the running of the country. Yet fervent Afrikaner nationalists never accepted the call of these politicians for reconciliation between Afrikaners and English-speakers, between South Africa and the United Kingdom. Such nationalists denounced reconciliation as mere capitulation to the British and acquiescence to "second-class" citizenship. They devised an appeal to Afrikaner distinctiveness to mobilize the Afrikaner majority of the white population and wrest political power from the British and those who favored compromise with them. The electoral victory of the National party in 1948 represented the realization of their dream.

From the very outset of National party rule, however, there was widespread belief among Afrikaners that control of the existing South African government would not necessarily provide lasting protection of Afrikanerdom. Although Afrikaners constituted the bulk of the white population of South Africa, whites themselves made up only a minority of the total population, and non-whites, particularly blacks, might at some future time seek to exploit their numbers to claim exclusive jurisdiction over the government, just as Afrikaners had.

To try to foreclose this possibility, Afrikaner authorities committed themselves to the concept of *apartheid* (separation). According to this concept, each racial group in South Africa would develop separately in keeping with its own institutions and customs, but whites, as the most advanced group, would retain the reins of central power.

Nevertheless, in the eyes of mainstream Afrikaners, the passing years brought even closer to reality what was a mere specter in 1948, for the country's non-whites, and especially its blacks, greatly intensified their efforts to gain full political, economic, and social rights.[15] Such efforts, to be sure, had already commenced prior to the National party's advent to power. For example, an organization championing black rights, the African National Congress (ANC), had emerged as early as 1912, and it had subsequently attracted to its ranks substantial numbers of South African blacks. Yet in the late 1940s the struggle of blacks to enhance their rights posed only a minor challenge to Afrikaner dominance of South Africa. Those blacks whom the ANC had managed to mobilize were mainly from cities, where only a small portion of the country's black population lived, and they did not constitute a majority even of the black urban population. Furthermore, the ANC itself advocated gradual reform through nonviolent, legal means.

Ensuing years, however, witnessed a major transformation in the nature and dimensions of the black threat from the Afrikaner standpoint. This transformation occurred in stages.

The first change came in the early 1950s, when the ANC adopted a program of militant African nationalism and mass action. Despite this shift, the organization remained officially wedded to non-violence throughout the 1950s—even in the face of mounting police retaliation against its mass undertakings.

Events in March 1960 and their aftermath ushered in a new phase of the black struggle. A demonstration launched in Sharpeville by the Pan-Africanist Congress (PAC), which had broken away from the ANC in April 1959 because of its leaders' disapproval of the ANC policy of joint activities with whites, ended in the killing of 67 blacks and the wounding of 186 others by white police. This outcome sparked major black unrest around the country. To help suppress it, the Pretoria government ordered a political crackdown, involving, among other things, the outlawing of both the ANC and the PAC. In reaction to this move, the ANC turned to sabotage and guerrilla warfare to accomplish its ends, and in late 1961 it formed Unkonto We Sizwe (Spear of the Nation) as the vehicle for carrying out its revised strategy. Later, the PAC, too, embarked on the path of violence.

But the long-range significance of the Sharpeville affair derived not so much from the shift that it produced in the approach of either the ANC or the PAC. By the summer of 1963, the South African security police had captured and imprisoned Unkonto's leaders, and this "decapitation" of the main black underground movement in South Africa rendered the armed opposition essentially ineffectual throughout the remainder of the 1960s and into the 1970s.

Rather, the real importance of Sharpeville lay in its impact on the generation of urban South African blacks that reached maturity toward the end of the 1960s and during the 1970s. This generation displayed less willingness to compromise and a greater inclination to engage in confrontation with the Pretoria government than its predecessors had. These attributes of the new urban generation were manifest in two developments—the rise in the late 1960s and early 1970s of the "black consciousness" movement, which stressed black self-reliance and pride, and the revolt in mid-1976 of students in Soweto and other black townships when the government attempted to make the Afrikaans language compulsory in black primary and secondary schools.

During the 1980s, the struggle of South Africa's blacks for full rights within the country entered still another stage. The unveiling and formal approval by the white electorate in 1983 of a new constitution that accorded a limited parliamentary role to Asians (Indians) and coloreds (individuals of mixed-race ancestry) but none to blacks brought about the politicization of virtually all urban blacks, and stirrings of opposition to Afrikaner authorities soon became evident in some formerly quiescent rural "homeland" areas as well.

No less important, during the decade blacks managed to organize themselves better than they had in the past to put forward their demands. To some extent, it is true, the proliferation of groups purporting to speak for blacks weakened the overall thrust of the black drive for enhanced rights, for the programs of even such overt groups as the United Democratic Front, the Zulu-based Inkhata, the Azania People's Organization, the National Forum, the South African Federal Union, and black African trade unions—to say nothing of the banned ANC and PAC—differed substantially in content and emphasis. Yet this diversity also proved a strength of the drive. It greatly complicated the task of the Pretoria government in trying to cope with the heightened black challenge.

Perhaps of most concern to Afrikaners, the inclination among blacks to resort to violence to attain their goals escalated visibly. This trend was apparent largely in attacks by blacks on other blacks deemed to have "collaborated" with Afrikaner authorities, but it manifested itself from time to time in black behavior toward whites as well. Although some of the increase in incidents of violence stemmed from stepped-up activities by those organizations committed to armed struggle, particularly the ANC, most of it reflected the radicalization of young blacks not tied to any specific organization. A substantial number of black townships fell effectively under the control of such young "comrades" in the mid-1980s, and despite the imposition of emergency rule for extended periods, the Pretoria government still had succeeded in reasserting its authority there only tenuously by the late 1980s.

These various encounters with other ethnic groups left Afrikaners with deep-seated feelings of beleaguerment.[16] Not even the profound social changes that Afrikanerdom underwent after the 1940s—from a poor, relatively uneducated, and overwhelmingly farmer/blue-collar people to a fairly affluent, educated, and predominantly white-collar one[17]—eliminated the feelings. Younger, more cosmopolitan, and more liberal Afrikaner elements tended to evince them the same as their older, more provincial, and more conservative counterparts did.[18]

Method of Preserving Afrikaner Identity. Although Afrikaners after 1948 consistently saw themselves as engaged in a battle to ensure the survival of their ethnic identity, their thinking about how best to accomplish this end evolved over the years. Initially, as already noted briefly, National party leaders stressed the notion of "separation." Applied to the specific context of South Africa, this meant separation of racial groups. Each group would have its own territory, maintain its own distinctive institutions, and live according to its own traditions; moreover, interaction between groups would be kept to a minimum.[19]

National party leaders proposed to use their control of South Africa's white-minority government to impose separation of racial groups upon the entire population of the country. They discerned no need to consult with non-white groups about the merits of such a policy. Certainly, they were not prepared to entertain any objections to the policy from these groups.

Between 1948 and the close of the 1950s, therefore, a large amount of new legislation designed to draw clear-cut lines between racial groups in South Africa went into the record books. This ranged from the Mixed Marriages Act, which banned marriages between whites and non-whites, to the Group Areas Act, which mandated the introduction of residential segregation of whites, Indians, coloreds, and Bantus (blacks).

Over the ensuing two decades, however, doubts mounted among Afrikaners about the viability of "separateness" as an approach to preserving their ethnic identity. Two major, interrelated factors contributed to this trend. First, despite the Pretoria government's concerted efforts to separate the races in South Africa institutionally and physically, it became increasingly apparent that economic realities there rendered them interdependent. There were simply not enough whites to meet the demands for skilled labor—let alone unskilled labor—that the expanding economy was generating, and if these needs remained unfulfilled, the performance of the economy was going to suffer. Non-whites, for their part, required jobs and training to improve their own economic lot.[20] Second, as noted earlier, non-whites, and especially blacks, were pushing with growing militancy for full rights within the country. Not only did this heightening opposition to the existing order raise questions about the long-term ability of the Afrikaner government to compel non-whites to accept separation of the races, but it also tended to make non-whites reluctant to cooperate closely with whites in the economic sphere.

By the end of the 1970s, the majority of Afrikaners had concluded that some alternative to separateness had to be found. This judgment was reflected in the slogan that P. W. Botha began to expound a few months after his installation as prime minister in 1978: "Adapt or die."

The alternative that the mainstream elements of Afrikanerdom subsequently embraced can perhaps best be characterized as "coaptation of non-whites." Central to the approach was the principle of "controlled change." As related specifically to South Africa, this principle embodied two somewhat conflicting desiderata. First, non-whites should participate willingly with whites in the political, social, and economic life of the country. Such an aim prompted endorsement of the ending of most social and economic discrimination against non-whites, the granting to non-whites of greater autonomy with regard to their own affairs, and a limited form of power-sharing between whites and non-whites. Second, Afrikaners should retain the final say on the pace and extent of alterations in the existing order. Refusal to yield to "revolutionary violence," opposition to integration of residential areas and primary and secondary schools, and rejection of a black-majority government illustrated this goal.[21]

The revision of Afrikaner outlook resulted in a number of concrete developments in the policies of the National party government. In 1979, black trade unions were recognized and then accorded the right to strike and bargain collectively. The following year, major hotels, restaurants, libraries, and sporting facilities were desegregated. In 1981, the permanence of blacks in white areas was accepted. By 1985, freehold land ownership rights had been extended to urban blacks, and central business districts had been opened to businessmen of all races. In 1982, local black councils were set up for black self-government in urban areas. The next year, a new constitution providing a limited parliamentary role for coloreds and Asians (but not for blacks) was submitted to the white electorate; after approval by the electorate, it was implemented in 1984. In 1985, laws forbidding interracial sex and marriage were abolished. That same year, all universities were desegregated. In 1986, the pass laws were taken off the books, and influx control and thirty-four related laws were amended or scrapped. Last but not least, formation of a National Statutory Council was proposed as a means of beginning discussions with blacks on a new constitution providing for some measure of power-sharing between whites and blacks.

At the same time, however, the authorities in Pretoria showed determination not to allow the process of change to get out of hand. They continued to denounce resorts to violence, and they ruled out dealings with any non-whites committed to a strategy of violence.[22] Moreover, they employed coercion and intimidation to try to quell the disorder that spread through black townships in the wake of the creation of the new parliamentary dispensation in 1984. As for the substance of change, they adamantly rejected a political system for South Africa based on simple majoritarian rule,[23] and they persisted in carrying out some measures designed to enforce the Group Areas Act.[24]

This revised approach to ensuring the survival of Afrikaner identity, it should be stressed, did not meet with universal acclaim even among erstwhile National party supporters. Criticism of it came from both the right and the left. The right favored adherence to separatism and argued that any deviation from that course simply compromised the white position in South Africa.[25] In 1982, seventeen members of parliament who propounded this viewpoint left the National party and founded the Conservative party. This body captured about 27 percent of the popular vote in the white parliamentary election of May 1987—largely in hardcore Afrikaner areas and especially in the Transvaal. As a consequence of its showing, the party obtained 22 seats in parliament and replaced the Progressive Federal party as the official opposition.[26] The left believed that changes more fundamental than the National party leadership contemplated must take place in South Africa and that negotiations with authentic black leaders were essential to effect these.[27] Prior to the 1987 parliamentary election, three prominent National party figures of this persuasion withdrew from the party and ran as independents in the elections. A significant number of other well-known National party members severed their association with the party and backed the independent candidates. The three independents garnered about 25 percent of the total ballots in their electoral districts, and one won a seat in parliament.

Perceived Domestic-Regional Political Linkages. From the earliest indications in the mid-1950s that at least some sub-Saharan African countries were going to gain independence under black-majority governments, Afrikaners judged that the emergence of such states could have a serious impact on the domestic South African scene. It might inspire South Africa's non-whites and particularly the country's blacks to intensify their struggle for full rights. More crucially, it might significantly expand the ranks of foreign critics of the Pretoria government's internal policies; indeed, these new states might even try to provide some form of concrete aid to local blacks.[28]

The behavior of the new African states in the late 1950s and throughout the 1960s tended to confirm Afrikaner apprehensions on this score to some degree. For instance, the founding meeting of the Organization of African Unity (OAU) in 1963 condemned the Pretoria government and called for an effective trade boycott of South Africa. It also resolved to buy arms for the national liberation movement in South Africa, to give the movement's members military training in camps to be set up in various independent African countries, and to afford these individuals shelter and transit on their way to and from South Africa.[29] Subsequently, the OAU Liberation Committee recognized both the ANC and PAC as authentic "national liberation" groups, and some black-ruled states began to provide military training to members of the two organizations.[30]

Yet in the eyes of mainstream Afrikaners several factors limited the effect on South Africa's domestic situation of the rise of black-dominated states in Africa during these years. First and foremost was distance. Most of the new black-controlled states lay in the central belt of the continent, and between them and South Africa were large territories governed, like South Africa, by white minorities. To be sure, the transitions to independence under black-majority governments in Zambia, Malawi, Lesotho, Botswana, and Swaziland in the mid- and late-1960s left a few gaps in the white redoubt. But of these new states, only Zambia showed any real inclination to confront the Pretoria government, and it lacked direct access to South Africa proper. The nearest thing that it had to such access was the border along a part of the Caprivi strip of South West Africa, over which Pretoria had exercised authority since the 1920s under a League of Nations mandate. It is also true that during the 1960s black "liberation" movements in Angola, Mozambique, Rhodesia, and even South West Africa launched armed struggles to win power. Nevertheless, Afrikaners did not view these insurgencies as imminent threats to the existing order in any of these countries. In short, Afrikaners felt that South Africa's distance from antagonistic black-ruled African states meant that local blacks could not obtain much help from these countries.

Second, Afrikaners recognized that the new black-dominated states on the continent possessed relatively feeble means for assisting South African blacks. For example, the black-run African states could—and some did—provide shelter and military training for exiled elements of the black South African opposition; however, none of the states had major quantities of arms and equipment to offer these opposition elements. Moreover, their own military forces were small, and these did not have the logistical capacity to operate far, if at all, beyond local borders.

Third, it quickly became apparent to Afrikaners that the resolve to bring about a black-majority government in South Africa varied in intensity among the black-ruled African states, despite their universal attacks on Pretoria's apartheid policy. Not all of the states endorsed a trade boycott against South Africa, and even a number that did failed to enforce it. Similarly, many black-dominated states refrained from furnishing financial and military aid to the ANC and PAC, either on an individual basis or through the OAU Liberation Committee.

In light of these factors, Afrikaners even leaned toward the view that the fulminations of the new black-governed states in Africa against apartheid in South Africa stemmed from the "immaturity" of these states. Over time, they would become more "realistic" and accept white-run South Africa as a lasting and desirable part of the African political scene.[31] The increasing division among the black-dominated African states into militants and moderates regarding South Africa in the late 1960s tended to reinforce this Afrikaner calculation.

Beginning in the mid-1970s, however, Afrikaner assessments underwent major revision. This shift reflected the altered circumstances that South Africa faced. As already noted, the years from 1975 to 1980 witnessed the establishment of black-majority governments in Angola, Mozambique, and Zimbabwe, leaving South Africa virtually surrounded by black-ruled states. Only Namibia (South West Africa), over which the Pretoria government continued to exercise sovereignty, remained under white-minority control. Thus, distance no longer constituted an impediment to efforts by black-dominated states in Africa to influence South Africa's internal situation.

Worse yet from the Afrikaner perspective, key moderate as well as militant states in Southern Africa now evidenced a determination to carry out such undertakings, and countries of both persuasions formed an informal grouping, known as the Front-Line States, to work jointly toward eradication of white-minority rule in South Africa and Namibia. By the early 1980s, the grouping included Angola, Mozambique, Botswana, Zambia, and Zimbabwe (plus Tanzania).

The Front-Line States, to be sure, differed somewhat among themselves about how far they should go in assisting South African and Namibian blacks to win power.[32] Only Angola was overtly willing to provide sanctuaries and training facilities to guerrillas of the ANC and the Southwest African People's Organization (SWAPO), the body pursuing armed struggle in Namibia. (Tanzania did allow both the ANC and PAC to conduct guerrilla training on its territory, but Tanzania lies outside Southern Africa as traditionally defined.) The other states gave asylum to ANC and SWAPO members and even permitted them to open local ANC and SWAPO offices, but these countries officially forbade use of their domains by guerrillas as sanctuaries and/or for training camps.

Nevertheless, none of the latter group except Zimbabwe vigorously monitored the activities of SWAPO or, particularly, ANC adherents. Thus, the two bodies sometimes organized and launched sabotage attacks against Namibia and South Africa from the territory of Front-Line States aside from Angola. (The same was true in the cases of two Southern African countries that did not formally associate themselves with the Front-Line States—namely, Lesotho and Swaziland.)

Finally, although the Front-Line States, like black-run countries elsewhere on the continent, lacked impressive means to carry out their goal with respect to South Africa and Namibia, they appeared to Afrikaners to be resolved to remedy at least their military deficiencies in this regard. Angola and Mozambique in particular seemed determined to improve their own military prowess.[33]

As a result of these considerations (and some others to be examined a little later), the Afrikaner government came to see a "total onslaught" against South Africa. According to it, South Africa confronted a coordinated challenge from abroad and from within the country. This was "not just military" in character; it was also "political, diplomatic, religious, psychological, cultural, economic, and social." In short, "South Africa is . . . involved in total war."[34]

That rank-and-file Afrikaners shared this perception of an intertwined domestic and regional threat is unquestionable. In a 1982 opinion poll of whites, for instance, more than 80 percent of the people queried believed that neighboring states offered sanctuaries to the ANC, and the same proportion of the sample approved strikes against such sanctuaries. Among National party supporters, the figure reached 86 percent.[35]

Developments of the 1980s if anything strengthened Afrikaner convictions about the close ties between internal and external challenges. During 1980–84, the ANC conducted a sabotage campaign of mounting intensity and high visibility against South African targets from neighboring countries. Although pressure from Pretoria subsequently managed to deprive the ANC of sanctuaries in places like Mozambique, Swaziland, and Lesotho, the ANC quickly found a way to advance its cause from more distant exile locations. In June 1985, after the upsurge of militancy and protest in South Africa's black townships had been under way nearly a year, the ANC switched to a strategy of "people's war." That is, it now sought to recruit an army of part-time guerrillas who would operate in their normal home areas rather than from outside the country.[36] The growing number of simple acts of sabotage during subsequent months attested to the implementation of this new strategy.[37] To the particular frustration of mainstream Afrikaners, these developments came during a period when the Pretoria government was moving away from a "separateness" approach toward non-whites in South Africa and making concessions designed to coopt them.

After Mozambique's conclusion of a non-aggression treaty with South Africa at Nkomati in 1984, it is true, spokesmen for the Afrikaner government tried to differentiate to a degree between the domestic and the regional threats that they discerned. In September 1986, for example, President Botha told two West German correspondents that the "terrorists" operating out of neighboring countries constituted a threat to South Africa, but that the countries themselves did not necessarily pose such a challenge.[38] Yet a variety of indications left little doubt that the government remained persuaded of the fundamental connection between the internal and regional threats to it.[39]

Expanding Regional Role of Hostile Non-African Powers

The evolution of the state system in Southern Africa permitted non-African countries unfriendly to the South African government to assume an increasing role in the affairs of the region. Chief among these were the communist powers—especially the Soviet Union.

As early as the late 1940s, authorities in Pretoria expressed fears that the handing over of political control in other portions of Southern Africa to blacks would have just such a consequence,[40] but they lacked much solid evidence to confirm the validity of these fears until the end of the 1960s. Prior to that juncture, the communist states had played quite a minor part in the region. In the mid-1960s, Zambia had entered into diplomatic relations with the USSR, China, and several other communist countries, yet interaction between the Lusaka government and these countries had remained fairly limited in ensuing years—even with respect to support for the ANC, the PAC, and other "national liberation" movements of Southern Africa.[41] No other sovereign entity in the region had so much as established official ties with any communist state.

Zambia's acceptance in late 1969 of a Chinese offer of financial and technical aid to build the Tan-Zam Railway altered the situation appreciably. In Pretoria's eyes, not only did the scope of the Chinese commitment—about $400 million and a substantial number of technicians and workers[42]—demonstrate clearly Beijing's intensified resolve to acquire influence in the region, but the nature of the project itself attested to Zambia's new willingness to enlist the assistance of communist powers against South Africa. The railway, by linking the Zambian copper belt with Dar es Salaam, would afford Zambia a route for exports other than through South Africa; thus, it would reduce Zambia's economic dependence on South Africa. In summing up the Afrikaner government's perspective, P. W. Botha, then Minister of Defense, charged: "[Zambian President Kenneth] Kaunda has chosen to side with the communists and he is becoming more and more their lackey and slave."[43]

It was events after the collapse of the Portuguese empire in Africa in the mid-1970s, however, that led South African authorities to conclude firmly that their anxieties were well founded. In Angola, the Popular Movement for the Liberation of Angola (MPLA) called upon various communist states to aid it in the civil war that began before independence, and a coalition consisting mainly of the USSR, Cuba, and the German Democratic Republic provided the essential military backing that enabled the MPLA to install itself in power in Luanda. This successful communist venture represented a direct slap in the face to Pretoria, for South Africa had intervened in the war in behalf of the MPLA's rivals, the National Front for the Liberation of Angola (FNLA) and particularly the National Union for the Total Independence of Angola (UNITA). In October 1976, not long after the close of the civil war, the MPLA government signed a treaty of friendship and cooperation with Moscow. Discerning a continuing threat to its existence from South Africa, the government also sought concrete military assistance from the USSR and its Warsaw Pact allies. By the end of the 1970s, about 1,000 Soviet military advisers and an additional 400 from East European countries were working in Angola. No less important, the USSR had become Luanda's chief arms supplier. The MPLA government even requested Cuban troops to remain in Angola indefinitely, although it acquiesced to reduction of the Cuban contingent from 36,000 men in 1976 to about 19,000 in 1979.[44]

In Mozambique, the Front for the Liberation of Mozambique (Frelimo) managed to acquire power without significant help from the communist states, but in April 1977 the new Frelimo regime signed a treaty of friendship and cooperation with the USSR. Furthermore, the regime's escalating conflict with white-controlled Rhodesia as well as its wariness of South Africa soon caused it to turn to the USSR and a variety of other communist countries for military aid. By 1979, there were 525 Soviet and East European military advisers plus 215 Cuban military advisers in Mozambique. In addition, Moscow was furnishing the lion's share of the weapons and equipment that Maputo was receiving from abroad.[45]

Worst of all from Pretoria's standpoint, the new governments in Angola and Mozambique allowed the USSR and its allies to step up assistance to exile elements from South West Africa (Namibia) and South Africa proper. Instructors from communist countries provided military training in Angola to SWAPO and ANC recruits, and political and military personnel from communist states had improved access to SWAPO and the ANC through the offices that the MPLA and Frelimo regimes let these organizations set up in Angola and Mozambique. Moreover, the USSR, by virtue of its ability to channel deliveries through Angola, now assumed the role of principal supplier of arms to SWAPO.[46]

The most telling sign of the import that the South African government attached to these events came from the twist that it put on the notion of "total onslaught." According to its officials, the communist states, and especially the USSR, were orchestrating the attack on South Africa for their own purposes. That is, Moscow was using not only the newly independent black states of Southern Africa but also the ANC and SWAPO to further its own expansionist designs.[47]

Developments of the 1980s merely reinforced Pretoria's conviction that the changed character of the regional situation had exposed South Africa to a mounting challenge from the USSR and its communist allies. By the early 1980s, all of the black-ruled countries of the region except Malawi had opened up diplomatic relations with the USSR and a number of its fellow communist states. Of these Southern African countries, all but Lesotho had also acquired some arms from Moscow. By 1984, the total of Soviet and East European military advisers alone seconded to states in the region exceeded 3,000.[48]

As the 1980s wore on, to be sure, Pretoria tended to deemphasize the term "total onslaught"—especially after the conclusion of the Nkomati agreement with Mozambique in 1984. Nevertheless, the idea that South Africa confronted a conspiracy masterminded by the USSR for its own ends continued to permeate official statements and commentary.[49]

Threat Perception Since 1989

The year 1989 marked a watershed in South Africa's threat perception. Not only did the severity of the challenge that the Pretoria government deemed it faced decline, but the nature of the discerned threat altered considerably.

Changes in Pretoria's assessment of the security challenge confronting it did not, of course, come about overnight. They reflected the accumulated experience of earlier years; moreover, they have intensified since they began. Nonetheless, the breakthroughs of note took place in 1989.

Southern African Countries

South African authorities decided that the other states in Southern Africa no longer posed a real threat to South Africa. Events after the December 1988 agreements on Namibian independence and withdrawal of Cuban troops from Angola produced this shift in judgment.

As late as November 1988, General Magnus Malan, South Africa's minister of defense, had charged that black-ruled states in Southern Africa were still compelling South Africa to wage "a struggle for survival."[50] Yet the behavior of Southern African countries after the signing of the Namibia-Angola accords raised doubts about the official South African view. MPLA authorities quickly closed down ANC camps in Angola, thereby compelling the ANC's military elements to seek refuge in Tanzania and Uganda, far from South Africa's borders. Furthermore, officials of many regional states counseled SWAPO, generally regarded as the likely victor in the Namibian elections scheduled for November 1989, to retain links with South Africa when it gained power.

Thus, by the time that F. W. de Klerk assumed the presidency of South Africa in September 1989, Pretoria's commentary about South Africa's neighbors was acquiring a new tone. In his inaugural address, de Klerk declared that "on the basis of good-neighborliness, nonintervention, and healthy cooperation," Southern Africa "can enter into a new era of stability and progress," and he promised that "my government and I will exert ourselves" to that end.[51]

Shortly thereafter, General Malan delivered a speech to the SADF Infantry School that differed strikingly from his observations a year previously. "The frontline states," he claimed, "have lost their ability to continue their struggle against South Africa," for "the same system that has destroyed growth in the East Bloc has also ruined development in the frontline states." As a result, he contended, there had been "a slow change in perceptions."[52]

President de Klerk provided the definitive statement of the revised official thinking on the matter in his speech at the opening of a new session of the South African parliament on 2 February 1990. "The season of violence" in Southern Africa "is over," he proclaimed; the region "now has an historical opportunity to set aside its conflicts and ideological differences."[53]

The Soviet Union and Its Communist Allies

Pretoria concluded that the USSR and its communist allies had ceased to be a threat. This revised judgment represented a somewhat belated recognition of shifting Soviet outlook toward Southern Africa.

Moscow's attitude toward the region had begun to alter in the first half of the 1980s,[54] and since the mid-1980s it had gradually become apparent that Soviet leaders favored a political resolution of the conflict in South Africa.[55] Indeed, the USSR had taken a number of steps to expand its contacts with South African whites and especially Afrikaners opposed to apartheid.[56]

What obviously kept the South African government from trusting these growing signs of a new Soviet approach to Southern Africa was the level of Soviet and Cuban military support of Angola. By January 1988, to be sure, the Cubans were signaling a willingness to negotiate the withdrawal of their troops from Angola in return for South African acquiescence to Namibian independence, and soon thereafter the USSR began to evince an interest in facilitating such an arrangement.[57] Nevertheless, there had been a major rise in the flow of Soviet arms to Angola after Gorbachev took over the top job in the USSR. According to official U.S. estimates, the value of the shipments was now amounting to more than $1 billion a year.[58] Furthermore, in late 1987 Cuba not only increased the number of its troops in Angola to 40,000 (in reaction to a UNITA-South African siege of Cuito Cuanavale) but also sent large numbers of them into the southern part of the country for the first time since the mid-1970s.[59]

The Pretoria government, then, clung to its traditional assessment of the challenge presented by the USSR and Soviet allies until after the signing of the Namibia-Angola agreements.[60] By no means all elements of the government, it is true, were equally wedded to such an assessment. Analysts at the ministry of foreign affairs had displayed mounting interest as the hints of "new" Soviet thinking about Southern Africa had accumulated over the years. In fact, the ministry had reestablished a Soviet desk, and in February 1988 it had even helped to organize a conference to explore the possibility that the USSR could be trusted in negotiations. Yet the dominant ministry of defense remained quite adamant that the threat from the USSR and its allies had not altered.[61]

The accords on the Namibia-Angola question and their successful implementation, however, gradually produced a change in Pretoria's viewpoint. Not only did the USSR press the Angolans and Cubans to enter into the agreements, but it expended considerable effort during the period leading up to the Namibian elections of November 1989 to ensure that the settlement did not become derailed.[62] In addition, the withdrawal of Cuban troops from Angola proceeded according to schedule.

By late 1989, even such a stalwart defender of the notion of "total onslaught" as General Malan had shifted his position on the threat to South Africa from the Soviet bloc. During the late 1970s, he observed, "the Soviet Union was still in an expansionist phase," but "now with the process of Namibia's independence in full swing," the Soviet Union had had "a change of heart." "The revolutionary tide that was to sweep across the world," he went on "has lost its momentum;" indeed, it "is receding."[63]

Local Blacks

The South African government now conceded that the assumption of a major political role in South Africa by local blacks would not necessarily mean the extinction of Afrikanerdom. This shift in perspective resulted largely from a change in state leadership. During the course of 1989, F. W. de Klerk replaced P. W. Botha as president.

To the end of his tenure in office, Botha, for all of the modifications that he had engineered in the old apartheid system, still clung tenaciously to the belief that the survival of Afrikaners as a group required them to maintain a firm grip on the reins of power in Pretoria. He was willing to give blacks and other non-whites a minor function in the political system, but this "power-sharing" he saw as a means of coopting them.

Initially, de Klerk's reputation as essentially a conservative tended to obscure the contrasts between his outlook and that of Botha. Yet differences there were—and important ones. The chief of these concerned what political role blacks should be offered.

As early as 1987, de Klerk had concluded that attempts to coopt "moderate" blacks by allowing them highly limited forms of participation in the political system would fail, but he recognized that Afrikaners particularly and whites generally had a self-interest in working out a modus vivendi with blacks.[64] By early 1989, he was convinced that achieving such an end necessitated according a significant role in the political life of the country to blacks, and he was ready to take that step.[65]

The sort of role that de Klerk envisioned for blacks in a new South African political order emerged in broad outline during 1989, although he insisted that the precise institutions for realizing it would have to be shaped in negotiations with blacks. Blacks, first of all, should have "meaningful participation" in decision-making. At the same time, the involvement of blacks in decision-making should not permit them to dominate whites. Where decisions had to be made jointly within the same institution, for example, the basis for such decisions should be consensus, and failure to reach such a consensus "should be settled by a fair referee." Furthermore, on matters of "intimate interest for the individual groups" there should be "self-government." In other words, de Klerk foresaw a condominium or "co-government" of blacks and whites on issues of common interest, and group autonomy on questions of relevance solely or largely to one or the other.[66]

De Klerk held firmly to this vision even though less than 50 percent of Afrikaner voters in the September 1989 elections supported him and the National party. He consoled himself with the fact that about 55 percent of Afrikaners and 70 percent of all whites had opted for "reform" by voting for either the National party or the newly formed Democratic Party, which had campaigned on a platform of one man, one vote.[67] Thus, in his inaugural address as president, he promised to push ahead with the creation of "a new constitutional dispensation in which all South Africans shall participate but without domination."[68]

As long as much of the black opposition remained suppressed, of course, the credibility of this revised official thinking about a political role for blacks remained open to challenge as simply rhetoric. But de Klerk soon moved to dispel skepticism on this score. In October 1989, he released seven senior leaders of the ANC and one of the PAC, all of whom had been in prison since the 1960s. Then on 2 February 1990 he lifted the long-standing ban on the ANC, the PAC, and the South African Communist Party (SACP) and removed the more recent restrictions on thirty-three other anti-apartheid organizations, including the United Democratic Front (UDF) and the Congress of South African Trade Unions (COSATU). A few days later, he set free Nelson Mandela, the ANC leader who had been in prison for more than 25 years.

International Isolation

The foregoing developments together produced a substantial reduction in Pretoria's overall sense of threat, but South African officials also identified a new challenge confronting the country that partially offset this trend. That challenge arose from the high degree of international isolation in which South Africa found itself, and especially from the economic sanctions that Western industrial states had maintained against it since the mid-1980s.

When the Western powers had first imposed economic sanctions in the mid-1980s, the Pretoria government had reacted with both defiance and self-confidence.[69] Yet by 1989 sanctions were having sufficient impact on South Africa that they had begun to cause serious worry in Pretoria. Although South Africa had managed to get around many of the trade sanctions and keep its level of foreign trade up, these sanctions had helped to fuel double-digit inflation within the country. To be sure, inflation did drop, according to official figures, from 18.6 percent to 12.9 percent between 1986 and 1988, but government authorities acknowledged that the rate might well climb back to 15 percent in 1989. It did in fact do so.[70]

The financial sanctions had proved even more damaging. These had essentially ended loans from abroad; however, South Africa had had to continue to repay debts that it had accumulated to foreign banks in the pre-1985 period. Even in 1989, the figure for its outstanding international debts stood at $21.2 billion or roughly a quarter of the state's GNP. It was estimated that servicing of the remaining debts would require $2.7 billion annually, which amounted to more than 12 percent of the country's yearly export earnings in the late 1980s.[71] In addition, the financial sanctions had not only dried up most new foreign investment but caused substantial disinvestment by foreign firms which had previously set up enterprises in South Africa. Between 1985 and 1989, for example, half of the 1,120 foreign companies that were operating in the country in 1985 departed. Two-thirds of those that left, it is true, were taken over at very low prices by South African companies, some of which were evidently only figureheads. Nevertheless, the outward transfer of funds involved still reached $13 billion during the period.[72]

Largely because of the major outflow of capital stemming from the financial sanctions, South Africa's growth rate had stayed fairly low. The rate of real increase in its gross domestic product (GDP) went from a negative 1.2 percent in 1985 to 1.0 percent in 1986, to 2.6 percent in 1987, and to about 3 percent in 1988. Even in the last two years, the rates of growth achieved barely kept pace with the expansion of the population, which was running at 2.6 percent annually. Economists estimated that at least a 5 percent rate of real increase in GDP would be necessary for the government to make a start on reducing black unemployment and meeting housing and other infrastructure needs of blacks.[73]

The rising concern about the effects that sanctions were having on South Africa was reflected clearly in de Klerk's public utterances after he was elected president in September 1989. His inaugural address called upon the international community to "take note" of "the determination among millions of South Africans to negotiate fair and peaceful solutions" and to "use your influence constructively to help us attain that goal."[74] In his speech to the opening of a new session of parliament on 2 February 1990, he acknowledged that "without contact and co-operation with the rest of the world we cannot promote the well-being and security of our citizens." He then stressed that "the dynamic developments in international politics" had permitted "important advances" to be made in "our contacts abroad," and he expressed the hope that "this trend will be encouraged by the important change in climate that is taking place in South Africa."[75]

Strategic Response Before the Late 1980s

Over the years from the late 1940s to the late 1980s, the rising sense of threat that the South African government felt from the rest of Southern Africa prompted it to take—at various times—steps aimed at accommodation, deterrence through defense, alliance, state strengthening, and counterthreat. At no juncture, however, did the government confine its response to a single type of approach, although that response often had a dominant thrust. Of even greater significance, neither the objective underlying the government's response nor the mixed approach employed by the government remained the same throughout the period. Even the major thrust of the response altered.

Therefore, it is imperative to examine Pretoria's strategic response during these years in terms of phases. Five of these can be distinguished: 1948 to the early 1960s, the early 1960s to the late 1960s, the late 1960s to the mid-1970s, the mid-1970s to the mid-1980s, and the mid-1980s to the late 1980s.

From 1948 to the Early 1960s

These years amounted to a prelude—a period when the South African government awakened to the merits of exercising hegemony in Southern Africa. This awakening stemmed from the political changes taking place in sub-Saharan Africa and from Pretoria's general lack of success in finding another security response to cope adequately with these changes.

Alliance and Accommodation. Throughout the years in question here, the South African government sought avidly to forge an alliance with the Western powers that would protect white rule in South Africa (including the mandated territory of South West Africa). In the 1940s and early 1950s, for instance, Prime Minister D. F. Malan proposed that all of the powers with interests and/or territory and possessions in Africa issue an "African Charter."[76] He wanted them, specifically, to assert that the continent must be preserved for "Western European Christian civilization." To keep the continent safe in this regard, he advocated that the parties to the Charter prohibit Asiatic (that is, Indian) and communist influence from entering Africa and forbid the arming of "natives" and their employment in white wars. In justification of his proposal, he argued that although Africa clearly needed economic development, it required protection and guidance more.

The South African government also made some tentative attempts at accommodation with the new black states in sub-Saharan Africa. By the mid-1950s, authorities in Pretoria were offering the emerging black governments there friendship and cooperation, although they predicated these offers on non-interference in one another's internal affairs.[77] To a degree, South Africa even tried to establish direct contacts with the new states. For instance, Pretoria sent a representative to Ghana's independence celebrations in 1957; in 1958, it welcomed a Ghanaian to a conference in South Africa of the Commission for Technical Cooperation South of the Sahara and accorded him much the same treatment that it did white delegates.[78]

Neither of these two kinds of undertakings, however, yielded appreciable fruit. The Western powers shied away from commitments that might conceivably guarantee whites control of South Africa in perpetuity. By the end of the 1950s, it had become evident as well that the new black states were going to shun South Africa, at least for the present, because of its policy of apartheid.[79]

State Strengthening. The one aspect of South Africa's security response that did produce some positive results from Pretoria's standpoint was the government's effort to consolidate Afrikaner domination of the state. This effort took several forms. First, authorities in Pretoria sought to Afrikanerize the civil service. By 1968, twice as many Afrikaners held government jobs as had been the case before the 1948 elections,[80] and most of this increase had clearly come before the early 1960s. Second, government officials promoted the transformation of South Africa into a republic, in order to deprive Great Britain of any opportunity to interfere in South Africa's domestic affairs. They finally achieved this end in 1961. Third, the government strove to implement apartheid so as to bolster its control of non-whites. As noted previously, all of the key apartheid legislation was on the books by the beginning of the 1960s.

Early 1960s to Late 1960s

This period witnessed vigorous pursuit and eventual achievement of hegemony in Southern Africa by South Africa. A combination of developments spurred the drive. For several years after the incident in Sharpeville in 1960, there was a substantial amount of domestic unrest in South Africa. The decisions of Great Britain and the United States to heed the 1963 call of the UN Security Council for a voluntary arms embargo against South Africa dashed all lingering hopes of South African authorities that the Western powers might ultimately opt to uphold white rule in South Africa (and South West Africa). During 1964–68, all of the British territories in Southern Africa except Rhodesia obtained their independence under black-majority governments.

Alliance. As in the previous period, Pretoria's security approach relied heavily on a search for allies, but the targets of its attention now shifted. With no perceived prospect of association with the Western powers, South Africa labored mightily to create an informal grouping of Southern African countries friendly to and reliant on it, for such a grouping would help to cordon off South Africa (and South West Africa) from what the Pretoria government viewed as hostile states to the north. The South African effort focused particularly on the territories where white minorities continued to hold sway—the Portuguese colonies of Mozambique and Angola and the British territory of Rhodesia. Yet Pretoria included in its undertakings, too, the more moderate black states emerging in the region.

By the late 1960s, South Africa had realized visible fruits from such endeavors. It had exploited its economic and technical assets to fashion fairly strong links with the white-dominated regimes of Angola, Mozambique, and Rhodesia, and it had induced Lesotho, Swaziland, Botswana, and Malawi to carry on substantial interaction with it—although all of these states, and particularly Botswana, showed considerably greater wariness than did the white-controlled territories of Southern Africa.[81]

State Strengthening and Deterrence Through Defense. With no expectations of protection by a great-power ally, the Pretoria government also felt a need to bolster its position at home and to improve South Africa's own capabilities to ward off dangers from abroad. To accomplish the first of these goals, the Afrikaner authorities resorted essentially to suppression of the local non-white opposition. In 1960, after events in

Sharpeville had sparked widespread demonstrations by blacks, the government declared a state of emergency, outlawed the ANC and PAC, and arrested many of the leaders of the two groups. Those leaders who managed to escape and go underground in South Africa, the police subsequently hunted down and jailed—especially after the two banned organizations turned to violence to pursue their ends. By the close of 1965, such repressive measures had largely succeeded in fulfilling their purpose. All of the key non-white critics of the government were in prison or in exile, and public challenges to the government from non-whites had virtually ceased, although the black community, particularly, continued to smolder with resentment of the Afrikaner authorities.

To enhance South Africa's capabilities to deter external challengers, the Pretoria government carried out an extensive military buildup. Prior to the early 1960s, South Africa had lacked significant military strength, but this situation changed dramatically during the course of the 1960s.[82] Between 1960/61 and 1967/68, South Africa's defense allocations rose nearly sixfold, from 44 million to 252 million rands; then they remained more or less constant in the last years of the decade. Whereas the figure for 1960/61 constituted less than 1 percent of the country's GNP and less than 7 percent of government expenditures, the figure for 1967/68 represented 2.5 percent of the national GNP and about 17 percent of the government budget. By the mid-1960s, the regular forces had expanded from 9,000 to about 15,000 men, and they stayed at roughly this level for the rest of the decade. Far more significant, the government in 1961 introduced compulsory military training of three months for selected young men; in 1967, it made military service mandatory for all medically fit young men and extended the length of required full-time service to nine months. As a result, by 1969 the number of Citizen Force conscripts and reservists exceeded 70,000, and that of Commando (part-time rural militia) reserves had grown by 18 percent, to 58,000. With these increases, the government now had 200,000 armed and trained men (counting the police) upon which it could call. Of the total of more than 1.8 billion rands in defense expenditures during the decade, more than 660 million went for weapons for the armed forces. Among these were new generations of armored vehicles, jet aircraft, transports, naval vessels, helicopters, and missiles.

In conjunction with this military buildup, the Pretoria government strove to decrease South Africa's dependence on outside sources for weapons.[83] Between 1960/61 and 1964/65, for example, the annual sum of South Africa's outlays for local manufacture of munitions jumped a hundredfold—from 315,000 to 33 million rands. In 1964, authorities in Pretoria created the Armaments Production Board to coordinate the country's drive for increased self-sufficiency. By the end of 1965, the government was proclaiming South Africa virtually independent in the manufacture of small arms and ammunition, and it could even boast of a nascent aircraft industry and a new National Institute for the Development of Missiles. In 1968, the powers of the Armaments Production Board were extended to cover all phases of production and procurement, and a state corporation, the Armaments Development and Manufacturing Corporation (Armscor), was established to produce arms.

Accommodation. Despite its preoccupation with defensive types of security measures, the Pretoria government did not entirely eschew accommodation with its external opponents. From its perspective, the steps that it took to create Bantustans, or "self-governing" African "homelands," in South Africa (and South West Africa) had such dimensions. By providing an institutional framework within which local blacks could have a limited say in developments affecting them, Afrikaner leaders hoped to placate black-controlled states that exhibited hostility toward South Africa.[84] Similarly, courtship of Southern African states like Malawi and Swaziland, although primarily motivated by defensive concerns, had positive overtones. In demonstrating that South Africa was willing to cooperate with black-run states, Pretoria sought to promote acceptance of South Africa and to restore the country to its "rightful place" as a continental leader.[85] To drive home the benefits to be derived from contacts with South Africa, Afrikaner authorities in March 1968 even set up a fund to furnish low-interest loans to developing African countries well disposed to South Africa.

But for the time being these overtures produced little response from any black-controlled state beyond Southern Africa. Only in the next period did they yield results.

Late 1960s to Mid-1970s

During these years, South Africa tried to exploit its hegemony in Southern Africa to win the tolerance, if not the approval, of states elsewhere on the continent. A relatively quiet domestic front (even taking into account the attempts of SWAPO after 1965 to conduct guerrilla warfare in Namibia) helped to make this enterprise possible.

Alliance. A key element of Pretoria's security approach continued to be pursuit of alliance with the white-dominated territories and moderate black states of Southern Africa, yet the focus of its energies in this regard shifted. Previously, Afrikaner leaders had directed their attention principally toward the white-controlled countries; now, they looked more to the countries under black rule.

To be sure, the Pretoria government did not neglect the white-minority regimes.[86] Nevertheless, South African courtship of the moderate black-run states of the region heightened visibly. In 1969, for example, Afrikaner officials approved a revision of the customs union with Botswana, Lesotho, and Swaziland that gave each of the three more than double their previous share of customs revenue. During the early 1970s, South Africa elected to proceed with projects proposed earlier to build a thermal power station in Swaziland and a rail link between South Africa and Swaziland. Prime Minister Vorster visited Malawi in May 1970—the first time that a sitting South African prime minister had ever been in an independent black African state. The following year, he received Malawi's president, Dr. Hastings Banda, in South Africa. Before the close of the period, he also had "unofficial" talks on at least one occasion with both Prince Makhosini Dlamini, prime minister of Swaziland, and Chief Leabua Jonathan, prime minister of Lesotho. South Africa and Lesotho even agreed in 1972 to enter into consular relations at the consul-general level. In 1971, South Africa reportedly sold Malawi some arms, including four aircraft with weapons and three armored cars.[87]

These undertakings with respect to the moderate black-controlled countries of Southern Africa paid significant dividends for Pretoria. Both Malawi and Lesotho in the early 1970s became strong advocates in African councils of dialogue with, rather than isolation of, South Africa. By the mid-1970s, however, Lesotho had abandoned that role as a consequence of a deterioration in its relations with South Africa.

Accommodation. Hand in hand with the Pretoria government's intensified efforts to fashion collaborative relationships with the moderate black-ruled states in Southern Africa went an attempt to achieve a modus vivendi with other black-dominated states on the continent. Such a modus vivendi, in the eyes of South Africa's leaders, would involve a quid pro quo. South Africa would proffer political friendship and expanded economic ties in return for acceptance of the existing order in South Africa by the black-run countries.[88]

In the late 1960s, authorities in Pretoria had begun privately sounding out a number of African states outside Southern African about a rapprochement, but the first open sign of a concerted South African push toward this end came in October 1969. At that juncture, a forty-man South African trade mission traveled to Madagascar, Reunion, and Mauritius. Quickly thereafter, the indications multiplied.[89]

The South African campaign brought about an open debate in 1970/71 among members of the OAU about "dialogue" with South Africa. Aside from the Southern African states of Malawi and Lesotho, states like the Ivory Coast, Gabon, Madagascar, and Mauritius endorsed such "dialogue." But the OAU as a whole concluded that there was no basis for "dialogue," for South Africa had no intention of modifying its internal policy of apartheid.[90]

Advocates of dialogue for a time tried to keep the idea alive outside the OAU framework,[91] but by the mid-1970s all of the black-controlled African states beyond Southern Africa had essentially lost interest in the project. Nonetheless, to the end of the period Pretoria still retained hope of eventually arriving at an accommodation with at least some black-dominated African states outside the immediate region.

Deterrence Through Defense. Although South African leaders stressed alliance and accommodation in their security approach during the years under consideration, they did not by any means scorn steps aimed at deterrence through defense.[92] In 1972, they extended the length of service required of conscripts from nine to twelve months. Active-duty military forces—regular and conscript—rose from 39,700 in mid-1969 to 47,450 in mid-1974. With the continuing transfer of conscripts from active-duty to reserve status, the Citizen Force reserves swelled from about 45,000 to 72,000 over the same timespan. Furthermore, the part-time rural militia increased from 58,000 to 75,000. Defense appropriations jumped from 272 million rands in 1969/70 to 692 million rands in 1974/75; however, the great bulk of this increase came after 1972/73, in response to a general strike of black workers in Namibia and a step-up of guerrilla activity in Rhodesia and Mozambique. Among the new kinds of weapons and equipment introduced into the inventory during the period were three Daphne-type submarines.

Mid-1970s to Mid-1980s

South Africa endeavored throughout these years to avert loss of its hegemony in Southern Africa. Its preoccupation with this goal reflected a mix of considerations. By mid-1980, as already noted, virtually the whole of independent Southern Africa was of a mind to shake off Pretoria's influence. Indeed, Angola had gone so far as to lend active support to black South African and Namibian elements challenging the authority of the Pretoria government, and several other states in the region had provided lesser degrees of assistance to these elements. Of equal consequence, the Angolan civil war of 1975/76 turned the USSR and its allies, all of which denounced not only South Africa's apartheid policy but also South Africa's hegemonial position in Southern Africa, into major players on the regional stage. Moreover, these communist powers did not disappear from the scene after the conclusion of the civil war.[93] To top things off, the Pretoria government felt a new sense of vulnerability at home, in both South Africa and Namibia. The severe disturbances in Soweto and other black townships of South Africa in 1976, the escalating guerrilla war in Namibia after the mid-1970s, and the growing assertiveness of the non-white population of South Africa in the 1980s all underscored non-white resentment of the existing order in the two domains.

In pursuit of its goal, the Pretoria government employed all of the general types of strategic response available. Yet its resort to some of them waxed and waned.

Accommodation. At the outset of the period, South African authorities placed heavy emphasis on accommodation. Not only did they hold out a hand of friendship to the new black government in Mozambique, but they also pressed for a resumption of dialogue with African leaders both in and beyond Southern Africa.[94]

Yet the substantial progress that South Africa appeared to be making toward rapprochement ceased with its large-scale military intervention in Angola in October 1975 to help FNLA-UNITA forces. This action, undertaken after consultations with some moderate black African governments, drew widespread fire from black-dominated African states, and that reaction caused even moderate countries on the continent to shy away from involvement with the Pretoria government.[95]

South Africa resumed its attempts at accommodation in 1978, but it now adopted a more indirect approach than it had followed initially. In April 1978, South Africa accepted the fundamental terms that the UN Security Council had formulated for a political settlement in Namibia, although it did subsequently string out negotiations on the precise implementation of these general principles.[96] In addition, the reforms of apartheid that South African authorities enacted from 1979 onward, even though largely intended to address the domestic situation, had an external dimension to them. According to the notion of a "total national strategy" that the Pretoria government embraced in the late 1970s, what other states thought about South Africa was important to the country's defense, and internal political and economic actions could influence not only the views of the domestic population about the government but those of foreign powers as well.[97]

Toward the close of the period, South African authorities deemed circumstances favorable to revive efforts at direct accommodation too, but they focused such undertakings essentially on the countries of Southern Africa this time. In February 1982, the Pretoria government signed a nonaggression pact with Swaziland, although the agreement did not become public knowledge until 1984. South Africa concluded a similar accord with Mozambique in March 1984.

Alliance. Just as in earlier years, a hunt for allies to strengthen South Africa's dominance in Southern Africa figured prominently in Pretoria's security approach during most of the period. Yet the high degree of flux in circumstances within and related to the region produced great instability in South Africa's principal targets of interest in this regard.

Moreover, the Pretoria government had little luck in actually finding any allies useful for its purpose.

In the mid-1970s, South African authorities concentrated on fashioning an alliance with the Western powers and especially the United States. By late 1977, however, Pretoria had concluded that, for the present, alliance with the West was not possible.[98]

For a brief time thereafter, South African leaders appeared to toy with the idea of primary alliance with "pariah" states.[99] Prime Minister Vorster had already paid an official visit to Israel in April 1976, and during his sojourn there the two countries had signed an agreement on economic, industrial, and technological cooperation. In the late 1970s, Pretoria also cultivated especially friendly relations with Taiwan.

But the growing challenge within Southern Africa and from outside powers to South Africa's regional hegemony persuaded authorities in Pretoria of the inadequacy of the "pariah" option. Consequently, South Africa turned again to the regional context in search of allies. In early 1979, it began to call for the formation of a "constellation of states" in Southern Africa.[100] This proposal envisioned a grouping including South Africa proper; the homelands of Transkei, Bophuthatswana, and Venda, to which Pretoria had granted "independence" in 1976, 1977, and 1979, respectively; the customs union states of Botswana, Lesotho, and Swaziland; Rhodesia, under the coalition of whites and "moderate" blacks that had emerged from the "internal settlement" of March 1978; and Namibia, when "independent" (presumably under a government similar to that in Rhodesia). South African officials entertained hopes that Zambia might join as well, and they even left the door open for Marxist states like Mozambique to participate, although this aspect of their plan may have stemmed more from tactical considerations than from genuine expectations.

According to Pretoria's vision, the "constellation" would collaborate in a variety of ways. It would work together militarily to keep "communism" out of Southern Africa. It would expand and further institutionalize cooperation in trade, agriculture, transportation, health, labor, power and energy, and scientific and technological development. It would even engage in some types of joint political activity.

Two developments in 1980, however, doomed the "constellation" scheme. Zimbabwe achieved independence under the guidance of Robert Mugabe's ZANU, a sharp critic of the internal policies of the South African government. At about the same time, SADCC emerged as an alternative—embracing all of the sovereign black-ruled countries of the region—to the "constellation" conceived by South Africa.

South African authorities then cast their eyes back toward the Western powers, notably the United States. Their renewed hope for alliance with the West stemmed largely from the victory of conservative Ronald Reagan in the 1980 United States presidential election.

The remainder of the period witnessed South African leaders' gradual disillusionment with the West in general and the United States in particular.[101] To Pretoria's dismay, Washington exerted increasing pressure on South Africa to eradicate apartheid domestically and to avoid provocative actions against its neighbors. Events following the South African government's declaration of a state of emergency in thirty-six black townships in July 1985 (and ultimately throughout the entire state in June 1986) finally prompted South African leaders to conclude that alliance with the United States or other Western powers was out of the question for the foreseeable future. Pushed by the United States Congress, the Reagan administration imposed limited sanctions on South Africa in September 1985, and then in September 1986 Congress overrode a presidential veto to toughen these measures. The members of the European Economic Community and Japan also instituted moderate economic sanctions against South Africa during 1985/86.

State Strengthening. After the onset of turbulence in Soweto and other black townships in June 1976, the Pretoria government devoted considerable energies during these years to trying to bolster its position at home. But the main thrust of its efforts fluctuated over time.

Initially, South African authorities concentrated on suppressing the domestic opposition to apartheid,[102] but by 1979 the situation had calmed sufficiently for the government to adopt conciliation and coaptation as the basic means whereby it sought to solidify its rule. Ensuing years brought the various reforms of the apartheid system already mentioned. Afrikaner authorities, to be sure, did not hesitate to employ harsh measures against critics if they felt circumstances justified such measures, but the accent of their approach plainly shifted to persuasion.

This emphasis prevailed until mid-1985—despite the escalating protests and violence in non-white areas after the elections in August 1984 under the new constitution. Then in July 1985 the government slid back toward repression by declaring a state of emergency in thirty-six black townships. Yet at that point, Pretoria still attempted to restrict the crackdown. Even after it extended the emergency to additional townships in October 1985, all of the affected townships were located in just three large areas of the country.[103] Not until June 1986 did the government proclaim a nationwide state of emergency.

Deterrence Through Defense. During the period at issue here, South Africa took a number of measures to improve its defense capabilities.[104] In 1977, the government increased the length of the country's compulsory military service from a year to two years, and it raised the requirement for service in the Citizen Force from nineteen days a year for five years after discharge from active duty to thirty days a year for eight years. Further changes in the conscription law in 1982 made all white males between the ages of seventeen and fifty-five subject to national military service. They also extended the obligation of a conscript to participate in the active reserves after his national military training until he was fifty-five and mandated that he remain in the inactive reserves for ten years thereafter.

The effect of these innovations was to increase the size of the active-duty forces and the pool of men available for rapid mobilization. Between mid-1974 and mid-1985, the figure for full-time personnel went up from 47,500 to 106,400 (including 64,000 conscripts), and the total of mobilizable elements mounted from about 200,000 to more than 550,000.

On 1 August 1980, the Pretoria government formed a South West Africa Territory Force (SWATF) under South African control, and it introduced conscription among all racial groups on a selective basis in the territory. By mid-1985, the SWATF had reached a strength of 21,000.

Allocations for defense rose dramatically between 1974/75 and 1985/86—from 692 million to 4.274 billion rands. Such outlays permitted the SADF to expand and modernize its inventory of weapons and equipment. For example, the number of combat aircraft at its disposal rose from 100 in mid-1974 to 356 in mid-1985. Among the additions were more than forty Mirage F-1 fighter and reconnaissance planes, acquired before France instituted an embargo on sale of arms to South Africa in 1977. The Pretoria government apparently even developed the capability to design, produce, and deliver a tactical nuclear weapon, although whether it actually turned out such a weapon remains a hotly debated point.

To help ensure that South Africa would have adequate arms available despite the 1977 UN Security Council resolution against arms sales to it, the Pretoria government poured increased funds into the local manufacture of weapons and equipment. By 1981, its annual expenditure on arms production had risen to 1.54 billion rands, as compared with 140 million rands in 1972. The following year, official sources claimed that local output met about 85 percent of the country's armament needs, and they depicted the country as fully self-sufficient in artillery weapons and rockets, armored and other operational vehicles, ammunition, and land mines. By 1985, the state-owned armaments corporation, Armscor, had become the third largest industrial group in the country, with some 16,000 employees, and South Africa's arms industry ranked as the tenth largest in the world.

Counterthreats. For the first time, the Pretoria government during these years employed counterthreats as part of its strategic response, and it relied more heavily on them as the period wore on.[105] One form that these counterthreats took was cross-border military operations, mostly aimed at SWAPO or ANC personnel and facilities. By 1985, Angola, Mozambique, Lesotho, and Botswana had experienced at least one major attack of this sort.

South Africa also provided assistance to opposition or dissident elements in several of its neighboring states. Although defeated by the MPLA in the 1975/76 Angolan civil war, Jonas Savimbi's UNITA survived in the south of the country, and it soon undertook guerrilla operations against the MPLA regime in Luanda. South Africa helped these efforts through logistical backup and even direct military intervention at times. During the 1970s, the white-minority government of Rhodesia spawned a guerrilla movement, the Mozambique National Resistance (Renamo), to destabilize the Frelimo government in Maputo, and South Africa assumed sponsorship of this movement after Robert Mugabe and ZANU gained power in Salisbury (Harare) in early 1980. The South Africans provided Renamo with sanctuary, arms, supplies, training, and logistical support. Such aid, it is true, did diminish greatly in the wake of the Nkomati accord between South Africa and Mozambique in early 1984, but the SADF, apparently without the concurrence of some key cabinet ministers, continued it at a reduced level. After Prime Minister Jonathan of Lesotho adopted a contentious stance toward South Africa in the latter half of the 1970s, the Pretoria government courted Lesotho dissidents. Initially, it favored Ntsu Mokhehle and his Lesotho Liberation Army; however, it later turned to the Basuto Democratic Alliance. In the case of Zimbabwe, South Africa between October 1982 and late February 1984 seems to have furnished training, weapons, and ammunition to some rebels in southern Matebeleland engaged in armed conflict with the government. Many of these individuals had formerly belonged to the guerrilla army of Joshua Nkomo's Zimbabwe African People's Union, ZANU's principal rival.

South Africa even used nonmilitary means on occasion for coercive purposes. In the spring of 1981, South African authorities, unhappy at Robert Mugabe's criticisms of South Africa's domestic conditions, withdrew twenty-five locomotives on loan to Zimbabwe. Zimbabwe at this time was trying to get a bumper grain crop to market. After a private demarche to South Africa by the United States, the Pretoria government eventually agreed to renew the leases on the locomotives. In August 1983, South Africa instituted a blockade against Lesotho to force it to expel 3,000 South African refugees.

The Mid-1980s to the Late 1980s

During these years, authorities in Pretoria treated South Africa's hegemony in Southern Africa as a shield behind which to try to stabilize the country's internal situation. By the mid-1980s, South Africa's leaders had concluded that they could successfully handle the challenges to the state's dominance of the region for at least the immediate future.[106] Moreover, they knew that South Africa had largely itself to thank for this development, for it had not benefited from the assistance of any major allies within or outside Southern Africa.[107] At the same time, the country's domestic environment had become racked with turmoil. Indeed, some of the state's black townships had reached the point where not only were they ungoverned but it was questionable whether they were governable.

State Strengthening. In keeping with its basic goal, the Pretoria government pursued a security approach stressing reestablishment of firm control of South Africa's internal affairs.[108] This entailed chiefly attempts to suppress the anti-apartheid opposition.

At first, South African authorities sought to employ repression in only a restricted way. As already noted, the state of emergency that they imposed in July 1985 applied to just thirty-six of the country's black townships. Even more telling, the emergency was actually lifted in March 1986.

But then in June 1986, the government declared a far more drastic, nationwide state of emergency. To carry out the tough new security measures, the authorities created the National Security Management System, a hierarchical network of behind-the-scenes councils and committees running from the State Security Council to the grassroots level.[109]

Operating under the emergency decree, the government rapidly took a number of major steps. It rounded up and detained some 20,000 persons. These individuals included not only a substantial contingent of children but also many prominent antigovernment activists—clergy, civic and community leaders, labor union officials, and especially prominent figures in the United Democratic Front (UDF). (The UDF, an umbrella body representing a broad geographic, ethnic, and demographic base, had emerged in 1983 as a key force in the opposition to the new constitution, and its list of patrons and founders had a strong ANC flavor.) In October 1986, the authorities went even farther and declared the UDF an "affected" organization—thereby preventing it from receiving funds from abroad. During the early days of the emergency, the government banned rent strikes and other types of protest that blacks had employed over the preceding months. In addition, it placed new restrictions on the reporting of unrest and violence. It expanded the curbs on the press even further in December 1986.

February 1988 witnessed the culmination of the repressive measures. Authorities in Pretoria forbade seventeen opposition groups, including the UDF and the Azania People's Organization (AZAPO), to engage in any political undertakings, and they restricted the Congress of South African Trade Unions (COSATU) to trade union activities.

Despite the government's heavy reliance on a big stick, however, it did not utterly forsake the carrot; it made some moves designed to reconcile non-whites to the existing order in South Africa. Urban blacks who had earlier become legal citizens of independent tribal homelands by fiat regained South African citizenship. The pass laws disappeared from the books. Blacks could now purchase land and houses in black townships. President Botha attempted to set up a National Statutory Council for constitutional discussions between the government and black leaders; however, he experienced difficulties finding black representatives willing to serve on such a council. Then he indicated that he would negotiate in less formal ways with blacks. Some key South African officials even suggested in mid-1987 that such negotiations might take place with "radical" blacks as long as these blacks were not committed in principle to a "strategy of violence."[110] To test the waters in this regard, Botha in early November 1987 released Govan Mbeki, a former chairman of the ANC, from prison after twenty-four years of incarceration. But when Mbeki embarked on what the authorities considered to be inflammatory undertakings, the government quickly restricted his activities.

Through such a combination of means—but principally the repressive ones—the government by mid-1988 had managed to reduce the incidents of violence in the country's black townships significantly. Yet even official observers conceded that discontent was still high there. Consequently, President Botha decided to leave the state of emergency in force.[111]

Deterrence Through Defense. Despite their emphasis on state-strengthening, the authorities in Pretoria still felt that South Africa must continue to enhance its military prowess so as to keep its hegemony in Southern Africa unchallenged.[112] By mid-1988, the country's pool of trained manpower available for military duty remained much the same as it had been in mid-1985, but its allocations for defense had climbed from 4.274 billion rands in 1985/86 to 8.09 billion rands in 1988/89. Even with an inflation rate running 15 percent or higher during these years, such a jump in the military budget was fairly dramatic.

Furthermore, the quality of weapons and equipment available to the SADF rose substantially. In July 1986, the SADF unveiled its new Cheetah jet fighter, an upgraded Mirage III believed to be a match for the Soviet-made MiG-23. This development followed closely on announcement of South Africa's production of a prototype combat helicopter, the Alpha XH1; an advanced gas turbine engine; and unmanned, remote-piloted reconnaissance airplanes. Shortly after the unveiling of the Cheetah, the SADF acquired at least two Boeing in-flight refueling tankers. By the end of 1986, South Africa was even building an airstrip on Marion Island in the Antarctic with the possible intent of preparing a site for testing nuclear missiles.

Counterthreats. The Pretoria government also persisted in making considerable use of counterthreats against the black-ruled states of the region. By late 1985, South Africa had resumed attacks on SWAPO personnel and facilities in Angola after a short-lived cease-fire and disengagement in the southern part of the country. In December 1985, South African forces carried out a reprisal raid in Maseru, Lesotho, for ANC activities within South Africa, and in January 1986, South African officials closed the border with Lesotho, thereby bringing normal activity in the country to a standstill and triggering a military coup against Prime Minister Jonathan. May 1986 witnessed simultaneous South African air strikes against the Makeni refugee camp near Lusaka, Zambia; ANC buildings in Harare, Zimbabwe; and an alleged ANC base at Mogoditshane, near Gaborone, Botswana. In May 1987, South African commandos conducted a raid on ANC houses in Maputo, Mozambique, in disregard of the Nkomati accord. The following March, South African military forces hit an alleged ANC base in Gaborone, Botswana, leaving four dead. Then in June 1988 a South African commando group attempted another incursion into Botswana that was thwarted by the Botswana Defence Forces.

Nor did Pretoria confine its counterthreats to direct assaults and pressure. South Africa continued to furnish support to both UNITA in Angola and Renamo in Mozambique, but its commitment to UNITA vastly exceeded that to Renamo.[113]

Accommodation. Although confrontation and resort to force overwhelmingly dominated South Africa's security approach during these years, some elements of accommodation did creep into it in the last months of the period. Beginning in early 1988, the Pretoria government showed mounting signs of a willingness to bring the long-drawn-out talks about Namibian independence to a conclusion. The basic deal that outside mediators, and particularly the United States, had proposed since the early 1980s involved a quid pro quo—South Africa's departure from Namibia in return for a phased withdrawal of Cuban troops from Angola. On December 22, 1988, South Africa, Angola, and Cuba signed accords along these lines.[114]

In conjunction with its growing flexibility on the Namibia issue, Pretoria also made diplomatic overtures to a number of countries not only in Southern Africa but farther afield on the continent as well. These in some cases even entailed visits by the South African president. Botha traveled to Mozambique and Malawi in September 1988 and then to Zaire and Cote d'Ivoire the next month.[115]

The exact import of all these undertakings, however, was not clear. They could represent a genuine search for rapprochement, but they could also reflect recognition of major military and economic realities concerning Namibia/Angola and a desire to reduce domestic opposition to a settlement there by demonstrating that South Africa was breaking out of its international isolation. In December 1987, for instance, large numbers of Cuban troops moved into southern Angola for the first time since the mid-1970s, and in January 1988 they helped to end the siege of Cuito Cuanavale that UNITA and South African forces had launched in the wake of a victory at Mavinga in October 1987. Indeed, the combined forces of the Angolan government and Cuba managed to gain advantage in the air war and to shoot down several South African aircraft in the process. On the economic front, the financial costs of the Namibia-Angola operation were severely constraining the government's efforts to increase expenditures on various urban projects designed to reduce unrest among non-whites. The military was now absorbing about 20 percent of South Africa's imports, and a big portion of these goods was going toward prosecution of the Namibia-Angola conflict. Moreover, such outlays were taking place at a time when Pretoria was having to trim its spending generally to make debt payments that foreign banks had refused to reschedule. To add to the confusion, there was still strong resistance within some South African quarters—especially among sectors of the military—to getting out of Namibia.[116]

Strategic Response Since 1989

As a consequence of the changes in its threat perception since 1989, the South African government has largely discarded military-oriented responses in its approach to the challenges that it sees facing it. This approach now places heavy stress on accommodation, but it involves major elements of alliance as well.

Accommodation

The central target of the Pretoria government's attempts at accommodation since 1989 has been the black opposition in South Africa, for de Klerk recognized from the outset that such an accommodation provided the key to South Africa's relationship with the outside world at large. During his first few months in office, the new South African president took a number of relatively small steps toward accommodation with the local black opposition. Of these, perhaps the two most significant had to do with the security forces. First, he dismantled the National Security Management System. This nationwide control structure, operating under the State Security Council, had functioned as the "real" government since the mid-1980s. Second, de Klerk reduced the defense budget. In January 1990, the SADF revealed a series of cost-cutting measures that it now planned to implement. These included elimination of some 2,000 personnel from the military rolls, closing of a variety of military bases, withdrawal from service of five types of aircraft, and cancellation of eleven major weapons and equipment projects and curtailment or delay of forty-nine others. At the same time, the length of compulsory military service for white males was reduced from two years to one.[117]

Beginning in February 1990, however, de Klerk moved toward accommodation with the local black opposition in a big way. As previously indicated, he lifted the ban on the ANC, the PAC, and the SACP and the restrictions on thirty-three other anti-apartheid groups, and shortly thereafter he released Nelson Mandela, the last major ANC figure still in prison. Then he set about trying to draw the black opposition and especially the ANC into negotiations on a new political dispensation for the country.

This undertaking turned out to be a fairly complex one. In early May 1990, de Klerk entered into talks in Cape Town with an ANC delegation headed by Mandela to define conditions under which negotiations on a new constitution could take place. The government side in these talks agreed to set up a working group to advise it on "norms and mechanisms" for freeing political prisoners and for granting immunity for political offences, to extend temporary immunity to senior members of the ANC so that they could return to South Africa to help organize and manage political activities and bring violence to an end, to review its security legislation in light of the changing situation, and to work toward ending the current state of emergency. In return, it obtained an ANC commitment to "resolution of the existing climate of violence and intimidation from whatever quarter" and to "stability" and "a peaceful process of negotiations."[118]

Over the next three months, de Klerk strove to carry out the provisions of this accord. The working group formed and began its task, the government allowed many prominent ANC members to come back to South Africa and to engage in political activity, and it lifted the state of emergency in all of the state's provinces except Natal.

In early August, de Klerk and his key advisers met again with an ANC delegation under Mandela—this time in Pretoria. On that occasion, de Klerk approved a timetable for releasing 1,500 political prisoners and for permitting thousands of South Africans to return from exile. He also consented to repeal parts of the Internal Security Act and to end the state of emergency in Natal when circumstances there made it possible to do so. These commitments persuaded the ANC delegation to suspend the organization's guerrilla war immediately. Furthermore, the joint statement issued at the conclusion of the discussions held that "the way is now open to proceed towards negotiations on a new constitution."[119] No specific date was mentioned for launching such negotiations, but there was widespread expectation that they would get under way by early 1991.

While these developments were in train, de Klerk also set about eliminating or revising the major discriminatory legislation still on the books. These included the Separate Amenities Act, the Group Areas Act, the Land Act, and the Population Registrations Act.

During the first half of the 1990s as well, the government significantly modified its posture on the basic principles that should be observed in the framing of a new constitution. Earlier, as already pointed out, it had seemed to favor some sort of constitutional provision for "co-rule" of the country by blacks and whites. In connection with its insistence that one element of the population not dominate another, it had spoken of "group rights," and it had clearly conceived of "groups" in racial terms. Yet now official spokesmen began to suggest that what they wanted to enshrine in a new constitution was not a coequal political role for whites and blacks but a guarantee that no majority (however constituted) could totally monopolize power. They showed a preference for the term "protection of minorities" rather than "group rights" in their discussions of what a new constitution should embody, and they conceded that "minorities requiring protection will have to be defined on the basis of freedom of association and in terms such as language, culture, and ethnicity," instead of "in racial terms and with statutory prescriptiveness." Moreover, they acknowledged that "the concerns of the minorities" would have to be accommodated in such a way that "the claims of the majority are not disregarded and in fact overridden by minority domination."[120] De Klerk firmly associated himself with this revised position in an interview that he gave to Clarence Keyter on 27 June 1990.[121]

Although the Pretoria government has focused its efforts at accommodation on the local black opposition, it has not completely neglected external actors in such endeavors. The black-ruled states of Southern Africa have figured prominently in this group. Prior to the September 1989 elections in South Africa, de Klerk visited Mozambique and Zambia to assure their leaders that a South Africa under his guidance would seek to live in peace with the rest of Southern Africa; before 1989 was out, the South African government pledged publicly that it would cease cross-border raids and support of insurgencies in the region.[122] Its cutback of the South African military budget was clearly aimed in part at convincing black-run Southern African countries of South Africa's peaceful intentions toward them. So too were Pretoria's overtures to the black opposition in South Africa.

Western industrial powers carrying out economic sanctions against South Africa have also been among the external objects of official South African attempts at accommodation. Domestic considerations plainly provided the basic motivation for de Klerk's movement toward rapprochement with the local black opposition, but such a development's possible effect on Western attitudes regarding sanctions obviously entered into his calculations too. In an impromptu press briefing before leaving for an eleven-day European tour in May 1990, the president observed that if there had been grounds for pressure against South Africa earlier, he believed that they had now vanished, and he said that his message to the European heads of state would be that instead of pressure South Africa currently needed encouragement. Throughout his subsequent trip and upon his return, he made plain that such encouragement would involve the ending, or at least the easing, of sanctions.[123]

Even the USSR and its Warsaw Pact allies have received some gestures of accommodation from the Pretoria government. Not only did de Klerk include the South African Communist party among the organizations that he legalized in February 1990, but he has endorsed expansion of contacts with the Soviet Union and East European countries. Indeed, he has permitted fairly wide-ranging interaction to develop.[124]

Alliance

As with its accommodative undertakings, the South African government has directed its attempt to fashion alliances mostly toward domestic targets. This emphasis has grown out of an awareness by de Klerk and his close associates that the sort of political order that they foresee for South Africa will no longer allow the National party to exercise exclusive control of the government. In fact, the party could conceivably wind up in such a minority position that it would be relegated to a marginal role.[125]

By early 1990, there was widespread acknowledgment among key government figures of the need for the National party to forge alliances to preserve at least some of its influence, and de Klerk himself promised that the party "will actively promote" the formation of alliances and "will actively take part" in the process.[126] But such a commitment still left unanswered the question of what kind of alliances the party should pursue.

In the discussions that took place in official circles at that juncture, two basic approaches to constructing alliances were advanced. First, the party could open its ranks to all races. Even if few non-whites enrolled as members, the party would thereby erase the racist stigma attached to collaboration with it; hence, some non-white as well as white groups might eventually agree to associate themselves with it for common purposes. Second, the party could try to establish cooperative relationships with other parties or movements right away.[127]

The first of these approaches, it was clear to many, might prove essential for the party's long-term survival, but such an approach had limitations in the short run. It was not likely to bring the party enough immediate support to smooth the way for a transition to such a system. Therefore, de Klerk opted initially for the second approach.[128]

Yet even this approach posed some dilemmas. The political milieu at present contained only one group at all likely to consent to work with the National party to further shared values; however, this party, the Democratic party, currently lacked the strength to have a major impact on the country's political affairs except in a few specific contexts like the municipal councils in Johannesburg and Randburg. What the National party urgently required was some substantial black backing.

Thus, at the same time that he sanctioned cooperation with the Democratic party in instances where such cooperation seemed politically useful, de Klerk set out to try to build a tacit alliance with the ANC and especially with Nelson Mandela. Not only did de Klerk quickly resolve most of the issues that the ANC wanted dealt with before it agreed to begin negotiations on a new constitution, but he consulted fairly frequently with Mandela on different matters after the first meeting between government and ANC representatives in early May 1990. Perhaps most revealing, when the ANC voiced unhappiness that scheduling problems had created a situation in which de Klerk would visit the United States and confer with President George Bush before Mandela did, de Klerk moved promptly to switch his trip to a later date to permit Mandela to precede him.

Two developments in the three months following the initial government-ANC talks attest to the relative success of de Klerk's efforts. By late May, Mandela had commenced overtly to encourage whites to support de Klerk, even though Mandela did say also that he and the ANC still regarded the pace of de Klerk's reforms as too slow.[129] Then in August 1990, as already mentioned, the ANC agreed to suspend its guerrilla struggle.

Subsequent developments, to be sure, dealt some setbacks as well. When fighting between ANC and Inkhata supporters spread to the townships around Johannesburg in August, Mandela and the ANC charged that the police were siding with Inkhata elements. Mandela also defended his wife Winnie when the government announced in September that she would have to stand trial for alleged involvement in the kidnapping and beating of four black youths in Soweto in the late 1980s. Nevertheless, such factors had not disrupted the movement toward constitutional negotiations at the time of writing.

With the ANC's endorsement in early August 1990 of full-scale negotiations on a new political system, however, de Klerk began to combine the two approaches to alliances put forth in official circles earlier in the year. At a provincial National party congress in Durban in late August 1990, he called on the party to admit individuals of all races to membership. In so doing, he by no means ruled out further cooperation with the ANC to bring about a new political dispensation in the country; rather, according to government officials, he sought to make it viable for the Democratic party, the colored and Indian parties represented in the existing three-chamber parliament, and even Inkhata to band together with the National party in the forthcoming negotiations.[130] The formation of such a coalition would obviously go a long way toward ensuring the National party an important role in the new political order.

Despite the Pretoria government's preoccupation with forging alliances on the internal front, it has devoted some energy to establishing them in the international arena as well—notably with other Southern African states. In February 1990, for example, de Klerk proposed to enter into talks with these countries to draw up a "realistic development plan" for the region, and he called for a conference of all Southern African states to accomplish this task.[131] There have been sporadic attempts ever since by the South African government to foster such a gathering.

Prospects

There remains the question of just how long South Africa's reduced interest in exercising regional hegemony in Southern Africa will last. Will it become more or less permanent, or will it prove essentially a passing phenomenon? Two factors will be determining here: the evolving nature of the regional political system and the character of the elements in power in Pretoria. The first will establish the objective challenges that South Africa will face in the years ahead, while the second will shape how Pretoria responds to these objective realities—both what threats it perceives in them and how it approaches the task of coping with these threats.

The Regional Context

The chances of a serious challenge to South Africa emerging in Southern Africa in the foreseeable future appear remote, for the other states in the region have little hope of making much of a dent in South Africa's hegemonial position in even the medium term. As of the late 1980s, most of them confronted low or even negative economic growth rates, large debt-service obligations, and uncertain demand for their key export items; Botswana and Swaziland were the main exceptions.[132] Moreover, the new claims of Eastern Europe on Western economic resources and the winding down of global competition between the United States and the USSR have made the outlook for large-scale inputs of economic aid from foreign governments dim. Militarily, the SADCC countries have long had to rely on nonregional sources for all of their sophisticated arms. The same goes for advanced military training.[133] There is no likelihood that this situation will alter in the years immediately ahead. Yet the economic straits in which most SADCC countries find themselves will render them heavily dependent on the largesse of outside powers for such weapons and training. In light of the heightened emphasis by both the Western states and the USSR and its East European allies on resolving regional conflicts, neither group is likely to be enthusiastic about extending much assistance of this sort to SADCC countries.

As long as the key features of apartheid continue to exist in some form, however, the basic structure of the state system in Southern Africa will stay the same as it was at the dawn of the 1990s. South Africa will dominate the region economically and militarily, while the black-ruled states will look upon South Africa with antagonism and seek to enhance their room for independent maneuver.

Were a transition to a post-apartheid South Africa to take place, of course, the impact on the regional state system could be profound. Most observers in both South Africa and the smaller Southern African countries expect increased regional integration to result, although tensions— especially in the economic realm—might not vanish entirely.[134] But such a development would render threats to South Africa even less probable than they would be if apartheid persists.

The South African Government

Three types of government seem genuinely possible for South Africa in the medium-range future: a white-minority government headed by the National party, a nonracial majority government involving whites but essentially dominated by blacks, and a white-minority government led by the Conservative party. Both a military-controlled regime and an exclusively-black-run government are theoretically conceivable, but neither appears likely enough to materialize to warrant serious consideration here.

Unless the establishment of a new constitutional order cuts short their term of office, de Klerk and the National party can stay in power until 1994. Should negotiations with local blacks about a new political dispensation for the country fail, they could also run in another whites-only election in 1994, and although they probably would not attract enough support to maintain exclusive control of the government, they could still win sufficient backing to form the core of a coalition government.

Formidable obstacles to the emergence of a South African government involving blacks still remain, but the progress thus far toward full-scale negotiations between de Klerk and the black opposition suggests that some sort of nonracial majority government could come into being within a fairly short period of time. Given the 1994 deadline for the holding of new elections under the existing constitution, it would seem reasonable to suppose that this nonracial majority government would take shape by then.

A white-minority governmented headed by the Conservative party would probably emerge in one of two ways. First, if de Klerk and his colleagues fail to reach an agreement with the black opposition by 1994 on terms acceptable to whites, there could be a white backlash, and the Conservative party or a right-wing coalition headed by it could triumph in the 1994 election. Second, violence might escalate to the point where it made the bulk of the white population highly insecure, and extremist right-wing forces might enlist the help of the police and military to install a government under the Conservative party to try to restore order. Despite the illegality of such a move, the hierarchy of the police and military might be tempted to take the step if they viewed the circumstances as dire enough, for substantial numbers of that hierarchy tend to be sympathetic to right-wing viewpoints.

Under either of the first two kinds of governments, the official threat perception and official security response would probably differ little from those prevailing at the beginning of the 1990s. Small variations might crop up in attitudes and approach toward local blacks and whites, but there would in all likelihood be no major differences—especially in outlook toward the rest of Southern Africa.

If a white-minority government led by the Conservative party wielded the reins of authority, however, the official threat perception and official security response would almost certainly contrast greatly with those of the early 1990s. The threat perception would probably resemble that of the Pretoria government in the late 1970s, while the security approach would no doubt revert to a combination of elements stressing force—internal repression to bolster state authority and deterrence of outside powers through a defense buildup and counterthreats. It is possible, however, that to these elements might be added efforts to partition South Africa into two countries, one white-controlled (i.e., Afrikaner-controlled) and the other black-controlled. The Conservative party and other right-wing groups have been proposing such a partition since the late 1980s, but they have been vague about what the territory or structure of an Afrikaner state would be.[135]

At the outset of the 1990s, the situation in South Africa remains too much in flux to gauge which of these sorts of government will hold power by the end of the decade, although considerable potential now exists for a transition to a nonracial majority government. Hence, no firm judgments can be advanced as to the longevity of South Africa's decreased concern about preserving and exploiting its regional hegemony in Southern Africa.

Notes

The views expressed in the chapter are those of the author and do not necessarily reflect those of the U.S. Air Force or the U.S. government.

1. The ensuing discussion draws upon Julian Burgess, *Interdependence in Southern Africa,* EIU Special Report No. 32 (London: Economic Intelligence Unit, July 1976); D.S. Prinsloo, *Revolutions and Railways in Southern Africa,* Study Report No. 9 (Pretoria: Foreign Affairs Association, March 1978); Republic of South Africa, Department of Foreign Affairs, *South Africa 1985* (Cape Town: CTP Book Printers, 1985), particularly chapter 24 on "Railways and Harbours;" South African Embassy, *South Africa and Africa,* Backgrounder No. 8/83 (Washington, DC: Minister of Information, May 1983); D. Hobart Houghton, *The South African Economy,* 3d ed. (Cape Town: Oxford University Press, 1973); Sam C. Nolutshungu, *South Africa in Africa: A Study in Ideology and Foreign Policy* (New York: Africana, 1975), pp. 91–92 and 162–63; Richard W. Hull, *Southern Africa: Civilizations in Turmoil* (New York: New York University Press, 1981), pp. 122 and 124; Monica M. Cole, *South Africa* (New York: E. P. Dutton and Co., 1961), pp. 393–405 and 668–72; Jill Nattrass, *The South African Economy; Its Growth and Change* (Cape Town: Oxford University Press, 1981).
2. Barbara Villet, *Blood River* (New York: Everest House, 1982), p. 221.
3. W.C.B. Tunstall, *The Commonwealth and Regional Defence* (London: Athlone Press for the University of London, 1959), pp. 47–51; Neville Brown and W. F. Gutteridge, *The African Military Balance,* Adelphi Papers No. 12 (London: Institute for Strategic Studies, August 1964), pp. 9–10; Chester A. Crocker, "Current and Projected Military Balances in Southern Africa," in Richard E. Bissell and Chester A. Crocker, eds., *South Africa into the 1980s* (Boulder: Westview Press, 1979), pp. 81–82.
4. Villet, *Blood River,* pp. 221–22; Houghton, *The South African Economy,* pp. 39–41 and 180–81; Nattrass, *The South African Economy,* pp. 84–87 and 230–43; Burgess, *Interdependence in Southern Africa,* p. 3.
5. For detailed analysis of the Simonstown agreement, see Dennis Austin, *Britain and South Africa* (London: Oxford University Press for the Royal Institute

of International Affairs, 1966), pp. 121–45; James Barber, *South Africa's Foreign Policy 1945–1970* (London: Oxford University Press, 1973), pp. 85–86; Nolutshungu, *South Africa in Africa,* pp. 68–72.

6. On South African perspectives during this period, see Barber, *South Africa's Foreign Policy 1945–1970,* pp. 183–89; William Henry Vatcher, Jr., *White Laager: The Rise of Afrikaner Nationalism* (New York: Frederick A. Praeger, 1965), chapter 11; David Harrison, *The White Tribe of Africa: South Africa in Perspective* (Berkeley: University of California Press, 1981), chapter 12.

7. The bulk of the text of his speech on "the winds of change" in Africa may be found in Nicholas Mansergh, ed., *Documents and Speeches on Commonwealth Affairs 1952–1962* (London: Oxford University Press for the Royal Institute of International Affairs, 1963), pp. 347–51.

8. The following analysis derives from Burgess, *Interdependence in Southern Africa;* Prinsloo, *Revolutions and Railways in Southern Africa;* Nolutshungu, *South Africa in Africa,* pp. 91–92, 130–35, 162–63, 186–88; Houghton, *The South African Economy;* South African Embassy, *South Africa and Africa,* pp. 6–7; J.A. Lombard, J.J. Stadler, and P.J. van der Merwe, *The Concept of Economic Co-operation in Southern Africa* (Pretoria: Econoburo [Pty.] Limited, 1968), pp. 22 and 34; International Institute for Strategic Studies, *The Military Balance, 1970–1971* (London, 1970); Barber, *South Africa's Foreign Policy 1945–1970,* p. 198; Jack E. Spence, *The Strategic Significance of Southern Africa* (London: Royal United Services Institution, 1970), p. 23; Chester A. Crocker, *South Africa's Defense Posture: Coping with Vulnerability,* Washington Papers no. 84 (Beverly Hills: Sage Publications for the Center for Strategic and International Studies, Georgetown University, 1981), p. 14; Crocker, "Current and Projected Military Balances in Southern Africa," pp. 82–84; Republic of South Africa, *White Paper on Defence and Armament Production, April 1969* (Pretoria: Government Printer, 1969).

9. For extended treatment of the perspectives and behavior of the states of Southern Africa with respect to South Africa, see Barber, *South Africa's Foreign Policy 1945–1970,* chapters 16 and 17; Nolutshungu, *South Africa in Africa,* chapters 8–11; Larry Bowman, "The Subordinate State System of Southern Africa," *International Studies Quarterly* 12 (September 1968): 231–62; James Barber and John Barratt, *South Africa's Foreign Policy: The Search for Status and Security, 1945–1988* (Cambridge: Cambridge University Press, 1990), chapter 8.

10. Insight into the Maputo government's thinking on the subject may be gleaned from the comments of Joachim Chissano, then Mozambique's foreign minister, in *Afrique-Asia,* 7–20 July 1980, Supplement.

11. For detailed examination of the Rhodesian settlement and its eventual impact on Zimbabwe–South African relations, see Michael Clough, "From Rhodesia to Zimbabwe," in Michael Clough, ed., *Changing Realities in Southern Africa* (Berkeley: Institute of International Studies, University of California, Berkeley, 1982), especially pp. 42ff.; Colin Legum, "Southern Africa: The Road to and from Lancaster House," in Colin Legum, ed., *Africa Contemporary Record 1979–1980* (London: Holmes and Meier, 1981), pp. A3–31; Miles Hudson, *Triumph or Tragedy?: Rhodesia to Zimbabwe* (London: Hamish Hamilton, n.d.), particularly chapters 7–9; "Zimbabwe" in Colin Legum, ed., *Africa Contemporary Record 1980–1981* (London: Holmes and Meier, 1981), pp. B934–35.

12. Text reprinted in Legum, *Africa Contemporary Record 1980–1981*, pp. C31–35.

13. For details, see, for example, U.S. Department of State, *A U.S. Policy Toward South Africa*, Report of the Secretary of State's Advisory Committee on South Africa (Washington, DC, April 1987), pp. 4 and 34; Eric Leistner, "South Africa's Agricultural Interaction with Africa," *Africa Insight* 17, no. 2 (1987): 95–101; Denis Fair, "Electric Power in Africa: Southern Africa," *Africa Insight* 17, no. 3 (1987): 167–73; Col. James P. McWilliams, "South Africa: Tough-Guy Tactics Mask Economic Clout," *Armed Forces Journal International*, January 1989, p. 80; Coleen Lowe Morna, "Ashes and Diamonds," *Africa Report*, January–February 1989, 21–23, and "Linking Southern Africa: SADCC's Transport Corridors," *Africa Report*, May–June 1989, p. 36; Sanjiv Prakash, "Invisible Exports: Southern Africa's Dependence on Pretoria," *Defense and Foreign Affairs*, October 1989, pp. 29–31; International Monetary Fund, *Direction of Trade Statistics Yearbook 1989*, pp. 263, 422, and 424; Barber and Barratt, *South Africa's Foreign Policy*, Table 11, p. 355; *The Star* (Johannesburg), 30 April 1990; International Institute for Strategic Studies, *The Military Balance 1990–1991* (London, 1990), passim.

14. For discussion of Afrikaner history and Afrikaner nationalism from varying standpoints, ranging from the relatively sympathetic to the highly critical, see Villet, *Blood River*; Vatcher, *White Laager*; Harrison, *The White Tribe of Africa*; Edwin S. Munger, *Afrikaner and African Nationalism: South African Parallels and Parameters* (London: Oxford University Press for the Institute of Race Relations, 1967); Monica Wilson and Leonard Thompson, *The Oxford History of South Africa*, Vols. 1 and 2 (Oxford: Clarendon Press, 1969); John Fisher, *The Afrikaners* (London: Cassell, 1969); Newell M. Stultz, *Afrikaner Politics in South Africa, 1934–1948* (Berkeley: University of California Press, 1974); T. Dunbar Moodie, *The Rise of Afrikanerdom: Power, Apartheid & the Afrikaner Civil Religion* (Berkeley: University of California Press, 1975); W. de Klerk, *The Puritans in Africa (The Story of Afrikanerdom)* (London: Rex Collings, 1975); Ivor Wilkings and Hans Strydom, *The Super-Afrikaners* (Johannesburg: Jonathan Ball, 1978); J.H.P. Serfontein, *Brotherhood of Power* (London: Rex Collings, 1979); Heribert Adam and Hermann Giliomee, *Ethnic Power Mobilized: Can South Africa Change?* (New Haven: Yale University Press, 1979); Leonard Thompson, *The Political Mythology of Apartheid* (New Haven: Yale University Press, 1985); Steven Debroey, *South Africa: To the Sources of Apartheid* (Lanham, MD: University Press of America, 1989); Stanley Uys, "The Afrikaner Establishment," in Shaun Johnson, ed., *South Africa: No Turning Back* (Bloomington: Indiana University Press, 1989), pp. 206–39; Hermann Giliomee, "Afrikaner Politics 1977–87: from Afrikaner Nationalist Rule to Central State Hegemony," in John D. Brewer, ed., *Can South Africa Survive?* (New York: St. Martin's Press, 1989), pp. 108–35; Allister Sparks, *The Mind of South Africa* (New York: Alfred A. Knopf, 1990).

15. On these efforts, see A.P. Walshe, *The Rise of African Nationalism in South Africa, 1912–1952* (Berkeley: University of California Press, 1971); Thomas Karis and Gwendolyn Carter, eds., *From Protest to Challenge: A Documentary History of African Politics in South Africa 1882–1964* (Stanford: Hoover Institution Press, 1972–1977), Vols. 1-4; Gail M. Gerhart, *Black Power in South Africa* (Berkeley:

University of California Press, 1978); Steven F. McDonald, "The Black Community," in Bissell and Crocker, *South Africa into the 1980s,* pp. 21–47; *South Africa: Time Running Out,* Report of the Study Commission on U.S. Policy Toward Southern Africa (Berkeley: University of California Press, 1981), chapter 9; Tom Lodge, *Black Politics in South Africa since 1945* (London: Longman, 1983); Thomas Karis, "Revolution in the Making: Black Politics in South Africa," *Foreign Affairs* 62, no. 2 (Winter 1983–84): 378–406; Steven McDonald, "A Guide to Black Politics in South Africa," *CSIS Africa Notes,* no. 36 (5 November 1984); Alan Cowell, "Defiance in South Africa," *The New York Times Magazine,* 14 April 1985, pp. 30–48; Ken Owen, "A Fundamental Shift in South African Politics," *CSIS Africa Notes,* no. 53 (31 January 1986); John de St. Jorre, "South Africa Embattled," *Foreign Affairs* 65, no. 3 (1986): 538–63; Robert Fatton, *Black Consciousness in South Africa* (Albany: State University of New York Press, 1986); Glenn Moss and Ingrid Obery, eds., *South African Review 4* (Johannesburg: Ravan Press for the Southern African Research Service, 1987), section 1; Jeremy Seekings, "Political Mobilization in the Black Townships of the Transvaal," in Philip Frankel, Noam Pines, and Mark Swilling, eds., *State, Resistance and Change in South Africa* (London: Croom Helm, 1988), pp. 197–228; Tom Lodge, "State of Exile: The African National Congress of South Africa, 1976–86," in ibid., pp. 229–58; Howard Barrell, "The Outlawed South African Liberation Movements," in Johnson, *South Africa: No Turning Back,* pp. 52–93; Shaun Johnson, " 'The Soldiers of Luthuli': Youth in the Politics of Resistance in South Africa," in ibid., pp. 94–152; Kumi Naidoo, "Internal Resistance in South Africa: The Political Movements," in ibid., pp. 172–205; John D. Brewer, "Internal Black Protest," in Brewer, *Can South Africa Survive?,* pp. 184–205; Tom Lodge, "The United Democratic Front: Leadership and Ideology," ibid., pp. 206–30; Mark Mitchell and Dave Russell, "Black Unions and Political Change in South Africa," ibid, pp. 231–54; Sparks, *The Mind of South Africa.*

16. A good illustration from the mid-1980s of such feelings may be found in the speech of South African President P.W. Botha to the National party federal congress in Durban on 12 August 1986, as telecast by Johannesburg Television Service in English, 12 August 1986, and published in Foreign Broadcast Information Service, *Daily Report: Middle East and Africa* (hereafter *FBIS-MEA*), 13 August 1986: U/2–8. For some insightful comments about Afrikaners' basic sense of insecurity by Beyers Naude, perhaps Afrikanerdom's most famous dissident, see Michael Getler's article in the *Washington Post,* 10 February 1987.

17. A first-rate discussion of the changes may be found in Adam and Giliomee, *Ethnic Power Mobilized: Can South Africa Change?,* pp. 145–76.

18. For an excellent illustration, see an early 1980s statement by a Johannesburg attorney who had made his reputation defending individuals accused of violating South Africa's security and censorship laws, quoted in Villet, *Blood River,* p. 196. During the 1980s, the present author personally heard similar observations from "enlightened" Afrikaners.

19. See, for instance, the comments of J. G. Strijdom, one of the top figures in the National party during the late 1940s and the 1950s, in *Die Transvaler,* 7 November 1947. Strijdom served as prime minister from 1954 to 1958.

20. On the economic factor and its impact on Afrikaner thinking, see Merle Lipton, *Capitalism and Apartheid: South Africa, 1910–84* (Totowa, NJ: Rowman and Allanheld, 1985), especially chapter 8; Christopher R. Hill, *Change in South Africa; Blind Alleys or New Directions?* (Totowa, NJ: Barnes and Noble, 1983).

21. For representative attempts to delineate the views of Afrikaners advocating "controlled change," see Hill, *Change in South Africa,* chapter 15; *South Africa: Time Running Out,* pp. 227–32; Helen Kitchen and Michael Clough, *The United States and South Africa: Realities and Red Herrings,* Significant Issues Series (Center for Strategic and International Studies, Georgetown University) 6, no. 6 (1984), pp. 22–25. The public comments of former President Botha are good primary sources for these views. See, for example, his *A New Beginning,* Speech to the Opening of the Third Session of the Eighth Parliament, 31 January 1986 (Johannesburg: PERSKOR, 1986); his address to the President's Council on 15 May 1986, as carried by Johannesburg Television Service in Afrikaans, 15 May 1986, in *FBIS-MEA,* 16 May 1986: U/4–5; his speech to the National party congress in Durban on 12 August 1986, cited above in note 16; his campaign speeches in Port Elizabeth on 29 April 1987, and in Pietermaritzburg on 30 April 1987, as broadcast by Johannesburg SAPA in English, 29 and 30 April 1987, in *FBIS-MEA,* 1 May 1987: U/4-5; his address to the opening of the new session of parliament in Cape Town on 19 May 1987, as carried by Johannesburg Television Service in Afrikaans, 19 May 1987, in *FBIS-MEA,* 19 May 1987: U/2–4.

22. For emphatic statements against negotiations with the ANC on the basis of its refusal to renounce violence, see the speech of General Magnus Malan, Minister of Defense, at Venterdorp on 24 March 1987, as reported by Johannesburg SAPA in English, 25 March 1987, and published in *FBIS-MEA,* 25 March 1987: U/9; President Botha's address at the opening of the first session of parliament after the May 1987 elections, cited above in note 21. In June–July 1987, however, Stoffel van der Merwe, Deputy Minister of Information and Constitutional Development, conceded that not all "radicals" who employed violence were "ideologically committed" to it as a strategy. He thus left the door open for negotiations with members of the ANC not wedded to violence. See the *Washington Post,* 12 June 1987; *Sunday Times* (Johannesburg), 14 June 1987; interview on the "Network" program, Johannesburg Television Service, 23 July 1987, in Foreign Broadcast Information Service, *Africa (Sub-Saharan),* (hereafter *FBIS-AFR*), 27 July 1987: D/5–7.

23. Good illustrations may be found in the op ed piece by Herbert Beukes, South Africa's Ambassador to the United States, in the *Washington Post,* 18 September 1986, and President Botha's address to parliament on 19 May 1987, cited above in note 21.

24. For instance, the South African government warned American and European businesses in May 1987 that they faced prosecution if they continued to allow black executives to live in company-owned homes in white residential areas. See Umtata Capital Radio in English, 14 May 1987, in *FBIS-MEA,* 14 May 1987: U/1; *The Sun* (Baltimore), 13 May 1987.

25. The speech of Dr. Andries Treurnicht, head of the Conservative party,

in parliament on 20 May 1987 affords a classic example of the perspective. This speech was broadcast by Johannesburg SAPA in English, 20 May 1987, and published in *FBIS-MEA*, 21 May 1987: U/3–5.

26. Statistics in this discussion come from a report by Johannesburg SAPA in English 9 May 1987, in *FBIS-MEA*, 12 May 1987: U/3; the *New York Times*, 8 May 1987; and a statement by Dr. Dennis Worrall carried by Johannesburg SAPA in English, 22 May 1987, in *FBIS-MEA*, 26 May 1987: U/4–5.

27. See the account of former Ambassador David Worrall's press conference of 14 February 1987, by Johannesburg SAPA in English, 14 February 1987, and the interview with Worrall on the London BBC World Service in English, 15 February 1987, in *FBIS-MEA*, 18 February 1987: U/6–7; Andre le Roux's interview with Wyland Malan on 9 March 1987, carried by Johannesburg Television Service in Afrikaans, 9 March 1987, and translated in *FBIS-MEA*, 11 March 1987: U/2–5; "Pretoria's 'New Nats,'" *Newsweek*, 9 March 1987, p. 44.

28. For good treatments of Afrikaner assessments up to the early 1970s, see Barber, *South Africa's Foreign Policy, 1945–1970;* Nolutshungu, *South Africa in Africa;* Barber and Barratt, *South Africa's Foreign Policy*, chapters 3–5 and 7–9.

29. Provisional Secretariat of the Organization of African Unity, *Organization of African Unity: Basic Documents and Resolutions* (Addis Ababa, n.d.), pp. 17–20.

30. See, for example, Richard Gibson, *African Liberation Movements* (London: Oxford University Press for the Institute of Race Relations, 1972).

31. Good illustrations of this perspective may be found in the public statements of Prime Minister Hendrik Verwoerd. See, for instance, his correspondence with Sir Robert Menzies, the Australian prime minister, after the 1960 Commonwealth Conference, in Sir Robert Menzies, *Afternoon Light* (London: Cassell, 1967), pp. 206–07, and especially his remarks in the South African parliament in early 1964, in Republic of South Africa, *Debates of the House of Assembly (Hansard)*, 21 January 1964, cols. 55–57.

32. For further discussion, see, for example, Robert S. Jaster, *South Africa and Its Neighbours: The Dynamics of Regional Conflict*, Adelphi Papers no. 209 (London: International Institute for Strategic Studies, Summer 1986), p. 51; idem, *A Regional Security Role for Africa's Front-Line States: Experience and Prospects*, Adelphi Papers no. 180 (London: International Institute for Strategic Studies, Spring 1983), pp. 4, 19–21.

33. The military buildup carried out by these two states can be traced through the data in the annual volumes on *The Military Balance* published by the International Institute for Strategic Studies in London.

34. General Magnus Malan, former chief of the South African Defense Force and now Minister of Defense, as quoted in *The Star* (Johannesburg), 10 September 1977.

35. See Deon Geldenhuys, *What Do We Think? A Survey of White Opinion on Foreign Policy Issues* (Braamfontein: Macmillan South Africa, November 1982).

36. For analysis of the conference in Kabwe, Zambia, that produced this decision, see Thomas Lodge's contribution to *South Africa International* (South Africa Foundation), November 1985, pp. 82ff.

37. *ISSUP Bulletin* (Institute for Strategic Studies, University of Pretoria), no. 4 (1986).

38. Interview carried by Baden-Baden Suedwestfunk Television Network in German, 2 September 1986, and translated in *FBIS-MEA*, 3 September 1986: U/5–8.

39. See, for instance, the comments of Minister of Defense Malan in the parliamentary debate in May 1986 on his budget allocation, as reported by Johannesburg SAPA in English, 14 May 1986, and published in *FBIS-MEA*, 15 May 1986: U/5–6.

40. This was the view of D.F. Malan, the National party's first prime minister. See, for example, Nolutshungu, *South Africa in Africa*, chapter 3.

41. See, for instance, Bruce D. Larkin, *China and Africa, 1949–1970* (Berkeley: University of California Press, 1971), passim; Jan Pettman, *Zambia: Security and Conflict* (New York: St. Martin's Press, 1974), chapter 6.

42. U.S. Central Intelligence Agency, *Communist Aid Activities in Non-Communist Less Developed Countries, 1979 and 1954–79*, ER 80-10318U (Washington, D.C., October 1980), p. 11.

43. *Sunday Times* (Johannesburg), 25 October 1970.

44. For these details, see U.S. Central Intelligence Agency, *Communist Aid Activities in Non-Communist Less Developed Countries, 1979 and 1954–79*, pp. 15 and 39; U.S. Arms Control and Disarmament Agency, *World Military Expenditures and Arms Transfers, 1970–1979* (Washington, D.C., 1982), p. 127; *Discurso pronunciado por el Comandante en Jefe, Fidel Castro Ruz, Primer Secretario del CC del Partido Comunista de Cuba y Presidente de los Consejos de Estado y de Ministros, en la clausura de II periodo de Sesiones de 1979, de la Asamblea Nacional del Poder Popular, Palacio de las Convenciones, 27 de deciembre de 1979, "Ano 29 de Victoria"* (an unpublished but printed document from Cuba's Departmento de versiones taquigraficas), p. 10.

45. See U.S. Central Intelligence Agency, *Communist Aid Activities in Non-Communist Less Developed Countries, 1979 and 1954–79*, p. 15; U.S. Arms Control and Disarmament Agency, *World Military Expenditures and Arms Transfers, 1970–1979*, p. 127.

46. See, for example, the testimony of U.S. Assistant Secretary of State Chester Crocker and of a number of former ANC and SWAPO recruits, as well as the 12 July 1977 letter from Dino Haamambo, chief of SWAPO's armed forces, to the Angolan secretary of defense, in *The Role of the Soviet Union, Cuba, and East Germany in Fomenting Terrorism in Southern Africa*, Hearings Before the Subcommittee on Security and Terrorism of the Committee of the Judiciary, 97th Cong., 2d sess. (Washington, DC: Government Printing Office, 1982); Jaster, *South Africa and Its Neighbours*, pp. 6 and 51.

47. See, for instance, the remarks of Prime Minister Botha before parliament in Republic of South Africa, *Debates of the House of Assembly (Hansard)*, 31 January 1978, cols. 103–05; 8 March 1979, col. 2067; and 21 March 1980, cols. 3317–19. A full-blown exposition of the argument appears in "The Kremlin's View of Southern Africa," *Southern African Facts Sheet*, no. 16 (October 1980).

48. On these points, see U.S. Arms Control and Disarmament Agency, *World Military Expenditures and Arms Transfers, 1985* (Washington, DC, August 1985),

pp. 131–32; idem, *World Military Expenditures and Arms Transfers, 1986* (Washington, DC, April 1987), pp. 145–46; U.S. Department of State, *Warsaw Pact Economic Aid to Non-Communist LDCs, 1984* (Washington, DC, May 1986), p. 20.

49. See, for example, President Botha's speech on April 6, 1987, at a Cape Town parade marking the seventy-fifth anniversary of the South African Defense Force, as reported by Johannesburg SAPA in English, 6 April 1987, in *FBIS-MEA,* 7 April 1987: U/1–2.

50. Lecture at the University of Pretoria, 2 November 1988, on "The Contemporary Strategic Situation in Southern Africa," published in *Paratus,* December 1988, pp. 12–15, 39.

51. Radio Johannesburg Domestic Service in Afrikaans, 10 September 1989, in *FBIS-AFR,* 21 September 1989: 5.

52. For an extensive report of this speech, see Helmoed-Romer Neitman, "South Africa's Changing Defence Policy," *Jane's Defence Weekly,* 16 December 1989, p. 1333.

53. See the text in *Southern Africa,* March 1990, especially pp. 10–11.

54. For analysis, with sources, see David E. Albright, *Soviet Policy Toward Africa Revisited,* Significant Issues Series (Center for Strategic and International Studies) 9, no. 6 (1987), chapter 3, passim, and pp. 34–35.

55. Relevant evidence on this point may be found in Gleb Starushenko, "Problems of Struggle Against Racism, Apartheid and Colonialism in South Africa," report to the Second Soviet-Africa Conference for Peace, Cooperation, and Social Progress, 24–26 June 1986; Colin Legum, "Soviet Theoretician Favours Peaceful Negotiations in South Africa," *Third World Reports,* 13 January 1987; idem, "New Light on Soviet Theoretician's Views on Peaceful Negotiations with South Africa," *Third World Reports,* 28 April 1987; Stanley Uys, "Soviets Want 'Pink Not Red' S.A.," *Front File: South African Brief,* August 1987; Colin Legum, "What 'Glasnost' Means for Southern Africa," *Third World Reports,* 16 December 1987; Winrich Kuhne, "A 1988 Update on Soviet Relations with Pretoria, the ANC, and the SACP," *CSIS Africa Notes,* no. 89 (1 September 1988); Colin Legum, "The Superpowers and the Third World: Alternatives to Competition, New Soviet Thinking About South Africa," *Third World Reports,* 21 June 1989; Sparks, *The Mind of South Africa,* pp. 362–66.

56. By way of illustration, see S. Neil MacFarlane, "The Soviet Union and Southern African Security," *Problems of Communism* 38, no. 2–3 (March–June 1989): 83; the *New York Times,* 25 October 1988.

57. Chas. W. Freeman, Jr., "The Angola/Namibia Accords," *Foreign Affairs* 68, no. 3 (Summer 1989), pp. 134–35. Freeman was principal U.S. Deputy Assistant Secretary of State for African Affairs in 1988.

58. See, for instance, Michael H. Armacost, "Regional Issues and U.S.-Soviet Relations," address before the Women's Club in Grand Rapids, Michigan, on 22 June 1988, in *Department of State Bulletin,* no. 2138 (September 1988): 22.

59. For analysis of these moves, see Gillian Gunn, "A Guide to the Intricacies of the Angola-Namibia Negotiations," *CSIS Africa Notes,* no. 90 (8 September 1988), pp. 3–4; Freeman, "The Angola/Namibia Accords," p. 134.

60. See, for instance, Malan, "The Contemporary Strategic Situation in Southern Africa," pp. 13–14.

61. This was true despite some behavior on the part of General Malan in early 1988 that seemed to imply the contrary. On the conflicting views of the two departments as well as Malan's actions in 1988 and their meaning, see Gunn, "A Guide to the Intricacies of the Angola-Namibia Negotiations," p. 8.

62. Freeman, "The Angola/Namibia Accords," pp. 137–40; the *New York Times*, 27 April 1989 and 31 June 1990.

63. Quoted in Heitman, "South Africa's Changing Defence Policy," p. 1333. Nonetheless, some elements of the SADF still harbored doubts about the USSR's change of heart with respect to South Africa. See Robert S. Jaster, "The South Africa Military Reassesses Its Priorities," *CSIS Africa Notes*, no. 102 (30 September 1989): 4.

64. See the article by Hermann Giliomee in *The Star*, 22 February 1990; Clarence Keyter's interview with de Klerk on the "Network" program, Johannesburg Television Service in English, 29 June 1989, in *FBIS-AFR*, 30 June 1989: especially 7.

65. See, for instance, his address after his election as leader of the National party, as recounted by Johannesburg SAPA in English 8 February 1989, and carried in *FBIS-AFR*, 9 February 1989: 13–14; his speech to a National party function in Pietermaritzburg on 14 April 1989, as reported by Johannesburg Television Service, 14 April 1989, and published in *FBIS-AFR*, 17 April 1989: 6; his speech at the opening of the parliamentary debate on his budget as chairman of the Minister's Council of the House of Assembly on 12 May 1989, as covered by Johannesburg SAPA in English, 12 May 1989, and printed in *FBIS-AFR*, 12 May 1989: 3–4; interview by Johan Pretorious with him on "Network," Johannesburg Television Service, 14 May 1989, Part II, in *FBIS-AFR*, 16 May 1989: 2–6; Clarence Keyter's interview with him, cited above in note 64; de Klerk's speeches opening and closing the National party's seventh federal congress in Pretoria, 29 June 1989, as reported by Johannesburg SAPA in English, 29 June 1989, and published in *FBIS-AFR*, 30 June 1989: 3, 5–6; his inaugural address as president on 20 September 1989, as carried in full by Radio Johannesburg Domestic Service in Afrikaans, 20 September 1989, and translated in *FBIS-AFR*, 21 September 1989: 4–6.

66. This image of the future was laid out in fair detail in de Klerk's speech to parliament on 12 May 1989 and the interview that he gave to Johan Pretorius on 14 May 1989, both cited above in note 65. The quotations in the text are drawn from these two sources.

67. Rupert Taylor, "Between Apartheid and Democracy: The South African 'Election' of 1989," *The Round Table*, no. 314 (April 1990): particularly 161–64.

68. Speech of 20 September 1989, cited above in note 65, p. 5.

69. See, for instance, President Botha's speech at a ceremony in Kempton Park, Johannesburg, on 16 July 1986, as reported by Johannesburg SAPA in English, 16 July 1986, and published in *FBIS-MEA*, 16 July 1986: U/3–4.

70. Briefing for foreign journalists by Gerrit de Kock, president of the South African Reserve Bank, on 6 February 1989, as reported in the *New York Times*,

7 February 1989; article by Hassan Ziady, *Jeune Afrique Economie*, March 1990, as translated in *FBIS-AFR*, 11 May 1990: 30.

71. See D. J. Geldenhuys, "The International Isolation of South Africa," *Strategic Review for Southern Africa* 11, no. 2 (November 1989): 52; Ziady article in *Jeune Afrique Economie*, cited above in note 70, p. 29.

72. Ziady article in *Jeune Afrique Economie*, cited above in note 70, p. 29.

73. *The Africa Review 1989*, p. 106; Kock briefing of 6 February 1989, cited above in note 70.

74. Inaugural address of 20 September 1989, cited above in note 65, p. 6.

75. Speech of 2 February 1990, cited above in note 53, p. 10.

76. See, for example, the discussion in Nolutshungu, *South Africa in Africa*, pp. 46–53; Barber, *South Africa's Foreign Policy 1945–1970*, pp. 100–04; Barber and Barratt, *South Africa's Foreign Policy*, pp. 36–38.

77. For a typical illustration, see the remarks of Prime Minister Johannes Strijdom to parliament in South Africa, *Debates of the House of Assembly (Hansard)*, 23 April 1956, col. 4104.

78. Barber, *South Africa's Foreign Policy 1945–1970*, p. 107; Barber and Barratt, *South Africa's Foreign Policy*, pp. 39–40.

79. Indicative of Pretoria's recognition of this reality were the observations of Prime Minister Verwoerd to parliament in South Africa, *Debates of the House of Assembly (Hansard)*, 4 May 1959.

80. Adam and Giliomee, *Ethnic Power Mobilized: Can South Africa Change?*, p. 165.

81. See Barber, *South Africa's Foreign Policy 1945–1970*, pp. 168–72, 175–80, 246–52, and 257–83; Nolutshungu, *South Africa in Africa*, pp. 130–218; Colin Legum and John Drysdale, *Africa Contemporary Record 1968–1969* (London: Africa Research Limited, 1969), passim; Kenneth W. Grundy, *Confrontation and Accommodation in Southern Africa: The Limits of Independence* (Berkeley: University of California Press, 1973), pp. 41–46; Barber and Barnett, *South Africa's Foreign Policy*, pp. 128–44.

82. For documentation of the discussion in this section, see Crocker, *South Africa's Defense Posture*, pp. 12 and 14; idem, "Current and Projected Military Balances in Southern Africa," p. 83; Republic of South Africa, *White Paper on Defence and Armament Production, April 1969*; Barber, *South Africa's Foreign Policy 1945–1970*, pp. 195 and 197–98; Philip H. Frankel, *Pretoria's Praetorians: Civil-Military Relations in South Africa* (Cambridge: Cambridge University Press, 1984), p. 91; Barber and Barratt, *South Africa's Foreign Policy*, pp. 91–95 and 101–03.

83. See Republic of South Africa, *White Paper on Defence and Armament Production, April 1964* (Cape Town: Government Printer, 1964); South African Institute of Race Relations, *Survey of Race Relations in South Africa, 1965* (Johannesburg, 1966); Frankel, *Pretoria's Praetorians*, pp. 81–83; Barber and Barratt, *South Africa's Foreign Policy*, pp. 91–95.

84. See Nolutshungu, *South Africa in Africa*, pp. 116–19; Barber, *South Africa's Foreign Policy 1945–1970*, chapter 15; Barber and Barratt, *South Africa's Foreign Policy*, pp. 91–95.

85. For elaboration, see Nolutshungu, *South Africa in Africa*, pp. 259–66; Barber, *South Africa's Foreign Policy 1945–1970*, chapter 16; Legum and Drysdale,

Africa Contemporary Record 1968–1969, pp. 314–17; Barber and Barratt, *South Africa's Foreign Policy*, pp. 95–96, 118–20, and 143.

86. See the relevant annual volumes of *African Contemporary Record*, edited initially by Colin Legum and John Drysdale and then by Colin Legum, and published in London at first by Africa Research Limited and later by Holmes and Meier; Barber, *South Africa's Foreign Policy 1945–1970*, p. 250; Nolutshungu, *South Africa in Africa*, pp. 168–69; Barber and Barratt, *South Africa's Foreign Policy*, pp. 130–43.

87. For these details, see the annual volumes of *Africa Contemporary Record* for the years under review; Barber, *South Africa's Foreign Policy 1945–1970*, p. 250; Nolutshungu, *South Africa in Africa*, pp. 130–55 and 192–218; Barber and Barratt, *South Africa's Foreign Policy*, pp. 128–30 and 143–50.

88. South African officials left no doubt on this score. See, for example, Prime Minister Vorster's comments as reported in *The Times* (London), 24 June 1971.

89. See the 1969–72 editions of *Africa Contemporary Record;* Nolutshungu, *South Africa in Africa*, pp. 266–77; Barber and Barratt, *South Africa's Foreign Policy*, pp. 146–50.

90. For treatment of the relevant developments of the period, see Colin Legum, "Dialogue: The Great Debate," in Legum, *Africa Contemporary Record 1971–1972*, pp. A66–82; Barber and Barratt, *South Africa's Foreign Policy*, pp. 147–48.

91. Details may be found in Nolutshungu, *South Africa in Africa*, pp. 277–78; Legum, *Africa Contemporary Record 1971–1972*, passim; Barber and Barratt, *South Africa's Foreign Policy*, p. 148.

92. The following discussion is based on the editions of International Institute for Strategic Studies, *The Military Balance* for 1969–1970 and 1974–1975; Crocker, *South Africa's Defense Posture*, p. 14.

93. For data on their persisting presence in the region, see U.S. Central Intelligence Agency, *Communist Aid Activities in Non-Communist Less Developed Countries, 1979 and 1954–79*, p. 15; U.S. Department of State, *Warsaw Pact Economic Aid to Non-Communist LDCs, 1984*, pp. 16 and 20; International Institute for Strategic Studies, *The Military Balance 1984–1985* (London, 1984), p. 75.

94. See Colin Legum, "Southern Africa: The Secret Diplomacy of Detente," in Legum, *Africa Contemporary Record 1974–1975*, pp. A3–15; idem, "Southern Africa: How the Search for Peaceful Change Failed," in Legum, *Africa Contemporary Record 1975–1976*, pp. A39–57; idem, *The Battlefronts of Southern Africa* (New York: Africana, 1987), pp. 1–19; Michael Clough, "From South West Africa to Namibia," in Clough, *Changing Realities in Southern Africa*, pp. 68–69; Barber and Barratt, *South Africa's Foreign Policy*, pp. 174–86 and 197–203.

95. On South African dealings with moderate black governments regarding Angola, see John Barratt, "Southern Africa: A South African View," *Foreign Affairs* 55, no. 1 (October 1976): pp. 151–52.

96. The terms and South Africa's position regarding them are dealt with in Clough, "From South West Africa to Namibia," pp. 71–76; Legum, *The Battlefronts of Southern Africa*, pp. 106–09.

97. For an excellent treatment of "total national strategy," see Frankel, *Pretoria's Praetorians,* pp. 46–70.

98. For treatment of South Africa's relations with the West during these years, see Barratt, "Southern Africa: A South African View," pp. 152–53; Deon Geldenhuys, "South Africa's Regional Policy," in Clough, *Changing Realities in Southern Africa,* pp. 144–46; Clough, "From Rhodesia to Zimbabwe," pp. 20–26.

99. See Geldenhuys, "South Africa's Regional Policy," p. 147; Barber and Barratt, *South Africa's Foreign Policy,* pp. 236–37.

100. For a good capsule discussion of the South African notion of a regional "constellation of states," see Geldenhuys, "South Africa's Regional Policy," pp. 148–51.

101. See the volumes of Legum, *Africa Contemporary Record* for 1981–1982 through 1985–1986; Barber and Barratt, *South Africa's Foreign Policy,* chapters 14–16, passim.

102. For details, see *South Africa: Time Running Out,* pp. 183–89; Barber and Barratt, *South Africa's Foreign Policy,* pp. 211–12.

103. Barber and Barratt, *South Africa's Foreign Policy,* p. 311; David Webster, "Repression and the State of Emergency," in Moss and Obery, *South African Review 4,* pp. 141–42.

104. This section draws upon Frankel, *Pretoria's Praetorians,* pp. 72, 83, and 90–92; Kenneth W. Grundy, *The Militarization of South African Politics* (Bloomington: Indiana University Press, 1986), pp. 22–23; the editions of International Institute for Strategic Studies, *The Military Balance* for 1974–1975 through 1986-1987; Crocker, *South Africa's Defense Posture,* p. 14; the volumes of Legum, *Africa Contemporary Record* for 1974–1975 through 1985-1986; Robert S. Jaster, "South Africa," in Jed C. Snyder and Samuel F. Wells, Jr., *Limiting Nuclear Proliferation* (Cambridge, MA: Ballinger Books, 1985), pp. 147–79; the *New York Times,* 5 December 1980; U.S. Department of State, *A U.S. Policy Toward South Africa,* p. 32.

105. For relevant discussion from diverse perspectives, see Jaster, *A Regional Security Role for Africa's Front-Line States* and *South Africa and Its Neighbours;* Grundy, *The Militarization of South African Politics,* chapter 17; the chapters on Southern Africa by Colin Legum in the volumes of Legum, *Africa Contemporary Record* for 1978–1979 through 1985–1986; Legum, *The Battlefronts of Southern Africa,* passim; Barber and Barratt, *South Africa's Foreign Policy,* chapters 13–16, passim; *Africa Now,* October 1982, pp. 91–98; the interview with General Constand Viljoen, chief of the SADF, in the *New York Times,* 6 June 1983; Deon Geldenhuys, *The Diplomacy of Isolation: South African Foreign Policy Making* (Johannesburg: Macmillan South Africa, 1984); John de St. Jorre, "Destabilization and Dialogue: South Africa's Emergence as a Regional Superpower," *CSIS Africa Notes,* no. 26 (17 April 1984); Robert Davies and Dan O'Meara, "Total Strategy in Southern Africa: An Analysis of South African Regional Policy since 1978," *Journal of Southern African Studies* 11, no. 2 (April 1985): pp. 183–211.

106. For an early indication of the shifting viewpoint, see the commentary on "South Africa's Regional Role in Southern Africa" by the government-run

radio network, Johannesburg International Service in English, 21 December 1984, in *FBIS-MEA*, 26 December 1984: U/6.

107. South Africa had, however, profited from close ties with Israel. According to the *Washington Post*, 22 March 1985, examination of Israel's arms industry showed that South Africa had probably been the main purchaser of arms from Israel in recent years. Its share of Israeli exports of weapons and equipment had amounted to as much as 35 percent of the total.

This relationship apparently underwent substantial change in 1987. Early in the year, the Israeli government reassessed its arms links with South Africa and decided not to sign new military sales contracts with Pretoria. See the *New York Times*, 29 January and 19 March 1987; *The Christian Science Monitor*, 2 April 1987.

108. Unless otherwise specified, the ensuing details may be found in De St. Jorre, "South Africa Embattled;" U.S. Department of State, *A U.S. Policy Toward South Africa*, pp. 24 and 27–28; Webster, "Repression and the State of Emergency," pp. 141–72; Amanda Armstrong, " 'Hear No Evil, See No Evil, Speak No Evil': Media Restrictions and the State of Emergency," in Moss and Obery, *South African Review* 4, pp. 199–214.

109. For description of the elements of this system, see the *Weekly Mail* (Johannesburg), 3–8 October 1986; the *Washington Times*, 24 June 1987; Mark Mitchell and Dave Russell, "Political Impasse in South Africa: State Capacities and Crisis Management," in Brewer, *Can South Africa Survive?*, pp. 321–22.

110. See the comments of Stoffel van der Merwe, Deputy Minister of Information and Constitutional Development, in June-July 1987, cited above in note 22.

111. The *New York Times*, 10 June 1988.

112. The ensuing analysis derives from International Institute for Strategic Studies, *The Military Balance for 1985–1986 and 1988–1989*; Johannesburg SAPA in English, 16 July, 16 November, and 29 December 1986, in *FBIS-MEA*, 16 July 1986: U/2–4, 19 November 1986: U/12, and 29 December 1986: U/1–2, respectively; *Sunday Telegraph* (London), 16 November 1986; *The Observer* (London), 28 December 1986.

113. On UNITA, see Jaster, *South Africa and Its Neighbours*, p. 40.; Gillian Gunn, "A Guide to the Intricacies of the Angola-Namibia Negotiations," p. 3. With respect to Renamo, see Chester A. Crocker, *U.S. Policy Toward Mozambique*, Current Policy no. 983 (Washington, D.C.: Bureau of Public Affairs, U.S. Department of State, 24 June 1987), p. 3.

114. For an insider's view of the negotiations regarding Namibia in 1988, see Freeman, "The Angola/Namibia Accords," pp. 126–41. For the texts of the agreements, see the *New York Times*, 23 December 1988.

115. On these diplomatic ventures, see the *New York Times*, 5 October 1988; Philip Nicolaides, "Opening to the North," *The World and I*, February 1989, pp. 125–29; Professor P. Smit, "South Africa and Black Africa," *Africa Insight* 19, no. 3 (1989): pp. 125–29.

116. For a first-rate analysis of the background to the Pretoria government's actions, see Gunn, "A Guide to the Intricacies of the Angola-Namibia Negotiations."

117. On the military cutbacks, see Lieutenant General Kat Liebenberg, "SADF Will Remain Formidable Force," *Paratus*, February 1990, pp. 4–6; "SADF Rationalization; Leaner Machine Planned: 'Si Vis Pacem, Para Bellum,' " *Armed Forces* (Johannesburg), February 1990, pp. 24–25.

118. See the text of the Groote Schuur Minute as put out by Johannesburg SAPA in English, 4 May 1990, and the commentary on the talks carried by Johannesburg Television Service in English, 6 May 1990, in *FBIS-AFR*, 7 May 1990: 15–17; Peter Fabricius analysis in *The Star*, 7 May 1990.

119. Alan Cowell reports in the *New York Times*, 7 and 8 August 1990.

120. See especially the statement of Dr. Gerrit Viljoen, acting state president and minister of constitutional development, in parliament on 9 May 1990, as reported in *The Citizen*, 10 May 1990, and by Johannesburg SAPA in English, 9 May 1990, and published in *FBIS-AFR*, 10 May 1990: pp. 13–14.

121. Interview of 27 June 1990, carried by Johannesburg Television Service in Afrikaans, 27 June 1990, and translated in *FBIS-AFR*, 28 June 1990: pp. 16–17.

122. See particularly Minister of Defense Malan's speech reported in Heitman, "South Africa's Changing Defence Policy," p. 1333; President de Klerk's speech of 2 February 1990, cited above in note 53, pp. 10–11 and 16–17.

123. See the report of the press briefing in *The Citizen*, 9 May 1990, and the SABC interview with him on 27 June 1990—after he came back from abroad—cited above in note 121, p. 16.

124. Radio Johannesburg Domestic Service in Afrikaans, 20 April 1990, translated in *FBIS-AFR*, 23 April 1990: 13; *The Citizen*, 27 April 1990; the *New York Times*, 26 and 31 July 1990.

125. For concrete evidence that de Klerk and his top advisers accept the notion that the National party will lose its dominant position in the government under a new constitutional dispensation, see the account of the views of party leaders in *Financial Mail* (Johannesburg), 23 March 1990; de Klerk's address to parliament on 19 April 1990, as carried by Johannesburg Television Service in English, 19 April 1990 and published in *FBIS-AFR*, 20 April 1990: 8.

126. See his speech to parliament on 19 April 1990, cited above in note 125, p. 8.

127. For reports on these discussions, see *Financial Mail*, 23 March 1990, and *The Star*, 25 March 1990.

128. His comments about alliances in the SABC interview with him on 27 June 1990, cited above in note 121, p. 17, were indicative of his thinking on the matter.

129. See his comments at a rally in Attridgeville on 26 May 1990, as carried by Johannesburg SAPA in English, 26 May 1990, and published in *FBIS-AFR*, 30 May 1990: 15–16.

130. The *New York Times*, 1 September 1990.

131. Speech at the opening of parliament on 2 February 1990, cited above in note 53, pp. 10–11.

132. See U.S. Arms Control and Disarmament Agency, *World Military Expenditures and Arms Transfers, 1988* (Washington, DC, June 1989), pp. 32–68,

passim; Ernest Harsch, "SADCC: The Dimensions of the Region's Debt," *Africa South*, March–April 1990, pp. 17–19; International Monetary Fund, *Direction of Trade Statistics Yearbook, 1989*, passim, for export figures of individual states since the early 1980s.

133. See, for instance, International Institute for Strategic Studies, *The Military Balance, 1986–1987*, p. 237.

134. Personal conversations in the region in April–May 1990.

135. For an explication of the Conservative party viewpoint, see the commentary by C. B. du Toit, editor of the party's journal, *Die Patriot*, as discussed in Colin Legum, "South Africa: The Challenge of the Afrikaner Right-wing Movement," *Third World Reports*, 18 April 1990, pp. 2–4.

5

India and South Asia: Resolving the Problems of Regional Dominance and Diversity

Shrikant Paranjpe and Raju G.C. Thomas

During the decade of the 1980s, South Asia experienced varying degrees of conflict and cooperation. Central to this fluctuating pattern of conflict and cooperation has been the role of India, the dominant power in the region. Crises, sometimes bordering on military conflict, have occurred between India and nearly all of its neighbors in South Asia. In 1990, India and Pakistan were poised on the precipice of another major war over the Kashmir issue; the on and off military conflict between India and Pakistan over the Siachen glacier has not yet been settled; the Indian military intervention in Sri Lanka to deal with the Tamil separatist movement there increased the tensions in Indo-Sri Lankan relations; India's decision to eliminate all but two of Nepal's trade routes through India in 1989 produced a new low in Indo-Nepalese relations; Indo-Bangladesh differences persist over a variety of issues concerning the sharing of the Ganges river waters, flood control and refugees; and the Indian military intervention in the Maldives in 1988 and the acquisition of a nuclear-powered submarine raised new concerns among its smaller neighbors.

On the other hand, the establishment of the South Asian Association for Regional Cooperation (SAARC) in 1983 provided a forum for the states of this region to explore areas where cooperation may be possible. SAARC constituted the first major step in creating a formal indigenous structure that identified the South Asian subordinate state system.[1] Although the purpose of SAARC does not seek to resolve conflict issues, it provides a mechanism for confidence-building in South Asia.

The SAARC countries today include Bangladesh, Bhutan, India, Maldives, Nepal, Pakistan and Sri Lanka. Afghanistan and Burma, both of which traditionally have been oriented toward South Asia, remained outside of SAARC. They are perceived, however, as "borderline" states having immediate significance for the South Asian region. Progress within the institutional framework of SAARC is a new development that must take into account both the traditional sources of threat perceptions and strategic responses in South Asia, and the newer forms of cooperation. In promoting this innovative pattern of regional interaction, the members of SAARC are trying to better manage the problems of dominance and diversity derived from the unequal distribution of power in South Asia.

Table 5.1 profiles the representative dimensions that are indicative of this unequal distribution.

This chapter examines the most important lines of conflict and cooperation, and the patterns of continuity and change that have occurred in South Asia since the British Indian empire was dismantled in 1947. The basic threat perceptions and strategic responses of each member of the South Asian subordinate system, especially that of India, the region's dominant power, need to be evaluated. The changing strategic picture in South Asia may be seen, for example, in the dominance and decline in India's relations with its neighbors:

1. From 1947–1954, in the immediate aftermath of independence and the partition of British India, India was the primary state by virtue of its size and central location in the region.
2. This was followed by a period of erosion between 1954–1962 beginning with the infusion of American arms to Pakistan's through its newly founded membership of SEATO in 1954.
3. The decline in credibility of Indian military power began with its crushing defeat in the 1962 Sino-Indian War and then continued to remain at a low ebb until and during the Indo-Pakistani war of 1965.
4. While Indian rearmament had begun following the war with China, the effects of this rearmament began to show after the 1965 Indo-Pakistani war culminating in the next war with Pakistan over the Bangladesh issue in December, 1971.
5. The military victory over Pakistan in the war of 1971 ushered in a period of Indian military supremacy in South Asia.
6. The Soviet invasion of Afghanistan in December 1979 brought about a second erosion of Indian dominance almost along the same pattern as the 1954–62 period when the United States began to arm Pakistan.
7. The formal incorporation of SAARC in 1983 constituted a relatively modest breakthrough in attempting to displace Indian hegemonistic aspirations through a system of regional equality and cooperation

Table 5.1 The South Asian Regional System

State	Population (millions) (1990)	Area (sq. km) (thousands)	GDP (US$/billions) (1990)*	Regional Type
Afghanistan	15.8	647.5	3.0	Peripheral-Borderline
Bangladesh	118.4	144.0	20.6	Bargainer-Secondary
Bhutan	1.6	46.2	0.3	Peripheral
Burma	41.2	676.6	11.0	Peripheral-Borderline
India	849.7	3,287.6	333.0*	Hegemon
Maldives	0.22	0.03	0.14	Peripheral
Nepal	19.1	140.8	2.9	Bargainer-Secondary
Pakistan	114.7	804.0	43.2*	Bargainer-Primary
Sri Lanka	17.2	65.0	6.1	Bargainer-Secondary

*GNP

SOURCE: U.S. Central Intelligence Agency, <u>The World Fact Book-1990</u> (Washington, DC: CR WF 90001, 1990).

among the countries of South Asia. This phase, however, did not last very long.

8. From about 1987 onwards, there was a resurgence of new conflict issues accompanied by demonstrations of Indian hegemonic power through its military expansion at sea and its military interventions in the Maldives and Sri Lanka.

The structure and pattern of regional politics in South Asia differs in many ways from the pattern of intra-regional and inter-state relationships as set out in some of the other regions discussed in this volume.[2] South Asia displays greater common historical, cultural, social, linguistic and ethnic bonds than suggested in the theoretical introduction to this volume. It also has a comparatively greater asymmetrical distribution of power than the other regions. Accordingly, we will need to modify some of the concepts of the core, peripheral and intrusive sectors as defined in one of the earlier works of Louis J. Cantori and Steven L. Spiegel.[3] In their 1969 study, the core sector consists of shared social, political, economic or organization activities among a group of states which produces a central focus of intraregional international politics. The peripheral sector is comprised of states alienated from the core sector because of economic, organizational, social or political differences. The intrusive sector is those powers that tend to intervene in the international relations of the region.

The British departure from India in 1947 produced two consequences for the subcontinent. First, it left British India and the nearly 500 Indian states ruled by the Indian Princes but under the paramountcy of the British Crown, divided into the two countries of India and Pakistan. Second, while India could claim the status of hegemon or dominant regional power, Pakistan sought equal status and to share or act as a major force within the core. This situation became more complicated for Pakistan in 1971 when East Pakistan separated from Pakistan to become the independent state of Bangladesh. However, Pakistan's search to keep pace with the growth of Indian military power continued unabated.

The smaller powers of South Asia are not properly peripheral to these two core and semi-core states in that they are not entirely alienated from the aspiring hegemon (India) and bargainer (Pakistan) states. Neither do they fit David Vital's description of a small, minor or tertiary power.[4] Vital identifies such a power as a state which in the long term (by itself, or as a satellite, client, or ally) constitutes no more than a dispensable and nondecisive increment to a primary states' total array of political and military resources. This relationship would exist regardless of whatever short-term contingent role the minor state may play as an auxiliary or obstacle to the primary power. Perhaps the only South Asian state that would fit Vital's description of a minor power would be Sikkim which was never quite an independent state and was eventually incorporated into the Indian Union in 1975.[5]

South Asia's smaller powers are most usefully perceived as secondary "bargainers" (Bangladesh, Sri Lanka and Nepal), or as peripheral "dependents" (Bhutan and Maldives). Maldives, a collection of some 1,200 coral islands that are strategically located in the Indian Ocean, has ethnic, religious, and cultural ties to the subcontinent. Until November 1988, Maldives had faced no conflict or threat from any of the states of South Asia. In 1988, however, Maldivian businessman, Abdullah Lutefi, used Tamil mercenaries from Sri Lanka in an attempt to seize power from the government of President Maumoon Abdul Gayoon.[6] The coup attempt was thwarted when Indian paratroopers dispatched by Prime Minister Rajiv Gandhi defeated the mercenaries and restored the government of Gayoon.

In summary, some of the basic characteristics of the South Asian political system may be identified as follows:

1. South Asia is a compact area of geographically proximate states that interact with each other and share common bonds of race, history, religion, language and culture.
2. India, by virtue of its geographic size and location, and economic and military strength, occupies a pivotal position in this region. Indian aspirations for leadership, dominance or hegemony are mainly a product of this systemic condition rather than emanating from individual leadership or governmental ambitions.
3. Apart from India, South Asia has one other significant power that operates in the region: Pakistan, a primary bargainer, has the potential to check Indian dominance or hegemonic aspirations. Yet Pakistan's own geographic, economic and military limitations make it unlikely that it could unilaterally achieve parity with India.
4. The major and most active power relationships in South Asia are, in turn, affected by the intrusive great powers that are external to the region. The main actors here are China, the United States and the Soviet Union. With external help, Pakistan can severely limit Indian ambitions; and with external backing, Pakistan can play the role of an upwardly mobile "bargainer" in relation to India, the aspiring hegemon.
5. Bangladesh and Sri Lanka, and to a lesser extent, Nepal and Bhutan, may be considered the small powers of South Asia. These powers hold a "nuisance" value or even cause a debilitating effect on Indian policy actions in that they can acquire a disproportionate bargaining capability in the event of a crisis.

Afghanistan and Burma, the other states mentioned in Table 5.1, have borderline status in relation to the South Asian subordinate system. At times, their regional concerns are those of South Asia. On other occasions, the former is part of the Middle East region, and the latter participates in the subordinate state system of Southeast Asia. The role played by all bargainer and peripheral states in South Asia is often shaped and enhanced by the involvement of external powers, especially China, the Soviet Union and the United States.[7]

South Asia has never been free from external intrusions. In the 1950s, the Cold War spilled over into the subcontinent when Pakistan was drawn into the American security alliance network. Under the 1954 Southeast Asian Treaty Organization (SEATO) and the 1955 Central Treaty Organization (CENTO), Pakistan became the recipient of large-scale American arms aid. Subsequently, the 1962 Sino-Indian war and the growing alliance relationship between Pakistan and China compelled India to turn to the Soviet Union for military assistance and diplomatic support. Chinese intrusion into the region was both direct through its conflict with India, and indirectly through its efforts to establish close ties with Pakistan, Bangladesh and Nepal. Such great power involvement is part of the external challenges that South Asia has always faced. A better understanding of the South Asian subordinate state system, therefore, would need to take into account the dynamics of Great Power interests in the region, and also the extent to which global and regional powers have used each other to advance their respective political and strategic objectives.

Indian Threat Perceptions and Policies in South Asia

Until the end of the Cold War in 1990, Indian postwar perceptions of threats emanating from the South Asian region were derived from a dual concern: the need to maintain the hard gained independence from Western colonial domination by avoiding involvement in East-West confrontations; and the concurrent realization that given the global reach of the Cold War, isolationism would be a difficult policy to implement. Accordingly, Indian responses to the evolving world order were manifested in the policies of "nonalignment" in the East-West struggle, "peaceful coexistence" with the communist bloc, and in efforts to establish regional solidarity and identity within South Asia.[8]

Prime Minister Jawaharlal Nehru's call for keeping Indian foreign policy "independent of politics of groups aligned against one another" became the guiding principle during the decade and a half following Indian independence.[9] The practice of peaceful coexistence with the communist countries was further intended to strengthen the policy of nonalignment in the East-West Cold War. The roots of India's nonalignment and peaceful coexistence go back to the Indian political psyche built on Mahatma Gandhi's ideas of nonviolent struggle against British rule. These policies were also facilitated because of India's geographical location that appeared remote from the Cold War arena in Europe and East Asia, and the fact that India faced no immediate or acute threats to its own security arising from the global confrontation. Similarly, the stress on anticolonialism in India's foreign policy in the immediate post independence era may be seen as an extension of the Indian nationalist struggle from British rule.

India's attempts at creating a regional consciousness free from Cold War politics was extended to the Third World where it sought to play a pivotal leadership role. This was demonstrated very early at the first Asian conference held in New Delhi in 1947.[10] Later, at the Bandung Conference of Afro-Asian nations, India sought to reinforce this leadership role.[11] However, because of unresolved territorial border disputes and the status of ethnic and religious minorities on the subcontinent in the post-partition period, India was compelled to direct greater attention to regional issues, especially the threats to national security posed by Pakistan.

The energy and resources needed to deal with this threat, as well as the need to pursue a policy of nonalignment amidst the global politics of the Cold War, were magnified by the intrusion of the two superpowers into the region. Moreover, at Bandung in 1955 there was no consensus on substantive political issues, or even on how the nonaligned group of nations should deal with the politics of the Cold War. Consequently, Bandung became the last comprehensive Afro-Asian conference to be held. Although an attempt was made to revive the "spirit of Bandung" on its 30th anniversary in 1985, most of the important African and Asian political heads of state did not attend. Instead, the Third World conference held in Belgrade in 1961 became the first of several nonaligned summits.[12] Between Bandung and Belgrade, India realized increasingly that the Cold War and its complement of alliances not only constituted a threat to the foreign policy autonomy of the newly independent nations, but also a threat to world peace.

South Asia, as it emerged after 1947, reflected the indigenous imbalance of power following the withdrawal of Britain. India replaced Britain by assuming the "responsibility" for the security and integrity of the smaller powers, albeit thwarted subsequently by Pakistani policies and the intervention of the extra-regional powers. Consequently, Indian strategic thinking in South Asia was conditioned by the following assumptions:[13]

1. Any system that seeks to establish a stable pattern of order in South Asia must reflect the objectives and role of the aspiring hegemon, India, and its major adversary, Pakistan.
2. Peace and order in South Asia will not emerge as a product of the military balance between India and Pakistan. This is more likely to occur if India possessed a preponderance of military power because under these conditions, Pakistan dare not attack while India need not attack.
3. India's desired objective is to maintain the territorial status quo in the region based on the principle of peaceful coexistence. India should be perceived as a benevolent giant with a role similar to that of the United States in the American hemisphere.
4. The smaller powers of South Asia should accept the Indian perspective and the subsidiary roles implicitly assigned to them by the aspiring hegemon. Non-acceptance of this assigned secondary role would be perceived as "obstacles" to be overcome by diplomacy or even military pressure.
5. The aspiring hegemon must seek to limit or offset the potential political and military interventionist policies of the external powers in the South Asian region through international diplomacy and, if necessary, by purchasing arms from one or more of the great powers.

The basic principle underlying India's strategic thinking since 1972 is the need to maintain Indian military preponderance in South Asia. Indeed, the policies of the two Gandhis have essentially followed the analysis of Professor A.F.K. Organski of the University of Michigan who had argued that under conditions of military preponderance, the weaker state dare not attack, while the stronger state need not attack. Even when wars do take place, often it occurs because the weaker state is attempting to catch up in the military balance with the stronger state—a situation which Organski has called the "rear-end collision" theory. The fact that there has been no Indo-Pakistani wars since the last one in December 1971—including during the revival of the Kashmir crisis in 1990—may perhaps be attributed to India's military preponderance. Similarly, we could argue that the lack of a military balance between India and China has prevented the Himalayan border dispute from erupting into another war between the two states.

In retrospect, we may identify two important "models" sponsored by India to achieve stability and order in South Asia. The first was the "1947 model" that was essentially the legacy of British rule and withdrawal that left India with inherent advantages following the partition of British India in 1947. Geopolitically, the newly independent Government of India found itself the dominant state in South Asia. The first test of it's relative superiority occurred during the India-Pakistan war of 1947–48 over Kashmir, when Indian military forces retained two-thirds of that state, including the prized Valley of Kashmir. Subsequently, the "1971–72 model" evolved in the aftermath of the December 1971 Indo-Pakistani war which had resulted in the military defeat of Pakistan and the creation of the new state of Bangladesh out of the former Bengali province of East Pakistan.

The 1947 model predominated until 1962 when the credibility of Indian military power and leadership received a severe blow. In the 1962 October-December war between India and China, the Indian army was routed along the disputed McMahon Line in the northeast sector of the country. Until then, two considerations had worked to sustain the image of Indian leadership and superiority. The first involved India's efforts to promote foreign policy independence among the newly independent states of Asia and Africa attempting to prevent the spread of the Cold War. The second emphasized the promotion of regional security institutions outside of the East-West conflict arena but was largely negated by Pakistan's entry into the American sponsored SEATO and CENTO anti-communist alliance networks.

In the wake of India's 1962 military defeat by China, Pakistani fears of Indian military power greatly diminished. In 1965 Pakistan sought to exploit a demoralized India by provoking a confrontation over the disputed state of Kashmir that eventually led to war between the two states in September of that year. Meanwhile, the ruling elites in the Himalayan states of Nepal, Bhutan and Sikkim decided that they had more to fear from a militarily stronger China than from a belligerent but weaker India. India also continued to adopt Britain's earlier policy of maintaining the "protectorates," i.e., taking on "the responsibility for the security of smaller states."[14] Since the more proximate Indian Ocean area was relatively peaceful, the offshore states of Sri Lanka and Maldives was seen to pose no nuisance value to India's regional policy.

India's defeat at the hands of China in 1962 negatively affected both its global status and its regional standing in South Asia. Pakistan's response to this erosion of Indian power was two-fold. First, Pakistan sought to redress its grievances in Kashmir by provoking a revolt in that region in 1965 which was followed by the dispatch of Pakistani troops across the cease-fire line.[15] India responded with military actions along the entire India-West Pakistan front, especially in the Punjab. Second, Pakistan initiated a dialogue with China to establish close military ties between the two countries.[16] During this period, the smaller powers started to swing out of the Indian orbit. Sri Lanka took upon itself the role of a neutral mediator between India and China by calling for a Colombo Powers conference to resolve the territorial boundary dispute between India and China.[17] Nepal began to speak in terms of its independent policy posture between India and China. Between 1962 and 1971, therefore, Indian attempts at exercising leadership in South Asia came to be questioned or even rejected by all the other states.

Such political and military reverses had placed India's dominant position in South Asia in jeopardy and brought about a reassessment of its post-independence foreign policy strategy. Immediately after the 1962 war, the Indian government sought to obtain Western arms. The Nehru government even considered joining the Western alliance network, and Indian military units were allowed to take part in a joint air military exercise with Great Britain and the United States. However, Pakistan maneuvered to thwart such moves, claiming that the Kashmir issue first had to be resolved. Thus, the hesitant Indian efforts to establish military links with the Western powers were stymied.

Following the end of hostilities between India and Pakistan in September 1965, India initiated a massive rearmament program, especially through the large-scale purchases of weapons from the Soviet Union on easy credit terms. At the same time, India deemphasized its global approach to foreign policy, especially its policy of promoting pan-Asian and African regionalism. Prime Minister Lal Bahadur Shastri focussed on improving bilateral relations with the states within the South Asian region. However, the relatively quiet international regional environment in which India operated began to change in the late 1960s.

The 1971–72 model was India's response to the transformations that occurred in the domestic, regional and global political environments. In 1970, President Richard Nixon recognized Pakistan as an important link in U.S. global strategic policy. The diminished status of the United States following its defeat in Vietnam, the new Nixon Doctrine that projected a lower American military profile in Asia, and the need to offset the growth of Soviet military power, mandated closer cooperation between the United States and China. Given the then prevailing close Sino-Pakistani ties, the Nixon administration recognized that Pakistan could play an important intermediary role for bringing about Sino-Pakistani rapprochement. Subsequently, Islamabad became the conduit for the secret visit of Secretary of State, Henry Kissinger, to Beijing in July 1971.

Within Pakistan, however, political consensus had eroded, and efforts to establish a new constitution and reconvene the National Assembly had collapsed.[18] Demands of the Awami League for greater autonomy, and failure to achieve a mutually acceptable constitution for both East and West Pakistan, eventually led to a widespread revolt against the military regime of General Yahya Khan, and then to civil war between armed Bengali nationalists and the Punjabi-dominated Pakistani military forces in the eastern province.

India now perceived a multifaceted threat. It feared the geopolitical consequence of a potential Washington-Islamabad-Beijing alliance, as well as the fall-out from the civil war in East Pakistan. The flow of refugees from here eventually reaching 10 million, had to begun to affect India's own tenuous political stability in the volatile states of West Bengal, Assam, and Tripura. Earlier, in 1969, the Soviet Union had revealed its own calculations about Asia's strategic future. The Chairman of the Communist Party of the Soviet Union, Leonid Brezhnev, proposed an Asian Collective Security pact, a pact that was clearly directed at China. To back this up, Foreign Minister Andrei Gromyko called for greater economic cooperation between the Soviet Union and the "other" states of Asia. Both proposals reflected the intensifying Sino-Soviet ideological conflict and the Soviet objective of containing the growth of Chinese military power in Asia.

India initially showed little interest in the proposed Collective Security pact. However, the impending Sino-American rapprochement, and the flood of Bengali refugees pouring into India as a consequence of the civil war in East Pakistan, suggested the need for greater Soviet military support. These conditions led to the signing of the Indo-Soviet Treaty of Peace, Cooperation and Friendship in August 1971. The treaty contained clauses of quasi-alliance nature. It called for Indo-Soviet consultations when the security of one or both of the signatories was threatened, and it prohibited alliance formations with states that constituted a threat to one of the two parties to the treaty.[19]

The 1971 Indo-Pakistani war ended with a decisive victory for India and the creation of the new state of Bangladesh out of what had been East Pakistan. With Pakistan cut in half, India regained its status as the premier regional power in South Asia. The following year, the Simla Agreement was signed by Prime Ministers Indira Gandhi and Zulfikar Ali Bhutto establishing the principle of bilateral negotiations on all outstanding Indo-Pakistani issues. In practice, this formalized India's dominant status on the subcontinent.[20] The Simla Agreement differed substantially from the 1966 Tashkent Agreement, mediated and hosted by the Soviet Union, which had been signed at the end of the 1965 Indo-Pakistani war. Unlike Tashkent which involved external third party mediation, the Simla Agreement of 1972 established bilateralism and regionalism as the framework of relations in South Asia.

With Pakistan having implicitly accepted India's dominant status, the government of Indira Gandhi was now in a better position to curb the drift of South Asia's smaller powers away from the Indian power center. Nevertheless, two basic assumptions underlay the 1971–72 model. The first presumed that the external great powers would acknowledge India's new preponderance on the subcontinent. American acquiescence came through repeated assurances that it recognized India's premier position throughout South Asia.[21] Soviet recognition was implicit in the continuing implementation of the 1971 Indo-Soviet Treaty. China's recognition of India's dominant role in South Asia was confirmed by the dialogue initiated between the two for the purpose of resolving differences that had separated them since the tensions began with the Tibetan revolt of 1959.

The second assumption grew out of the first. It revolved around perceptions of Indian behavior held by the other South Asian states. In exercising the role of the dominant power, the Indian government also had to instill confidence and a sense of security among the other countries in the region, especially Pakistan.

Pakistan: The Challenger to Indian Hegemony

Certain geographic compulsions and historical experiences which surfaced at the time of the partition of British India in 1947 have contributed significantly to Pakistan's strategic thinking. Pakistan's perceptions of its role rests on two vital forces. On the one hand, there exists a geographic, historic and cultural pull towards India. On the other hand, there is a religious and ideological pull away from the subcontinent towards the Islamic countries of the Middle East. The inevitability of being a part of the subcontinent made interactions with India unavoidable. At the same time, fear of militarily and industrially powerful India representing potential Hindu domination—which had precipitated partition in the first place—remained the essence of Pakistan's South Asian outlook. Consequently, the problem of Pakistan's defense revolved around the central theme of containing Indian attempts achieve regional hegemony or even to undo partition and absorb it back into a greater India.

Islam, a rallying point for separate statehood for Indian Muslims during the nationalistic period, continued to be an essential ingredient of Pakistan's foreign policy formulation. Pakistan immediately established ties with other Islamic states and solicited their support in its confrontation with India. Pakistan's first prime minister, Liaquat Ali Khan, stressed the strategic importance of the Middle East, West Pakistan's geographical contiguity with Iran and Afghanistan, and East Pakistan's proximity to the Islamic states of Indonesia and Malaya (now Malaysia).[22] Pakistan's vision of Pan-Islamic cooperation heightened India's perception of being isolated in an Islamic world and its fear of being surrounded by hostile Muslim states. However, Pakistan's efforts to bring about Islamic solidarity were unsuccessful. These efforts came at a time when Arab nationalism in the Middle East overrode Islamic solidarity.

Having failed to consolidate Islamic support for its policies, Pakistan sought to break its isolation by aligning itself with the West. Pakistan joined the Southeast Asian Treaty Organization (SEATO) in 1954, and a year later became a member of the Baghdad (later Central Treaty Organization) defense pact. These steps ended Pakistan's isolation and provided a means of counter-balancing the perceived Indian hegemony through the infusion of large-scale American military aid. However, Pakistan's motive for joining the Western alliance network was not to counter the communist threat from the Soviet Union or China, but to secure itself against a larger and more powerful India in the South Asian region.

During the early 1970s some shifts occurred in Pakistan's South Asian perspective. The loss of East Pakistan in 1971 altered the Pakistani government's focus and reduced its commitment to exercising influence in South Asia. Political retreat from the subcontinent received another impetus in 1973, when Daoud Khan came to power in Afghanistan after overthrowing the monarchy of his cousin, King Zahir Shah. Daoud Khan's pro-Soviet leanings and his declared interest in reviving the Pakistan-Afghanistan border issue created a new threat for Pakistan from beyond the subcontinent. Despite Pakistan's disenchantment with the United States and China because of their half-hearted support during the 1971 conflict, Pakistan turned once again to these two countries for military assistance. At this time, both the United States and China reportedly rejected the idea of a new defense pact with Pakistan.[23] Subsequently, Pakistan attempted to enlist informal Arab and Iranian support for its defense needs.[24]

President Zulfikar Ali Bhutto also initiated a major rethinking of Pakistan's strategic policy.[25] He focussed on three basic issues that in some ways appeared contradictory. First, there were efforts to rationalize and defend Pakistan's continued military links with the United States. The tactics here were to play upon the underlying domestic fear of the Indian military threat, and to stress Pakistan's isolation in the Islamic world. The India factor was also used to justify Pakistan's continued military links with China. Secondly, there was the need to create a rationale for reducing Pakistan's military ties with the United States in order to establish better relations with the Soviet Union. Here Bhutto used the argument of "changes in the international system" and the limited utility of global alliances to deal with regional issues. The intent of these seemingly incompatible objectives was to obtain military assistance from wherever possible without the constraints and obligations of alliance systems. Finally, Bhutto introduced the idea of nonalignment and bilateralism. He stressed the advantages of independence in foreign policy-making and the need for direct negotiations with other nations. However, he also sought to maintain Pakistan's active membership in the Islamic Conference as well as the CENTO alliance system. Pakistan's military and political ties to the Shah's Iran, Turkey and Saudi Arabia—three states with strong military links to the United States—were portrayed as outside the scope of nonalignment and bilateralism. They served to advance Pakistan's Islamic identity and interests. By talking of nonalignment while keeping nonalignment separate from its traditional Islamic ties, Pakistan appeared to be communicating with India in the same language that New Delhi had used over the years.

The Afghanistan Crisis and Indo-Pakistani Relations

Not until the Soviet invasion of Afghanistan in December 1979 did the 1971–72 model begin to undergo significant change. The problems began in April 1978 with the Marxist coup in Afghanistan led by Hafizullah Amin of the Khalq faction against the regime of President Daoud Khan. Subsequent efforts at implementing Marxist reforms by Khalqi ideologues and the rivalry between this faction of the People's Democratic Party of Afghanistan (PDPA) and the more pragmatic Parcham faction, produced widespread revolt in the countryside and greater Soviet military involvement. In December 1979, amidst a major revolution against the new Marxist government, Soviet forces invaded Afghanistan overthrowing the regime of Hafizullah Amin of the Khalq faction and installing the new regime of Babrak Karmal of the Parcham faction.

The Soviet military intervention in Afghanistan suddenly increased the importance of Pakistan in U.S. global military strategy. Pakistan had become a "frontline" state and began to receive large-scale American economic and military aid. From the Pakistani perspective, however, the Soviet invasion and occupation of Afghanistan represented a dual Indo-Soviet threat that could possibly squeeze Pakistan out of existence. The old 1971–72 model based on benevolent Indian hegemony became no longer credible or acceptable to Pakistan. The importance of American and Chinese military support, therefore, had become crucial. It is in this context, that President Zia ul-Haq came to proclaim Pakistan's right to purchase sophisticated defense equipment from the United States. However, Zia made it clear that it still considered the Indian threat to be greater than the Soviet threat, and that its military cooperation with the United States against the Soviet threat through Afghanistan was in exchange for expected American support to Pakistan to deal with the Indian threat.[26]

Between the Soviet invasion of Afghanistan in December 1979 and its withdrawal in March 1988, India labored to contain the conflict and convince the Soviet leadership of the futility of its policy. India viewed the fallout from the Soviet military intervention in Afghanistan as a threat to its leadership in the South Asian region, and its response pivoted around the strategies of accommodation and alliance manipulation with the Soviet government. Prime Minister Indira Gandhi initially proclaimed that the invasion should be viewed in the larger perspective of the deteriorating global and regional environment of the Middle East, Central America, and Southern Africa.[27] India called for the withdrawal of all foreign troops from the soil of foreign nations, including the Soviet military presence in Afghanistan and implicitly the American military involvement in Central America.[28]

The new round of American arms to Pakistan to counter the Soviet occupation of Afghanistan raised several new questions. First, although Pakistan continued to claim to be part of the nonaligned group of nations, it also emphatically declared itself a staunch and trusted ally of the United States. Second, Pakistan began to receive very sophisticated arms from the United States which included F-16 fighters, TOW anti-tank missiles, and the Stinger anti-aircraft missiles. Third, Pakistan sought to establish military links with the Muslim states in the Middle East, in particular with Saudi Arabia where it had stationed some two divisions of its troops. Fourth, its clandestine nuclear weapons program was accelerated and appears to have reached critical proportions when reports alleged that Pakistan had managed to enrich uranium to weapons grade levels. All of these events and actions suggested a renewed Pakistani effort to balance and deter Indian military capabilities which appears to have paid off during the confrontation over Kashmir in 1990.

The Bargainers: The Smaller Powers of South Asia

India perceives no significant threat from the small powers of South Asia. For the greater part, India's policies toward them, unlike its policies toward Pakistan, have been benevolent. Undoubtedly, there have been some major disputes with Bangladesh over the Farrakha Barrage and illegal immigration into Assam, with Sri Lanka over the treatment of Tamils, and with Nepal over the terms of the bilateral trade and transit treaties.[29]

In responding to threats to its Indian empire from external powers, Great Britain had devised the concept of the "extended frontier." Britain's strategic interests and responsibilities included all of India's neighbors—Afghanistan, Tibet, Nepal, Sikkim, Bhutan and Sri Lanka—in an extended security framework. India sought to continue these policies by assuming responsibility for the security of some smaller neighbors. Because of Pakistan's non-cooperation, Afghanistan's distance and difficult accessibility, China's reassertion of its sovereignty over Tibet, only three states eventually fell within India's defense perimeter—Nepal, Bhutan and Sikkim. The British practice of administering Sri Lanka separately from its British Indian empire also kept this state outside India's defense perimeter. At the same time, India sought to avoid interference in the internal affairs of these countries, except during crisis situations that India perceived to affect its own national security interests. The Indian political intervention and eventual absorption of Sikkim into the Indian Union in 1983 was an extreme example and the exception to this policy.

Indian statements of this basic policy came intermittently. For example, both Prime Minister Nehru and former Indian foreign policy advisor and ambassador to China, K. M. Pannikar, had talked of close ties with Ceylon (now Sri Lanka) even to the extent of making it an autonomous unit of the Indian federation.[30] Similarly, speaking in the Indian parliament during the visit of the King of Nepal, Nehru stated that "much as we stand for the independence of Nepal, we cannot allow anything to go wrong there . . . because that would be a risk to our own security." Responding to the crisis in Bangladesh in 1975 caused by the assassination of Prime Minister Sheikh Mujibur Rahman, India reiterated that it was vitally interested in the security and stability of all neighboring countries.[31] Such statements and reactions reflect the general security orientation in India's relations with the small powers.

Nepal

India's policy towards Nepal is determined by several considerations. Geographically, Nepal is a landlocked country between India and China. However, road, rail and air access to Nepal is almost exclusively through India. Historically, both countries have shared common security perceptions. There also exists a close socio-cultural affinity between the two, Nepal being the only other state in the world with a Hindu majority. Because of these strategic and cultural links, India and Nepal signed two treaties in 1950 that laid the foundations of their future relations.[32] These were the Peace and Friendship Treaty and the Trade and Transit Treaty.

Unlike the two other smaller Himalayan states of Bhutan and Sikkim, Nepal's relatively larger size has allowed its government to use China as a counterweight against excessive Indian domination. On the other hand, rarely has Bhutan deviated from the treaties signed with India in 1949, treaties that are similar in content to those signed with Nepal. Sikkim, as noted earlier, was merged as a new state into the Indian Union in 1983.[33]

During most of the 1950s, India further consolidated its influence over Nepal by using the 1950 treaties as the instrument of control. For instance, during the 1954 visit of King Tribhuvan to India, an official note was handed to the Nepalese foreign minister stating among other things that there would be close and continuous contact between the two countries. In reality, Nepal was to consult India in all matters relating to foreign policy or relations with other states.[34]

Indo-Nepalese relations during the 1960s and 1970s have gone through several ups and downs. In 1960, the Nepalese king had dismissed the popularly elected Prime Minister, B. F. P. Koirala, for his allegedly pro-India leanings. As in the earlier case of Sikkim, implicit in the Nepalese monarch's fear was the example of a popular democratic republic set by India which had dismissed all of its own native princely rulers. By the 1970s, Nepal began to use its opening to China more frequently based on the diplomatic relations at the ambassadorial level that the two countries had established in 1958. Nepal's further assertion of an independent identity and autonomy in its foreign policy came in 1975 when the King proposed "peace zone" in the Himalayas.[35] Within the context of the new proposal, efforts were made to end India's special status in Nepal and establish Nepal as a neutral state between India and China.

The question remained, however, whether India would respect the Nepalese concept of a peace zone. India's unwillingness to allow Nepal to drift away may be seen in the Indian government's refusal to abandon the restrictive interpretation of the 1950 Trade and Transit Treaty when it came up for review in 1971, suggesting that India was determined to perpetuate its privileged status.[36] From the perspective of Nepali nationalists, this realization has been discouraging, although officially the Indian government claims that it places no pressure on Nepal.[37]

That India is able to exert considerable pressure on Nepal was illustrated in the crisis of 1988–89. The issue arose again over the renewal of two treaties that India and Nepal had signed in 1978 regarding trade and transit rights through India.[38] These treaties, which were continued extensions of the 1950 treaties, had expired in 1983 but was renewed by Prime Minister Indira Gandhi for another five years. Negotiations for further renewal in 1988 had been stalled by India's insistence that there should be a single treaty governing trade and transit rights. Nepal, claiming the treaties to be archaic and unreasonable, demanded two separate treaties governing trade and transit on the grounds that trading relationships could change over time, while transit rights for a landlocked state were permanent based on international law. The negotiations became deadlocked, and India declared the two treaties to have lapsed. India then closed 12 of the 14 transit routes between the two countries claiming that it had more than met the minimum of one transit route required by international law.

The tough Indian stance against Nepal was provoked by an Nepalese decision in 1988 to purchase anti-aircraft guns and other arms from China. The Nepalese decision may have been provoked by the constant overflight of the surveillance and combat aircraft of the Indian Air Force patrolling the Chinese borders, and the specific incident in 1987 when the IAF dropped relief supplies to Tamil rebels in the Sri Lankan province of Jaffna in violation of that country's sovereignty. On the other hand, India felt that Nepal had violated the understanding of the 1950 Peace and Friendship Treaty which required Nepal to purchase its weapons from India, or failing India's inability to provide them, to purchase them from Britain or the Western powers. Indian fears arose from the open borders between India and Nepal which allowed Nepalese citizens to move freely across and seek employment in India. A Chinese military connection in Khatmandu would erode Indian security across the Sino-Nepalese borders.

Other irritants claimed by India included the Nepalese decision to require all residents of Nepal to demonstrate their citizenship or acquire work permits, something which Nepalese citizens in India do not need. There are about 150,000 Indians who live an work in Nepal, while 5 million Nepalese work in India, most of whom have acquired Indian citizenship.[39] Again, Nepal imposed a 55 percent tariff on Indian goods entering Nepal to which India retaliated by imposing a similar tariff on Nepalese goods entering India. Combined with the closure of 12 transit points, this Indian policy severely affected Nepal's economy.

Most of these differences were eventually resolved with the election of the Janata Dal-led National Front government of Prime Minister V.P. Singh in India. In June 1990, Indo-Nepalese differences were settled with the renewal of the trade and transit treaty.[40] Nepal was given 15 trade and transit points and the Indian tariff on Nepalese goods was lifted. In return, Nepal exempted Indian citizens from work permits and agreed to be more sensitive to Indian security concerns regarding its purchase of arms from China.

Bangladesh

The creation of Bangladesh out of East Pakistan through Indian armed intervention initially gave that state a special place in Indian foreign policy during the 1970s. Until the creation of this state, born out of the Indo-Pakistani war of December 1971, Indian defense policy in South Asia had been built around the possibility of a two-front war against both wings of Pakistan. Intense Pakistani military pressure on Kashmir could always be countered in the last resort by an Indian threat to sweep across Pakistan's vulnerable eastern province. Following the independence of Bangladesh, the area of Pakistan to be defended became more compact, and the Indian threat to conduct a two-front war could no longer be used as a leverage against Pakistan.

Since Bangladesh became independent, India has attempted to play on the breakup of Pakistan to discredit the view of Islam as a unifying force on the subcontinent or as the basis for nationhood. This strategy was given high priority by India to counter Pakistan's pan-Islamic drive to muster support for its claim to India's Muslim majority state of Kashmir. India also sought to avoid encouraging broader Bengali nationalism that may produce separatist tendencies in West Bengal and the creation of a greater Bangladesh state. Such a state would reunite the two Bengals that was divided at the time of independence and partition in 1947.

The signing of the Indo-Bangladesh Friendship Treaty in 1972 brought Bangladesh into the Indian sphere of influence while providing assurance to the new state that India would do nothing to threaten its territorial sovereignty and national independence.[41] Under Sheikh Mujibur Rahman, Bangladesh also recognized the geopolitical fact of India's strategic interests in the region and India's contribution to the country's liberation struggle. However, the same conditions also produced a growing suspicion and fear of Indian domination and control over Bangladesh in the future. Consequently, Bangladesh also sought to reinforce its separate identity and newly acquired nationhood resisting various Indian overtures.

During the lifetime of Sheikh Mujibur Rahman, the emotional ties between the two countries remained strong. After Mujib's assassination in 1975, Bangladesh sought to increase and diversify its ties with Pakistan, China and the United States, and, correspondingly, to reduce its dependence on India and the Soviet Union. Bangladesh finally chose the course that India had sought to prevent: closer ties with Pakistan. However, by simultaneously adopting the rhetoric of support for a South Asian alternative, Bangladesh was also able to satisfy Indian demands for limiting extraregional interventions.

In reality, this change reduced Indian domination and control. Moreover, Islam had become the ideology once again for bridging differences between Bangladesh and Pakistan. Khodakar Mushtaque, who took over power after the assassination of Mujibur Rahman, proclaimed Bangladesh an Islamic Republic. Later, presumably under Indian pressure, he declared the state to be secular again.[42] In 1977, through a presidential order, the next president of Bangladesh, General Ziaur Rahman, dropped the word "secularism" from the Bangladesh constitution. He argued that with 90 percent of the population being Muslim, the introduction of

Islamic thinking into government policy was inevitable.[43] Since the assassination of Ziaur Rahman, his successor, General Hussain Muhammed Ershad, officially declared Bangladesh to be an Islamic state.

The issues between India and Bangladesh are not explosive, but they remain and continue to strain relations between the two countries. These issues include the sharing of the Ganges waters, policies on flood control, the illegal immigration of Chakma refugees into India, and the dispute over the South Talpatti island.[44]

Sri Lanka

As an island located strategically in the Indian Ocean, Sri Lanka's only close neighbor is India. From the time of independence, India had always considered this island country as important to its security. Besides, Sri Lanka had a significant minority Tamil population. Although Sri Lanka has no formal treaty links with India such as Nepal or Bhutan, like these two states, it has usually shared India's views on global issues. By accepting and promoting India's proposal to maintain the Indian Ocean as a "Zone of Peace," Sri Lanka demonstrated that it identified with Indian concerns about keeping the area free of extra-regional political and military influence. Nevertheless, Sri Lanka has remained neutral on Indo-Pakistani and Sino-Indian disputes.

At the bilateral level, Sri Lanka and India have attempted to resolve two major continuing issues—the status of Tamil settlers in Sri Lanka, and the location of the maritime boundary between the two states. On the maritime boundary dispute, India accommodated Sri Lankan demands in the Treaty of 1974.[45]

In contrast, the Tamil question remains a serious problem despite bilateral agreements signed in 1964, 1987, and 1989.[46] Rioting among the Tamils during the early 1980s, escalated into a major revolution against the Sri Lanka government and the country's majority Sinhalese populations. Insurgency and terrorism, exemplified by the April 1987 Ayuath Oya massacre that attracted international attention, have become commonplace in the attempts by Tamil extremists to achieve an autonomous or separate Tamil state in Sri Lanka. India's involvement in Sri Lanka's Tamil movement arises from the political and emotional support, and even covert material and military aid, provided by the Tamils in the Indian state of Tamil Nadu.

In 1990, there are about three million Tamils and 13 million Sinhalese in Sri Lanka, compared to 55 million Tamils in an Indian population of about 850 million. Although the Tamils are mainly Hindu and the Sinhalese mainly Buddhist, there are sizeable numbers of Christians in both groups. It is important to note though that the intensity of the conflict is not generated so much by religious differences as by a linguistic-racial divide. The Tamils constitute the heart of the Dravidian race and culture, while the origins of the Sinhalese race, language and culture are essentially from the Indo-Aryan North of the subcontinent, a group that migrated to the island during a distant historical past.

Given earlier efforts by Indian Tamils to create an independent Dravidastan in southern India—an entity consisting of the four Dravidian states of Tamil Nadu, Andhra Pradesh, Karnataka and Kerala—the Indian government may have feared that disregarding the Tamil cause in Sri Lanka could so alienate the Indian Tamils, that they might seek to reorganize the Dravidan separatist movement against the dominance of the Indo-Aryan north.

India's role and objectives in the Sri Lankan crisis needs to be understood in the context of its perceptions as the primary regional power. It seeks first, to prevent the military intrusions of other powers in the Sri Lankan civil war, and second, to keep the dispute within the South Asian regional framework. The Indian interest in the crisis intensified when Sri Lanka sought political support and military assistance from Pakistan, Israel, Britain and the United States. India cautioned the foreign powers to stay clear of the crisis and sent a special envoy to conduct negotiations with the Sri Lankan government.[47] The Colombo talks in 1984 and the Thimpu talks in 1985 sought to bring about a reconciliation between the military Tamils and the Sri Lankan government. The Indo-Sri Lankan dialogue failed; and, in 1986–87 the crisis escalated into an all-out civil war between the Tamil militants controlling the northern peninsula, and Sri Lankan forces. At this point, under pressure from the Tamils of Tamil Nadu, India sought to intervene directly in the conflict.

The "Indo-Sri Lankan Agreement to Establish Peace and Normalcy in Sri Lanka," signed on July 29, 1987 by Prime Minister Rajiv Gandhi and President J. R. Jayewardene, led to unprecedented Indian military involvement in Sri Lanka.[48] The agreement was viewed initially as balancing Tamil demands for autonomy with the Sri Lankan objective of maintaining its territorial integrity and national unity. It provided for the creation of provincial councils for the eastern and northern regions of the country, with the option later to merge the provinces into one administrative unit through a referendum. The agreement also provided for the deployment of an "Indian Peace Keeping Force" (IPFK) at the invitation of the Sri Lankan president, to disarm the Tamil rebels and ensure the safe conduct of elections in the newly created provinces.

Indian peace keeping efforts in Sri Lanka proved more costly and divisive than anticipated. Soon after their arrival, Indian troops became bogged down in a guerrilla conflict with the major and most powerful of the Tamil factions fighting for independence, the Liberation Tigers of Tamil Ealam (LTTE). The LTTE refused to surrender their arms under the accord claiming that they were not consulted or a party to it. The IPFK found themselves fighting the Tamils whom they come to protect and the size of its forces soon swelled to 45,000 soldiers. The presence of so large an Indian military force, provoked a revolt by the Sinhalese nationalist group, the Janatha Vimukthi Peramuna (JVP). The guerrilla terror that once had been confined to the island's Tamil north erupted with even greater ferocity in the Sinhala south. The level of violence among the opposing insurgent forces increased. While the IPFK fought the Tamil insurgents in the north, the Sri Lankan army fought the Sinhalese insurgents in the south. Mysterious terrorist death squads were formed. Between July 1987 and September 1989, more than 5,000 insurgents, soldiers and civilians died, including 1,000 members of India's Peace Keeping Force. Within the Indian Army, one of the world's largest and most disciplined fighting forces, morale deteriorated.[49]

India's inability to impose a military solution in the ethnic violence between Tamils and Sinhalese led to irresistible pressures both in Sri Lanka and India for the withdrawal of the IPKF. On the one hand, President Ranasinghe Premadasa (a Sinhalese) concluded that no solution to the ethnic crisis was possible until the Indian military returned to the mainland, On the other hand, Prime Minister Rajiv Gandhi's Sri Lankan policy loomed as a major issue in the upcoming November 1989 Indian general elections for the central parliament. In September 1989, bowing to pressure from all sides, New Delhi agreed to pull its troops out of Sri Lanka by the end of the year. (The withdrawal was eventually completed in March 1990 under the new National Front government of Prime Minister V. P. Singh.)

Although several foreign observers have termed India's political and military involvement in Sri Lanka a dismal failure, the results may not have been as bad.[50] Clearly, the original objective of disarming the Tamil militants, especially the LTTE, failed. However, India did forge the creation of two Tamil majority provinces which were eventually joined into a single provincial council, while the IPKF dealt the LTTE a series of devastating blows which compelled it to negotiate and cooperate with the Sinhalese government. The IPKF also left behind a counterweight to the extreme militancy of the LTTE through the training and arming of a moderate and pro-India Tamil militia called the Ealam People's Revolutionary Liberation Front. However, the Indian military involvement and subsequent withdrawal failed to provide Sri Lanka's Tamils with the increased power and autonomy that the Rajiv Gandhi administration had promised.

SAARC: An Institutional Check to Indian Hegemony

Calls by India for restraint by its South Asian neighbors in their reactions to the strategic environment of 1979–88, may be viewed as the expected reaction of an aspiring hegemon whose immediate and basic interests was the maintenance of the regional status quo. The 1980s also produced new initiatives by the regional challenger and the bargainer states of the South Asian regional system. These initiatives were essentially a reaction to the collapse of the 1971–72 model. Pakistan's proposal for a "No-War Pact" between India and Pakistan constituted an important manifestation of the desire of the weaker states to stabilize their own geopolitical region.[51] This pact called for a simple declaration of non-aggression, but on a deeper and more significant level, it sought to reinstate the basic principles of bilateral interaction that would replace the earlier Simla Agreement. Because the focus of the Pakistani initiative was on bilateral negotiations, it remained an incomplete solution for restructuring relations within the South Asian subordinate system. In particular, Pakistan made no commitments on the future security arrangements to be established in South Asia. In these circumstances, the proposal by Bangladesh for setting up a South Asian Association for Regional Cooperation (SAARC) became especially important.

In November 1980, President Ziaur Rahman of Bangladesh sent a "Working Paper on Regional Cooperation in South Asia," to the countries of South Asia. This document represented the first comprehensive attempt by a country other than India to formulate a governing regime for South Asia. The successful establishment of SAARC in 1983 suggested a new trend within South Asia, one that seeks to reduce perceptions of threat by managing potential conflict issues. It also seeks to maximize the advantages of regional economic cooperation.

The Bangladesh Working Paper, and the subsequent letter of clarification sent by the Bangladesh Foreign Ministry, jointly provide the projected purpose and process of SAARC.[52] The basic characteristics underlying the proposal were as follows:

1. The institutional framework to be established will reflect the participating states' commitment to nonalignment. While bilateral negotiations are to be encouraged, SAARC is to identify areas of cooperation that will be of mutual benefit to all regional states. These areas include telecommunications, meteorology, transport, shipping, tourism, and agriculture.
2. The proposal took into account the natural apprehensions of smaller nations given the asymmetry of power distribution in the region.

It recognized that unfettered South Asian regionalism may institutionalize the leadership of the dominant state, thus making India the first among equals. On the other hand, the proposal also acknowledged the Indian fear that the smaller states might coordinate their policies for the purpose of pressuring or isolating the dominant power.

3. The proposal made clear that it was not an attempt to regionalize bilateral issues. Rather they sought to identify those areas of cooperation that were essentially regional in character.

The Bangladesh proposal had sought to recognize the fears of both the smaller powers and the dominant power in South Asia, and to find an arrangement whereby all the states could live without being vassals or experiencing perpetual confrontation. It was an historic effort to build a working relationship that were equal in principle but unequal in reality.

The final declaration of SAARC reflected many of the more important Indian concerns. It steered clear of two controversial yet crucial issues that could make or unmake a regional order. First, SAARC retained cooperation in the non-controversial areas of socioeconomic and cultural cooperation. Political and security issues were excluded from the organization. Second, contentious bilateral issues that were not security-related were also excluded from the deliberations of SAARC. This was done for cautionary reasons partly because of the newness of SAARC in order to avoid its collapse at an early stage. However, by keeping all such issues out the SAARC agenda, India appeared to have succeeded in restricting the scope of the organization to areas which do not impinge significantly on its efforts to maintain its dominant status.

Living with Hegemony: The Search for Alternatives

To claim that India would like to return to the 1971–72 model would be quite simplistic under the conditions of the 1990s. No doubt the continuous growth of Indian military power, especially demonstrations of naval power in a wider arc of the Indian Ocean, and the increased possibility that India will embark on a nuclear weapons program in the 1990s, may reinforce beliefs that India seeks hegemonic status. However, fundamental changes have taken place in South Asia since the Soviet occupation of Afghanistan that appear to make India's preferred regional system unrealistic.

First, especially during the present crisis over Kashmir, efforts by India to seek military dominance will be matched by Pakistan. With the end of the Cold War in 1990, already Pakistan is seeking arms from both East and West. Apart from weapons already received from the United States or in the pipeline, Pakistan has benefitted from the unloading of weapons by Western and Eastern European countries in the Middle East, South Asia and Southeast Asia.

Second, Indian efforts to achieve clear and unabashed military superiority is likely to produce fallout in the adjacent regions of the Persian Gulf and Southeast Asia. India's naval expansion, for instance, may provide Pakistan with the opportunity to convince other major Islamic states such as Iran and Indonesia, to forge an Islamic alliance against India, thus making Indian miliary expansion counterproductive.

Third, any attempt by India to acquire nuclear weapons will provide Pakistan with the excuse to go nuclear as well.[53] A Pakistan with (say) 10 nuclear bombs would then become the equal of an India with a 100 nuclear bombs because both sides would be able to deter each other with their retaliatory strike capabilities. It would also make India's conventional military superiority less meaningful since all Indo-Pakistani confrontations could be quickly escalated to nuclear levels.

Fourth, there is a price that India may have to pay for engaging in military interventions in the region. The Indian military interventions in both the Pakistani civil war in its eastern province in 1971 and in the Sri Lankan civil war between 1987 and 1990, carried with it grave risks that Bengali and Tamil nationalism may spill into the Indian states of West Bengal and Tamil Nadu. Moreover, military interventions by the United States in Vietnam and the Soviet Union in Afghanistan have demonstrated the futility of deploying conventional power capabilities under conditions where insurgencies are likely to operate. Similarly, a future Indo-Pakistani war would have to take into account the effects of continuing insurgencies and acts of terrorism in the strategic border states of Indian Punjab and Kashmir.

Fifth, the growth of separatist movements in India, Sri Lanka and Pakistan implies that these multi-ethnic states will eventually have to decentralize radically granting greater internal autonomy to its states and provinces. Such a decentralizing process may make India look less a colossus to its smaller neighbors than it appears at present.

Sixth, the world in general is moving from an era of High Politics to Low Politics. While this may simply mean a shift from Indian military hegemony to economic hegemony in South Asia, the experience of East Asia has shown that this constitutes less of a threat. Countries such as South Korea and Taiwan have prospered despite the presence of the Japanese and Chinese giants adjacent to them. Economic interdependence is not likely to be confined to the regional level—it is not even necessary—but is more likely to be global as even smaller states reach out around the world for economic cooperation.

In the ultimate analysis, despite the persistence and even intensification of conflict pressures in South Asia at the turn of the 1990s decade, the patterns of cooperation will continue to surface transcending inter-state disputes. To be sure, there are specific regional differences, but there are also a variety of common characteristics among the peoples of this region—race, religion, languages, culture and cuisine. Geography and history also tend to unite the region in many ways. The SAARC system and process have managed to survive amidst a variety of disputes and confrontations among the states of South Asia. However, the nature of Indian political behavior will remain crucial if the conflict pressures are not to overwhelm cooperative incentives. As the largest state in the region, India must learn to play the role of big brother rather than bully.

Notes

1. See *Indian and Foreign Review,* Vol. 20, No. 21, 15–31 August, 1983, pp. 38–39, 42; and *India Express* (Bombay), December 9, 1985.

2. See the discussion surrounding Table 1.1 in the overview chapter.

3. L.J. Cantori and S.L. Spiegel, "International Regions: A Comparative Approach to Five Subordinate Systems," *International Studies Quarterly,* December 1969, pp. 361–80.

4. David Vital, *The Survival of Small States: Studies in Small Power/Great Power Conflict,* (London: Oxford University Press, 1971), p. 9.

5. Sikkim became a state in the Indian Union by means of the 36th Amendment to the Indian Constitution in response to the decision taken by the Sikkim Congress.

6. See *Time,* November 14, 1988, p. 33.

7. For an earlier study of these relationships, see Raju G. C. Thomas, *Indian Security Policy,* (Princeton New Jersey: Princeton University Press, 1986), pp. 11–14.

8. Werner Levi, *The Challenge of World Politics in South and South East Asia,* (New Jersey: Prentice Hall, 1968), p. 154.

9. Jawaharlal Nehru, *India's Foreign Policy: Selected Speeches September 1946–April 1961,* (New Delhi: Publications Division, 1961), p. 2.

10. *India Quarterly,* Vol. III, No. 3, July–September, 1947, pp. 296–97.

11. *Foreign Policy of India: Text of Documents, 1947–1964,* (New Delhi: Lak Sabha Secretariat, 1966), pp. 525–35.

12. Milos Dromnjak, *The Policy and Movement of Nonalignment 1961–1979,* (Belgrade: Jugoslovenska Stavarnost), pp. 29–31.

13. See Shrikant Paranjpe, *India and South Asia Since 1971,* (New Delhi: Radiant Publishers, 1985), pp. 5–6; Raju G. C. Thomas, *Indian Security Policy,* pp. 10–19; Lloyd I. and Suzanne Rudolph, et al, *The Regional Imperative; The Administration of U.S. Foreign Policy Towards South Asian States,* (Atlantic Highlands, N.J.: Humanities Press, 1980), pp. 1–100; Surjit Mansingh, *India's Search for Power: Indira Gandhi's Foreign Policy, 1966–1982,* (New Delhi: Sage Publications,

1984), pp. 32–67; and Mohammed Ayoob, "India in South Asia: The Quest for Regional Predominance," *World Policy Journal*, vol. 7, no. 1, Winter 1989–90, pp. 107–134.

14. Biseshwar Prasad, *Our Foreign Policy Legacy: A Study of British Indian Foreign Policy*, (New Delhi: Peoples Publishing House, 1965).

15. Asgar Khan, *The First Round: Indo-Pakistan War 1965*, (Sahibabad: Vikas Publishing House, 1979).

16. Anwar Hussein Syed, *China and Pakistan: Diplomacy of an Entente Cordiale*, (Amherst: University of Massachusetts Press, 1974), pp. 97–107.

17. *Foreign Affairs Record*, Vol. XVII, No. 8, August 1971, pp. 159–62.

18. For an excellent detailed study of the origins and causes of the Bangladesh crisis in 1970–71, see Richard Sisson and Leo E. Rose, *War and Secession: India, Pakistan and the Creation of Bangladesh*, (Berkeley and Los Angeles: University of California Press, 1990).

19. Most of these clauses are found in Articles 8, 9 and 10. For a full text of the treaty, see *Current Digest of the Soviet Press*, Vol. 23, No. 32, September 7, 1971, p. 5. For a discussion, see Raju G.C. Thomas, *The defense of India: A Budgetary Perspective of Strategy and Politics*, (Delhi: The Macmillan Company of India, 1978), pp. 56–60.

20. *Foreign Affairs Record*, Vol. 28, No. 7, July 1972, pp. 192–93.

21. A. Appadorai, *Select Documents on India's Foreign Policy and Relations, 1947–1972*, (Delhi: Oxford University Press, 1982), Volume I (Delhi: Oxford University Press, 1982), pp. 387–89.

22. Liaquat Ali Khan, *Pakistan: Heart of Asia*, (Cambridge, Mass.: Harvard University Press, 1950), pp. 11–13.

23. *Asian Recorder*, Vol. 18, No. 12, pp. 18–24, March 1972, Col. 10673.

24. Samuel Baid and Sreedhar, "Pakistan's Defense Potential," *Foreign Affairs Reports*, Vol. 25, No. 4, April 1976, p. 63.

25. Z.A. Bhutto, *Bilateralism: New Directions*, (Islamabad: Ministry of Information and Broadcasting, 1976).

26. See Raju G.C. Thomas, "U.S. Arms for Pakistan: Without Parallel or Precedent," *Times of India*, (February 14, 1990). See also Raju G.C. Thomas "The Afghanistan Crisis and South Asian Security," *Journal of Strategic Studies*, Vol. 4, December 1981. pp. 415–434.

27. India, Ministry of External Affairs, *Report 1979–80*, (New Delhi; Government of India, 1980), p. iii.

28. See the statement by the Minister for External Affairs in Parliament on January 23, 1980. *Asian Recorder*, Vol. 26, No. 8, February 1980, pp. 19–25, Cols. 15324–15325.

29. Lalit Kumar, *India and Sri Lanka: The Shrimavo-Shastri Pact*, (New Delhi: Chetana Publications, 1977), p. 12. See also K.M. Panikkar, *India and the Indian Ocean* (London: George Allen and Unwin, 1945), p. 95.

30. Jawaharlal Nehru, *India's Foreign Policy: Selected Speeches, September 1946–April 1961*, pp. 7 and 436.

31. See *Report 1975–76*, New Delhi: Ministry of External Affairs, Government of India, 1976, p. 13.

32. Leo E. Rose, *Nepal: Strategy for Survival*, (Berkeley: University of California Press, 1971), pp. 185–187.

33. See *Foreign Policy of India: Text of Documents, 1947–1959*, (New Delhi: Lok Sabha Secretariat, 1959), pp. 15–20.

34. Leo E. Rose, *Nepal*, pp. 26 and 206.

35. See *A Souvenir Issued on the Happy Occasion of the Thirty First Birthday Celebration of H.M. Kind Birendra Bir Bikram Shah Day*, (Khatmandu: Nepal Council of World Affairs, 1975), p. 3.

36. Leo Rose, p. 26, pp. 185–87.

37. See S.D. Muni, "Nepal as a Zone of Peace," *Strategic Analysis*, (New Delhi), Vol. 8, No. 10, January 1984, p. 789; and *Lok Sabha Debates*, (March 11, 1983).

38. For a discussion of the problems surrounding Indo-Nepalese relations, see Niranjan Koirala, "Nepal in 1989: A Very Difficult Year," *Asian Survey*, Vol. 30, No. 2, February 1990, pp. 136–143; and special report entitled, "Nepal: Himalayan Crisis," in *India Today*, May 15, 1989, pp.48–55.

39. See Niranjan Koirala, "Nepal," p. 137.

40. See *India Abroad* (New York), June 15, 1990.

41. See India, Ministry of External Affairs, *Bangladesh Documents*, (Madras: Government of India Press, 1973), Vol. 2, pp. 645–48.

42. This was first reported on Radio Karachi on 15 August 1975. Dhaka Radio on 17 August 1975, however, continued to refer the title People's Republic of Bangladesh. See *Summary of World Broadcasts* (SWB), FE/4983, 16 August 1975, c/3; SWB, FE/4985, 17 August 1975, c/2.

43. Ved Mahendra, "Bangladesh Under Ziaur Rahman: An Analytical Survey," *Foreign Affairs Reports*, Vol. 30, No. 9, September 1981, pp. 179–85.

44. See Syedur Rahman, "Bangladesh in 1989: Internationalization of Political and Economic Issues," *Asian Survey*, Vol. 30, No. 2, p. 157.

45. *Asian Recorder*, Vol. 20, No. 34, pp. 20–26 August 1974, Col. 12159.

46. *Foreign Affairs Record*, Vol. 10, No. 10, October 1964, pp. 263–65.

47. Prime Minister Indira Gandhi announced this in the Lok Sabha on August 18, 1983. See India, Ministry of External Affairs, *Statements by Mrs. Indira Gandhi, Prime Minister of India in Parliament on the Sri Lankan Situation*, (New Delhi: Government of India, 1983), pp. 11–13.

48. See *Indo-Sri Lankan Agreement to Establish Peace and Normalcy in Sri Lanka, July 29, 1987*, (New Delhi: Publications Division, 1987).

49. See Barbara Crossette, "India's Loss and Sri Lanka's Despair," *New York Times*, September 17, 1989; also, see Sheila Tefft, "Sri Lankan Civil Strife Escalates," *Christian Science Monitor*, August 11, 1989.

50. See Bruce Mathews, "Sri Lanka in 1989: Peril and Good Luck," *Asian Survey*, Vol. 30, No. 2, February 1990, p. 146. See also assessment by Marshall R. Singer, "New Realities in Sri Lankan Politics." *Asian Survey*, Vol. 30, No. 4, April 1990, 409–425.

51. See discussions in the *Lok Sabha Debates*, Series 7, Vol. 21, No. 3, November 25, 1981, Col. 341.

52. *Bangladesh Working Paper on Regional Co-operation*, (Dhaka: Government of Bangladesh, 1981); and Letter from the Ministry of External Affairs, Government

of Bangladesh, to the Bangladesh High Commission in India. Letter No. SA/SUN/3/FS/BO, November 27, 1981.

53. Raju G.C. Thomas, "Should India Sign the NPT?" in Robert Pendley and Joseph Pilat, eds., *Beyond 1995: The Future of the NPT,* Los Alamos National Laboratory Security Studies Series (New York: The Plenum Press), pp. 133–150.

6

China and Southeast Asia: Overseeing the Regional Balance

Parris H. Chang and Zhiduan Deng

The Southeast Asia subordinate state system encompasses three geopolitical subregions: Indochina, the Mainland States and the Island periphery. Vietnam, Cambodia and Laos comprise the Indochina area. The Mainland Asia subregion includes Malaysia, Brunei, Thailand and Burma. Finally, Macau, Papua-New Guinea, the Philippines, Singapore, Taiwan (officially part of China but ruled by the Guomindang elite), and Indonesia lie in the Island Periphery.

While China's vital national interests extend far beyond Southeast Asia, the region is one Beijing traditionally has viewed as its special sphere of influence. For almost two thousand years, prior to the mid-nineteenth century deterioration of Chinese power, Indochina was a dependency of China; also Chinese authority extended into northern Burma.[1]

In the Chinese cultural tradition China was the "middle kingdom," the center of the civilized world. Reinforcing this perception was the tributary system under which Southeast Asian kingdoms sent emissaries and gifts to Chinese rulers, sometimes in return for Chinese protection and support in wars with rival Southeast Asian leaders.

To China these areas of Southeast Asia offered trade and payment of tribute, as well as opportunities for colonization when Chinese merchants and settlers moved into what is now Malaysia, Indonesia and the Philippines. These regions could be lucrative for venturesome Chinese, who sometimes intermarried with local elites. They could also be barbaric and hazardous when resentful native populations turned on Chinese newcomers to carry out vicious massacres.

Later the unilaterally contrived transformation of Europe's Southeast Asian colonies into independent nations gave rise to territorial disputes between China and these states. China also advanced claims to territorial waters in the South China Sea which are challenged by Vietnam, the Philippines, Malaysia, and Indonesia. These disputes remain a source of intraregional tension.

China in the Context of Southeast Asia

Mainland China boasts an enormous population, and millions of overseas Chinese reside in other parts of Southeast Asia. While contributing to China's influence, Chinese migration also has given rise to apprehensions among regional bargainer states. Bargainer state governments view the overseas Chinese as a force through which Beijing can interfere in their internal affairs. Beijing, on the other hand, perceives a special obligation to protect the ethnic Chinese from the sometimes brutal treatment accorded them in their adopted homelands. Thus ethnic loyalties, in addition to economic interests and geopolitical perceptions, figure in China's desire to exert special interest throughout Southeast Asia. Chinese capabilities in relation to those of the bargainer states, suggest that hegemonic aspirations are not unrealistic. They are profiled in Table 6.1.

Since Mao Zedong unified mainland China in 1949, Beijing has played a crucial role in balancing power within the Southeast Asia subordinate state system. The region's bargainer states have sometimes treated Chinese influence as a threat; on other occasions they have viewed Beijing as a protector of the region from the United States, the Soviet Union and Western Europe. For its part, Beijing has fine tuned its relations with Southeast Asia's bargainer states on the basis of their inclination and ability to augment China's interests and influence in the larger international arena. Also, like aspiring hegemons in other regions, China has attempted to coordinate regional bargainer states to counterbalance external powers, and to prevent the domination of the United States and the Soviet Union over Southeast Asia. These efforts have been only partially successful. As a backup strategy, China has attempted to play off the intervening external powers against each other.

Contemporary relations between Beijing and Southeast Asia's bargainer states appear as a China-Vietnam-ASEAN tripolar power condominium. Each of the aforementioned components perceives the others as an actual or potential threat to its security interests. The dimensions of these threats are economic, political, and military; they also rest on the obvious geopolitical fact of Chinese propinquity and power. In their efforts to balance China's potential to exercise regional influence, Southeast Asian states have sought out external allies. In reaction, China has invited other external actors into the region.

Table 6.1 The Southeast Asian Regional System

State	Population (millions) (1989)	Area (sq. km) (thousands)	GDP (US$/billions) (1988)*	Regional Type
China	1,112.3	9,596.9	350.1	Aspiring Hegemon
Indochina				
Cambodia	6.8	181.0	.57	Peripheral Dependent
Laos	3.9	236.8	.6	Peripheral Dependent
Vietnam	66.8	329.6	12.6*	Bargainer
Mainland Asia				
Brunei	.35	5.8	3.1	Peripheral Dependent
Burma	40.5	678.5	9.3	Bargainer
Malaysia	16.7	329.8	34.3	Bargainer
Thailand	55.5	514.0	52.2	Bargainer

(Continues)

Table 6.1 (Continued)

State	Population (millions) (1989)	Area (sq. km) (thousands)	GDP (US$/billions) (1988)*	Regional Type
Island Periphery				
Hong Kong	5.7	1.0	46.2	Colony
Indonesia	187.7	1,919.0	69.0	Bargainer
Macao	0.4	.01	2.0	Colony
Papua-New Guinea	3.7	461.7	2.9	Peripheral Dependent
Philippines	64.9	300.0	33.6	Bargainer
Singapore	2.7	.6	23.7	Peripheral Dependent
Taiwan	20.2	36.0	91.7	Ruled by Kuomintang

*GNP

SOURCE: U.S. Central Intelligence Agency, The World Factbook-1989 (Washington, DC: CR WF 89001, 1989).

External penetration of Southeast Asian regional politics has remained at a high level since World War II. During the twentieth century's final decade, the Soviet Union and the United States seem destined to continue playing essential roles in shaping bilateral and multilateral interactions among China, Vietnam and ASEAN. While Beijing remains uncomfortable with this state of affairs, it is unable to craft a realignment of the existing regional balance of power. The unknowable consequences of initiating realignment appear more alarming than the distasteful but predictable arrangements involved in sharing power with Moscow and Washington. Nevertheless, in the long run, China seeks freedom to deal in Southeast Asia as the first among states that are far from being equal.

Southeast Asia and Chinese Strategic Considerations

Beijing, as suggested above, has struggled to increase its influence in Southeast Asia since the Communist regime came to power. Chinese cultural pride was an important motivating force in these attempts to regain special regional status. To this historic motivation has been added the Chinese communist elite's ambition to become an international revolutionary force. These ambitions, coupled with China's location, size and economic potential, have forced the United States and the Soviet Union to neutralize Chinese capabilities and policies when either sought to influence events in Southeast Asia.[2] Not surprisingly, China's communist government has perceived the U.S. and the USSR as hostile and intrusive powers. Their military bases threaten China's physical security and their influence with regional bargainer states constrains China's capabilities to act as a hegemon within the subordinate state system its rulers view as their sphere.[3]

Beijing pursued a two dimensional Southeast Asian policy during the 1950s and 1960s. It sprang from Beijing's perception of threat from intrusive American power and fear that Washington might succeed in crafting a comprehensive anti-Beijing alliance among Southeast Asian bargainer states. Under this policy Beijing sought firstly to counter American penetration of the region and secondly to increase its regional influence. Support for communist insurgencies throughout Southeast Asia in the 1950s served both purposes. During the 1960s large scale resource transfers to the North Vietnamese, for their war against the United States, brought success along these two high priority dimensions of Chinese regional strategy.

Chinese perception of threats originating in Southeast Asia changed during the 1970s. Moscow came to be viewed as far more dangerous than a weakened United States. Thus Beijing turned to Washington for support in countering Moscow's increased Southeast Asian influence, as well as its aggressive behavior along the Sino-Soviet border. When dealing with the former, Beijing's most immediate problem involved deteriorating relations between itself and Hanoi.

Following the collapse of South Vietnam's pro-American government, Hanoi had taken control of Laos and occupied Cambodia. The Soviet Union supported Hanoi's efforts to expand its influence in Indochina and beyond. Viewing Soviet-Vietnamese cooperation in this venture as a serious threat to its regional ambitions, China changed tack. Instead of trying to expel the United States from Southeast Asia, China welcomed an American presence in the region and cooperated with the U.S. and ASEAN to check Vietnamese expansion. Washington responded affirmatively, and the new arrangement strengthened China's presence in Southeast Asia. Chinese influence, while far from being hegemonic, has become critical in the regional interest calculations of Southeast Asian bargainer states.

Perceptions of Threat from the Soviet Union

The Sino-Soviet rift that opened in the early 1960s fundamentally changed the Chinese political leadership's perceptions of relations between these one-time fraternal communist giants.[4] Mao Zedong and his colleagues reinterpreted the history of relations between the two from a perspective that was more negative. The pressure Moscow was exerting on Beijing reminded China of deceitful Soviet strategies practiced during earlier decades: appeasing Japan at the expense of China during the 1930s in return for Tokyo's acceptance of Moscow's Far Eastern interests; bargaining at the end of World War II with the United States (again at China's expense) about the division of post-war areas of influence; attempting to prevent a unified China by discouraging Chinese communists from taking over the whole country during the late 1940s civil war; pressuring China into Korean War in the early 1950s in order to make Beijing more dependent upon Moscow; and supporting India in the Sino-Indian dispute at the end of the 1950s. The perception that crystallized among China's leaders of these historical events reinforced their view that Moscow consistently had sought to penetrate, exploit, control, and contain China. Undoubtedly under the influence of Mao, who never trusted the Soviets, China came to view Moscow as its most immediate and dangerous enemy.

The Sino-Soviet border conflict in 1969 increased Beijing's apprehension that the Soviet Union was planning a massive invasion of China. Even though the ongoing Cultural Revolution seriously paralyzed effective Chinese power, the Communist leadership managed to deploy a significant force of trained and well armed troops into Northern China, and to evacuate inhabitants along the Sino-Soviet border. On several occasions the Soviets seem poised for a military strike. This immediate threat forced Beijing to pay serious attention to security conditions along China's southern flank. Beijing's strategy was to avoid a situation in which there was immediate danger on two fronts: in the north from the Soviet Union; and in the South from the United States military in Vietnam, and from what Beijing then perceived as a U.S. backed anti-communist and anti-China alliance among the ASEAN powers.

Perceptions of the U.S. Threats to China's Southeast Asian Interests

The Chinese communist elite, as suggested earlier, divided Southeast Asia into two critical two geopolitical arenas. One was Indochina and the other was ASEAN. Beijing's efforts on behalf of North Vietnam in the 1960s, at that time China's only ally against the United States in Southeast Asia, were unceasing. China worked just as hard to break down what it saw as the United States policy of using the ASEAN states to contain China. Beijing initially viewed ASEAN as a reincarnation of the Southeast Asia Treaty Organization (SEATO),[5] the anticommunist coalition set up by the United States in 1954. The Vietnam War further strengthened Beijing's perception that the United States sought to contain the communist world, especially China. Even worse, Beijing felt a growing sense of encirclement and isolation because of its deteriorating relationship with the Soviet Union. Perceiving threats from both global powers, and spurred on by the dominant radical ideology of its Cultural Revolution, Beijing recast its policy towards Southeast Asia; replacing an essentially defensive posture with one that was more activist.

During the late 1960s, Beijing official statements severely derided and attacked U.S. policy in Southeast Asia as imperialist aggression and neo-colonialism.[6] Meanwhile, Beijing labeled the ASEAN states (except perhaps Singapore) as "running dogs of U.S. imperialism," a clique of "imperialist puppets," and even a "fascist military regime."[7] Moreover, Beijing praised and supported communist, anti-government movements in Thailand, Indonesia, Malayia, and Burma (even though Burma was not an ASEAN member state).[8] In their advocacy of these insurgences, Beijing cited Mao's words that violent change was inevitable. The ASEAN states' reactionary regimes could not stand against the march of history. "Revolution and revolutionary wars are inevitable in class society, and without them it is impossible to accomplish and leap in social development and to overthrow the reactionary ruling classes and therefore impossible for the people to win political power."[9] In addition to this verbal advocacy, Beijing helped to plan insurgency strategies and supplied them with arms.

To summarize, Chinese policy during most of the 1960s in Southeast Asia was based on perceptions that cast the United States as the greatest impediment to attaining special regional influence. China also saw United States policy as retarding its drive for general upward international mobility. Toward the end of the decade, however, new developments altered these calculations, especially after fighting erupted along the Sino-Soviet border. Overnight the Soviet Union became the most dangerous threat to China's security. Concurrently, Beijing seemed to recognize that for more than a decade United States containment of China had supported the status quo in Southeast Asia, rather than promoting aggressive attacks against Chinese territory. Thus, after the early 1970s, Beijing appeared less preoccupied over Washington's presence in Southeast Asia; concluding that Richard Nixon and future American presidents would mute their opposition to Chinese regional and international influence.[10] This change propelled Beijing toward Sino-American reconciliation at the cost of its relations with Hanoi.

China's Perception of the Vietnamese Threat

Historically Beijing has opposed Vietnam's designs for the Indochinese peninsula. Also, Indochina has been the subarena of highest priority in China's Southeast Asian regional strategy of fragmenting border states to prevent the rise of a strong contiguous power. China's communist elite never doubted that a united Vietnam would seek to unify and control all of Indochina. However, Cold War politics overrode these concerns during the first two decades of China's communist regime. When relations between the superpowers warmed during the late 1950s, Beijing concluded that Soviet-American detente was being achieved at China's expense. The Chinese saw Moscow and Washington sharing attitudes toward China's international aspirations (opposition and hostility), although they acknowledged that the superpowers remained adversaries in other fields. Thus China's strategy toward the United States and the Soviet Union was obvious: sabotage detente.[11] The Vietnam war presented an ideal opportunity to pursue this strategy.

The third and most important component in Beijing's policy towards Vietnam was competition with Moscow for influence over Hanoi. Beijing had spent billions of dollars on behalf of Hanoi in the name of struggling against colonialism and imperialism.[12] From this perspective, Soviet and Chinese policies complemented each other. On the other hand, the Soviet elite also saw China's backing of North Vietnam as yet another manifestation of intensifying Sino-Soviet competition for influence within the communist bloc. Soviet threat perceptions were accentuated by geopolitical concerns over vulnerabilities along the eastern border with

China. A major part of Moscow's response to these threat perceptions involved forcing China back into a position of dependency on the Soviet Union.[13] Moscow anticipated success here would reverse negative trends appearing in the international competition with the United States. United States appeal and prerogatives would be limited if it became entangled in an Indochinese "containment" of China.[14] China, of course, perceived that only through involvement in Indochina could development of the security situation in Southeast Asia be influenced in its favor. Thus Beijing opted to play a major role in the Vietnam War, even at the cost of increased dependency of the Soviet Union.

Beijing appeared not to be well prepared for the United States policy change which brought an end to military operations in Vietnam. Also, because Hanoi won the war earlier than expected, Beijing's aid to North Vietnam had an unanticipated impact. It had been given, as discussed above, in hope of increasing China's influence throughout Indochina. In practice it provided resources for Hanoi's Indochina federation scheme.

Hanoi's victory in the Vietnam War created a new Southeast Asian balance of power. After the war, Vietnam (with its Soviet arms) boasted the fourth largest army in the world. Victory, unification of the country and military advantage changed Hanoi's regional outlook. Southeast Asia came to be viewed in terms of strategic threats and geopolitical opportunities, of the regional balance of military forces and of other orthodox security matters that had been downplayed during the struggle against France and the United States.[15] Of all the policy objectives after the war, the most important and immediate for Hanoi was to begin organizing the long-sought Indochina federation that Ho Chi Min had envisioned in the early 1930s. The Vietnamese easily incorporated Laos into their sphere of influence, a shift formalized by the signing of a twenty-five year "Treaty of Friendship and Cooperation." This agreement legitimated the de facto Vietnamese military and administrative presence in Laos. On the other hand, Vietnamese designs evoked intense resistance on the part of Pol Pot's China-backed Khmer Rouge government in Cambodia. Hanoi, ever loyal to Ho Chi Min's vision, responded with a military invasion of Cambodia in January 1979. This ushered in a new era of Southeast Asian instability.

China perceived the success of Vietnamese military operations in Indochina, and the growing Soviet presence throughout Southeast Asia, as a newly invigorated threat against its aspirations for special regional influence. Especially worrisome was crystallization of a hostile Soviet-Vietnamese concert that appeared to be actively constraining China's regional prerogatives.[16] Soviet geopolitical designs, when integrated into Vietnam's vision of a unified Indochina, loomed as a greater threat to

China's Southeast Asian interests than any challenge that could be mounted by the United States.

Threat Perceptions of the Regional Bargainers

Most bargainer states of the Southeast Asia subordinate state system see themselves as vulnerable to the designs of both superpowers, Japan and the aspiring regional hegemon. Over the past three decades political and military developments in the Southeast Asia have rearranged the local power balance, and hence altered bargainer state perceptions of the regional threats to which they are subject. Changes caused the bargainer states to modify their regional postures; including a reevaluation of national interests, recalculation of policy costs and benefits and reconsideration of political allies and opponents. In spite of this fluidity, the bargainer states continue to view Chinese aspirations for regional hegemony as the most important long-term constraint on their ability to act in the subordinate state system.

Hanoi's Perception of the Chinese Threat

With the benefit of hindsight, the most recent rift between China and Vietnam appears almost to have been preordained. China's relationship with Vietnam for two thousand years revolved about designs to dominate. Not surprisingly, Vietnamese policy makers have viewed Beijing as the most important continuing threat to Vietnam's security; also, the Chinese are perceived as having played fast and lose in pursuing their Indochinese interests. After so many centuries of distrust, the fact that both came to be ruled by communist elites (China in 1949 and North Vietnam in 1954) merely facilitated a surface cordiality. Even this proved transitory. Hanoi's communist regime always regarded control over all of Indochina as the centerpiece in its historic task of creating a strong and independent Vietnam; Beijing, in contrast, was apprehensive over how a unified Indochina would act in the regional international system. Apprehension intensified after North Vietnam showed signs of accepting Soviet influence.[17]

Escalating tensions in the Indochinese peninsula, especially after they exploded into the Vietnam War, provided a powerful but temporary bonding that united China and North Vietnam. The latter depended on the former for aid; and equally important, as a counterweight when bargaining for technologically sophisticated assistance available only from Moscow and the Communist Bloc countries of Eastern Europe. Beijing, because it bordered on Vietnam, perceived the civil war between Hanoi and Saigon as a golden opportunity to penetrate and dominate all of

Indochina.[18] Hanoi, ever mindful of its allies' hidden agendas, feared that its Indochina ambitions would fall victim to maneuvering between the superpowers and the aspiring regional hegemon. The Indochinese involvements of the United States were the immediate problem between 1961 and 1976. However, North Vietnam saw the Soviet Union and China as greater long-term threats to its interests. New intrusions by one of these competitors seemed to elicit counterescalations by the other. While United States troops were fighting in Vietnam, their defeat was Hanoi's first priority. During those years, North Vietnam had no option but to court Moscow and Beijing competitively. Support was solicited from both, even while they jockeyed for influence over Indochina.

When Hanoi increased pressure on South Vietnam in the early 1960s, it directly challenged the anti-communist Diem regime. Mounting an effective challenge required that Hanoi obtain additional resources from its allies. Initially, during the early 1960s, Ho Chi Min demanded increased aid from China and the Soviet Union. At that time, the Soviet Union gave only half the amount of assistance that China was transferring to Vietnam.[19] Correspondingly, Hanoi leaned towards Beijing; and in 1962 North Vietnam sided with China in the controversial disputes between Beijing and Moscow over the Test Ban Treaty. Moreover, Hanoi shared Beijing's resentment against the Moscow-Washington detente. Both perceived it as a freeing of resources with which the United States had propped up its Saigon ally; in turn, the South Vietnamese government was able to intensify guerrilla warfare against Hanoi's supporters in the South. When, in 1963, Sino-Soviet relations further worsened, Hanoi suddenly muted its support for Beijing. Thus China's president Liu Shaoqi was received correctly during his visit to Hanoi, but without warmth. The shift appeared as accommodation to pressure from the Soviet leader Nikita Khrushchev. Khrushchev implied that the Soviet Union would disengage from Indochina (threatening to resign co-chairmanship of the International Control Commission) if Vietnam continued its tilt toward Beijing.[20]

Hanoi's victory in the Vietnam War set the stage for an end to Sino-Soviet cooperation in Indochina. China ceased to be a partner for Vietnam because China opposed Vietnam's designs in Laos and Cambodia. Second, China's reconciliation with the United States while the Vietnam War was in progress outraged North Vietnam's communist elites. In victory they saw themselves as freed from the need of ignoring China's "betrayal," an oversight they had accepted earlier as the price of military assistance. Thirdly, Hanoi victorious felt itself in a position to press Beijing on a number of disputes that had lain just below the surface for several decades. They included ideological differences, conflicting border claims, competition for influence in Laos and Cambodia, antagonism toward the overseas Chinese, maritime disputes and personal affronts.[21]

Perhaps the most important element coloring Hanoi's perception of China's role in the post-war balance of power in Southeast Asia has been Beijing's relations with Washington. As suggested earlier, North Vietnam viewed the Nixon visit to China as a harbinger of Sino-American cooperation directed at constraining Hanoi's ability to pursue its regional agenda. Douglas Pike portrayed North Vietnam as having four security objectives in Southeast Asia: (1) managing the Indochina peninsula as a pliant, nonthreatening sphere of influence; (2) preventing crystallization of any front hostile to Vietnam (such as ASEAN) in Southeast Asia; (3) eliminating the U.S. military presence from the region and diminishing general U.S. influence; and (4) limiting the activities of more powerful states in the regional international system. Here Hanoi had in mind the Soviet Union, as well as China and the United States: however, the North Vietnamese did not mention the Soviets by name.[22]

China, on the other hand, was labeled openly as the principal threat to Hanoi's national Security. Beijing's maneuvering against Hanoi's Indochinese alliance had made the achievement of effective federation difficult, if not impossible. Thus Vietnam's dominance of Indochina remained incomplete and fragile. In addition, China continues to work the ASEAN states to isolate Vietnam. Even more dramatic, China now encourages the United States to maintain a military presence in Southeast Asia as a counterweight to Soviet influence, which is viewed in Beijing as amplifying the power of Hanoi's militant ruling elite. Thus Vietnam finds itself in multifaceted competition throughout Southeast Asia with a China that has grown increasingly hostile. Vietnam's relationship with of China has shifted one-hundred-and-eighty degrees; from wartime ally to first on the list of post-war enemies.

ASEAN Perceptions of the Chinese Threat

ASEAN, established in 1967 with United States support, began as a political reaction by the non-communist states of Southeast Asia to perceived common threats from Chinese communism. In the decades following the communist seizure of power in China, ASEAN states had come to regard their large northern neighbor as a growing menace. They saw Beijing's most dangerous threat as derived from the ideology that motivated its foreign policy during Mao's reign. With few exceptions, Beijing's foreign policy goals between 1950 and 1980 were dictated by the ideology of Marxist-Leninist proletarian internationalism. Proletarian internationalism popularized and legitimized such notions as anti-imperialism, anti-colonialism, anti-revisionism, and anti-reactionaries.

Proletarian internationalism dictated one central objective of China's foreign policy, support for struggles of "oppressed" peoples against the "oppressors" in the non-communist countries. Throughout Southeast Asia, between 1950 and the late 1970s, this was expressed by assisting bargainer state communist parties and communist insurgencies.[23] These efforts were most pronounced in Indonesia, Malaysia, Singapore, Burma, and Thailand. Beijing's behavior frightened the governments of all Asean countries, causing them to recoil from establishing working relations with China.[24] Beginning in the late 1970s, China sought to calm these fears with promises not to export revolution; however, most ASEAN governments remained unconvinced. Indonesia and Malaysia went so far as to state publicly that as far as their security interests were concerned, China posed a greater threat than Vietnam.[25]

A second element in ASEAN perceptions of China as a threat is the presence of numerous overseas Chinese throughout Southeast Asia. Three of the five ASEAN states (Singapore, Indonesia, and Malaysia), have continually stated that the overseas Chinese issue must be settled before they will consider establishing diplomatic relations with China. In the view of these governments, strong ties between China and the overseas Chinese undermine their national integration and contribute to ethnic unrest. China's willingness to intervene on behalf of the overseas Chinese makes their very presence a volatile political issue. It also causes ASEAN governments to be doubly apprehensive that an increasing powerful China will seek a permanent role in their domestic affairs.[26]

The third source of ASEAN fears concerning China derives from structural geopolitics. A strong and united China historically has sought influence beyond its borders. Thus neighboring states respond with caution when China offers them an embrace.[27] In the present situation, ASEAN governments fear that Beijing is cloaking its regional aspirations under the mantle of preserving stability in Southeast Asia. They also believe that Chinese managed stabilization will strengthen Beijing's ability to influence them. In other words, ASEAN governments anticipate that cooperation will pave the way for domination. China's portrayal of itself as a regionally satisfied is not believed and increases ASEAN insecurity. On the other hand, China cannot be ignored. It remains the subordinate state system's most powerful and influential country.

ASEAN Threat Perceptions as Tempered by Conflict Between China and Vietnam

While ASEAN states remain aware of the long term threat posed by China, they generally perceive post-war Vietnamese expansion throughout Indochina as a more immediate threat to their security. This has given

China a major opportunity to improve government to government relations with its ASEAN neighbors. Beijing, as suggested above, stresses its commitment to contain Vietnamese expansion and downplays support for revolutionary movements in Southeast Asia.

Viewed from a different perspective, the China-Vietnam conflict has provided a protective umbrella for Southeast Asia's ASEAN bargainer states. With China's energies focused on Vietnam and Vietnam's energies directed against China, neither power is in a position to threaten significantly any ASEAN state. ASEAN governments have breathing space to concentrate on domestic economic and political problems without having to worry about ideological or military infiltration from the North. Thus, while ASEAN leaders proclaim in public that the Cambodia issue must be settled quickly, their advisors privately concede that the ongoing struggle in Indochina between China and Vietnam is a boon for ASEAN states.

China, notwithstanding its sophisticated diplomacy, has enjoyed only mixed success in convincing ASEAN that its earlier support of local revolutionary movements is a thing of the past. Long experience with China-backed communist insurgency makes ASEAN governments aware that Beijing's present conciliatory policy could change overnight. Malaysia especially sees itself as vulnerable, knowing that at any time its discontented Chinese minority could turn to China for support. Malay elites have not forgotten that China took up the cause of the oppressed Chinese minority in Vietnam as one justification for its 1979 invasion of that country.

Indonesia has even stronger reservations about China's long range plans in Southeast Asia. Indonesian government suspicions derive in large measure from China's backing of an unsuccessful coup attempt by Indonesian communists in 1965. President Suharto and other ranking Indonesian leaders, after narrowly escaping assassination by the communists, brutally repressed that rebellion. They remain in power and have had no intention of giving their China-oriented communists a second chance. Correspondingly, Indonesia has tilted more toward Vietnam than have other ASEAN states during the ongoing struggle in Indochina.

Thailand's leaders also have allied themselves with Communist China's efforts to undermine Vietnam's hold on Cambodia. However, their support is luke warm. They know well that a decisive Chinese victory over Vietnam would leave China a much more difficult neighbor to deal with than Vietnam.

China's honeymoon with the ASEAN states owes much to ASEAN perceptions that growing Soviet military power, especially its naval bases in Vietnam, must be counterbalanced. Since the United States appears no longer willing to intervene in Southeast Asia, the most obvious candidate for regional counterweight is China. Yet many of the political and economic problems that have fueled China-backed insurgencies in the past continue to plague Southeast Asian bargainer states. These include disaffected minorities, large gaps in wealth distribution, exclusion of the masses from participation and rural poverty. Insurgents, while usually able to obtain military and economic assistance from the Soviet Union, often they see China's Maoist revolution as more relevant to their situation than Lenin's toppling of the Kerensky government in 1917. Therefore, for many ASEAN governments China's communist revolution is in and of itself subversive and threatening. This suggests that China's honeymoon with the ASEAN governments is extremely precarious.

Ties between the Philippines and China, while cordial, never were as close as those between China and the other ASEAN states. Tensions associated with land redistribution, warlordism, bureaucratic corruption and Muslim rebellion have set in motion cycles of insurgency, repression, and reform since Manila gained its independence. They also have facilitated continuing rural insurrection. Against this background, Filipino leaders are apprehensive that in the future China could support such rebellions. The same is true of the Soviet Union. However, at present Moscow seems more likely to push for a diplomatic realignment that would take the Philippines out of the American military orbit and into more neutral stance.

For the present Manila has tied its financial future to the United States. The Philippine economy depends on lucrative payments from military base agreements, and on trade and economic aid from the United States. Filipino nationalists, however, have grown increasingly vocal and influential. They appear eager to distance their country from its former colonial master. These nationalists have urged the Aquino government to close down U.S. bases in the Philippines and improve relations with Moscow and Hanoi. However, economic deterioration in the Soviet Union and Vietnam raises questions about the ability of either to increase its economic presence in the Philippines. Finally, the dampening down of the Cold War has reduced the ability of all third world states to play capitalist and communist countries off against each other, at least as it was done between 1950 and 1985.

In the new international environment of the 1990s, the arguments of Philippine nationalists are not without merit. Gorbachev has downplayed Soviet military expansion and moved away from revolutionary Marxism. ASEAN leaders now perceive that they have less to fear from Soviet expansionism. The same may be true from Vietnam. Vietnam's troop withdrawal from Cambodia has softened its regional image and made Soviet penetration into the region appear less threatening. In this more relaxed setting, ASEAN leaders seem less likely to welcome a vigorous and outwardly looking China as a necessary evil for counterbalancing the Soviet Union. They will demand continued Chinese reassurance that Beijing's support of local insurrections has become a thing of the past.

The Post-Vietnam Era: China's Southeast Asian Interests and the Superpowers

The will and physical capability of the United States and the Soviet Union to project power around the globe remain crucial elements in the Southeast Asian regional balance of power. As both superpowers harbor interests in Southeast Asia and retain capabilities to penetrate into the region, China, Vietnam, and ASEAN have had no choice when crafting Southeast Asian policy but to develop special relationships with Washington and Moscow. Thus Hanoi facilitated Soviet (along with Chinese) intrusion into Indochina, calculating that these two communist giants were needed to offset U.S. military pressure during the Vietnam War. After the war, Hanoi confronted the reality of a Beijing-Washington alignment committed to its containment. Vietnam responded by opting for increased dependence on Moscow as the most palatable means of accessing the resources needed to carry out its designs for an Indochinese federation. The ASEAN states, fearing loss of sovereignty as intensifying rivalry between Vietnam and China restricted their options, pressured the United States not to abandon the region. This suggests that while Southeast Asian states prefer to manage regional problems with local resources, they do not hesitate to solicit outside assistance if they believe that such assistance provides critical additional resources.

The perspective of China's foreign policy differs from that of Vietnam and ASEAN. As a major power in North Asia, with significant ties to the Middle East and Africa, China considers its relations with the Soviet Union and the United States not only in Southeast Asian terms but from a global perspective. For more than two decades China has clung to the position that the Soviet Union is its principal superpower adversary. Beijing policy makers view Moscow as pursuing a global strategy to contain China; encompassing not only activities in South and Southeast Asia and the Middle East, but also a mobilization of allied states in Eastern Europe and Africa. Direct Soviet pressure against China also is seen as threatening China's security. For example, since the early 1970s Moscow has stationed ten additional divisions of troops along the Sino-Soviet border, an increase of about 60 percent over that of the mid-1960s.[28] It was rising insecurity associated with threats from the Soviet Union that decided China to seek accommodation with the United

States in the early 1970s; Beijing had grown desperate to create a strong counterweight to Moscow.

The policy of reconciliation with the United States caused Beijing to modify its strategic thinking, replacing the earlier paradigm of Sino-Soviet bilateral relations with one of trilateral Sino-Soviet-American maneuvering. Reconciliation with Washington also relieved Beijing of anxieties stemming from United States hostility. Moreover, the improvement in Beijing-Washington relations led to Soviet uncertainty about possible U.S. responses if Moscow attacked China. This gave China new flexibility to pursue policies shoring up its eastern and southern flanks.

Of course, China's reconciliation with the United States came at the cost of worsening relations with Vietnam. It was a price that Beijing was prepared to pay. For in China's perception of its total security environment, the real threat to Chinese security from the Soviet Union lay in the North. Vietnam's strategic importance was secondary. The Southeast Asian balance of power, however, was not. Beijing calculated that as long as there was a significant U.S. presence in Southeast Asia, Moscow would be unable to mount a serious threat on China's southern flank.[29]

Frustration accompanying Washington's ability to constrain aspirations for Southeast Asian regional hegemony is acceptable to Beijing in the short run. This less than optimal regional state of affairs does not threaten China's vital security in spite of what Chinese leaders say publicly. On the contrary, the Vietnamese invasion of Cambodia had two positive consequences for China. First, China used international disgust with the invasion to attack Soviet penetration and influence in Southeast Asia. That Vietnam has become more isolated is considered by Beijing as a setback for Moscow's policy of containing China. Second, Vietnam's projection of military power into Cambodia enabled Beijing to play on ASEAN insecurities associated with Vietnamese unification and military power. Vietnamese aggressiveness has made the ASEAN states more anxious to improve relations with China than at any time since 1949, when the Communists drove the Nationalists from the mainland. Beginning in 1978, Beijing's ASEAN diplomacy emphasized China's desire to replace four decades of hostility with a new friendship. In November 1978, the then Chinese Vice Premier Deng Xiaoping visited Thailand, Malaysia, and Singapore. He portrayed China as a benign regional influence, praising the ASEAN states' independent foreign policies and "farsighted" position of "strengthening their own unity and cooperation." By such unity and cooperation, Deng said, ASEAN not only served "the interest of peace, stability, and prosperity in Southeast Asia," but also made "a valuable contribution to world peace and security."[30]

Hanoi had less room to maneuver between the two superpowers than did Beijing. Fifteen years of fighting in Indochina between Hanoi and Washington had left a deep-rooted hostility which would not easily be overcome. After the fall of South Vietnam, the United States instituted a trade and aid embargo against North Vietnam. Its lifting remains conditioned on Hanoi's fulfillment of several conditions, not the least of which is locating the remains of missing U.S. soldiers in Vietnam. On the Cambodia issue, Washington's demand for Vietnamese withdrawal is no less intransigent than that of Beijing.

It is difficult to underestimate the obstacles to normalizing relations between the U.S. and Vietnam. The conflict of interest between China and Vietnam forces Hanoi into a close alliance with Moscow, China's greatest enemy and the only state capable of challenging the military power of the United States. The greatest costs of alliance with the Soviet Union are associated with that state's potential to compromise Vietnamese sovereignty. Benefits come as transfers of resources which enable Vietnam to take its place as a Southeast Asia regional power. Because Vietnam's most vital geopolitical and nationalistic interests lie in Southeast Asia, especially Indochina, and because its dream of an Indochina federation ensures a negative reaction from China, Hanoi has determined that the benefits of allying with Moscow far outweigh their costs.

Soviet backing has assisted Hanoi in reaching many of its strategic objectives. Since 1977, the Soviet Union had supported Vietnamese reaffirmation of its sovereignty claim over the Xisha (Spratly) and Nansha (Paracell) Islands. On November 3, 1978, the Soviet Union and Vietnam signed a Twenty-five Year Treaty of Friendship and Co-operation by which Moscow agreed to provide military, political, and economic aids to Hanoi.[31] With Moscow's backing, the Vietnamese began a Christmas day offensive against the China-backed Pol Pot regime and created a Cambodian National United Front for National Salvation headed by Heng Simring. Between 1965 and 1975 the value of Soviet arms transfers to Vietnam totaled roughly U.S. $1.9 billion. In 1978, Moscow underwrote a 50 percent expansion of the Vietnamese army, at a cost of U.S. $50 million in military aid. The following year, when Vietnam invaded Cambodia and became involved in a border conflict with China, total arms transfers by the Soviet Union to Vietnam approached U.S. $1.1 billion, a twentyfold increase over the amount transferred in 1978.[32]

Pursuit of the dream of federation for Indochinese has come at great expense to Vietnam. Immediately after Vietnamese troops entered Cambodia, the ASEAN states expressed disapproval and hostility. Among the communist nations, Hanoi's enterprise was criticized by Romania, Yugoslavia, and North Korea. Among the industrial countries, costs were immediate and physical. Japan suspended all of its aid for post-war reconstruction; Denmark cancelled a program worth U.S. $20 million; Sweden reduced its aid by 10 percent; and Britain cut off bilateral assistance except for "disaster and humanitarian help."[33] As international opinion shifted increasingly against Vietnam, Hanoi experienced its most difficult period of isolation since the end of French colonialism in 1954.

The dream of Indochinese federation continues to have high domestic costs for the Vietnamese people. In addition to uncounted casualties, plans to restore and improve the quality of life have been cut dramatically. Forty seven percent of Hanoi's public expenditures go for military and military-related items, despite its unreconstructed, war-torn economic infrastructure.[34] Soviet aid to Vietnam has consisted largely of arms; hence it contributes little to economic recovery. There is increasing debate over whether Soviet support for the Indochinese federation and an increased role in Southeast Asia for Vietnam will facilitate either of these objectives in the long run. At the very least, the immediate consequences of the isolation that Vietnam experienced between 1980 and 1990 was to weaken Hanoi's position as a regional bargainer and retard its post war reconstruction.

Breaking out of the isolation that has had such negative and unanticipated consequences will not be easy for Hanoi. In the first place, close ties with the Soviet Union undercut Vietnam's efforts to improve relations with its non-communist neighbors; they remain highly suspicious of Soviet penetration into Southeast Asia. Second, as of late 1990 joint efforts by the United States and China, in opposition to Vietnam's project of creating an Indochinese federation, had been successful. Neither Beijing nor Washington appeared inclined to reverse their position. No matter how Vietnam justified its Cambodian designs from the perspective of regional politics, China and the United States continued to view efforts to implement them in terms of global competition with the Soviet Union. Beijing and Washington saw opposition to Vietnam in Indochina as part of their "overall strategy to deter Soviet advances in this part of the world. Any retreat in their demands in the Southeast Asian theater of war would be viewed as conceding to Soviet expansionism via Vietnam."[35]

The ASEAN states, like China, maintain close ties with the United States in their foreign policies. Unlike Beijing, which links itself with Washington only for checking the Soviet threat, the ASEAN states seek U.S. support as a counterweight to both Soviet and Chinese regional designs. Also, unchecked Vietnamese expansion in Indochina raises the level of insecurity within the ASEAN states. It creates concerns about Vietnamese capabilities and intentions, and contributes to doubts over Moscow's long range designs. From this perspective, China looms as a positive force in its potential to contain the Soviet Union and Vietnam.

Nevertheless, the ASEAN states have questioned the extent to which increased Chinese influence in Southeast Asia would rebound to their benefit in the long run. The overriding ASEAN interest remains to ensure a power balance among Southeast Asian states that permits ASEAN the greatest latitude of action. Thus Chinese hegemony is to be resisted. As discussed earlier, this is expressed as pressure by the ASEAN states on Washington retain a Southeast Asian presence.

The United States has been a major supporter of ASEAN since the organization's inception, but Washington's relations with individual ASEAN states varies greatly. The Philippines and Thailand have defense pacts with the United States, while Indonesia, Malaysia, and Singapore adhere to a nonaligned foreign policy. In the last two decades Washington's ASEAN strategy has changed. At the beginning of the 1970s, the United States shifted the emphasis of its more general Asian policy (except in Vietnam); from military commitment when confronted with communist penetration to economic and social development of the threatened countries.[36] Washington had concluded that economic growth and restructuring, rather than military confrontation, was the most effective way of blocking communist expansion in the developing world. On the basis of this perception, the United States encouraged and aided assorted developmental programs in such strategically important areas of Asia as Pakistan, South Korea, Taiwan and the ASEAN states. Simultaneously, Washington began to draw down its military commitments in East and Southeast Asia. In response to the ZOPFAN policy (which called for foreign power withdrawal from the region) adopted by ASEAN in 1971, and reaffirmed in 1976, Washington extracted its military forces from the mainland of Southeast Asia. Acquiescence to Thailand's request to close the U.S. air bases in that country completed America's withdrawal. During the Carter Administration's shrinkage of United States military assets, many ASEANs even anticipated that Washington would withdraw from its major military bases in the Philippines.[37]

Most ASEAN states initially viewed Vietnam's invasion of Cambodia as a regional problem, an issue that could and should be solved by diplomacy among Southeast Asian countries. Doubts arose when fighting in Cambodia spilled over into Thailand, resulting in pitched battles up and down the Thai-Cambodian border. They became more serious in 1979, when China attacked Vietnam and pushed Hanoi toward further dependence on Moscow. This new level of dependence was institutionalized when Vietnam granted the Soviet Union air and naval access to Cam Ranh Bay and Da Nang. A long-term Soviet military presence in Vietnam was seen by the ASEAN states as a serious setback for their policy of self-reliance, self-development, and self-confidence in the conduct of regional politics. Given the turn of events, their best option became seeking extraregional support from the United States.

Although the ASEAN states share with the United States a strong interest in maintaining stability throughout Southeast Asia, the two differ in their views of regional security dynamics. First, for many ASEAN states, especially Indonesia and Malaysia, China's threat potential appears as great as that of the Soviet Union. In the past, among the ASEAN states, only Thailand has not seemed unduly concerned about U.S. arm sales to China. But to Washington, priority is given to Beijing's status as the only regional actor capable of effectively checking Moscow.[38] Even though ASEAN governments have increased substantially their defense spending since 1981,[39] the military strength of ASEAN as a whole remains vastly inferior when compared to that of a Soviet-armed Vietnam. In the eyes of the Pentagon, therefore, there is no alternative to arming Beijing if the military imbalance in Southeast Asia is to be corrected.

The second difference in perspective between ASEAN and the United States centers on how best to defuse and manage the Indochinese imbroglio. From the perspective of ASEAN, Washington should modify its "hard line" towards Hanoi; this policy is seen as having yielded little in reducing Vietnamese dependence on Moscow. The analyst Jusuf Wanandi, portrays ASEAN's hopes for Washington as including: (1) pursuit of a more flexible policy towards Hanoi; (2) encouragement of compromise between ASEAN and Vietnam; (3) influence on China to modify its hostile attitude towards Vietnam; (4) planning between U.S. allies and ASEAN to prepare an aid program for Vietnam, conditioned on compromises by Hanoi that facilitate a regionally acceptable political order in Indochina; and (5) normalization of diplomatic relations with Vietnam.[40] But, as stated above, the United States long has seen Vietnam's Indochinese aspirations as part of Soviet global expansionism. Whether the winding down of the Cold War in Europe, and Soviet cooperation with the West in response to Iraq's invasion of Kuwait, have changed Washington's perceptions remains to be seen.

Chinese Strategic Responses

Pursuit of Southeast Asian interests has been a major foreign policy concern of China's communist elite since it came to power in 1949. Only resisting Soviet pressure along the Sino-Soviet border received higher priority. In Southeast Asia China's central concern, as we have seen, has revolved about containing Vietnam and neutralizing potential threats from external powers. Beijing achieved major successes in pursuit of these objectives. Still, Southeast Asian regional have highlighted significant limitations on China's influence and power.

Chinese management of Southeast Asian threats emphasizes four strategic responses: counterthreat, defense by allying, state strengthening (especially of the military), and accommodation. Each of these responses will be examined in detail.

Counterthreats

In responding to concerns posed by the emergence of an Indochina Federation dominated by Vietnam, China began by raising the costs to Vietnam of controlling Laos and Cambodia. Beijing hoped to make consolidation of Vietnam's influence in Indochina so painful that the effort would have to be abandoned. Four months after Vietnam attacked Cambodia, in December of 1977, China terminated its technical cooperation with the Vietnamese military. Economic aid was cut off in July of the following year. Also, from the beginning, China encouraged and assisted Cambodian resistance groups in opposing Vietnam's invasion. The Khamer Rouge received a broad range of military assistance; weapons and ammunition, advisers, and equipment for communications, engineering and surveillance. Beijing also denounced the Vietnamese for provocations along the border and threatened military action in defense of its territorial sovereignty and to ensure the safety of Chinese in the frontier region. Vietnam, however, was not to be deterred. Thus, on February 17, 1979, China's armed forces struck into Vietnam.[41]

Beijing's effort to "teach Hanoi a lesson" on the battlefield failed; China's military capability proved insufficient to the task. Thus the objectives undergirding military deployment were not fulfilled. These included: diverting Vietnamese armed forces to relieve pressure on Cambodia; tarnishing the fighting reputation of Hanoi's military; and damaging Vietnam's economy, and slowing its recovery from the war. The key to China's failure was Soviet military and economic support for Vietnam. It made the high costs of simultaneously attempting to unify Indochina and resisting the Chinese attack bearable. Indeed, in the midst of its tribulations Vietnam gained military control over Cambodia and saw its ally, the Heng Samrin regime, consolidate political authority.

Vietnam's unexpected success caused China to rethink the regional role of the ASEAN states. Where once they had been perceived as allies of the imperialists, they came to be seen as a positive force, capable of contributing to a Southeast Asian balance of power more favorable to China. Thus China turned to ASEAN for support in containing Vietnamese influence.

Alignment with ASEAN

Beijing's strategy toward ASEAN derives from two concerns: fear of regional instability and insufficient military capability. ASEAN state insecurities associated with Southeast Asian international politics were similar. During the 1960s ASEAN governments lived with fears that came from vulnerabilities to United States armed force; in the aftermath of the Vietnam war they became anxious over the regional influence that Hanoi would gain from success in dominating Indochina. Instability and unknowns associated with the Sino-Vietnamese border conflict also fanned ASEAN insecurities. Having recently escaped the worry of civil war cloaked as communist insurgency and United States sponsored counterinsurgency, no ASEAN state was anxious to be caught up in another round of great power competition for influence in Southeast Asia.

Earlier discussion explained how the organization of ASEAN states was founded to promote cooperation and stability in Southeast Asia. ASEAN leaders wanted all external actors, especially the superpowers, to accept their peaceful approach to cooperative economic development. Thus in 1971 the ASEAN states adopted the Kuala Lumpur Declaration. It proclaimed a Zone of Peace, Freedom and Neutrality as an alternative security paradigm to competitive military buildups by external powers within Southeast Asia. Kuala Lampur was intended to legitimate a post-Vietnam war framework for crafting a stable and non-threatening Southeast Asian balance of power. However, Vietnam's turn to the Soviet Union for backing in its efforts to assemble an Indochina federation dashed these hopes. It forced the first ASEAN summit meeting (in 1976 at Jakarta, Indonesia) to focus on cooperative action for checking Vietnamese expansion and Soviet penetration.

There was no initial consensus among the ASEAN states on how best to ensure their Southeast Asian security interests. Most favored a political and diplomatic compromise with Vietnam, rather than falling in with the hardline Beijing-Washington alliance. On the other hand, the ASEANS acknowledged that some working arrangement with the United States and China was necessary for containment of Vietnam. They also were apprehensive that a conditional commitment by them to United States policy goals would weaken Washington's willingness to maintain commitments in Southeast Asia, a region in which less vital interests were at stake than in Europe or the Middle East. Balancing this concern were suspicions that Washington's preference for a "China-Centered" Asia would facilitate Chinese control over Southeast Asia, thus undermining the ASEAN vision of a regional multipolar balance.[42]

To summarize, the ASEAN states were faced with the problem of convincing the United States to remain a permanent presence in Southeast Asia while utilizing shifting currents in Indochina to preserve balance between Vietnam and China.

Chinese regional alignment strategies have taken advantage of the dilemma faced by ASEAN governments. Above all, China has courted ASEAN. Once portrayed as puppets of imperialism, ASEANS, in the new Chinese lexicon, have become "peace loving countries," and Beijing is unequivocal in its support for "the truly successful progress of ASEAN as an organization."[43] Seldom does China voice its once incessant demands for a firm ASEAN stance against Vietnamese expansionism. This reflects increased sensitivity to ASEAN states' uneasy feeling that China is "too close for comfort." Chinese leaders believe that the byproduct of conceding more latitude to the ASEANS, within which they can deal with the Indochina problem, will lead ASEANS to have a more favorable attitude toward China's role in Southeast Asia.

China's drive for diplomatic alignment with the ASEAN has enjoyed considerable success. ASEAN states have entered into closer relations with China. Beijing is seen as a desirable partner, not only to contain Vietnam's expansionist policy, but also for the benefits available from long term political, social and economic cooperation. Post Maoist China is viewed as fundamentally more benign than its predecessor. Nevertheless, unable to forget that domestic Communist parties once served as agents of Communist China's foreign policy, ASEAN governments remain apprehensive when Beijing repeats that friendly "state-to-state" ties should not preclude close "party-to-party" relations.

Beijing's policy of giving priority to friendly state-to-state relations, over ties with local communist parties, has begun to convince the ASEANS that China can be a reliable ally. Thailand has strengthened ties with China, and relations with Indonesia, Singapore, and Malaysia are improving. Indonesia, reversing a decade of hostility toward Beijing's ruling communists, invited China to attend the 30th anniversary of the Bandung Conference; and in his September 1985 visit to China, Singapore Prime Minister Lee Kuan Yew proclaimed that his aim was "to renew friendship with Chinese leaders and to search out new ways for expanding economic contacts."[44] Two months later, Malaysia Prime Minister Mahathir Mohamad led a 200 member delegation to China, where he revealed that the two governments had agreed to talk about areas in which they could reach agreement while putting aside such long-standing differences as support for the Communist Party of Malaysia.[45] Finally, trade between China and ASEAN increased significantly in the 1980s.[46] Together these developments profile an ASEAN community that is cooperating increasingly with China to manage regional international politics.

Military Strengthening

China's experience in the Sino-Vietnamese conflict exposed substantial military shortcomings. Most significant, the Chinese armed force suffered because of its outdated military equipment. Best estimates suggest that Chinese military infrastructure remains twenty to thirty years behind the world's more advanced forces.[47] This placed China's military forces at an obvious disadvantage in combat with the Vietnamese, who had been armed with Soviet weaponry and weapons left behind by American troops.

A second shortcoming of the Chinese troops was lack of training and inexperience. It had been more than twenty-five years since Chinese soldiers fought in the battlefields of Korea against a tenacious and well-equipped enemy. The border conflict between China and India in 1959, and with the Soviet Union in 1969, failed to provide Chinese troops with sustained fighting experience. Worse, for a long period of time many military units were used for such civilian tasks; road construction, agriculture and civil administration. The debilitating consequences this employment became apparent when China struck at Vietnam. Although China's army boasted some 4 million men, the largest number of troops in the world, it was unprepared for battle. Its best units performed poorly in engagements with the Vietnamese.

The third deficiency of China's armed forces derived from its military strategy and doctrine. Both had crystallized around Mao Zedong's portrayal of a "People's War." In a "People's War" the invader is lured deep into China, fighting ends in victory with the enemy surrounded by "an armed populace trained and led by the regular army."[48] The more orthodox strategy of defense by "development of large-scale conventional forces capable of stopping an attack at the border" received a low priority. Associated concepts (among them forward deployment, readiness, mobility and substainability by reinforcement) were seldom discussed and not integrated into the training of China's military.

The "People's War" doctrine to which China's military leaders clung created a armed force that was ill equipped to conduct modern warfare, especially offensive operations. Officers, especially in the low and middle ranks, lacked training for carrying out armed reconnaissance, combined arms operations (especially when they involved armored deployments), and electronic warfare.[49] Tactical air control over the battlefield was a matter far beyond China's reach. The Vietnamese Army, on the other hand, had dealt with an enemy possessing these capabilities during two decades of warfare. Differences between the experience and organization of China and Vietnam's armed forces enabled the later to fight the former to a standstill after only minimal penetration into Vietnam.

Insufficient military capability has been a problem of major concerns to China's post-Mao leadership. Since the late 1970s Deng Xiaoping has made modernization of the armed forces a matter of the highest priority. Current efforts center on the introduction of advanced weaponry and related technology, upgrading military research and development, restructuring combat and combat support units, application of new training methods, regularization of military education for officers and extrication of the armed forces from non-military tasks.

Introduction of Weaponry and Technology

Beijing has shown sustained interest in a broad range of U.S. military equipment and technology since 1979, although minor military purchases have been made from Britain, France and Italy.[50] In 1980 President Carter approved military sales to China, and the Reagan and Bush administrations have continued this policy. Bilateral military relations between the United States and China warmed considerably in 1984, when three delegations of top-ranking officers from the Chinese military staff visited the United States.[51] Since Chinese President Li Xiannian came to Washington in 1986, Beijing has gained access to American technology of the highest strategic importance for Chinese military development.

R & D and Military Industry

Beijing has implemented sweeping military R & D programs in diverse fields: strategic missiles, artillery, aircraft and naval ordinance. Results have included successful test firings of ICBMs, placing satellites with military payloads into orbit using a single carrier rocket and submarine launches of ballistic missile.[52] Meanwhile, Chinese military industries have concentrated resources on developing weapons that will correct the most obvious shortcomings revealed during the unhappy Vietnam adventure. Key projects include radar and surveillance technology for tanks, armored vehicles, communications systems and self-guided munitions.[53]

Military Training and Education

Under China's defense modernization program training exercises and officer higher education and professionalization have been re-emphasized. During the 1980s numerous large-scale naval and land-force exercises took place. Military deployments for modern warfare were stressed, including maneuvers by a deep water combat fleet and its logistical tail, the mounting of combined-arms operations and the integration of combat engineering units into offensive maneuvers.[54] Success in these endeavors has necessitated intensified training for middle level officers. As of early

1985, 70 percent of this group had received formal military education and training for combat. In addition, a newly-founded China National Defense Academy, modeled on the National War College in Washington, now educates professionals under consideration for general officer rank.[55] Finally, as part of the post-Mao professionalization of the armed forces, the Army gave up important non military responsibilities. The duty of guarding public facilities and foreign legations shifted to the newly-established People's Armed Police, and the Ministry of Railways took over the railway construction programs for which the army had been responsible.[56]

Accommodation

China experimented with accommodation after its policy of bleeding Vietnam ran up against two major obstacles. The first derived from China's limited military strength. The second was a product of pressures exerted by the international community. After armed combat along the Sino-Vietnamese border subsided, many countries (including the United States, the ASEAN states, Japan, the EEC countries, and others) expressed anxiety over the possibility that fighting might flare anew. Although Vietnam's expansionist policy in Indochina received most of the blame for what had happened, the international community was opposed to any solution that depended on armed force. Beijing was now looking to reintegrate itself into the global community of nations, and decided it would be a mistake to unleash its military to "teach Vietnam a second lesson." Nevertheless, China never gave up the "right" to deploy its armed forces into Indochina should it become "necessary." Meanwhile China inaugurated a diplomatic offensive to undermine Hanoi's influence in Southeast Asia. Accommodation with Moscow was a centerpiece of this effort.

The offer of accommodation was floated as an inducement for the Soviet Union to adopt a more favorable stance toward Chinese interests. Most significantly, Beijing hoped that the prospect of reduced tensions with its populous southern neighbor would induce Moscow to rethink its support for Vietnam's occupation of Cambodia. In this context it is critical to keep in mind that Beijing regards the core problem behind the Sino-Vietnamese estrangement to lie more in Moscow than in Hanoi. Without Soviet backing for Vietnam, geopolitical realities are seen as propelling Vietnam into China's orbit. Thus China perceives itself as possessing critical leverage over Vietnam; by improving relations with the Soviet Union, China can undercut vital Soviet support for Vietnam's challenge to Chinese influence in Southeast Asia.

Beijing has laid out three pre-conditions for the normalization of Sino-Soviet relations: substantial drawdown of troops positioned along the

Sino-Soviet and Sino-Mongolian border; withdrawal of Soviet troops from Afghanistan; and termination of Soviet support for Vietnam's occupation of Cambodia. However, China has not insisted that all three conditions be met before reconciliation can be considered. Recently Beijing has give priority to the Indochinese issue, perhaps because it is perceived as the one most amenable to Chinese diplomacy. In Afghanistan, Soviet combat troops already have departed, and only advisors remain; also, the country is of little strategic importance to China. In the Soviet Union, Beijing views recent turmoil as reducing the already low probability that Moscow would launch a massive military strike to the south. Thus Deng Xiaoping, in the interview with CBS correspondent Mike Wallace, stressed that Vietnam's invasion of Cambodia remained the main obstacle to normalization of Sino-Soviet relations. He even expressed that despite having already accomplished, at his age, his "historical task of making overseas visits," he was willing to "break the rule and go to any place in the Soviet Union to meet Gorbachev," were it possible to resolve the Cambodian issue.[57]

Negotiations between China and the Soviet Union appear to have gotten off to a good start: mutual visits of high ranking officials have increased; bilateral trade reached U.S. $1.5 billion in 1985, and seems likely to surpass the level targeted for 1990 of U.S. $5 billion. Also, after being suspended for nine years, Beijing and Moscow resumed negotiations over their disputed common border. The Soviet negotiators summarized their receptivity to Chinese overtures by stating what while they would not improve relations with China at the expense of third parties, they also "would not allow Vietnam to influence their great power policy interests, even though that might lead to the Chinese having increased diplomatic leverage over Vietnam."[58] In response, China dangled the possibility of a global strategy whose course would be equal-distance between Washington and Moscow. The message was clear: Beijing no longer perceived threats from the Soviet Union as so immediate and great that its tilt toward the United States could not be modified. Meaningful Sino-Soviet reconciliation, however, is still remote. Nevertheless, this does not exclude the possibility that Beijing and Moscow will reach compromises on the Cambodia issue in order to reduce tensions between them.

Finally, China has attempted accommodation with Laos. Here accommodation's purpose was to undermine Hanoi's influence. Implementation of this strategy began with a five day visit, during January of 1987, to Vietnam by Chinese Deputy Minister Liu Shuqing. The immediate goal was negotiation of a normalization of bilateral relations with Laos. Liu Shuqing stressed that China differentiates between Vientiane and Hanoi, not to mention the Heng Samring regime in Cambodia. Subsequently, a high-ranking Chinese visitor to Vietnam characterized the stationing of 40-50,000 Vietnamese troops in Laos as "bilateral matter" between Hanoi and Vientiane.[59] The substantial flexibility of Beijing's position on Laos, in stark contrast to that toward Vietnam, has evoked a positive response from the Laotian government.

Conclusion: Policy Options and the Future of Southeast Asia

Although China has not been able to achieve all of its strategic objectives in Southeast Asia, its can boast important successes. From the broadest perspective, China enters the 1990s in a more advantageous position than its Vietnamese rival. Hanoi has been unable to assuage insecurities among the ASEAN powers derived from its aggressive pursuit of Ho Chi Min's dream for an Indochinese federation. Potentially fruitful policy option remain, but none of them is easy. On the other hand, China also faces strategic difficulties; its domestic infrastructure is in need of modernization, while its size and propinquity create unease among regional bargainer states. Also, Beijing like Hanoi, has no clear plan on how to make Southeast Asian international politics more responsive to its interests.

Hanoi

Although Vietnam has achieved considerable military success in Cambodia, its international image is negative. Nearly seven years after Vietnam overthrew the Pol Pot regime by force, Hanoi remains frustrated that its client Heng Samring regime has not been recognized by the global community. Moreover, unless recent Vietnamese troop withdrawals from Cambodia come to be seen as truly ending its occupation there (an unlikely prospect), Vietnam's relations with the outside world will continue to be dominated by reservations derived from the perception that Vietnam is an expansionist state. It is imperative that Vietnam find a way to alter this perception while retaining influence over Laos and Cambodia. Here Hanoi must deal with several strategic considerations.

First, the intensification of insurgent activity during 1990, following the withdrawal of Vietnamese troops, reinforces doubts that Vietnam's Phnom Penh client government can survive and control Cambodia. Within one year of withdrawal, twenty percent of the countryside had fallen under control of the Khamer Rouge. A crucial factor bearing on Vietnamese success is the degree of Soviet support. Hanoi fears that the ending of the Cold War in Europe, and problems with nationalities inside of the Soviet Union, will lead to a scaling down of Moscow's commitment to Vietnam's plans for Indochinese federation. As of late 1990, Moscow appeared reluctant to continue with its U.S. $3 million aid per day to Vietnam.[60]

Second, Hanoi has to deal with increasing Sino-Soviet initiatives toward normalizing relations. To Hanoi, a reconciliation between its great power provider and its great power enemy appears more harmful to its interests than any other conceivable international realignment. Vietnamese leaders visited Moscow in early 1990, and they were not reassured. Their apprehension suggests that Hanoi has concluded that Moscow is placing its interests as a global power over traditional ties with an ally whose utility has diminished. For the Soviet Union's most important security interest in Asia during the 1990s is to prevent crystallization of the incipient Beijing-Tokyo-Washington security alignment. Thus, despite accommodation with the United States in Europe, many of the Soviet Union's Asian policy experts advocate reconciliation with China, intimidation of Japan, and isolation of the United States.[61] This confirms Moscow's preoccupation with the all-Asian balance among the great powers; from this perspective, Hanoi's concerns are secondary.

The third and perhaps the most important strategic concern for Hanoi has become development of an influencing preserving strategy that will break the diplomatic stalemate with regard to Cambodia. Trial balloons were floated as long ago as seven years before the September 1989 troop withdrawal from Cambodia. In April 1982, Vietnamese Foreign Minister Nguyen Co Thach visited France, West Germany, Sweden, Belgium and India. Following his return, Hanoi announced its willingness to withdraw troops unilaterally from Cambodia as a "first step" towards restoring peace to Southeast Asia.[62] Subsequently, Vietnam attempted to play upon differences among the ASEAN states, but with few tangible results.

To summarize, Hanoi has insisted since the end of the Vietnam War that Cambodia is a Southeast Asian regional issue. Overtures have been made to other bargainer states, with proposals setting forth a framework for regional stability. Hanoi remains unmoved in its commitment to a peaceful Indochina, under its domination, as a critical pillar of the new regional order. When the ASEAN states have presented counterproposals, Vietnam has turned them down.

Beijing

Until there is regional (including the intrusive powers), agreement on the political outlines of an Indochina confederation, Beijing appears committed to increasing military assistance to the tripartite resistance forces in Cambodia. But in this respect, Beijing has to take into account the situation inside of Cambodia. Hanoi has experienced important political successes in strengthening the Heng Samring Regime, and military victories against the resistance forces; although as noted earlier, ability to build on these accomplishments is more uncertain than ever.

There are increasing tensions within the tripartite resistance; especially among military units loyal to Son Sann, Prince Sihanok and the Khmer Rouge. The conditionality of their commitment to China causes great apprehension in Beijing. Also, China finds support for the Pol Pot forces, viewed internationally as a pariah, a source of continual embarrassment. Thus Cambodia future is uncertain and the impact of China's policy unclear. Not surprisingly, China is extremely cautious as it gropes for a solution to the Indochinese imbroglio that preserves its interests while constraining Vietnamese influence.

Beijing will have to make additional policy adjustments if it hopes to accommodate ASEAN. To the ASEAN states, Vietnamese dominance over Indochina and the Sino-Vietnamese conflict are both undesirable. ASEANS find the regional instability associated with these conditions extremely threatening. China has become more acceptable to ASEAN as a stabilizing force to counter Vietnamese aggressiveness, but most ASEAN states reject Beijing's policy of "bleeding Hanoi." This policy is perceived as raising the risk of military actions, which only can lead to more regional involvement by the superpowers. Moreover, the ASEAN states do not want to see Vietnamese influence completely eliminated. Without Vietnam as a counterweight, China would possess effective Southeast Asian hegemony. As China's communist elite has a long history of anti-government activities in the ASEAN states, the latter find Chinese hegemony as threatening as Vietnamese expansionism.

In conclusion, the pivotal change defining Southeast Asian international relations since 1950 is restoration of China as a viable aspiring regional hegemon. China has regained its historical influence in spite of being encircled and isolated by first the United States, and then the Soviet Union. The new subordinate state system balance of power provides China with maneuvering room to manage threats that have persisted since the Western powers forcibly intruded into Southeast Asia during the nineteenth century. Nevertheless, the regional power balance is far from what Beijing would prefer. The United States retains a significant military presence and Soviet backing for Vietnam has emboldened Vietnam in its dealings with China. In turn, Sino-Vietnamese estrangement has enabled the ASEAN states to retain great autonomy as they pursue their Southeast Asian interests.

Well into the twenty-first century a competitive pursuit of national interest between China, Vietnam, and ASEAN will sustain regional tensions. States that fail to shape the power balance to accommodate their interest will find themselves clients of the more successful.

Notes

1. Dennis Duncanson, *Government and Revolution in Vietnam,* (London: Oxford University Press, 1968), p. 23.

2. Michael Yahuda, "China and the Region," *Southeast Asian Affairs,* 1985, p. 54.

3. Ibid.

4. The literature on Sino-Soviet relations has widely dealt with the issues as stated in the paper. Specifically, for a detailed account of Soviet strategy toward the Japanese invasion of China, refer to Aitchen K. Wu, *China and the Soviet Union,* (Port Washington, N.Y.: Lemmolat Press, 1950), pp. 234–36, and David J. Dallin, *Soviet Russia and the Far East,* (Hamden: Archon Books, 1977), pp. 61–62; for Soviet policy toward China at the Cairo and Yalta conferences, Henry Wei, *China and Soviet Russia,* (Westport, CT: Greenwood Press, Publishers, 1956), pp. 162–72, and Robert C. North, *Moscow and Chinese Communists,* (Stanford, CA: Stanford University Press 1963), pp. 206–17; for Soviet strategy toward China during the Korean War, Adam B. Ulam, "Washington, Moscow, and the Korean War" in Allen Guttman ed., *Korea, Cold War and Limited War,* (Massachusetts: D.C. Heath and Company, 1972) pp. 263–77, and Joseph L. Mogee & Robert H. Donaldson, *Soviet Foreign Policy Since World War II,* (New York: Pergamon Press, 1981), pp. 75–78; and for Soviet strategy during the Sino-Indian dispute, Neville Maxwell, *India's China War,* (New York: Pantheon Books, 1970), pp. 275– 84, and Howard L. Boorman, *Moscow-Peking Axis, Strengths and Strains,* (New York: Harper & Brothers, 1957), p. 223.

5. Alain-Gerard Marsot, "The Chinese Perspective" in Sudershan Chawla, Melvin Gurtov, and Alain-Gerard Marsot eds., *Southeast Asia Under the New Balance of Power,* (New York: Praeger Publishers, 1974), pp. 70–72.

6. *Beijing Review,* 1969, No. 35, pp. 14–18.

7. Ibid. 1968, No. 10, p. 29, No. 27, p. 29.

8. Ibid. 1968, No. 2, p. 17, p. 20, and 23, No. 4, p. 21, No. 10, p. 29.

9. Ibid, 1968, No. 4, p. 21.

10. Robert G. Sutter, *China-Watch, Sino-American Reconciliation,* (Baltimore: The Johns Hopkins University Press, 1978), p. 73.

11. Donald S. Zagoria, *Vietnam Triangle* (New York: Pegasus Publishers, 1967).

12. Sarasin Viraphol, "The People's Republic of China and Southeast Asia: A Security Consideration for the 1980s," in Robert Scalapino and J. Wanandi ed., *Economic, Political, and Security Issues in Southeast Asia in the 1980s,* (Berkeley: Institute of East Asian Studies University of California, Berkeley, 1982), p. 148.

13. Richard C. Thornton, "Soviet Strategy and the Vietnam War" *Asian Affairs,* No. 4 (March/April, 1974), p. 205.

14. Ibid., pp. 210–13.

15. Douglas Pike, "Hanoi Looks to the Southeast" in R. Scalapino and J. Wanandi eds., p. 85.

16. Jay Taylor, *China and Southeast Asia: Peking's Relations with Revolutionary Movements,* (New York: Praeger Publishers, 1976), p. 385.

17. Les Buszynski, "Vietnam Conflicts China," *Asian Survey,* Vol. XX, No. 8 (August, 1980), pp. 831–32.

18. Eugene K. Lawson, *The Sino-Vietnamese Conflict,* (New York: Praeger Publishers, 1984), p. 304.

19. Bernard B. Fall, *The Two Vietnams,* (New York: Frederick A. Praeger, 1963), p. 175.

20. Zagoria, p. 111.

21. Lawson, p. 303.

22. Scalapino and Wanandi, p. 85.

23. Melvin Gurtov, *China and Southeast Asia—The Politics of Survival,* (Baltimore: The Johns Hopkins University Press, 1975), pp. 159–64.

24. Lucian W. Pye, "The China Factor in Southeast Asia" in Richard H. Solomon ed., *The China Factor—Sino-American Relations & The Global Scene,* (Englewood Cliffs, New Jersey: Prentice-Hall Inc. 1981), pp. 219–24.

25. Donald E. Weatherbee, "Southeast Asia in 1982," *Southeast Asian Affairs,* 1983, pp. 15–16.

26. Yahuda, pp.61–67.

27. Lucian W. Pye, "China and Southeast Asia," in Scalapino and Wanandi, p. 159.

28. John G. Stoessinger, *Nations in Darkness: China, Russia, and America,* New York: Random House, 1981), p. 221.

29. Yahuda, p. 57.

30. *Beijing Review,* 1978, No. 45, pp. 3–4, No. 46, p. 4.

31. C.G. Jacobsen, *Sino-Soviet Relations Since Mao,* (New York: Praeger Publishers, 1981), pp. 95–96.

32. F.A. Mediansky, "Soviet Strategic Interests in Southeast Asia," *Southeast Asian Affairs,* p. 43.

33. Donnell, p. 21.

34. Huynh Kim Khanh and Hans Indorf, "Southeast Asia 1981," *Southeast Asian Affairs,* 1982, p. 16.

35. Ng Shue Meng, "Vietnam in 1981," *Southeast Asian Affairs,* 1982, pp. 390–91.

36. Sheldon W. Simon, "The Great Powers and Southeast Asia: Cautious Minuet or Dangerous Tango?," *Asian Survey,* Vol. XXV, No. 9 (September, 1985), p. 920.

37. Karl D. Jackson, "U.S. Policy, ASEAN, and Kampuchean Crisis," Scalapino and Wanandi, p. 124.

38. Christopher F. Chyba, "U.S. Military-Support Equipment Sales to the People's Republic of China," *Asian Survey,* Vol. XXI, No. 4, (April 1981).

39. According to the International Institute of Strategic Studies in London, the military spending of ASEAN in the fiscal year between 1981 and 1982 was about U.S. $7.44 billion, which represented a 18.21% increase over the previous year. Refer to *Southeast Asian Affairs,* 1982 p. 17.

40. Jusuf Wanandi, "The United States and Southeast Asia in the 1980s," Scalapino and Wanandi, p. 122.

41. John C. Donnell, "Vietnam 1979: Year of Calamity," *Asian Survey,* Vol. XX No. 1, (January 1980) pp. 19–22.
42. Pye, "The China Factor in Southeast Asia" pp. 218–19.
43. *Beijing Review,* 1983, No. 28, p .11, No. 16, p. 18.
44. Ibid, 1985, No. 36. pp 8–9.
45. Ibid., 1985, No. 49, pp. 7–8.
46. Yahuda, pp. 62–66.
47. Scott James, "PRC Military Electronics Systems Evaluated," *Defense Electronics,* June 1980, p. 77.
48. Christopher M. Clarke, "Defense Modernization," *The China Business Review,* July–August, 1984, p. 41.
49. James Gregor, "The Military Potential of the People's Republic of China and Western Security Interests," *Asian Affairs,* Vol. 11, Spring 1984, pp. 2–3.
50. Richard E. Gillespie, "Marketing to the PLA," *The China Business Review,* 1984, p. 34.
51. Ibid. p. 35.
52. June Teufel Dreyer, "China's Military Modernization," *Orbis,* Winter, 1984, p. 1016.
53. Clarke, p. 44.
54. Dreyer, pp. 1016–17.
55. Clarke, p. 41.
56. Ibid.
57. *Beijing Review,* September 15, 1986, p. 5.
58. Yahuda, pp. 58-59.
59. *Far Eastern Economic Review,* (FEER), January 15, 1987, p. 26.
60. Harry H. Kendall, "Vietnamese Perceptions of the Soviet Presence," *Asian Survey,* Vol. XXII, No. 9, (September 1983), pp. 1060–61.
61. Simon, "The Great Powers and Southeast Asia," p. 931.
62. Carlyle A. Thayer, "Vietnam's Two Strategic Tasks," *Southeast Asian Affairs,* 1983, p. 332.

7

Brazil: The Quest for South American Leadership

David J. Myers

Over the past quarter century Brazil has experienced upward international mobility.[1] Possessing a national territory larger than the continental United States, a population of 151 million, and the eighth largest market economy, Brazilian aspirations and capabilities command increasing attention. The conditions that facilitated general upward international mobility are leading to even greater Brazilian influence within South America. In addition, with the vital Western Hemisphere concerns of the United States restricted to the geographically contiguous Caribbean Basin, South America is emerging as an autonomous international arena in its own right. Brazil's potential to exert influence throughout South America, in spite of recent economic and political difficulties, is unprecedented.

This chapter examines the threats Brazilian policy makers perceive to their aspirations of exercising special influence in South America. It also analyzes the strategic responses that flow from these perceptions. Attention focuses on the threat perceptions and strategic responses that predominated between the advent of military rule in 1964 and the inauguration of President Fernando Collor de Mello in 1990. These perceptions and responses will shape Brazil's South American policy well into the twenty first century.

Brazilians long have viewed South America as a region in which their country is destined to exercise special influence.[2] During the 1950s, military geopoliticians, the best known advocates of this perspective, defined and analyzed Brazil's South American interests. Between 1964

An earlier version of this chapter was published in *In Depth*, the journal of the Washington Institute for Values in Public Policy Vol. 1, No. 1 (March 1991), pp. 25–75.

and 1985, geopolitical thinking prevailed within the ruling military regime. With the return of civilian government, foreign service officers, academics and businessmen participated increasingly in the debate over national security policy. Geopolitical perspectives were downplayed, especially as Brazil and Argentina's civilian presidents stressed economic, political and military cooperation. Nevertheless, concern over potentially covetous neighbors and regional spheres of influence remained enormous, not only in Brazil, but throughout South America.

In spite of growing capabilities and new opportunities, Brazil is far from being a regional hegemon. Industrial and technological development inside of the country continues to be selective and concentrated in the Europeanized south; complex domestic political conflicts also detract from Brazil's ability to project power and influence beyond its frontiers. In addition, there are significant international constraints. Argentina, proud but frustrated because of its inability to match broad-based Brazilian industrial advances, oscillates between cooperative integration and distrustful rivalry.[3]

South America's Northern Tier states also display mixed feelings toward Brazil. Mindful of their Portuguese speaking neighbor's successful nineteenth century territorial expansion, they are apprehensive over the long range implications of integrated Amazon Basin development. At the Manaus summit of May 1989, eleven years after signing the Amazon Pact Treaty, these countries rejected Brazilian proposals for multinational conditionalities on the exploitation of Amazonian resources.[4] Northern tier leaders appeared fearful that movement toward the Pact's goal of integrated regional development threatened national sovereignty over their largely vacant Amazonian peripheries. Brazil views this intransigence as a major hurdle to be overcome on the road to continental leadership.

Brazilians also perceive the larger international environment as a source of threats to their South American aspirations. Their foreign service (ITAMARATY) is especially sensitive to political, military and economic posturing by the industrial countries. Brazilian diplomacy regularly seeks to influence the international politics of North-South military intervention, trade, technology transfer, foreign investment, and debt servicing. Each of these issues is seen as effecting Brazil's capability to gain special regional influence and upward international mobility.

The discussion that follows revolves about four central topics. The first examines how domestic politics gives rise to insecurities among Brazilian policy makers regarding their capacity to exercise special influence over South America. Concern next focuses on South American international politics, especially the trends and behavior that Brazil views as threatening to its regional aspirations. Third, the capabilities and inclinations of actors in the global environment to derail Brazilian designs for primacy in South America are addressed. Finally, attention centers on Brazilian responses to the threat perceptions that originate in each of the above geopolitical arenas. These responses proved to be variants of those identified in the overview chapter: accommodation; defense through deterring and allying; state strengthening; and, counterthreat.

Domestic Politics and Threat Perception

Domestic politics as a source of threat was popularized by conservative Brazilian military intellectuals after the Second World War. They crafted a comprehensive approach to national security, elements of which were written into the Constitution of 1946. This approach inserted the Armed Forces into the political process, and during the life of the 1946 constitution the military exercised veto powers over a broad range of policy options. Open interventions occurred when the officer corps decided that the populism of elected presidents was stimulating domestic political conflict and compromising Brazil's potential for upward international mobility.

The military's national security ideology initially assigned the officer corps the role of "moderators" who, after removing disruptive politicians, were to return to their traditional concerns of defending the nation against external enemies.[5] Thus the military ousted President Getúlio Vargas in 1954; subsequently, upon the inauguration of Juscelino Kubitchek, it returned to the barracks. In March of 1964, the officer corps toppled the civilian government of President João Goulart. This time the armed forces decided to govern directly. Efforts to legitimate this exercise of political authority included an unsuccessful attempt to popularize national security doctrine. Following the restoration of civilian government in March of 1985, advocates of the national security approach continued to operate behind the scenes.

Contemporary national security doctrine portrays domestic political conflict as posing serious threats to the state; it tenets mesh easily with Brazil's authoritarian traditions.[6] During the twentieth century proponents of authoritarian corporatism have controlled the Brazilian national executive far longer than advocates of liberal democracy. After 1985, as the exhilaration of democratic restoration gave way to the realities of exercising power, civilian leaders experienced increased difficulties in governing. Thus, during the 1989 presidential election campaign, even populist democrats discussed the importance of maintaining order to facilitate progress. Since the inauguration of President Collor de Mello this concern has become even more central.

Apprehension over Brazil's historic dependence on the North Atlantic pervades both the military and civilian variants of Brazilian national security doctrine. Both portray the most serious internal threats as deriving from the tendency of great powers to interfere in the domestic affairs of lesser ones. Leftist stress the intrusive activity of multinational corporations; rightists emphasize the dangers of foreign military intervention. Both view intrusion as intended to exploit pre-existing "insecurities" among local populations.

The military variant of geopolitically based national security thinking is explicit. It classifies three kinds of insecurities as common to "lesser states."[7] Most important are *national insecurities*. These are related to the lack of resources, deficiencies in industrialization, and financial weaknesses. *Cultural insecurities,* a second category identified in the *Manual Básico* of the National War College (Escola Superior de Guerra), are tied to the "ignorance" of some sectors when they participate in politics. While "cultural insecurities" remains a vague concept, the implication is that legitimating mass demands to redistribute wealth makes it impossible for significant capital formation to occur in the "lesser states."

The military's national security approach recognizes a third category of insecurities, *moral insecurities*. Moral insecurities are linked with generational confrontation. Public references to this linkage during the early years of the post 1964 military regime suggested preoccupation on the part of the armed forces with the failure of Brazilian youth to accept guidance from their elders. In addition, national security ideologues viewed moral insecurities as growing out of the struggle between classes as they adapted to rapid technological change. Initially, the Soviet Union was portrayed as the principal, but by no means only exploiter of the aforementioned insecurities. After the middle 1970s the United States also emerged as an exploiter.

During the decades of military government, Brazil's National War College held national security seminars for opinion leaders in the most important cities. Instructors stressed that when domestic tensions generated by insecurities reach critical levels, political order hangs by a slender thread. With breakdown imminent, the state is justified in taking strong measures to preserve the internal political order.[8]

Military, as well as civilian national security thinking, also views unacceptable international consequences as flowing from heightened levels of internal political conflict. Because acute domestic tensions force the executive to prepare for contingencies which, if unattended, may lead to the regime's overthrow, state capabilities are severely strained. Few resources remain for projecting power beyond national frontiers. Viewed from this perspective, the commitment of each 1964–1985 military president to increase Brazilian international power and prestige weighed heavily in the high priority they gave to suppressing and managing domestic political conflict.

The tenuousness of domestic political order remained a concern of the civilians who assumed power in March 1985. During the final year of General Figueiredo's government, the frequency of mass demonstrations had increased and banditry became almost commonplace in the urban slums. Only expectation that military rule was ending prevented the outbreak of organized violence. Brazil's post 1985 government, like its military predecessors, perceived direct connections between the ability of domestic political institutions to produce broadly acceptable policies and the country's capability to project power throughout South America. However, civilian politicians differed from the officer corps in that they accepted as normal levels of nonviolent conflict during the making of political decisions that the uniformed services found unacceptable. Also, the compromises that emerged from bitter struggles in the 1987/88 constitutional convention confirmed that party leaders would tolerate a broader range of policy outcomes than the military.[9]

José Sarney, the Northeastern politician who assumed the presidency following the death of President-elect Tancredo Neves, had been a leader of the pro-government ARENA party during the military regime. Nevertheless, he attempted to chart an independent course. Sarney calculated that the military's application of national security doctrine, especially during the early 1980s, had so fueled popular dissatisfaction that widespread alienation threatened to undermine the societal concord on which Brazil's international power projection capabilities depended. Correspondingly, President Sarney gave high priority to reducing the explosive potential of long-simmering internal discontent.

No dimension of discontent was more important than the outrage deriving from human rights violations by the ruling military. Sarney acted here to strengthen civil liberties and prevent human rights abuses, but *in the newly democratizing milieu.* He ignored violations that had occurred between 1964 and 1985. Oversight was seen as the price of avoiding reimposition of military authoritarianism. President Collor calculated that his popular mandate placed him in a stronger position. One of his first acts was to reduce the autonomy, power and budget of the SNI (Serviço Nacional de Informações), the institution charged with implementing national security law during the military regime. Nevertheless, the Brazilian intelligence community remains influential.

A second dimension of discontent involved perceptions that military presidents had managed political conflict for the benefit of the officer corps and its allies. As in the matter of human rights violations, all but a few militant leftists maintained silence despite popular calls for an accounting. While negotiations surrounding the issue of accountability were highly secretive, conventional wisdom asserted that again silence was the price extracted by the armed forces for their return to the barracks. Therefore, Presidents Sarney and Collor, as well as the major opposition parties, focused attention on how best to consolidate democratic "rules of the game," rather than on retribution for past abuses.[10]

The precarious state of the economy during the 1980s, and its fallout, were the greatest domestic threats to Brazilian aspiration for special South American status in the 1990s. Inconsistent economic growth and the debilitating international debt underlay economic weakness. Gross Domestic Product grew erratically. Brazil experienced a sharp recession in the early 1980s, but in the first years of the Sarney government (1985/1986) Gross Domestic Product expanded at an annual average rate of 8 percent. Subsequently growth rates plummeted, bottoming out in 1988 at 0.3 percent. During early 1987, in hopes of making more goods available domestically and of restoring his political standing, President Sarney, suspended interest payments to foreign banks on Brazil's $108 billion foreign debt.[11] Trade surpluses in 1988 and 1989 facilitated an interim debt restructuring, although deficits in the national budget constrained the government's ability to reduce significantly the foreign debt or to control inflation.

Inflation rates during the Sarney government varied, while continually skirting the hyperinflationary danger zone. Although the government's Cruzado Plan checked inflation during most of 1986, prices soared during 1987 and the hyperinflation threshold was approached in 1988. President Sarney's January 1989 Summer Plan, his fourth attempt to control inflation and stimulate economic recovery, enjoyed only marginal success. Real wages fell by 60 percent early in the year, and the November presidential elections created irresistible demands for compensatory increases. In early 1990 hyperinflation appeared. Newly inaugurated President Collor deflated the economy by freezing bank accounts, wages and pensions. This action plunged Brazil into deep recession.

To summarize, the domestic politics of returning to elected national government gave rise to critical threats effecting Brazil's ability to project influence throughout South America. The magnitude of these threats ruled out the role of regional hegemon, at least in the near future. Ironically, many fears expressed in the armed forces' national security doctrine came to the forefront after three decades of military imposed governments. The generals had presided over the creation of an industrial and commercial base capable of supporting aspirations of upward international mobility and special regional influence. However, the social disorganization and economic liabilities that the first popularly elected president in three decades inherited mandated that he concentrate on domestic problems during the opening years of the 1990s.

South America and Brazilian Threat Perception

For many purposes, Latin America remains a single, albeit complex, region.[12] The view is growing, however, that South America and the Caribbean Basin, while interrelated, are distinct geopolitical arenas. Where the United States once crafted policies for all of Latin American (the Monroe Doctrine, the Good Neighbor Policy, and the Alliance for Progress) more recent initiatives have centered on the Caribbean Basin.[13] Washington increasingly looks at South America as an arena in which the United States has only slightly more at stake than in West Africa. This shrinkage of Western Hemispheric aspirations, as suggested earlier, has opened the possibility for Brazil to become more influential with her neighbors. Correspondingly, it has diminished some perceptions of threat to Brazil's regional leadership role and intensified others.

The South American Regional System

Geopolitically, South America encompasses twelve independent nation states and two colonies. Four nations—Argentina, Uruguay, Chile and Paraguay—belong to the Southern Cone subregion. Six nations—Peru, Ecuador, Colómbia, Venezuela, Guyana and Suriname—comprise the Northern Tier. Bolívia, the eleventh country, falls for some purposes into the Southern Cone and for others into the Northern Tier. The colony of French Guinea belongs to the latter grouping and the English Falkland (Malvinas) Islands are linked with the former. Brazil, continental in size, is revealed in Table 7.1 as dwarfing its South American neighbors. Also, its free market economy, the eight largest in the world, is more dynamic than that of any other state within the region. These cursory comparisons illustrate the perspective of Brazilian geopoliticians when they argue that during the twenty first century South American structural dynamics will bestow a large measure of regional hegemony upon their country.[14]

Character Traits and International Roles

Important character traits have long colored how Brazilians view their role in the international community. From the beginning of Portuguese colonization, Brazilian settlers spoke of their good fortune at having come to a blessed land that held great promise.[15] They believed that they and their descendants were part of an epic adventure: that Brazil was destined for greatness. Destiny mandated that they wrest the fertile coastal valleys in the north from hostile natives. Similarly, belief in Brazil's destiny drove the southern pioneers (Bandeirantes) to occupy and win vast interior territories claimed by Spain. The myth of future

Table 7.1 The South American Regional System

State	Population (millions) (1989)	Area (sq. km) (thousands)	GNP (US$/millions) (1989)*	Regional Type
Northern Tier				
Colombia	31.1	1,138.9	34.0*	Bargainer
Ecuador	10.2	283.6	13.1*	Bargainer
French Guinea	0.09	91.0	2.0	Colony
Guyana	0.77	215.0	0.5	Peripheral
Peru	21.3	1,098.6	19.8	Bargainer
Suriname	0.4	163.3	0.9	Peripheral
Venezuela	18.8	912.1	53.9	Bargainer
Southern Cone				
Argentina	31.5	2,766.9	77.2	Bargainer
Bolivia	6.5	1,098.6	3.9	Peripheral
Chile	12.6	756.9	16.4	Bargainer
Malvinas	0.02	12.2	NA	Colony
Paraguay	4.4	406.8	3.8	Peripheral
Uruguay	3.0	176.2	6.9	Peripheral
Brazil	150.7	8,512.0	270.0	Aspiring Hegemon

*GDP

SOURCE: U.S. Central Intelligence Agency, The World Fact Book-1989 (Washington, DC: CR WF 89001, 1989).

greatness also motivated Portuguese-speaking Brazilians to mount military campaigns that repulsed French and Dutch efforts to establish colonies on their coast. By the mid-eighteenth century, Brazil had become the jewel in Portugal's imperial crown.

Brazilian independence from Portugal was a by-product of the turbulence in Europe surrounding the Napoleonic Wars. When King Dom João VI returned the Portuguese court to Lisbon from exile in Rio de Janeiro, his son, Dom Pedro, remained behind as regent. Brazilian dissatisfaction with Portugal followed efforts to rescind privileges granted when Rio de Janeiro had been the empire's political center. Dom Pedro deflected this dissatisfaction away from the monarchy, making Portugal's Assembly of Nobles (Cortes) the source of Brazilian grievances. Success enabled him to rally Brazilians around his indigenous monarchy.[16] Because the young emperor, now Dom Pedro I, retained the loyalty of most Portuguese colonial officials, Brazil was spared the bloody and prolonged independence struggles that fractured the Spanish viceroyalties and left in their place nine independent South American republics. Thus state consolidation in Brazil lacked the brutality and extensive destruction that characterized the transition to nationhood in Spanish America. Preservation of colonial Brazil's political and economic patrimony, whether due to luck or to the prevailing pragmatic ethos, was a necessary precondition for the upward international mobility Brazil experienced during the late twentieth century.

Early in the twentieth century fortune again smiled on Brazil. An unusually capable diplomat, the legendary Baron José María do Rio Branco, became Foreign Minister at a critical moment. Rio Branco's tenure as Foreign Minister occurred when "final" boundaries between Brazil and her neighbors were being legitimated before the international community. The Baron prepared his briefs and maneuvered diplomatically with such skill that he gained most of the contested territory.[17] This success reaffirmed the elite's self-image as being more clever and capable than its Spanish-speaking competitors. Also, by securing international recognition for the borders that Brazil needed in order to aspire to hegemony in South America, the Baron do Rio Branco strengthened his countrymen's faith in the greatness of Brazil's future.

Brazilian elites have favored initiatives that would strengthen their country with little thought to ideology. Thus, in the middle 1930s, when seeking a counterbalance to growing United States influence, President Getúlio Vargas courted Berlin. After 1940, when the British navy cut Brazil's commercial links with Germany, Brazil became the strongest South American ally of the United States.[18]

Other self images with relevance for the conduct of foreign affairs suggest that Brazilians view their international situation less favorably than the often-stated belief in future greatness would imply. Especially important is the sense of isolation that Brazilians feel at being so far removed from the locus of international power, economic as well as political and military. Isolation has bred feelings of inferiority that cause Brazilians to react defensively toward anything they perceive as a slight by the industrial countries. Also, Brazilians view their nation as a victim of discrimination by first world states that jealously guard their power and privileges.[19]

Finally, most Brazilian elites are apprehensive because of the wide gulf separating them from the masses. Rapidly growing population, from the perspective of elite aspirations for upward international mobility, appears as a two-edged sword. On one hand, populating Brazil's empty spaces is seen as a prerequisite for great power status. On the other, elites fear that demands from a rapidly growing population will diminish the state's ability to assemble the capital necessary for industrial and technological modernization. This dilemma underlay efforts by the ruling military to shape political socialization between 1964 and 1985. They attempted to convince young Brazilians that sacrifice in the present would assure future development.[20] Deferral of gratification was presented as a necessary condition for national greatness. From this perspective, the economic instability since the foreign exchange crisis of 1982 becomes especially threatening. The officer corps and other elites committed to Brazilian greatness fear economic stagnation will clear the way for leftist governments in the 1990s. The preference of leftists for centralized economic control is perceived as mandating the confiscation of elite wealth; their promise to redistribute accumulated capital is viewed as undermining the foundations for technologically sophisticated industrialization. To summarize, Brazilians exhibit six cultural characteristics that shape their preferences about possible international roles:

1. faith in Brazil's future greatness;
2. belief in the importance of luck, and that it rides with Brazil;
3. flexibility and pragmatism in the pursuit of foreign policy goals;
4. confidence that under pressure they perform as well as anyone, and significantly better than their Spanish speaking neighbors;
5. a sense of isolation, derived from South America's geopolitical location, which sometimes lead to feelings of inferiority and sensitivity to any perceived slight from the industrial world;
6. apprehension that foreigners or their ideologies have and will exploit the gulf between rulers and ruled for the purpose of thwarting Brazil's great power ambitions.

South American Issues

South American international politics raises important policy issues with threatening dimensions for Brazil. The most immediate of these derives from Brazil's deep seated fears of Argentina.[21] Brazilian-Argentine relations during the middle 1980s appeared to enter an era of unprecedented cooperation. It must be kept in mind, however, that the two presidents who orchestrated this cooperation, José Sarney of Brazil and Raúl Alfonsín of Argentina, came to office following periods of authoritarian rule. In the post Malvinas conflict milieu, the consolidation of democracy in Brazil and Argentina seemed to mandate the strengthening of cooperative bonds between the two countries. Recently discredited military regimes in both had emphasized nationalistic rivalry and used accompanying tensions to justify a central political role for themselves. Sarney and Alfonsín presided over transitions to electoral democracy. They were forced to maneuver around military intrigues, conflicting prescriptions for economic growth, and growing demands for social justice. Policy making proved difficult, and potentially destabilizing choices abounded.[22]

The darker or threatening dimensions of relations between Brazil and Argentina have not disappeared. They are the product of four centuries of rivalry with roots in the even older struggle between Spain and Portugal. The issues involving Argentina which Brasília views as potentially threatening include: (1) the nuclear arms race; (2) struggles for influence in the buffer states of Uruguay, Paraguay, and to a lesser extent Bolívia; and, (3) related but distinguishable threats derived from possible changes in the Pacific coast balance of power.

Relations with South America's Northern Tier countries, while less important historically, also involve issues which Brazilians perceive as potentially threatening.[23] Most obvious are fears that the Andean Pact might assume anti-Brazilian colorations. This contingency raises the specter of an alliance between Andean Pact countries and Argentina for the purpose of limiting Brazilian influence. A unified and hostile alliance of Spanish South America could deny Brazil increasingly important export markets and low cost natural resources. At the extreme, it might even reopen boundary issues that were "resolved" earlier. Lesser Brazilian concerns in the north include: (1) fears that guerrilla warfare could spill over into Brazil; (2) apprehension that an insurgency might triumph and install a hostile Marxist-Leninist regime; and, (3) concern that the rapid development of an Andean country's Amazon periphery could threaten Brazilian control over its own Amazon territory. Each of the aforementioned threats will be examined in greater detail.

The reality of a nuclear arms race raised the level of insecurity surrounding relations between Brazil and Argentina during the early

1980s. As suggested above, there is a long history of mistrust and rivalry between the two. In the violence that accompanied independence, Brazil took advantage of Argentine weakness to annex territories that now comprise parts of the Brazilian states of Rio Grande do Sul, Santa Catarina and Paraná. Brazil also annexed, and lost, territory that now comprises the buffer state of Uruguay. The lands Brazil detached from the Viceroyalty de la Plata were the wealthiest and most valuable areas given up by Buenos Aires.[24] Argentine nationalists have never reconciled themselves to these losses.

During the 1930s, Argentine diplomacy raised Brazilian apprehensions that Buenos Aires might take advantage of the fluid situation associated with fighting between Paraguay and Bolívia and transform them into Argentine dependencies. Unexpectedly, Argentina turned inward. Within a decade, however, President Juan Peron was proclaiming his nation's obligation to restore the La Plata viceroyalty's lost territories. Peronist thinking about South America continues to be closer to that of the military geopoliticians than to the cooperation and economic integration advocated by Raul Alfonsín's Radical Civic Union. Thus the return of Peronism to power, with Carlos Saul Menem's inauguration as president in July 1989, strengthened the hand of those in Argentina whose tradition resents and distrusts Brazil.[25] However, Menem himself appears not to share that distrust.

The nuclear arms competition between Argentina and Brazil has been given high priority by Brasília since the early 1970s. At that time, President Emílio Garrastazú Médici became alarmed that Argentina's limited success with nuclear power generation was strengthening its capability to produce nuclear weapons. In 1976, Brazil's fear of falling behind became a motivating factor in President Ernesto Geisel's substitution of West German nuclear technology for that of the United States. Whereas Washington offered "turnkey" installations and demanded the return of spent reactor fuel, a substance from which weapons grade plutonium could be extracted, Bonn offered to transfer the entire nuclear cycle. Following the signing of an agreement with West Germany, Brasília anticipated having a minimum of ten operational nuclear power generating plants by early in the twenty-first century. Brazil also viewed itself as a future supplier of low-cost components for nuclear electric plants throughout South America. The spillover to Brazilian nuclear weapons capability was expected to be substantial.[26]

In response to the Brazilian-West German agreement, Argentina strengthened its nuclear power programs.[27] By the time of the Malvinas Islands conflict, Argentine technology and spent fuel stores had evolved to where Argentina possessed the capability to build several nuclear weapons; however, Buenos Aires chose not to exercise this option. After being defeated by Great Britain, the Argentine armed forces pushed for the creation of a small nuclear force. They argued that had such a force existed, London would not have reconquered the Malvinas. At that time, Buenos Aires enjoyed a lead over Brasília in nuclear weapons development of between five and seven years.[28]

Lobbying by Argentina's military for a small nuclear force intensified Brazilian concerns. Brazilian perceptions of threat had grown during fighting in the Malvinas, although Brasília extended qualified support to Argentina. Like Buenos Aires, Brasília's sense of vulnerability increased as London demonstrated its capability to conduct successful military operations in the South Atlantic. Brasília also felt apprehensive over Buenos Aires' resort to force. The security implications for southern Brazil appeared obvious.[29]

Confusion within its own nuclear program also fed Brazilian insecurities. At the time of Argentina's invasion of the Malvinas Islands, evidence mounted that Brazil's costly and delayed nuclear power generating program was in disarray. The decision to transfer control over most dimensions of this program from a state corporation (NUCLEBRAS), to the National Security Council, suggested heightened concern over the strategic implications of disarray.[30] Military planners feared that if Buenos Aires developed its capability to produce and deliver nuclear weapons, Brazil would become vulnerable to Argentine nuclear blackmail. One obvious option, seeking protection behind Washington's nuclear shield, flew in the face of perceptions that the United States opposed upward international mobility by Brazil. In the aftermath of Argentina's Malvinas defeat, therefore, Brazilian-Argentine competition to master nuclear technology almost erupted into a costly race to build small nuclear forces.

Other pressures brought into play by fighting in the Malvinas throttled the potential for a nuclear arms race. In Argentina, ignominious defeat so discredited the military that civilian leaders forced the generals to call elections and turn power over to a popularly elected president, Raúl Alfonsín. As indicated earlier, Alfonsin gave high priority to reducing the officer corps' capability to intervene in politics. He quickly signaled Brasília that Argentina did not intend to produce nuclear weapons; subsequently, he cut military spending and proposed that avenues of cooperation be explored. Brazil responded by offering to supply Argentina's nuclear generating plant with slightly enriched uranium from its Resende facility. In turn, Argentina promised to provide low and medium enriched uranium for Brazil's Angra 1 nuclear power plant and three research reactors.[31]

Bilateral nuclear accords between Presidents Alfonsín and Sarney did not reduce the determination of Brazil and Argentina's armed forces to develop the capability to produce nuclear weapons. Even while the two leaders were becoming more open about their countries' efforts to develop nuclear plants for generating electricity, the Brazilian and Argentinean armed forces moved ahead with their "parallel" nuclear programs. They also continued with aerospace projects that included ballistic missiles capable of transporting significant payloads up to 2000 miles. In this endeavor Brasilia achieved an advantage. Thus the *Christian Science Monitor* reported that by 1993 "Brazil will be well positioned to break into an exclusive circle of nations that not only possesses nuclear weapons, but are also able to missile-launch them to targets."[32]

Despite persisting military rivalry, relations between South America's two leading states improved during the 1980s. The resolution in 1979 of long-standing disputes over water rights in the La Plata River Basin, and President João Figueiredo's visit to Buenos Aires in May of 1980, ended a decade of growing tension. During July 1986, Presidents Sarney and Alfonsin signed an economic integration compact that exempted over 500 products from import tariffs in trade between the two countries. Barter arrangements were concluded for products ranging from Argentine wheat to Brazilian iron, cacao and coffee. The two presidents also committed their countries to several important joint ventures: in the production of light aircraft, in constructing the Garabí hydroelectric project, in bio-technological research, and in the development of computer software. The automotive industry and industrialized food products were added in a special 1988 agreement. Economic integration as envisioned by Presidents Sarney and Alfonsín marked a watershed in efforts to reduce competition and expand cooperation.

Economic integration, despite Uruguay's incorporation into the agreements, proved a disappointment. While Sarney and Alfonsín envisioned a tripling of bilateral trade within five years, trade between the Brazil and Argentina fell by 7 percent in 1987, the first year of the new arrangement. Joint projects were beset by tangles of red tape and fears of political instability that discouraged long-term commitments by businessmen on both sides. Presidents Collor and Menem moved to restore momentum in July 1990; they formally agreed to create a common market by December 31, 1994. Collor reasoned that with the world fracturing into great trading blocs even Brazil's larger economy needed an expanded regional market if it was to remain internationally competitive.[33]

Democratically elected governments also downplayed the geopolitical significance of competition between Brazil and Argentina for influence in Uruguay, Paraguay and Bolívia. Between 1968 and 1981, geopolitical concerns served to justify covert, and not so covert, intervention in these buffer states. President Garrastazú Médici went so far as to order contingency planning for a Brazilian invasion of Uruguay when leftist Uruguayan political parties with ties to Argentine guerrillas verged on winning the 1971 presidential election. However, victory by pro-Brazilian José María Bordaberry mollified Brasília. The ruling military subsequently forged strong links with Uruguay's armed forces and orchestrated the purchase of land by Brazilians on the Uruguayan side of the Brazil-Uruguay border.

The tide that ended military rule throughout much of South America swept over Uruguay in 1984. José María Sanguienetti became president after winning free and open elections. Sanguienetti, like Sarney and Alfonsín, viewed geopolitically oriented foreign policy as a stimulus to military interference in politics. Sanguienetti intended to restore effective civilian supremacy. Unlike Brazil and Argentina, however, Uruguay's autonomy rests on its ability to maneuver between large and powerful neighbors; it requires that Brazil and Argentina accept Uruguay's status as a buffer. By rejecting incorporation into either a Brazilian or an Argentine sphere, Sanguienetti was left with a single viable option: balancing the influence of one large neighbor with that of the other. His successor, Luís Alberto Lacalle, continued with this strategy and maintained distance from both Brazil and Argentina. In hope of increasing financial autonomy he signed a banking decree with tighter secrecy provisions than those prevailing in Switzerland. Brasília and Buenos Aires, asserting that Lacalle intended to make Uruguay a haven for drug cartel money, turned to Chile as a third partner for their integration scheme.[34]

Paraguay, more primitive and less European than Uruguay, is viewed in Brasilia as a source of threat only insofar as Paraguay becomes a surrogate for Argentine geopolitical ambitions. During the first Peronist era (1946–1955), Brazil worried about the Argentine tilt of Paraguay's General Strossner. During the decade of the Brazilian "economic miracle" (1968–1978), however, Argentina's economy stagnated; Paraguay gravitated toward its Portuguese speaking neighbor. Ties between Paraguay and Brazil intensified during construction of the Itaipú hydroelectric complex in the late 1970s. Brazilian influence became so pervasive that nationalistic Paraguayans feared for their independence, especially as thousands of Brazilians crossed the poorly patrolled frontier to take advantage of lands opened for agriculture as Itaipu neared completion.

Paraguay's General Strossner viewed Brazil's turn away from military rule with apprehension. Added to long standing concerns about Brazilian designs on Paraguay, the prospect of a civilian government in Brasília intensified Strossner's discomfort. Determined to reduce Brazil's influence inside of his country, he ordered the repatriation of illegal Brazilian immigrants.[35] The arrival of peasant refugees in Southern Brazil created a potentially explosive situation for President José Sarney. Sarney responded by focusing on the problems of all landless peasants in the south. In so doing he opted not to champion the presence of Brazilian migrants in Paraguay. Had Sarney chosen this course, he would have increased tensions throughout the region by confirming suspicions that Brazil was orchestrating migration for expansionist purposes. During the remainder of Sarney's term in office, Paraguayan fears of Brazilian expansion continued to dissipate. Following General Strossner's ouster in early 1989, Paraguay's new president, General Andreś Rodríguez, initiated negotiations that would facilitate cooperation with the emerging Brazilian-Argentine common market.

Landlocked Bolívia lies between South America's Southern Cone and Northern Tier. From the perspective of Brazilian national security interests, Bolivian concerns have been more closely linked with the former. While some Brazilian geopoliticians have portrayed Bolívia as Brazil's window to the Pacific, effective Brazilian interest in Bolívia is concentrated in the neighboring lowland province of Santa Cruz. Historic separatist tendencies in Santa Cruz, coupled with Brazilian economic influence and interest in energy reserves, feeds Bolivian concern that its lowland periphery might be swallowed by Brazil. Consequently, Brazilian peasant migrations into Santa Cruz during the late 1970s were viewed by La Paz as especially threatening. Unlike Paraguay, La Paz has not attempted to repatriate illegal Brazilian immigrants. However, the Bolivian government has negotiated accords with Buenos Aires that insure an Argentine economic presence in Santa Cruz.[36]

Brazilian concerns in Bolívia link its historic rivalry with Argentina to balance of power politics on South America's Pacific coast. Bolívia has been embroiled in conflict over territory and influence with Chile and Peru for more than a century; and Bolivian weakness has invited intervention on the part of its neighbors. Brazilian geopoliticians have been quite explicit in pointing out their country's interest in this context. Thus, as early as 1947 Mário Travassos defined the triangle formed in Bolívia by the cities of Cochabamba-Sucre-Santa Cruz de la Sierra as an economic space that, under Brazilian influence, would "neutralize" the La Plata Basin. Subsequent confirmation of the triangle's fabulous Mutun iron ore deposits intensified Brazilian interests. Geopolitical and economic concerns, along with ideologically based apprehensions, underlay Brazilian intervention against Bolívia's General Juan Torres during the early 1970s. Brazil's ruling military viewed Torres as a nationalistic leftist, in the mold of Peru's Juan Velasco and Argentina's Juan Peron. The generals were troubled that Torres' policies would diminish Brazil's South American influence by transforming the Pacific Coast and La Plata Basin balances.

Cooperation (and possibly a formal alliance) between leftist governments in Peru, Bolívia, and Argentina, raised concerns in Brasília that the three would seek to weaken Chile. In this context the Itamaraty feared that these leftist governments might coordinate pressures to recover territories lost by Bolivia and Peru during the War of the Pacific (1878–83). Even before that conflict, Brazil nurtured Chilean strength to prevent Argentina from focusing exclusively on its rivalry with Brazil.[37] Conservation of Chilean strength remains central to Brazil's Southern Cone subregional strategy.

South America's Northern Tier countries were arenas of secondary importance for Brazilian foreign policy during two-thirds of the twentieth century.[38] Demarcation of Colómbia's Letícia corridor in the 1930s settled the last significant boundary dispute directly involving Brazil and a Northern Tier country. At that time, only marginal trade existed between Brazil and the Tier. Vast distances separated the pivotal Northern cities of Caracas, Bogotá, Quito and Lima from Brazil's predominantly coastal population. During the late 1960s, however, concern over threats to Brazilian interests caused Itamaraty strategists to upgrade the importance of relations with their northern neighbors. Threat perception coalesced along several dimensions. First, concern grew that tenuous Brazilian control over the Amazon was being compromised by seemingly successful development projects in Peru, Colómbia and Venezuela. The Amazon Basin's emergence as a conduit for illegal drugs from Andean South America further exacerbated this concern. Second, the Itamaraty feared that a politicized Andean Pact was evolving into a vehicle that would limit Brazilian influence throughout South America. Finally, given the Northern Tier's new importance, Brazil's military paid increasing attention to whether political conditions within Tier countries were ideologically hostile to their national security ideology, and the extent to which those conditions threatened domestic political stability inside of Brazil.

The consequences of populating Brazil's largely vacant Amazonian north have been an important focus of South American geopolitical writings. Applying Mackinder's heartland theory, theorists have identified effective control of the Amazon Basin as the key to dominating South America.[39] Until after the 1964 military revolution, however, the Brazilian government had no significant program to develop the Amazon.

During the 1960s, there was a great deal of loose talk in Western Europe and North America about the Amazon Basin as a global food reserve. In 1972 the Hudson Institute, a Manhattan-based think tank, proposed to flood two-thirds of the Amazon Basin in order to feed the developing world. This came on top of rumors circulating in Brazil that the United States planned to seize a portion of the Amazon for use as a relocation center for rioting urban blacks. While few gave much credence to warnings that United States blacks would be transported to South America, the Hudson Institute plan attracted considerable attention and was widely attacked.[40] It came at a time when President Garrastazú Médici already had decided to experiment with Amazon colonization as a safety valve for starving peasants in the drought-stricken Northeast.

The Brazilian government viewed Amazon colonization as an answer to both internally and externally generated national security concerns. In terms of the former, colonization promised an alternative to traditional southern migration from the northeast. Overpopulation in the slums of southern Brazilian cities, even in 1970, was spawning an unprecedented lawlessness that would intensify as the decade progressed. Brasília feared that if the productive southern cities were convulsed by violence, plans for upward international mobility would go up in smoke. Loss of the Brazilian Amazon to international control, on the other hand, would be an even greater blow to dreams of Brazilian greatness. Consequently, throughout the 1970s Brazil's ruling military assigned Amazon development a high priority.[41]

South America's Northern Tier states greeted the emphasis on Amazon development by Brasilia with apprehension. Although the core territory of each clustered around cities on the Pacific, in the Andes, or along the Caribbean, all possessed lightly populated Amazon peripheries. Northern Tier leaders viewed their own Amazon development efforts as preemptive, certainly not designed to threaten Brazil. Indeed, they feared that if these territories remained undeveloped, they might become neocolonial appendages of their powerful Portuguese-speaking neighbor. In the worst case, events could be set in motion that would create separatist movements desirous of union with Brazil. Spanish South America did not take lightly the threat of a replay of the events by which the nominally Bolivian territory of Acre was swallowed by Brazil in the early twentieth century.

The role of spokesman for Northern Tier concerns fell to Venezuela's Rafael Caldera during the early 1970s. The Caldera government (1969–1974) initially sought close relations with Brazil, viewing its neighbor as an important ally in the struggle to force economic concessions from Washington. Contact with Brazil's military government, however, convinced Caldera and his Foreign Minister that Brazil did indeed have hegemonic aspirations in South America. Consequently, during the second half of his administration Caldera sought to forge a common political front among Andean Pact members for the purpose of confronting Brazil with a roughly equal alliance of Spanish-speaking states.

During the last months of Caldera's government, Venezuelan foreign policy alarmed the Brazilians. President Caldera journeyed to the capital of each Andean Pact country, where he proclaimed the need for South American economic and political cooperation. The Venezuelan leader also visited Argentina. In Buenos Aires he urged President Alejandro Lanusse to explore avenues of economic and foreign policy coordination with the Andean Pact. Subsequently, Caldera met with Brazilian President Garrastazú Médici at the Amazon border town of Santa Elena de Uairen. While the two leaders signed a joint declaration reaffirming the principle of non-intervention, the latter refused to treat the former as a spokesman for other Andean Pact presidents.[42]

The Santa Elena meeting intensified suspicions between Brazil and Venezuela. Caldera and Foreign Minister Arístides Calvani returned to Caracas convinced that Spanish America must display greater unity in the face of increasing Brazilian power. The Itamaraty, on the other hand, came to realize the intensity of Norther Tier concerns about Brazilian development and colonization in the Amazon. Indifference to these concerns was seen as leading to crystallization of an anti-Brazilian alliance.

Finally, the Santa Elena meeting confirmed the Amazon jungle's decline as a physical barrier. Realization of this change increased Brasilia's sensitivity to politics and economics throughout the Northern Tier. Andean Pact integration could not be ignored. The potential for destabilizing fallout into Brazil from guerrilla warfare in Peru and Colómbia, or from coups in Suriname and Guyana, appeared significant. Southern Cone issues were no longer the only essential components of South American regional international relations. For the first time, the Itamaraty perceived the continent's Northern Tier as a zone with the potential to effect vital Brazilian interests.[43]

The International System and Brazilian Regional Aspirations

Following Washington's experience in Vietnam, and Moscow's difficulties in Afghanistan, both superpowers became skeptical about the cost effectiveness of military intervention in the third world. South American states quickly grasped the geopolitical implications of these doubts.[44] Thus, in planning continental strategy, Brasília now acts as if superpower military resources are only marginally relevant. Nevertheless, the power and preferences of the "Northern" industrial states remain capable of constraining important Brazilian plans for South America.

In global military terms, Brazil has remained a third rank power since independence. Traditional Brazilian national security policy emphasized managing the vulnerability of military inferiority. Informal alliance with the United States served as a fundamental management strategy for more than half of the twentieth century. Following the advent of nuclear weapons, when Brazilian vulnerability to first order military power increased, the Brazilian-American alliance was perceived as a reliable nuclear umbrella. However, as the balance of terror between Washington and Moscow crystallized during the 1960s, Brazil came to question whether nuclear weapons could be used in other than an all out exchange between the superpowers. The doubts which arose reduced the ability of threats associated with these weapons to constrain the exercise of Brazilian influence in South America. Following the successful Arab oil embargo of 1973, Brazilians focused increasingly on North-South issues. They found that their sympathies lay predominantly with the "South." Also, the additional influence that southern countries appeared to have gained after oil prices tripled reinforced the new conventional wisdom that the costs to the industrial north of intervening in the third world had become prohibitive. On occasion, Brazilian maritime strategists did warn that Soviet naval bases in Western Africa were potentially threatening; however, the United States-sponsored Treaty of Inter-American Reciprocal Assistance provided a sense of protection. Thus Brazilians were surprised and threatened by Great Britain's military deployment into the South Atlantic in 1982.[45]

The Brazilian armed forces shed few tears when Great Britain destroyed most of Argentina's military inventory, although President Figueiredo transferred some locally manufactured armaments to Argentina. Nevertheless, military operations in the Malvinas alarmed the Brazilian navy. They suggested that Brazil's coast was indefensible against the conventional forces of even a second rank industrial power.[46] In the wake of British success, and given Washington's preference for London over Buenos Aires, the engaging of conventional forces from an industrialized country became a contingency for which the Brazilian military needed to plan. Correspondingly, the probability that Brazilian behavior toward its neighbors might evoke a military response from the North Atlantic again was factored into Brasília's continental strategy. Finally, an ironic by-product of the Malvinas conflict was renewed Brazilian concern over the dangers of a Soviet blue water naval presence in the South Atlantic.

South America, as suggested earlier, always has been less subject to United States influence than the Caribbean Basin. Washington never mounted combat operations on the continent, and United States cultural and economic influence there never approached the level of dominance enjoyed in the Caribbean. On one hand, lesser influence in South America is the consequence of the region's potential to threaten Washington's vital interests appearing smaller than that of the Basin. On the other, it reflects the greater difficulty of projecting North American military, diplomatic and economic power into an arena that is larger, more populous and geographically remote. These constraining factors loom ever larger in the 1990s; Washington increasing retreats from even the pretense of South American hegemony.

Brazil's economy is more competitive than complementary with that of the United States. However, unrestricted economic warfare between the two remains unlikely. The undermining of Brazil's economy would have undesirable political consequences for both the United States and the European Economic Community. Sustained economic crisis in Brazil would create new opportunities for authoritarian leftists or other opponents of liberal democracy. Either would be less favorably inclined toward private enterprise and the multinational corporations than the post 1985 ruling party elites. Were a Marxist-Leninist Brazil to gravitate toward a reinvigorated Soviet Union, South America could be transformed into an arena of intense superpower rivalry. Competition would consume additional resources, and the specter of military confrontation would be ever-present. Brazil, the United States, and the European Economic Community (also, in the wake of Perestroika and Glasnost, perhaps even the Soviet Union) have a common interest in keeping East-West conflict away from South America.

Short of the emergence of an expansionist pro-Soviet regime in Brazil, or in another South American state, declarations that the continent lies within Washington's sphere of influence will remain significant only for jingoistic elements within the United States. Brazil would see continuing pretensions of hegemony from Washington as marginally credible but potentially threatening. During the 1980s, the United States floated only one initiative intended to assert special South American influence. Brazil was promised sophisticated military armaments and training in exchange for joining Argentina, South Africa, and the United States in an anti-Soviet South Atlantic Treaty Organization (SATO). President Figueiredo declined, pointing out that as a multiracial society Brazil could not ally itself with South Africa as long as Pretoria practiced apartheid.[47] Also, the growing availability, after 1985, of petroleum that did not have to traverse the South Atlantic reduced the importance of South Atlantic sea lanes to the United States. Thus South America and the South Atlantic became even more removed from the principle geopolitical arenas of superpower competition.

In spite of South America's geopolitical isolation, insulation from superpower competition remains tenuous. Low intensity conflict in the Caribbean Basin could intensify and spill into South America, especially should hard-line, Marxist-Leninists regain the upper hand in Moscow. The Caribbean and South American state systems overlap; in the former the United States and the Soviet Union remain locked in a contest for influence. Washington struggles to stem the decline of hegemony; Moscow and its Cuban ally assist local forces committed to undermining United States influence. Basin conflict intruded briefly into the South American regional international system during 1982, just prior to the United States invasion of Grenada. At that time, Suriname's Col. Desi Bouterse signaled his interest in an alliance with Grenada, Cuba and Nicaragua. Washington responded by planning military action to topple Bouterse.[48] The plan was never implemented, in large measure because the Itamaraty opposed the presence of United States troops on Brazil's northern frontier.

Colómbia, Venezuela, and Guyana are states that straddle the Caribbean and South American regions. As Caribbean Basin countries, they have been buffeted by competition between the United States and the Soviet Union. The extent to which that competition has been defused by Mikhail Gorbachev's pragmatic policies remains unclear. In any case, domestic politics in the above Caribbean Basin/South American states could bring to power elites interested in probing the benefits of allying with Moscow. Such experimentation would embitter and radicalize domestic politics; it would also inject the Soviet-American rivalry into continental South America. Brasília, unable to match the resources commanded by Washington or Moscow, views situations with the potential of attracting superpower competition to South America as a threat to its continental interests.

Industrial world economic power looms large in Brazilian calculations of potential threat to South American interests. Linkages between multinationals in the United States, Western Europe, Japan and Brazil are of long duration, complex and economically pervasive. Bankers in the United States, Western Europe and Japan control Brazil's $115 billion foreign debt. Among industrial world bankers and corporate leaders, those of the United States remain the most influential.[49] Unilaterally Washington can derail projects intended to link the economies of neighboring South American countries to that of Brazil. President Bush demonstrated this potential during early 1989, while attending the funeral of Emperor Hirohito in Japan. Word leaked to the press that the United States had requested that Japan reconsider funding for a road intended to facilitate timber extraction from the Brazilian Amazon through Peru. Brazilians were enraged. They perceived this as yet another example of interference by the industrial countries, especially the United States, in internal Brazilian affairs.[50]

Two additional potential extra-regional threats to Brazilian influence in South America, each primarily economic, merit special mention. The first involves rising protectionism in the North Atlantic. Again, the United States appears as Brazil's major protagonist. In May of 1989, Washington named Brazil as one of the countries liable to trade reprisals under the United States Omnibus Trade Act of 1988. It was alleged that Brazil was engaging in such "unfair" practices as quantitative import restrictions, import bans and restrictive licensing. The citation brought United States economic power to bear for the purpose of making trade between the two countries more favorable to the United States. As Washington was Brasília's most important foreign market, Brazilian leaders correctly viewed this action as a serious threat to their country's international trading position. It threatened not only Brazil's existing capability to sell abroad, but also Brazilian access to advanced technology and foreign capital.[51] Denial of technology and investment from the industrialized world would severely damage Brazil's long-term international economic competitiveness, including its status as a major arms supplier. This ever-present contingency fostered high levels of insecurity among Brazilian elites.

The other economic lever viewed as capable of influencing Brazilian continental policy derives from vulnerability to foreign energy imports. At the time of the 1973 oil embargo, Brazil imported 80 % of its petroleum. While Brazil has reduced its dependence, foreign energy remains critical.[52] Fallout from the first oil shock forced Brazil to scale back programs in the Amazon intended to gain influence with its Northern Tier neighbors. There is no evidence that any petroleum supplier consciously used its economic leverage for this purpose. Retrenchment was mandated by the steep rise in energy prices that drove the costs of Amazon Basin development beyond what had been envisioned in the late 1960s. Since the middle 1980s, energy dependence has been manageable. Nevertheless, United States willingness to employ military power, as in its enforcement of the 1990 United Nations boycott against trade with Iraq (the most important foreign source of petroleum for Brazil), keeps levels of insecurity high. It reminds Brazilians of their vulnerabilities, and of Washington's propensity to act in support of its interests with little regard for those of others.

Brazilian Strategic Responses

Brazilian elites look upon South America as their country's most critical geopolitical arena. Army General Staff strategist, Col. Geraldo Lesbat, summarized this perspective when he described the continent as "the only region in which Brazil has strategic interests because its diplomatic presence is complemented by a strategic presence."[53] However, as discussed earlier, Brazil's capability to influence its neighbors was constrained historically by Washington's pretensions of hegemony over the entire Western Hemisphere. Brazilian strategy for dealing with these pretensions throughout most of the twentieth century involved the pursuit of special benefits from Washington by adopting the role of junior South

American ally. In spite of several assertive interludes, this policy prevailed until the presidency of Jimmy Carter. Brazilian feelings that President Carter was insensitive in applying human rights policies to them, and his perceived hostility toward Brazilian desires for upward international mobility, made junior partner status unacceptable to nationalistic Brazilians.

The Carter presidency crystallized a consensus in Brasilia to abandon automatic support for Washington in the competition between "East" and "West." While some issue specific backing for Washington continued into the Reagan administration, Brasília inclined toward neutrality. At the same time, Brazilian determination to reduce United States influence throughout South America became more pronounced. In November 1985, speaking before the Council on Foreign Relations in New York, President José Sarney took aim at the political and economic policies of the United States. He was thinking about the United States when he identified the underlying causes of world insecurity as deriving "from the attempt at international crystallization of areas of influence" as well as from the "prevailing unfair structures of the international and financial system which lead to economic and social crisis." President Fernando Collor, although less open in his declarations, appears to share this point of view.[54]

Brazilians see South America as moving into their economic orbit, but resistant for the present to a *Pax Brasiliana*. They see Brazil's growing influence as resting on foundations built by the 1970s economic miracle. Difficulties during the 1980s are perceived as a temporary setback. Confidence remains that possession of the world's eighth largest market economy ensures that in South America the twenty first century belongs to Brazil. The longer current trends continue, the stronger Brazilian leaders see their position becoming. Thus they have favored subtle and largely non-military responses when they perceived threats to Brazil's South American interests. Here five strategies were especially important: (1) accommodation, (2) deterrence through defense, (3) deterrence through allying, (4) state strengthening, and (5) counterthreats.

Accommodation

Accommodations are one sided concessions undertaken to preserve influence within a subordinate state system, or to win regional clients. Accommodations seek to avoid the increases in resource allocation mandated by deterrence strategies. Traditionally, they have underlain important Brazilian policies for managing threats to its South American position. During the first half of the twentieth century, for example, neighboring Argentina surpassed Brazil in wealth and technological sophistication. Deterring Argentina by military means alone became prohibitively costly. It would have strained Brazil's economy and demanded sacrifices that the elite was unwilling to make. Consequently, until the Second World War, Brazil's Argentina policy focused on maintaining a ceremonious friendship; also, in order to play for time, Brazil conceded to Buenos Aires the coveted South American leadership role.[55]

In the early 1940s, as Argentina's military forged links with fascist Germany and Italy, Brazil concluded that ceremonious friendship was providing little security. In response, Brazilian President Getúlio Vargas turned to an alliance with the United States. During the 1950s, especially in economic matters, Brazil pursued accommodation with Washington. In return, Brazilian leaders anticipated that foreign investment and technology from the United States and its allies would enable their country to become the most powerful state in South America. Disillusionment with this strategy led to an "independent" foreign policy during the early 1960s.

The leftists who crafted Brazil's independent foreign policy also sought to shift wealth and power away from their country's traditional elites. Had their plans been implemented, Brazil's historic ruling class would have been forced to share power with the popular sectors. However, conservative revolution in 1964 ended the redistributive experiment. The United States supported the revolution, and Brazil's military government returned to playing the role of Washington's junior ally in South America. President Lyndon Johnson's continuing support for the ruling military discouraged domestic opponents and decreased the willingness of democratic forces in neighboring states to assist them.[56] For more than two decades, the cost to the generals of maintaining a "national security state" remained well within the acceptable range.

The Brazilian military regime initially pursued geopolitical goals with an eye toward minimizing friction with the United States. While perceiving United States influence in South America to be in decline, Brasília recognized that Washington retained immense influence, especially in the Northern Tier. Even after the earlier mentioned difficulties with President Carter, Brazil's military presidents practiced accommodation whenever possible.

Post 1985 civilian presidents, like their predecessors, sometimes accommodated to Washington's geopolitical world view in hopes of gaining compensatory economic benefits. They calculated that sustained Brazilian influence in South America mandated industrial and technological growth. Thus, in a September 1986 address to the United States congress, President José Sarney asked that his country's manufactured goods be granted greater access to the North American market. In addition, he called for increased technology transfer and for more favorable terms in repaying

Brazil's foreign debt. President Sarney's pleas fell on deaf ears; economic relations between the two countries remained strained throughout his presidency.

In June 1990, several months after taking office. Fernando Collor de Mello experimented with economic accommodation toward the United States. He announced a New Industrial Policy (NIP) that promised elimination of many trade barriers that had long troubled both the United States government and foreign investors in Brazil. Specifically, Collor proposed to eliminate all quota-based import restrictions over the course of four years, reduce tariffs and market reservation barriers and revise the code of Industrial Property to improve patent protection for many products, including pharmaceuticals. He hoped that the United States would respond with measures that would restore momentum to Brazil's economy. Most important, Collor wanted assistance in managing the foreign debt. He also sought redesignation by the Bush administration of 90 Brazilian imports for duty free treatment under the Generalized System of Preferences (GSP).

Washington responded quickly to Collor's initiative. Not only were the 90 products restored to duty free status, President Bush included Brazil in his "Enterprise for the Americas" plan with its promise of debt relief for $12 billion in outstanding U.S. government credits to Latin American countries. On the other hand, despite praise for the NIP from the international financial community, it remained unclear whether the commercial banks holding $68 billion in Brazilian foreign debt would ease the burden of its servicing.[57]

Military security issues, from time to time, also were treated as part of accommodation. An unenthusiastic President Sarney had joined with the United States in a Memorandum of Understanding on military affairs (MOU).[58] During negotiations (1983–84), the Reagan administration hinted that refusal to sign could interrupt the transfer of coveted technology, particularly to Brazil's burgeoning arms industry. Also, at that time some Brazilian military strategists remained apprehensive about Soviet intentions and capabilities in the South Atlantic. Civilian leaders were less concerned. The professional foreign service argued that Brazil's preference for a South Atlantic Peace Zone would deter the Soviet Union; and that it was not in Moscow's interest for Brazil to become more dependent on the Washington. However, the military position that the MOU represented a Brazilian hedge in case the Soviet Union deployed blue water naval units to its Angolan bases carried the day.[59]

Brazil also has responded with accommodation to perceptions of threat when it was the stronger party, although minimizing Washington's presence on the continent remained an overriding consideration. Thus, at the time of the United States invasion of Grenada (1982), Brazil extended significant development aid to Suriname's Bouterse government. This assistance continued throughout the 1980s, despite Brazil's considerable economic difficulties. Geopolitical considerations underlay the Suriname policy. Suriname borders on the Brazilian Amazon, and in 1982 the United States stood poised to invade Suriname. Col. Bouterse saved his government by acquiescing to Washington's demand that he repatriate his Cuban advisors and technicians. Without them, however, order and critical services began to breakdown. President João Figeuiredo, seeking to stabilize the situation and to avoid an increase in United States influence along Brazil's northern frontier, offered economic aid, technicians and political advisors.[60] Relieved of the necessity to further overextend its limited assistance capability, Washington gladly accepted this replacement of the Cubans by Brazilians. Brasília breathed a sigh of relief at having deflected an intrusion of superpower rivalry into northern South America.

In no situation has accommodation been more important in defusing a potential threat to Brazil's South American strategy than in the Itamaraty's use of the Amazon Pact to undermine the potential of the Andean Pact to operate as a counterweight to Brazil. Ever since Venezuela floated the idea of using the Andean Pact to unify Spanish South America, Brazilian foreign policy has given high priority to undermining Andean political integration. One immediate Brazilian response was to negotiate bilateral trade treaties with its northern neighbors. Another involved persuading the Andean and other northern tier states to join Brazil in a regional Amazon Pact.

Brazil hosted the initial Preparatory Meeting for the Amazon Pact in November 1977. Subsequently, several Spanish-speaking countries declared the Brazilian draft to be expansionistic.[61] They objected to its inclusion of the term "physical integration" and rejected economic integration within an Amazon framework on the grounds that it already was occurring through the Andean Pact. Determined to obtain agreement on even a minimalist Trans-Amazon institution, Brazil accommodated. The treaty signed on July 2, 1978 excluded all mention of physical integration, avoided commitment to economic integration and declared that the Amazon Pact would not interfere with national programs or planned bilateral or trilateral agreements.

What the Amazon Pact signatories found acceptable was to create a forum in which South America's Amazon countries would be able to discuss their common Amazon programs. All eight members—Brazil, Bolívia, Peru, Ecuador, Colômbia, Venezuela, Guyana and Suriname—pledged support for the sovereignty of each over their Amazon territories. The Amazon Pact treaty contained only a vague promise to create opportunities for coordinating its signatories' regional development plans.

While this was less than Brazil hoped for, Brazilian negotiators viewed the Pact's creation positively. Its very existence undermined the cassandras who warned of Brazil's intention to dominate South America. Also, it served as a symbol of South American unity against possible threats to Amazon Basin resources from outside of the continent.

Long-standing suspicions among the signatories over each other's designs on the Amazon resulted in the Pact lying dormant for more than a decade. Not until May of 1989 did the signatory countries hold the first of what were once envisioned as annual summits. The May 1989 summit was a response to increased criticism from the North Atlantic countries over what they portrayed as wanton destruction of the Amazon rainforest. Brazil took the lead in convening a summit that would reaffirm the sovereignty of Pact members over their Amazon territories. The resulting Declaration of Amazona called upon the international community to convert its concern over rainforest exploitation to cooperation on financial and technical levels. It rejected all attempts "to impose conditionalities on the granting of resources," and emphasized that the eight countries had a sovereign right to use the region's resources. With this declaration the thrust of Brazil's Amazon policy shifted to defense through allying.[62]

Deterrence Through Allying and Defense

Allying involves cooperative relationships with other states; defense focuses on reconfiguring resources that are predominately military. Both are short term responses, intended to make the best use of existing resources or position. Several Brazilian responses to perceived threats discussed in the context of accommodation—the Amazon Pact and military cooperation with Washington—also are relevant for deterrence through allying. Other Brazilian allying strategies involve the La Plata Basin Pact, transnational development projects and military sales to neighboring states. This diversity suggests a need to deal individually with the political, economic and military dimensions of deterrence through allying.

Politically, the allying response depends on strength derived from diplomatic coordination to deter. Brazilian diplomacy has joined with other southern countries for the purpose of refracting the industrial world's influence, especially in Latin America. Thus Brazil became part of the Contadora Support Group, an auxiliary to the four-country Caribbean consortium (Contadora Group) that sought a peaceful solution to conflict in Central America. However, the diversity of interests among southern states, even in the Caribbean Basin, has limited the effectiveness of deterrence through allying. Even when regional unity was achieved, as with South American opposition to London's reconquest of the

Malvinas Islands, the United States and other industrial powers were only marginally responsive.[63] The Malvinas affair proved surprising for Brazil; it demonstrated that despite the bitterness of defeat in Vietnam, industrial countries remained willing and able to project military power into the third world.

Brasília has mixed politics and economics in bilateral treaties intended to create and strengthen a community of interests with neighboring states. Ranging eclectically, these treaties encompass cooperation in constructing hydroelectric dams (Paraguay, Uruguay and Venezuela), aircraft (Argentina), gas pipelines (Bolívia), aluminum processing (Guyana) and exploration for petroleum (Peru).[64] Usually, they have allowed Brazil to become the dominant partner.

Brazil also relies on multilateral economic ties to strengthen cooperation and defuse historic rivalries. This includes membership in the Latin American Integration Association (ALADI), the Latin American Economic System (SELA), La Plata Basin Pact, and the Amazon Pact. Traditionally, however, more than 85 percent of Brazil's foreign trade has been with states outside of South America. Between 1980 and 1986, the proportion of Brazil's world trade accounted for by all South American countries fell from 15 percent to 9 percent.[65] Brazilian leaders saw this as incompatible with their continental aspirations. Thus, as discussed earlier, President Sarney negotiated an economic compact with Argentina's Raúl Alfonsín that exempted over 500 products from import tariffs in trade between the two countries. The two presidents envisioned a tripling of bilateral trade within five years. They also saw this compact as the nucleus for a South American economic community.

President Sarney's economic efforts at defense through allying were stillborn. The strains of servicing a large foreign debt, and of the economic turbulence accompanying presidential elections, staggered the overextended Brazilian and Argentine economies. Trade between the two countries fell by 7 percent in 1987, the first year of the new arrangement. Subsequently, Sarney and Alfonsín were so consumed by efforts to politically and economically stabilize their countries that the problem of making economic integration work was ignored.[66] Still the dream of a Southern Cone common market persisted. As discussed earlier, Presidents Collor and Menem signed a protocol advancing establishment of the market to December 31, 1994. The failure of the 1986 accords to produce significant benefits, however, cautions that the rhetoric of economic integration will have to be accompanied by innovative policies and institutions if the Southern Cone Common Market is to become a vehicle for effective Brazilian leadership.

Debt management strategies provide another opportunity for Brasilía to lead. Although Brazil's total foreign debt is the highest in the third world ($115 billion at the beginning of 1990), the economy's size and large productive capacity makes indebtedness more manageable for Brazil than for other South American countries. These smaller but more burdened states often follow Brazil's example in negotiating with their creditors. For the purposes of regional leadership, it is important that Brazil's debt management strategy appear attractive to its neighbors. Civilian and military Brazilian governments have cultivated the image of being economically responsible while remaining aggressively nationalistic. In 1988, this yielded substantial rewards. Brazil was one of the few debtor countries to reach a new rescheduling agreement with the banks. The Brazilian government presented its success as a precedent that would benefit all South American debtors.[67] Unfortunately hyperflation during the transition to the Collor government undermined Brazil's ability to fulfill its contractual obligations.

The military dimensions of deterrence by allying are interwoven with deterrence through defense. Like other South American countries between 1947 and 1982, Brazil viewed the Inter-American Treaty of Reciprocal Assistance (TIAR) as protection from threats originating outside of the Western Hemisphere. However, all of South America downgraded the importance of TIAR when the United States declared it inapplicable to the Malvinas Islands conflict. Since then Brazil has viewed TIAR as having limited relevance for its continental security.

Brazil continues to participate in such TIAR activities as officer exchanges and the annual UNITAS naval exercises.[68] Participation provides the opportunity to keep abreast of developments in other military establishments, including that of the United States. Thus UNITAS serves a different purpose for Brazil than for Washington. The Pentagon continues to worry about the possible expansion of Moscow's naval presence into the South Atlantic. For Brazil, this threat has become sufficiently remote that even the Brazilian military opposes allowing the United States its long-sought base for naval aircraft on Trindade Island, some 1,200 kilometers off the Brazilian coast of South America.

Brazil's indigenous arms industry has increased its capability to deter through defense; however, this has been predominantly a state strengthening response. Deterrence through defense, as suggested above, centers on reconfiguring available resources. Between 1964 and 1986 Brazil reconfigured its armed forces along the northern and southern frontiers. Changes in the north began soon after the military came to power. The Army created Amazon Battalions and stationed them along critical frontier avenues of approach and configured special engineer companies to construct public works. The Navy strengthened its river patrol units and moved its Amazon headquarters from coastal Belém to Manaus. These changes signaled the military's determination to control and develop Brazil's vast and sparsely populated heartland.[69]

President José Sarney shared the military's perception that a lightly controlled Amazon Basin invited interference from the North Atlantic and provided a sanctuary for insurgents and migrants from neighboring states. Thus, in June of 1985, Sarney initiated the Calha Norte (Northern Basin) project. While Calha Norte envisioned assistance to indigenous populations and intensification of bilateral economic relations with neighboring countries, its principal thrust was to increase the number of military personnel along the northern border. The project envisioned new military detachments stretching along the 6,500 kilometers of frontier. Additional rapid deployment battalions were to supplement the single existent battalion stationed in Boa Vista, capital of the territory of Rorãima. Other special forces would be stationed in the north; on the Venezuelan frontier, on the border between Venezuela and Colómbia, on the border of Venezuela and Guyana, in the state of Pará adjacent to Suriname, and in the territory of Amapá alongside French Guiana. During early 1987, while visiting sites for the new bases, Brazil's military commander of the Amazon described them as "necessary" because of international interest in taking over the area.[70]

Military redeployment in the south occurred in 1982, during the Malvinas crisis. Additional conventional units were dispatched to the states of Rio Grande do Sul, Santa Catarina and Paraná, along the Argentine border. They reinforced the elite Third Army which traditionally defended Southern Brazil. This deployment responded to apprehensions spawned by Argentina's unpredictable actions in its conflict with Great Britain. It was intended as a warning against Argentine adventurism and to calm the fears of Brazilians living in the south.

To summarize, the government often responded with deterrence through allying and defense when experiencing threats to Brazilian interests in South America. In calibrating responses, it confronted unpleasant realities derived from limited Brazilian power. Time and time again, Brazil lacked the resources and influence necessary for playing out the roles envisioned in geopolitical dreams of South American *grandeza*. Consequently, policy makers also pursued a longer range strategy, state strengthening.

State Strengthening

State strengthening has been a core Brazilian security response since independence. Historically, Brazilian conventional wisdom held that if its half continent could be held together until it could be developed, Brazil would surpass Argentina and dominate South America. Playing for time in which to undertake state strengthening development has been central for the pursuit of *grandeza*. Since 1960 Brazil has emphasized four state strengthening responses. They are: (1) crafting a central political infrastructure capable of administering the state and ensuring domestic tranquility; (2) facilitating technically advanced industrialization; (3) pursuing military self-sufficiency and modernization, and; (4) internal colonization.

The first response derives from fears that regional rivalries could fragment Brazil, and that subversive nationals might subordinate the state to international interests. In 1964 these fears were intense. Before and after the military's seizure of power, Brazil teetered on the brink of civil war. The new government moved to consolidate power by purging influential leftists whose flirtation with international communism they perceived as having endangered Brazil's opportunity for *grandeza*. High priority was given to strengthening the central government. This led the generals to create and manage a country-wide network of centers from which intelligence operatives could observe and neutralize opposition. Outrage at the abuses spawned by this system eventually damaged the military's legitimacy. During the government of General João Figueiredo (1979–1985), this network was purged of its most onerous components. Its power and privileges were further reduced in the first months of the Collor government.

Brazil's post 1985 civilian politicians have shared power with the generals. The two groups have similar regional and domestic security goals. Since returning to the barracks, military spokesmen have proclaimed that modernizing combat capability has first priority.[71] Nevertheless, the generals retain immense political influence. During 1987 they prevented the constitutional convention from establishing a parliamentary system; also, their opinion on when and how to use armed force against striking workers remains decisive. In addition, the military retains control of selected bureaucracies, oversaw the anarchic 1989 presidential campaign, and guaranteed the passing of executive power as stipulated by the new constitution.[72]

State strengthening industrialization is not an innovation of the generals. It became official policy during the governments of Getúlio Vargas (1930–1945, 1951–1954). In 1945, after having dispatched a Brazilian division to Italy for use against the Axis, President Vargas expected repayment from the victorious Allies. He understood that Brazil had been promised the capital and technology necessary to attain South American preeminence. After the war, more investment did flow into Brazil than into Argentina; however, it failed to meet expectations. Disillusioned, Vargas inaugurated a policy of import substitution during his second presidency. He sought a domestic productive capacity that would replace many imported manufactured products; especially steel, aluminum and sophisticated consumer goods. Vargas also speeded the search for internal energy sources and established the state petroleum corporation, Petrobrás. Until the 1964 revolution, subsequent governments followed this lead. They also envisioned an "inward oriented" growth that would reduce Brazilian dependence on the North Atlantic.

Inward oriented industrial substitution reached its limits during the early 1960s, as Brazilian balance of payments deficits grew ever larger. However, post 1964 military governments also viewed industrial development as the economic key to upward international mobility. Thus they explored strategies for stimulating growth that bypassed balance of payments obstacles. Their preferred option was to attract investment by the multinationals; for a brief period, Brazil became the favored recipient of capitalism's efforts to shift labor intensive manufacturing to the developing world. Another strategy of the military involved borrowing abroad to expand the number of state enterprises. Nuclear power, hydroelectric dam construction and transportation infrastructure were prominent beneficiaries of this approach. It led to the controversial "economic miracle" during which Brazilian per-capita growth led the developing world. The 1973 rise in petroleum prices ended the "miracle;" further escalation in 1979 set the stage for economic stagnation.[73]

After 1979, the military feared a reversal of the economic advances on which *grandeza* depended. Decline would discredit their political stewardship. Consequently, against the advice of Brazil's most prominent economists, President Figueiredo chose to stimulate the economy in 1980 and 1981. His decision reignited inflation, pushed the foreign debt to more than $100 billion and led to the recession of 1982–84. In light of this legacy, even given widespread antipathy toward the multinationals and international banks, the transitional Sarney government could not pursue the inward oriented industrialization favored by Getúlio Vargas.[74] Neither can its elected successor.

One dimension of industrialization, Brazil's creation of a domestic arms industry, merits special mention. During the presidencies of Emílio Garrastazu Médici (1968–1973) and Ernesto Geisel (1973–1979), Brazil began moving in directions that were to make her the world's sixth largest producer of military equipment. The United States unintentionally stimulated this development when, after Brazil refused to sign the nuclear non-proliferation treaty, President Jimmy Carter applied the Glenn-Symington Amendment restrictions on security assistance and arms sales. Brazilian foreign and national security strategists viewed this decision as an attempt by Washington to freeze the international balance of power. Expansion of the domestic arms industry became a crusade to reduce dependence. Within a decade Brazil boasted the largest and most sophisticated military-industrial complex in the Third World. Capabilities include the manufacture of light tanks, military engineering equipment, frigates, river patrol boats, jet fighters and heavy rockets.[75] Increasing reliance on domestically manufactured equipment pervades Brazil's FT-90 strategic plan for military modernization.

Brazil also discovered that the export of weapons could be a significant source of foreign exchange. Thus many Brazilian weapons systems have been exported before being deployed to Brazilian maneuver units. Thirty two countries on four continents presently use Brazilian armaments; in 1984, foreign billings exceeded two billion dollars.[76] The Middle East (especially Iraq) and North Africa have been the largest markets for Brazilian arms, and South American countries also make significant purchases. Sales include jet aircraft, navy patrol boats, armored vehicles, and assorted small arms. The professionalism of Brazilian advisors, and the high quality simplicity of its weapons, have increased Brazilian influence throughout South America and the Third World.

Development of the interior is Brazil's final state strengthening response. Beginning with General Costa e Silva (1967–1969), successive presidents supported colonization and integration of the Amazon and Southwest regions into Brazil's effective national territory. Access into these regions was provided by such newly constructed highways as the Transamazon, the Northern Perimeter Road, and RB364. Brasília foresaw agricultural villages and regional marketing centers at regular intervals along the new roads. However, development was undertaken with inadequate information about jungle ecosystems and the viability of marketing arrangements for supplying consumption centers in the south. Many agricultural settlements were abandoned, and large sections of the Transamazon Highway and Northern Perimeter Road fell into ruin.

There have been successes. RB-364, the 1,100 mile highway linking Cuiabá in Matto Grosso, Porto Velho in Rondônia, and Rio Branco in Acre, has evolved into an important artery stimulating Amazon development. The city of Manaus prospers from its status as a Free Trade Zone. Also, south of Belém, the exploitation of Carajás Mountain iron ore, manganese, copper, aluminum and tin is creating a major mining center. In the Carajás Mountains, as in Rondônia and Manaus, the highways of the Amazon are filling up once disquietingly empty expanses.[77]

Fears that foreigners, especially in the North Atlantic, coveted Brazil's lightly held interior were an early stimulus for internal colonization efforts. Military hopes that settlers from the poverty-stricken Northeast could transform frontier territories into rich agricultural lands was another. In addition, channeling migration from the Northeast to the Northern (Amazon) and Western frontiers was viewed as a means of slowing movement from the Northeast into the urban concentrations ringing Rio de Janeiro, São Paulo and Belo Horizonte. During the 1970s new growth poles did blossom in the Amazon and the West; however, their impact on the rate of slum formation in the cities of Brazil's prosperous South and Southeast regions was marginal.

Counterthreats

Counterthreats promise positive or negative actions against the intimidating source. Post World War II gains in power and influence enabled Brasília to experiment with strategies of positive counterthreat. Thus, in 1972 Brazil's Third Army staged maneuvers along the Uruguayan border. They were intended to communicate the potentially serious consequences for Uruguay of electing a leftist president. Ten years later, President João Figueiredo deployed additional jungle warfare units to northern Rorãima, along the Venezuelan border. Caracas had just completed military maneuvers near the Guyana-Venezuela frontier that Brasília viewed as threatening to Guyana, its sometime ally. President Figueiredo intended deployment as a signal of his displeasure to Venezuela. Any use of force to press Venezuela's claim to Guyana's Essequibo territory would place Caracas on a collision course with Brasília. Brazil's nuclear programs illuminate another dimension of positive counterthreat. Despite agreements between Presidents Sarney and Alfonsín to share nuclear power generation technology, Brazil continues with its militarized "parallel" nuclear programs. Technical capability to build and deliver nuclear weapons increases. This communicates that Brazil will counter Argentina's acquisition of nuclear weapons by developing its own capability.

Brazilian military governments between 1966 and 1985 pursued counterthreats against South American revolutionaries by sharing counterinsurgency technology. President José Sarney continued this policy. Brazilian advisors remained with embattled Colombian counterinsurgency units throughout his presidency. This signaled revolutionaries that civilian governments would not abandon force in opposing low intensity conflict when Brazil's frontiers appeared to be threatened. Sarney also was signaling solidarity with his neighbors in their battle against leftist insurgency.[78]

Finally, Brazil has not resorted to negative counterthreats in dealing with its South American neighbors. As defined in the overview chapter, negative counterthreats seek to communicate that the hegemonic power will not act in a manner that a bargainer state government desires or values. Only in the southern buffer states has Brazilian power been sufficient so that negative counterthreats might have stood any chance of causing its neighbors to act as otherwise they would not.

Conclusions

The closing decade of the twentieth century is a time of transition for South American regional politics. United States hegemony is history; Brazilian influence grows. Yet Brasília is far from being a regional hegemon. Argentina remains a formidable rival; sometimes friendly, occasionally antagonistic, but always resentful at having been surpassed by its Portuguese-speaking neighbor. Andean South America harbors lingering doubts about Brazilian expansionism; Brasília, in turn, is influenced by events in the Caribbean Basin and South Atlantic over which it has little control. Also, Brazil's economy is shackled by foreign debt and dependence on North Atlantic and Japanese technology. Thus powerful forces constrain Brazil's ability to influence its neighbors.

Domestic political strain deriving from economic struggle undermines Brazil's capability to become more influential in South American. Derivative class warfare complicates agreement on democratic rules of the game. A majority of Brazilians remain poor and clamor for a better life. During the military regime, the national executive suppressed their demands on the pretext of stimulating capital formation and facilitating exports. Now the survival of elected governments turns on appearing responsive to popular aspirations. However, these aspirations generate demands that greatly exceed the productive capability of Brazil's economy. Only a dramatic revival of Brazilian economic growth can significantly reduce the importance of class struggle as a barrier to democratic consolidation.

Investment destined for military industries is an obvious source of resources for the poor. While the military-industrial complex is always scrutinized by elected politicians, arms production does provide jobs and foreign exchange. Even populist and leftist political parties hesitate to weaken this profitable activity in which so much has been invested. Therefore, as long as Brazilian arms producers remain internationally competitive, Brazil's military seems likely to have access to the equipment and technology which comprise one essential ingredient of regional power projection.

The form in which Brazil's party system coalesces will strongly influence the course of political development. Institutionalization of a radical leftist majority; for example, expansion of Lula's Workers' Party (Partido dos Trabalhadores-PT) or the Brazilian Communist Party; would undermine the legitimacy of civilian political authority with industrialists and the military. An elected president's loss of party support in congress might also lead to a regime threatening crisis. Thus renewed intervention by the armed forces remains possible. Intervention would not necessarily lead to civil war. The military retains sufficient coherence and power to reimpose its will, at least for a time. This suggests that persisting political and economic strains are unlikely to alter the intention of government to increase Brazil's South American influence. They will, however, effect capability.

The policies and fate of the Collor government are shaping the perceptions of Brazil that will carry into the twenty first century. If Brazilian power appears as a force that creates wealth and reduces North Atlantic influence in South America, Brazil's neighbors will accept and possibly welcome Brazilian leadership. On the other hand, if Brasília seems to be imposing hegemony, her neighbors will cooperate to constrain Brazilian power and influence. Buenos Aires is especially pivotal in this regard. Prior to the resurrection of Argentine and Brazilian democracy, geopolitical thinking stressing rivalry and the incompatibility of Brazilian and Argentine interests pervaded foreign policy making in both countries. In contrast, the transitional presidencies of José Sarney and Raúl Alfonsín emphasized cooperation and the existence of common interests. Elements favoring the cooperative and competitive perspectives remain strategically positioned in both countries.

Should Brazilian-Argentine economic cooperation founder, and Buenos Aires remain mired in the difficulties that accompanied transition to the Menem government, Argentine frustration will intensify. Disappointment could lead to the testing of nuclear weapons or toward renewed efforts to assemble an anti-Brazilian alliance among South American states. The former would create a regional "balance of terror" in which both Argentina and Brazil become less secure. The latter would isolate Brazil where she aspires to lead. Thus Brazil's popularly elected government, unless confronted by a hostile and nuclear armed Argentina, has little choice but to continue emphasizing cooperative ventures and downplaying geopolitical rivalry. Continuity also prevails in the north. The Itamaraty remains committed to strengthening bilateral arrangements with Northern Tier countries and nurtures cooperation inside of the Amazon Pact. To summarize, Brazilian South American policy in the early 1990s appears to be playing for time. It signals that despite difficulties during the 1980s, Brazil views South American regional politics as favoring its historic aspirations.

International forces beyond South America are perceived as threatening Brazilian continental ambitions to the extent that they undermine capability to project power regionally. Most critically, Brazil remains dependent. Its economic health is determined by four critical factors; rate of domestic capital formation, ability to export, the flow of foreign technology, and access to foreign investment. OECD country international capabilities in these areas give the North Atlantic and Japan power to stimulate or deflate Brazilian economic growth. Thus Brazil's ability to lead is constrained when leadership involves challenging the industrialized world. On the other hand, the size of Brazil's economy and market yield significant leverage in negotiations to attract capital, modify the terms of debt repayment, and lower tariff barriers to Brazilian products. This leverage reinforces Brasilia's central position in South American regional economic bargaining with the OECD countries.

Political and military events outside of South America seem increasingly less likely to effect Brazil's position in the region. However, lingering United States pretensions of Western Hemisphere hegemony remain as a sometimes important constraint. Another concern for Brasília is the possibility of an alliance between one of its neighbors and an extra-continental state. Either involves the projecting of power into South America by an external actor with the potential to counterbalance or overwhelm the assets on which Brazilian leadership is based. The situation with the United States appears manageable because of Washington's declining capability, except in special circumstances like the 1990 Iraq invasion of Kuwait, to deploy conventional military power into the Third World. On the other hand, Washington's nuclear deterrent would be useful to Brasília should supporters of Perestroika and Glasnost be replaced by a leadership desirous of developing a Soviet naval presence in the South Atlantic; or, in the unlikely event that Moscow transformed economic ties with Buenos Aires into a comprehensive political-military arrangement.

To conclude, the growth of Brazil's influence in South America, despite economic difficulties, adds to the conviction of Brazilians that their country can manage threats to its leadership aspirations from outside of the continent. In turn, the consolidation of South American leadership is viewed as a critical stepping stone to increased status elsewhere.

Notes

1. Wayne Selcher, ed., *Brazil in the International System: The Rise of a Middle Power* (Boulder, CO: Westview Press, 1981).

2. The best known work by a Brazilian geopolitician is Golbery do Couto e Silva, *Geopolítica do Brasil,* (Rio de Janeiro: Editorial José Olympio, 1967). Also see, Wayne A. Selcher, "The National Security Doctrine and Policies of the Brazilian Government," *Parameters,* VII, No. 1 (1977), pp. 10–42, and Jack Child, "Geopolitical Thinking in Latin America," *Latin American Research Review,* 14 (Summer 1979), pp. 89–111.

3. "Trade barriers and Argentine-Brazilian deal revive integration debate," *Latin American Economic Report* (May 31, 1988), p. 1; David J. Myers, "Brazil" and Daniel Poneman, "Argentina" in Jed C. Snyder and Samuel F. Wells, Jr., eds., *Limiting Nuclear Proliferation* (Cambridge, MA: Ballinger Publishing Co., 1985).

4. Brazilian Amazon development is analyzed in Martin T. Katzman, "The Brazilian Frontier in Comparative Perspective," *Comparative Studies in Society and History*, Vol. 17, No. 3 (1975), pp. 278–281. The Manaus Summit and other delays by Spanish speaking signatories in implementing the Amazon Treaty is discussed in *Brazil Report* (London, U.K.), June 1, 1989, p. 4; *La Nación* (Buenos Aires), July 5, 1978, p. 8; and, *Jornal do Brasil* (Rio de Janeiro), March 15, 1979, p. 19.

5. The classic presentation of the moderator thesis is Alfred Stepan, *The Military in Politics: Changing Patterns in Brazil* (Princeton: Princeton University Press, 1973).

6. Alfred Stepan, "The New Professionalism of Internal Warfare and Military Role Expansion," in Alfred Stepan, ed., *Authoritarian Brazil* (New Haven: Yale University Press, 1973), pp. 58–60. The best introduction to Brazilian corporatism is Philippe C. Schmitter, *Interest Conflict and Political Change in Brazil* (Stanford, CA: Stanford University Press, 1971).

7. The *Manual Básico of Brazil's Escola Superior de Guerra* (Rio de Janeiro: ESG, 1976), pp. 415–437 analyzes military thought concerning the national security implications of internal political conflict. For an excellent overview in English of the national security doctrine see Maria Helena Moreira Alves, *State and Opposition in Military Brazil* (Austin, TX: University of Texas Press, 1985), pp. 1–27. Also see David J. Myers, "Brazilian National Security Policy" in Edward A. Kolodziej and Robert E. Harkavy, eds., *Security Policy of Developing Countries* (Lexington, MA: D.C. Heath and Company, 1982), pp. 53–72.

8. Ibid.

9. The higher level of give and take characteristic of the constitutional convention is reported in the July 7, 1988 issue of *Brazil Report*. Also see, "Another round for Chaves: Sarney Calls for Broad Political Pact" in *Brazil Report*, May 31, 1985, p. 3.

10. During 1985 and 1986, discussion in the Brazilian press of what had taken place during twenty-one years of military rule was most notable by its absence.

11. Edmar L. Bacha and Pedro S. Malan, "Brazil's Debt: From Miracle to the Fund," in Alfred Stepan, ed., *Democratizing Brazil* (New York: Oxford University Press, 1989), pp. 120–142; *Latin American Economic Report*, January 31, 1988, April 30, 1989, and April 30, 1989; also, see Alan Riding, "Brazil To Suspend Interest Payment To Foreign Banks," *New York Times*, February 20, 1987 and Roger Cohen, "Brazil's President Isn't Likely to Impose Austerity Needed to Get Through Crisis," *Wall Street Journal*, February 25, 1987.

12. A useful overview of strategic regional concepts is John Child, "Strategic Concepts of Latin America: An Update," *Inter American Economic Affairs*, 34 (Summer, 1980), pp. 61–82. Cf. Harold Molineu, *U.S. Policy Toward Latin America: From Regionalism to Globalism* (Boulder, CO: Westview Press, 1986), Part I "Region Specific Approaches."

13. David Ronfeldt, *Geopolitics, Security, and U.S. Strategy in the Caribbean Basin* (Santa Monica, RAND R-2997-AF/RC, November, 1983).

14. John Child, *Geopolitics and Conflict Within South America: Quarrels Among Neighbors* (New York: Praeger Publishers, 1985), p. 35.

15. E. Bradford Burns, *Nationalism in Brazil: A Historical Survey* (New York: Fredrick Praeger, 1968), especially chapter 1.

16. E. Bradford Burns, *A History of Brazil* (New York: Columbia University Press, 1970), chapter 3.

17. Frank D. McCann, "Brazilian Foreign Relations in the Twentieth Century" in Selcher, ed. *Brazil in the International. . . .*, pp. 2–3.

18. Stanley E. Hilton, *Brazil and the Great Powers, 1930–1939: The Politics of Trade Rivalry* (Austin, TX: University of Texas Press, 1975) and Frank D. McCann, *The Brazilian-American Alliance, 1937–1945* (Princeton, NJ: Princeton University Press, 1973).

19. Albert Fishlow, "Flying Down to Rio: Perspectives on U.S.-Brazilian Relations," *Foreign Affairs*, Vol. 57, No. 2 (Winter 1978–79), pp. 387–394.

20. McCann, "Brazilian Foreign Relations in the Twentieth Century," in Selcher, ed. p. 3. and Mars, "Brazilian National Security Policy," pp. 52–60.

21. Stanley E. Hilton, "The Argentine Factor in Twentieth-Century Brazilian Foreign Policy Strategy," *Political Science Quarterly* Vol. 100, No. 1 (Spring 1985), pp. 27–52 and J. Moneta and Rolf Wichmann, "Brazil and the Southern Cone" in Selcher, ed., pp. 143–181.

22. Wayne A. Selcher, "Brazil-Argentine Relations in the 1980s: From Rivalry to Friendly Competition," *Journal of Interamerican Studies and World Affairs*, Vol. 27, No. 2 (Summer 1985), pp. 25–53.

23. Robert D. Bond, "Venezuela, Brazil and the Amazon Basin," *Orbis*, Vol 2. No. 3 (Fall 1978), pp. 635–650.

24. Olive Holmes, "Peron's 'Greater Argentina and the United States," *Foreign Policy Reports* No. 24 (December 1, 1946), pp. 158–71. By the same author see "Argentina and the Dream of Southern Union" in *Political, Economic and Social Problems of the Latin American Nations of Southern South America* (Austin: University of Texas—Institute of Latin American Studies, 1949), pp. 43–57.

25. Jonathan Kandell, "What Crisis? Argentines, As Usual, See Country Averting Plunge Into Poverty," *Wall Street Journal*, June 22, 1989; Selcher, "Brazil-Argentine Relations in the 1980s: . . . . ," pp. 29–35.

26. David J. Myers, "Brazil: Reluctant Pursuit of the Nuclear Option" *Orbis* (Winter 1984), pp. 881–911.

27. Argentina's revised nuclear plan was the subject of El Poder Ejecutivo Nacional, *Decreto No. 302*. In January 1979 CNEA chief, Castro Madero, announced that Argentina would begin to produce plutonium in a new, expanded reprocessing facility, *Nucleonics Week* No.4 (March 3, 1983), reported the planned capacity of this plant at around ten to fifteen kilograms of plutonium output per year.

28. Myers, "Brazil: Reluctant Pursuit of the Nuclear Option" pp. 906–907.

29. See the editorial "Crisis e Pânico" in *Jornal do Brasil* (Rio de Janeiro), April 14, 1983. Cf. the interview by Navy Minister, Admiral Maximiano da Fonseca in *O Estado de São Paulo* (São Paulo), June 18, 1983.

30. *Brazil Report*, February 11, 1983, pp. 6–7. Also, Cynthia Ann Watson, "Will Argentina Go to the Bomb After the Falklands?," *Inter American Economic Affairs*, 37 (Spring 1984), pp. 63–80.

31. See *Latin American Newsletters: special reports,* "Latin America's nuclear development programmes today," April-June 1985, pp. 2–5; *Latin American Weekly Report,* (London, U.K.), July 31, 1986, p. 8; August 2, 1990, pp. 10–11.

32. William A. Preston, "Brazil's nuclear secret," *Christian Science Monitor,* November 16, 1987; also see, John H. Williams, "Brazil Reaches for the Stars," *The Retired Officer* (March 1989), pp. 25–30, and *Brazil Report,* June 1, 1989, "Increased nuclear fuel output justified," pp. 4–5.

33. Thomas G. Sanders, "Brazilian Geopolitics: Securing the South and North," Universities Field Staff International, Inc., *Latin America* (1987/No.23), pp. 3–5; *Latin American Weekly Report,* September 3, 1987; *Southern Cone Report,* August 9, 1990, pp. 4–5; and *Latin American Economic Report,* May 31, 1989, p. 3.

34. Gustavo V. Dans, "Brazil: The Continental Strategy," *NACLA Latin America & Empire Report,* Vol. IX., No. 4. (May–June 1975), pp. 15–20; *Latin American Weekly Report,* July 31, 1986, p. 9; August 2, 1990, p. 8; and Philip Kelly, "Geopolitical Tension Areas in South America: The Question of Brazilian Territorial Expansion," in Robert Biles, ed., *Inter-American Relations: The Latin American Perspective* (Boulder: Lynne Rienner Publishers: 1989), pp. 190–209.

35. See Gerd Kohlhepp, "Colonización y desarrollo dependiente en el oriente paraguayano," *Revista Geografica* (Mexico), No. 99 (January-June 1984), pp. 5–33. Also, Cilia Schulman, "Land Invasion Threat Rises in Parana; Pact in Puerto Alegre" as reported in *O Estado de São Paulo,* July 13, 1985, translated in JPRS 1985–070–35. Also, *Latin American Economic Report,* May 31, 1989, p. 12.

36. *Latin American Weekly Report,* WR–22–86, June 6, 1986, p. 12.

37. Bernardo Quagliotti de Bellis, "The La Plata Basin in the Geopolitics of the Southern Cone," in Philip Kelley and Jack Child, eds., *Geopolitics of the Southern Cone and Antarctica* (Boulder, CO: Lynn Rienner, 1989), pp. 136–137; Carlos J. Moneta and Rold Wichmann, "Brazil and the Southern Cone" in Selcher, ed., *Brazil in the International System: . . . . ,* pp. 164–170.

38. See the "Documento Cavagnari," *Brazil Report,* April 20, 1984, p. 4.

39. Child, *Geopolitics and Conflict Within South America: Quarrels Among Neighbors,* p. 36.

40. This plan is set forth in Robert Panero, *The Amazon: A Catalytic Approach to Development* (Croton-on-Hudson, NY: Hudson Institute, 1972).

41. Alan Riding, "Brazil to Set Up Bases on Borders," *New York Times* (November 1, 1986). Also, Nigel J.H. Smith, *Rainforest Corridors* (Berkeley and Los Angeles: University of California Press, 1982), pp. 9–17 and "The Most Ambitious Settlement Project Ever Attempted" *Christian Science Monitor* (January 4, 1982), p. 22. In addition, Frances M. Foland, "A Profile of Amazona—Its Possibilities for Development," *Journal of Interamerican Studies and World Affairs,* Vol. 13, No. 1 (January 1971), pp. 62–77.

42. Charles D. Ameringer, "Foreign Policy of Democratic Venezuela" in John D. Martz and David J. Myers, eds., *Venezuela: The Democratic Experience,* 2nd. ed. (New York: Praeger, 1986) pp. 416–417. Also see Lewis A. Tambs, "Geopolitics of the Amazon," in Charles Wagley, ed., *Man in the Amazon* (Gainsville, FL: University of Florida Press, 1974). pp. 74–77.

43. General Golbery do Couto e Silva, *Conjuntura política nacional, o poder do executivo e geopolítica do Brasil* (Rio de Janeiro: Jose Olympio, 1981), pp. 131–133; Thomas G. Sanders, "Brazilian Geopolitics: Securing the South and North," pp. 5, 6; and, Martin T. Katzman, *Cities and Frontiers in Brazil: Regional Economic Development* (Cambridge, MA: Harvard University Press, 1977).

44. Alexandre de S.C. Barros, "The Diplomacy of National Security: South American International Relations in a Defrosting World" in Ronald Hellman and H. Jon Rosenbaum, eds., *Latin America: The Search for a New International Order* (Beverly Hills: Sage Publications, 1975), pp. 131–150.

45. Robert J. Branco, *The United States and Brazil* (Washington, D.C.: National Defense University Press, 1984), pp. 75–80, and Clifford A. Kiracofe, Jr. "Brazil: An Emerging Strategic Factor In The South Atlantic" in *Journal of Social and Political Studies*, Vol. 5 (Fall 1980), pp. 199–229. Also, Dov S. Zakheim, "The South Atlantic: Evaluating the Lessons," in James Brown and William P. Snyder, eds., *The Regionalization of Warfare* (New Brunswick: Transaction Books, 1985), pp. 37–53.

46. Rear Admiral Armando Amorim Ferreira Vidigal, "Marinha Não Está Equipada Para Defender Toda A Costa," *O Globo* (Rio de Janeiro), May 29, 1982, p. 25.

47. Alexandre de Souza Costa Barros, "Defense and Security Issues: Implications for the New Atlantic Triangle" in Wolf Grabendorff and Riorden Roett, eds., *Latin America, Western Europe and the U.S.: Reevaluating the Atlantic Triangle* (New York: Praeger, 1985), pp. 166–176. Paul Horowitz and Holly Sklar, "The South Atlantic Triangle" in *NACLA Report On The Americas*, Vol. XVI, No. 3 (May–June 1982), pp. 5–8 and "La Armada Brasileña" in *Technologia Militar* (September 1985), pp. 16–24.

48. *Folha de São Paulo* (São Paulo), December 24, 1982 in FBIS, December 28, 1982; *O Estado de São Paulo*, February 4, 1983 in FBIS, February 10, 1983; *O Estado de São Paulo*, April 20, 1983 in FBIS, April 25, 1983.

49. Brazilian Mission to the United Nations, "Address by His Excellency José Sarney, President of the Federative Republic to Brazil, to the Council on Foreign Relations" (New York: Mimeographed, September 24, 1985), p. 9; *New York Times*, July 16, 1990, D-9.

50. Leonard Silk, "Brazil's Battle Against Banks," *New York Times*, March 4, 1987, p. D-2, and Fishlow, p. 397.

51. For example, the area of supercomputing is discussed in John Markoff and Stephen Engleberg, "U.S. Debates Selling Supercomputers to 3 Nations," *New York Times*, August 20, 1989; also, see *Latin American Weekly Report*, June 8, 1989, pp. 4–5; *Statistical Yearbook for Latin America-1984* (New York: Economic Commission for Latin America and the Caribbean, 1985), p. 201 and Thomas E. Weil, *Area Handbook for Brazil* (Washington D.C. DA PAM 550-20, 1975), pp. 322- 323.

52. R. Harvey, "Running Out of Oil," *Economist*, 260 (July 31, 1976) pp. 11–12 and "Good results in onshore drilling" in *Brazil Report*, April 25, 1986, p. 3.

53. These remarks were made during the 1984 symposium on the "Military and Society in Brazil" at Campinas University (UNICAMP). The widely circulated

Documento Cavagnari also emerged from this symposium. Excerpts from the "Documento Cavagnari" appear in *Brazil Report,* April 20, 1984, p. 4.

54. Brazilian Mission to the United Nations, "Address by His Excellency José Sarney. . . . ," p. 9; *New York Times,* July 16, 1990.

55. Hilton, "The Argentine Factor in Twentieth-Century Brazilian Foreign Policy Strategy," pp. 35–41.

56. Riordan Roett, "Brazil and the United States: Beyond the Debt Crisis," *Journal of Interamerican Studies and World Affairs,* Vol. 27, No. 1 (February 1985), pp. 1–15.

57. *The Brazilians* (New York), August 1990, p. 5; *New York Times,* September 11, 1986, p. D-2, September 12, 1986, p. A-3. Useful background information appears in Albert Fishlow, "The United States and Brazil: The Case of the Missing Relationship," *Foreign Affairs* (Spring 1982), pp. 904–923.

58. "Cooperation with US gets under way, but there are still some Misgivings on the 'MOU,'" *Latin America Weekly Report,* March 2, 1984, p. 11 and July 10, 1986, p. 12.

59. "O Choque da Guerra," *Veja,* (Rio de Janeiro) June 30, 1982, p. 74, and Paul Horowitz and Holly Sklar, "South Atlantic Triangle" in *NACLA report on the Americas,* Vol. XVI, No. 3 (May–June 1982), pp. 2–40, and Margaret Daly Hayes, "Brazil and the South Atlantic: Changing Perspectives on an Emerging Issue" (Washington, D.C.: SAIS Occasional Papers Series: mimeographed, 1982). Finally, Brazil called for a South Atlantic Peace Zone (SAPZ) resolution at the 41st meeting of the United Nations General Assembly.

60. *Latin America Weekly Report,* June 3, 1983, p. 12, June 10, 1983, p. 12 and November 11, 1983, p. 3.

61. *O Estado de São Paulo,* March 26, 1978, March 28, 1978 and April 4, 1978. Also, Elizabeth Ferris, "The Andean Pact and the Amazon Treaty," *Journal of Interamerican Studies and World Affairs,* Vol. 23, No. 2 (May 1981), pp.147–175. The text of the treaty appears in "Treaty for Amazon Cooperation," *International Legal Materials,* Vol. XVIII, No. 5 (September 1978), pp. 1045–53.

62. *Brazil Report,* June 1, 1989, p. 4.

63. Gabriel Marchella, *The Malvinas/Falklands War of 1982: Lessons for the United States and Latin America* (Carlisle Barracks, PA: Strategic Studies Institute of the U.S. Army War College, 1983), pp. 9–24, and Dov S. Zakheim, "The South Atlantic: Evaluating the Lessons," in James Brown and William P. Snyder, eds., *The Regionalization of Warfare* (New Brunswick: Transaction Books, 1985), pp. 37–54.

64. A sampling of these treaties are discussed in the following; *Brazil Report,* July 10, 1986, *Gazeta Mercantil* (São Paulo), July 30, 1981, *Brazil Report,* September 13, 1985, and *Latin America Weekly Report,* June 6, 1986, p. 12. Also see, Peter Ford, "Argentina Reshapes Foreign Policy," *Christian Science Monitor,* July 25, 1989.

65. Compiled from the International Monetary Fund, *Direction of Trade Statistics Yearbook-1987.*

66. Juan de Onis, "Brazil on the Tightrope Toward Democracy," *Foreign Affairs,* 68 (4), Fall 1989, pp. 130–132; also, Peter Flynn, "Brazil and inflation: a threat to democracy," *Third World Quarterly* (July 1989), pp. 50–70.

67. *Latin American special reports,* "External debt round-up" (June 1989), pp. 1–4; Art Pine, "Brazil Creditor Nations Agree to Start Talks Without IMF Pact," *Wall Street Journal,* December 19, 1986.

68. Monica Hirst, "The United States and Middle Powers in Latin America: Mexico and Brazil," in Robert Wesson and Heraldo Muños eds. *Latin American Views of U.S. Policy* (New York: Praeger, 1986), pp. 100–101 and *FBIS,* November 29, 1983.

69. Brazilian Army Public Relations Center, *Sentinals of the Amazon* (Rio de Janeiro: Honor of the National Chamber of Industry to the Brazilian Army, n.d.), pp. 63.

70. "Governo tem plano de ocupação militar da fronteira norte," *Folha de São Paulo* (São Paulo), October 31, 1986; and "Arnd defende o Calha Norte," *Jornal do Brasil* (Rio de Janeiro), January 24, 1987.

71. Controversy in anticipation of the 1987 constitutional convention, over the Armed Forces' claim to a political role, is recounted in *Brazil Report,* July 5, 1985, p. 3 and September 18, 1986. p. 5.

72. *Maria do Carmo Campello de Souza,* "The Brazilian 'New Republic': Under the 'Sword of Damocles,'" in Stepan, ed. *Democratizing Brazil,* pp. 351–383.

73. Warner Baer and Carlos Von Doellinger, "Determinants of Brazil's Foreign Economic Policy," in Joseph Grunwald, ed., *Latin America and World Economy: A Changing International Order (Beverly Hills: Sage: 1978), pp. 147–160.*

74. *Bolivar Lamounier and Alkimar R. Moura, "Economic Policy and Political Opening in Brazil" in Jonathan Hartlyn and Samuel A. Morley, eds., Latin American Political Economy: Financial Crisis and Political Change* (Boulder, CO: Westview Press, 1986), pp. 165–195.

75. John Hoyt Williams, "Brazil Reaches for the Stars," *The Retired Officer* (March 1989), pp. 25–27 and "Aerospace Booms in Brazil," *Air Force Magazine* (June 1985), pp. 112–118; Alexandre de S.C. Barros, "Brazil" in James Everett Katz, ed. *Arms Production in Developing Countries* (Lexington Books: Toronto, 1984), pp. 73–88.

76. *Latin America Weekly Report,* June 26, 1986, p. 12, April 25, 1986, p. 4; *Brazil Report,* January 6, 1984, p. 5. The best analysis of the Brazilian arms industry is Patrice Franko-Jones, "Public Private Partnership: Lessons from the Brazilian Armaments Industry," *Journal of Interamerican Studies and World Affairs,* 29 (4), Winter 1987–1988, pp. 41–68. U.S. Army sources maintain that Brazil's defense industries provide 10 percent of their production lines to the military and 90 percent for export. The profit/loss orientation of Brazilian military industries causes them to seek high technology systems in order to remain competitive globally. In years when export orders are plentiful, they may be unable or unwilling to meet the low to middle level technology requirements of their own armed forces.

77. NACLA, "War in the Amazon," *Report on the Americas,* XXII, 1 (May 1989), pp. 13–39; also see, Helio Teixeira, "The Amazon Boom," *World Press Review* (October 1982), pp. 30–33; *Andean Group Report,* September 4, 1986, p. 11; and Alan Riding, "Brazil Takes a Look Inside Itself, Hoping to Fill in the Blanks," *New York Times,* Section E, November 9, 1986.

78. Sanders, p. 73; *Brazil Report,* March 14, 1986, p. 5.

8

Nigeria in West Africa

Anthony V. Williams

Nigerians justifiably see themselves as the giants of Africa. It is the one element they are agreed upon. And they are now seeking to use their oil and emerging industrial muscle to influence opinion and guide events. The December (1980) Lagos summit to determine the future of Chad showed how once the Nigerian elephant had taken a position, the rest of Africa had to acquiesce and swallow its bile. To that extent Lagos is already a point of political pilgrimage for the smaller, weaker, more dependent African heads of state. In a good week, African ministers flock to this capital like compliant sheep seeking their shepherd Shagari's blessing, and return home strengthened by promises of Nigerian support and more importantly, large gifts of money. . . . It is Nigeria's foreign policy, more than that of any other black African country, that most determines Africa's collective future. . . . The threshold upon which Nigeria is today poised is then not just a watershed in its pursuit of democracy, but also a potential turning point in its international outlook and position. . . . Nigeria is determined not just to play its natural leadership role in Africa, but also to build upon it.[1]

On any measure of objective factors such as population, military power, economic strength and the like, Nigeria should dominate its West African region. As the above quote indicates, it could lay claim to primacy in all of black Africa. Indeed, some Nigerians have done so.[2] Yet, while it has taken leading roles on several occasions, the reality is a great deal less impressive than the potential. The list of countervailing pressures is formidable. They are not, as is the case with some other aspiring hegemons, a function so much of outside forces but of internal problems which have bedevilled the country since before independence in 1960, and which show little signs of being alleviated in the foreseeable future.

The nature of these threats to hegemony and the responses of the several post-independence governments to them are detailed below. But the fate of the several heads of state is a good introduction to what follows. Sir Abubakar Tafawa Balewa, the first Prime Minister and the de facto head of state, the Sardauna of Sokoto, both moslems from the north of the country, were assassinated in an eastern led military coup in January, 1966. The eastern and Christian General Aguiyi Ironsi who took over the reigns of government after that coup was assassinated in a countercoup lead by northerners in July of that same year. The compromise leader chosen after that coup, Yakubu Gowon, a Christian from the ethnically and religiously mixed middle belt, lasted through an ensuing civil war and several turbulent years afterwards, but was deposed in a bloodless military coup in July, 1975. In 1976, his successor, the northern moslem General Murtala Muhammed was assassinated in an unsuccessful military-civilian coup attempt in which persons from several regions were implicated. The second in command of the Army, General Olosegun Obasanjo from the western region, reluctantly accepted power and managed to stay on and peacefully turn over the reins of government to a newly elected civilian regime in 1979. President Shehu Shagari from the north survived through a first government term but was deposed a few months into his second by a military coup on December 31, 1983. General Muhammad Buhari from the northern moslem area lasted until July, 1985, when he was deposed in another military coup. The current head of state (as of September, 1989), General Ibrahim Babangida, a moslem from the middle belt, has survived several coup attempts as did his predecessors. He anticipates turning over power to a new civilian regime in 1992. That only one government successfully and willingly handed over power between 1960 and the present is perhaps the most basic indiction of the substantial level of internal problems faced by the country.

Major Elements of the Regional System

The players in the regional system are depicted in their several roles in Table 8.1. At various earlier times, several of the entries would be modified. For instance, in the first years after independence there was considerable suspicion of Ghana which was thought to be interested in destabilizing the country. Britain has been viewed with suspicion several times as has the United States, particularly over its actions vis-a-vis Angola, Zimbabwe and South Africa. And France, with its support for the losing side in Nigeria's Civil War and continuing interventions in its former colonies, has been an object of dislike and fear. But the current perceptions are probably accurately portrayed below.

With regard to its neighbors, Nigerian power far outweighs that of the other West African states, separately or in combination. The data on conventional economic and demographic variables are one indicator of this (Table 8.1) as is the military balance (Table 8.2). Only the far off threat from South Africa and the still distant but closer possibility of subversion from Libya represent credible potential threats from other African states acting without external support. Foreseeable projections of economic, demographic, and military power among African states in the region will not change that situation.

Threat Perception and Response

Akindele and Bassey in a review of the All-Nigerian Conference on Foreign Policy held at Kuru in April, 1986[3] summarized the (then at least) official views of threats to the country. The head of state, President Babangida was noted to have equated national interest to national security interests. The then Foreign Minister, Bolaji Akinyemi, elaborated in two ways. First, he linked national security to economic growth and development which in turn was dependent on political stability. He then laid out the following list of threats:

1. impotence in industrial and technical development;
2. foreign military bases and presence in West-Central Africa;
3. regional military destabilization;
4. irredentist and ethnic conflicts that spill over boundaries;
5. subversion;
6. dependence on foreign military supplies;
7. apartheid;
8. proliferation of nuclear weapons, and
9. socio-economic insecurity of the Nigerian masses.

Given Bolaji's perspective, it is not surprising that five of his nine perceived threats are unambiguously external. What is telling is that the rest are purely or partly internal and that the most important is included among them. Factually, Nigeria has had several border conflicts with neighbors over the years. During its Civil War, between 1967 and 1970, Nigeria also experienced big and superpower involvement. But the former colonial powers had officially left the scene before or shortly after Nigeria's independence and have since posed no overt threats; neither have the superpowers. Domestic problems, on the other hand, have bid fair to destroy the nation several times. Indeed, Alhaji Isa Kaita's phrase, "Only God can save Nigeria,"[4] and the many comments on the unregenerate characteristics of "the Nigerian"[5] reflect a widespread despair over the chances for forming a united, strong, progressive and peaceful country. The discussion of threats and responses that follows is based on the assumption that before Nigeria can play a role as a regional

Table 8.1 The West African Regional System

State	Population (millions) (1990)	Area (sq. km) (thousands)	GDP (US$/billions) (1990)*	Regional Type
Nigeria	118.8	923.8	30.0*	Aspiring Hegemon
Benin	4.7	112.6	1.7	Peripheral Dependent
Cameroon	11.1	475.4	12.9	Bargainer
Chad	5.1	1,284.0	0.9	Peripheral Dependent
Ghana	15.2	238.5	5.2*	Bargainer
Ivory Coast	12.5	322.5	10.0	Bargainer
Liberia	2.6	111.4	1.0	Peripheral Dependent
Niger	8.0	1,266.5	2.4	Peripheral Dependent
Togo	3.7	56.8	1.4	Peripheral Dependent
Libya	4.2	1,759.5	20.0*	External Challenger
South Africa	39.6	1,221.1	83.5	External Challenger
Zaire	36.6	2,345.4	6.5	External Challenger

*GNP

SOURCE: U.S. Central Intelligence Agency, The World Fact Book-1990 (Washington, DC: CR WF 90001, 1990).

TABLE 8.2 Comparative Strength: Nigeria and Its Neighbors

State	Total Armed Forces	Army Regular (Reserve)	Air Force Regular (Reserve)	Navy (Regular) (Reserve)	Coastline (km)
Nigeria	94,500	80,000 (10,000)	9,500	5,000 (2,000)	853
Benin	3,160	3,000 (1,650)	60 (1,000)	100	121
Cameroon	7,650	6,000	350	700	402
Chad	17,500	17,500	------	100	None
Ghana	10,600	9,000	1,000	800 (200)	539
Ivory Coast	13,220	11,650 (15,000)	930	690	515
Liberia	6,750	6,300	Army Aviation	450	579
Niger	3,290	3,150	140	------	None
Togo	4,355	4,000	250	105	56
Libya	76,000	60,000	9,000	7,000	1,770
South Africa	105,000	75,000 (130,000)	13,000 (25,000)	9,000 (2,000)	2,954
Zaire	26,000	22,000	2,500	1,500	37

SOURCE: "The Balance of Military Power," Military Technology, XIII (1,1989).

hegemon it has to overcome or finesse the several sources of internal discontent. Instances of external threats real and perceived and responses to them are described after analysis of the former.

Sources of Internal Threat Perceptions

There are a number of interacting sources of internal threats to the stability and survival of the state. First, in common with many states but in a more virulent fashion, Nigeria is bedevilled with ethnic tensions. These have played themselves out in several arenas, ranging from political party and coalitions instability, changes in the internal geography of the country, an inability to conduct national censuses, and a civil war. Compounding the ethnic tension is a previously submerged but recently explosive confrontation between Moslems and Christians. Exacerbating these is an economy that does not have the wherewithal to satisfy the material needs and expectations of the people. Within this melange, the several elite groups in society have played roles that often exacerbated problems.

Ethnic Tensions

Like most African states, Nigeria is not a nation[6] but a construct imposed by colonialism. From footholds on the coast, the British pushed inland, subduing various groups until they established boundaries with other colonizing powers.[7] The resulting envelope enclosed between 200 and 250 cultures of varying size and cohesion. The major groups are the Yoruba in the southwest, the Ibos in the east central area and the Hausa-Fulani in the north. The middle belt of the country is a classical "shatterbelt" of smaller groups but there are significant minorities in the south and southeast also.[8] The lack of a recent census (see below) makes accurate estimates of the relative sizes impossible, but one local guess[9] is that the ratio among the three major groups, Hausa-Fulani, Yoruba, and Ibos approximates 45:30:25. The first and last of these have considerable influence on other cultures in their immediate vicinities. Whatever the actual numbers are, the generally accepted situation is that the north dominates but needs support from one of the other two major groups to govern. So delicate coalition building has been an art form since the British left in 1960. Given the instability of triads and the perception that when one group gains another loses[10] in an economy of scarcity, the likelihood of political instability is great.

The Politics of Coalition

Prior to independence, the British ruled the southern part of the country directly. The north was a classic situation of British indirect rule.[11] The southern areas with a longer period of contact with western political structures adapted their forms and at least nominally their ideologies. Thus, the agitation for independence which picked up speed rapidly after World War II was largely southern driven. Indeed, when it became apparent in the 1950s that the British were going to leave, northern leaders favored delay to get their house in order and avoid potential submission to the more "sophisticated" southerners.[12] On independence day, 1 October, 1960 the country took shape as a Westminster democracy with a northern-eastern coalition. True to their fashion of the time, the British, in conjunction with the regional leaders, established a federal structure. However, the central government coalition broke down in a couple of years and the Northerners cast around for a western partner, selecting one of the two contending groups among the Yoruba. The loser, Chief Awolowo, protested and was accused of disloyalty and treason. Not for the last time, a major politician was removed from politics and arrested. The repercussions also played out in charges of election fraud, a contentious pair of censuses (see below), strikes, intimidation and thuggery. This led to the overthrow of the first civilian regime in January, 1966.[13]

The overthrow was, of course, led by the Army. In their contacts with the peoples of Nigeria, the British found the Ibos of the east easier to deal with than the westerners. They also proved more eager to adopt Christianity and to westernize. At independence, the Ibos exercised disproportionate influence in the civil service and dominated the upper ranks of the military forces. That situation had changed but little five years later. Thus, the first military government was led by an Ibo General, Aguiyi Ironsi. Unfortunately, the precipitating coup was a bloody one. In particular, the northern Prime Minister and the leading religious leader of the north were killed. This, coupled with a proposal by Ironsi that Nigeria be converted to a unitary state led to a countercoup of northern officers in July of 1966. The northern elite, and to a lesser extent their western allies, could not stand the possibility of an Ibo-dominated country with no regional autonomy.[14] Ironsi was assassinated and Ibos in the north were subjected to a series of attacks and massacres; they streamed back to their eastern homeland.

The Army command was faced by major problems. During the period between the first and second coups there were cries in the north for secession. The reaction of the Ibos during and after their exodus was the same. The two major responses were: (1) to select as head of the new military government a Christian from a northern dominated part of the middle belt, Yakubu Gowon, and (2) to set in motion discussion of a new geographic arrangement with more states. It was hoped that subdivision of the major northern, western, and eastern "blocs" would lessen fears that any one of them would be in a position to dominate the Nigerian state. The north and west were amenable but the Ibos, psychologically shattered by their recent experiences, saw the plans as an attempt to destroy their cohesion. In mid-1967 they seceded and the Civil War of 1967–1970 began. The Federal Military Government established a 12 state federation, and by 1970 had won the war.[15]

The major contribution of General Gowon to Nigeria was his role in healing the wounds of that war. By 1974, a fortuitous rise in oil prices and increasing petroleum production had enabled reconstruction to occur faster than anyone anticipated. On the surface the country looked ready to resume its role as Black Africa's most influential power. But the problems that had surfaced immediately following independence had not been solved. The Gowon government was overthrown in a bloodless coup, in 1975. Failure can be traced to its indecisiveness over creating new states, inability to successfully conduct the 1973 census, cancellation of a plan to restore civilian government in 1976, corruption and ineptness.[16]

A reforming military regime led by General Murtala Muhammad, a northern officer, took over. It proceeded to dismiss and put on trial the worse malefactors of the Gowon regime. Muhammad also set up a constitutional commission of professors and eminent citizens to decide the shape of a future Nigeria, started a real push for a new national capital that would serve as a unifying symbol for the country, and established a new 19 state federation based on citizen inputs. Unfortunately, he was assassinated in early 1976. His successor, western General Olatunji Obasanjo was next in the line of Army command; reluctantly, he accepted the post of Head of State. Aided by the same feelings that eased Lyndon Johnson's access to the Presidency after the Kennedy assassination and by buoyant oil revenues, Obasanjo presided over the most peaceful period in Nigeria's post-independence history. He handed over power to a civilian regime in 1979.[17]

The constitution drafting committee was a carefully balanced group of academics, jurists, and political figures. It conscientiously sought public comment on what the future shape of the country should be. In a remarkably short time, a staged return to civilian rule was implemented via local, then state, then national elections. The form of government blended British and U.S. structures, with the latter predominant. A core idea was to hand over more powers to the states. Ultimate fiscal authority remained at the center as well as the usual defence and foreign policy roles at that level, under a President who would also serve as head of state of a unicameral federation.

In an attempt to defuse the tensions caused in the first civilian regime by regionally based parties and the subsequent coalition building tensions, provisions were established to encourage nationally based parties. One such provision was a rule that the winning party had to have a majority or plurality in at least two thirds of the 19 states of the federation.[18]

While the drafting was good and the intents laudable, reality fell somewhat short of hopes. A northern President was elected from a party that had adherents in the north, middle belt and the old east. So coalition building took place before the election rather than after. This, of and by itself was not at all incompatible with what the constitution drafting group had intended. But the two thirds rule proved contentious. In the end it was decided by the Supreme Court that the 12 states, taken by the winning coalition, constituted two thirds. The manner in which the decision was made led to vociferous charges of fraud, intimidation and corruption. Of the latter, there was certainly a surplus. At a time when the gap between Nigeria's needs and resources was widening, stimulated by falls in oil prices, the civilian regime proceeded to make up for lost time. Commenting on the level of corruption, a Nigerian friend told me, "The military was dipping money out with tablespoons and the civilians are bringing buckets."

Shagari stayed through his first term and won re-election in 1983. The accounts of corruption were coupled with those of intimidation and vote-buying even more blatant than in 1979. Despite some laudable comments in the foreign press during this period, especially over economic and foreign policy initiatives, the levels of dissatisfaction reached boiling point. The military stepped in again in a coup that took place 31 December, 1983 a few months into the new term.[19]

Two military regimes have succeeded the second republic. The first, led by General Muhamad Buhari from far north Dauru in what is now Katsina Province was initially popular. It soon forfeited its legitimacy by engaging in ethnic politics and repression against critics, notably students and journalists.[20] To be fair, the new government felt it had to try to root out obvious corruption quickly although it came to power in a period of worsening economic stress. But its heavy handedness led not only to fears of northern moslem domination but also of state fascism.[21]

The upshot was a widely popular coup in May 1985 by General Ibrahim Babangida. From the moslem town of Bida in the middle belt state of Niger, Babangida has, since taking power kept people guessing about his goals and programs.[22] For example, people initially wondered whether his name indicated he was a Yoruba, which he is not. Then speculation increased about his religious views since he had married a Christian woman from the east whose name was converted over the years from the traditional Mary to the moslem variant.[23]

Politically, Babangida has succeeded in finessing situations in a variety of ways. These range from various statements on what should be done to politicians implicated in the scandals of the old regime to plans for returning to civilian rule. Harsh punishments have been commuted to house arrests to release with the proviso of not engaging in political activity for life for prominent members of the Shagari regime.[24] On the other hand, all politicians and military men who had held power up to 1987 have been forbidden from running for office in the next elections.[25] Those too have been subject to changes in timing. Initially, the target date was 1990. In 1987, the Head of State indicated that because Nigerians needed to "purge" their old ways and that required time, the elections would be postponed until 1992.

In the meantime, local and state elections would be held to educate the country in basic principles. Local elections were held in December, 1987. Although none of the old parties participated, traditional charges of vote fraud and intimidation undermined the legitimacy of the results. A curious side complaint about these elections was the printing of 77 million ballots for an electorate estimated at no more than 50 million.[26] That as it turns out is related to another internal problem, the lack of census information. As of late 1989 Babangida may manage to steer the nation to 1992 like Obasanjo. But the eight (at least) attempted coups since his accession give one reason to wonder.[27]

How Many States Are Enough

The British ruled their northern and southern territories as separate entities for years. The rationale was the great difference between the Christian and animist south, which had been under British influence and rule longest, and the newly conquered moslem north which presented a different set of problems. However, Lord Lugard (of India fame) decided ruling Nigeria as two entities was untidy and that efficiency would be served by merging the whole area. Thus the creation of a united Nigeria as a northern and a southern section rather than two separate colonial possessions although they were *legislatively* apart until the Richards constitution of 1946. In fact, Akinola suggests that the idea of a separate North was not given up by the British during their period of colonial rule.[28] Differences between the eastern and western sections of southern Nigeria later gave rise to the creation of an eastern and a western state.

In 1963, a new midwestern state was carved out of pieces of the east and west. This state was created because of a feeling that the old city of Benin and close by areas was culturally different from either southern state. This recognition of ethnic diversity encouraged agitation for further separation and new state creation. Additional minorities sought recognition of their cultural autonomy and safeguards to prevent domination by other ethnic groups. Over the years, this issue of new state creation—

the most geographical manifestation of ethnic fears—has continued to bedevil the country. The next big decision of this kind, to move to a 12 state federation, precipitated the civil war. The lack of any decision on new state creation in 1973 and 1974 was a major factor in Murtala Mohammed's decision to mount a coup against the Gowon regime in 1975. His decree accepting a 19 state federation was widely applauded; however, those who had not received a state of their own voiced dissatisfaction. In the prevailing petroleum bonanza of the middle 1970s, having a state offered major economic as well as cultural and political advantages. Federal revenues from oil were distributed by states as well as by population. And as it became clear that a new state meant creation of a new bureaucracy and a new university, among other perquisites, the clamor continued even in the leaner economic climates of the late 1970s and 1980s. In late 1987, the number of states was increased by 2 to 21, and 53 or more states have been proposed.[29]

The Census as Source and Mirror of Tension

Lebanon is the classic example of a multi-cultural country whose political system ossified based on an increasingly outdated census (1931 the latest). The distribution of power centers in the government fixed based on that census led by the middle 1970s to Lebanon's collapse as a functioning state as the gap between officially accepted ratios and reality became too great. Nigeria's political structure is more fluid; nevertheless, great attention is paid to the ethnic composition of the government, government corporations, and universities, as well as the military. Each group wants to make sure it gets its share. But what is its fair share?

The "obvious" rational way to establish fair shares of power in a multi-ethnic federal system is to hold elections based on a well accepted census of the population. But in a country with shortages of resources and highly self-conscious ethnic groups, censuses are both mirrors and sources of tensions. This is true even in the United States, and far more so in Nigeria.[30]

The British took a census in 1952 which, while subject to the common problem of undercounting, was regarded as unbiased. It established the north as the major center of population and was the basis for the initial elections. Following established principles, a new census was scheduled for and held in 1962. The data were to be used to establish voting districts for state elections and the Federal elections scheduled for 1964. There were of course, other uses. Among them were the selection of towns to receive scarce public resources for provision and upgrading of infrastructure such as piped water, electricity, and secondary schools.

These economic and social outputs of the census created biases towards overcounting. The political outputs worked in both directions—overcounting in areas of strength for the ruling state parties and undercounting in areas of opposition strength. Egregious results, especially in the west, led to a disavowal of the 1962 census results. A new exercise was held in 1963 with even more suspicious results. But for reasons ranging from fatigue to a desire on the part of the federal and regional governments to avoid looking incompetent, the results were officially accepted.[31] To state that those two censuses were major causes in the collapse of the first civilian regime due to the suspicion and fear engendered by them is hardly too strong a statement.

With plans for elections leading to a return to civilian rule in 1976, the Federal Military Government decided to hold another census in 1973. The results would, of course, directly affect the political power distribution among the various states and parties. In addition, it was obvious that the census results would critically affect the success or failure of the many attempts by ethnic groups to create their own states. And economically, the steady increase in oil prices in the early 1970s and the sharp jumps in late 1973 and in 1974 which gave the federal government more money to distribute (grants to states as a right and adjusted by population) must have created almost incredible pressures to inflate population counts. The results are not known. The then government maintained silence while rumors abounded. After the 1975 coup, the new government declared the 1973 census null and void. The census schedules (returns) were supposedly stored in a warehouse and the elaborate processing facilities disbanded.[32]

The 1963 census, flaws and all, still serves as the basis for population-based government services. In a country with a fast growing population (estimated at 2.5 to 3 percent a year) and massive urbanization, census based distortions undermine political legitimacy. Yet the tensions revealed in 1962, 1963 and 1973 continue to prevent an update. The civilian regime of 1979–1983 was planning a census to be taken during the succeeding term. That was aborted by the 1983 coup. The current military regime is now planning a census to be taken in 1991 to prepare new election districts for the return to full civilian rule in 1992. The successful accomplishment and acceptance of such an exercise would be perhaps the single best indicator that Nigeria's internal ethnic tensions are manageable.

Religion

Constitutionally, Nigeria has been a secular state since independence. Given the existence of strong Moslem, Christian and indigenous religions this appears a necessary condition for social peace. A broad generalization would paint the north Moslem, the east and west Christian and indigenous, and the middle a mixture. (This is of course vastly oversimplified since there are Christian communities in many northern towns and a strong Moslem presence in the west.)

Grumbling by Christians about Moslems and vice versa has long been a feature of Nigerian life and the imprints of the 19th century *jihads* can still be seen on the cultural landscape. However, open religious conflict was not an obvious causes of Nigerian instability until the late 1970s. The issue "broke" over the demands raised during the drafting of the new constitution for the entrenchment in it of an Islamic sharia (religious law) appeals court. The level of bad feelings created among the religious communities over this seemed extreme at the time, although subsequent events elsewhere make them now seem quite normal. The issue was defused, but events in the 1980s have confirmed that religious feelings can be exploited as easily as other factors to create instability and advance the causes of a vast array of parochial interests.

The first major eruptions occurred among the Moslem communities in the north. Preaching by an itinerant fundamentalist, Maitatsine from the Nigerian-Cameroonian border area, in the main northern city of Kano, generated riots and looting for over two weeks. Eventually, the army was called in to mount a full scale control operation. Accounts of deaths vary, but the figure of around 4,000 is widely accepted. Property losses were in the millions. Further major riots among Moslems occurred in 1982 and 1984 in the north.

From 1986 on, there have been repeated clashes at several university campuses between Moslem and Christian students. In March, 1987 Moslem riots followed a Christian rally in a heavily Islamic area of Kaduna state in the north, and spread widely. Government initiated inquiries adopted the position that religion was being used by civilian political forces to destabilize the country. Most worrying at the moment are statements by extremists advocating the creation of Moslem and Christian political parties. Since the current Head of State has said that he wants just two parties to contend the election of 1992, the potential for a religious civil war has to be treated seriously. Tensions can arise over many issues. In September, 1989, for instance, Muslims were reported to be threatening to boycott new identification cards because they felt it had a Christian cross on the background. They complained the federal government was trying to *technically* impose Christianity on the nation. Early in 1990, Christians by the thousands, especially in the "middle belt" area between the north and south, demonstrated against a December 1989 cabinet reshuffle that they felt favored the country's muslims and was a harbinger of Islamicization of the country. In a 1989 article, Anthony Akinola proposed a two man joint presidency to defuse the religious situation. One man would be a Moslem from the north, the other a Christian from the south and they would change position within the term of office. Whether this would resolve the problem is doubtful. Akinola cites a prominent Moslem, Sheikh Abubakar Gumi, as saying in October 1987 that a two party system would be most likely to generate a religious rather than a geographic divide. Further, Gumi noted that Muslims would not tolerate a Christian leader and said that if Christians refused to accept Muslim leadership, "then we have to divide the country."[33]

President Babangida, the Head of State, exacerbated tensions by an apparently unilateral decision in early 1987 to make Nigeria .a full member of the Official Islamic Conference (the grouping of Moslem countries like Saudi Arabia, Pakistan, etc.). The second in command of the military government, a Christian, interviewed on television that same night, said it was the first he had heard of the decision. Faced with a growing uproar by intellectuals and Christian ministers, the decision was first described as not being terribly significant. Several months later, word was put around that Nigeria was still just an observer member of the OIC.[34]

The Economy

The colonial economy rested on three regional pillars. The north produced groundnuts (peanuts) and cotton, the west cocoa and the east palm-oil. Marketing Boards were prominent in handling these agricultural products, serving the ostensible role of evening out fluctuations in prices but also providing a means of mobilizing capital generated from agriculture to other areas of the economy. The industrial sector was nascent, consisting of such things as breweries, processing mills, and a limited clothing sector. Lagos, the capital, dominated such industry as existed; however, there were outposts at the western capital, Ibadan, at Enugu in the east, and Kaduna in the north.[35] In addition, there were substantial labor movements between Nigeria and Ghana, the British Cameroons and Fernando Po. The petroleum industry in the Niger delta and offshore started in the 1960s. The economy, while typical of the third world, obviously needed to be modernized if it was to meet the needs of a fast growing independent nation.

In accord with the temper of the times, the answer was to engage in five-year plans, encourage import substitution as a base for later industrialization, control imports by licensing, improve the transport and energy generating sectors, indigenize the industrial sector and create state corporations in critical sectors. Educational opportunities were expanded, particularly in the south. New universities took shape. The central government charged educators with increasing the emphasis on science and technology, elevating it from the minor role to which it had been consigned during the colonial period. These policies led to increased migration to towns, especially the bigger urban centers, a de-emphasis of noncash crops, and poorer terms of trade for the rural sector. One important manifestation of the attempts to break away from the dependence on the industrial north, and at the same time assert Nigeria's regional importance, was the creation of ECOWAS (Economic Community of West African States). While still in existence, the Community has not played the important role in economic development and integration originally envisaged.[36]

The rise in oil prices after 1970, and the explosive jumps in 1973 and 1974, brought opportunities and dangers. Petroleum became not just the largest source of foreign exchange, but the overwhelming one at over 90 percent. Perceived opportunities were obvious—the chance to break out of the poverty trap. The dangers, not so easily foreseen, soon became evident. Massive increases in wages (doubling or more) in the government sector occurred in 1974, spilling over to the private and even the informal sectors of the economy. Pent up demand for Mercedes and similar luxury products as well as imports in general exploded. Frozen beef and canned beer were flown in as local supplies were inadequate to meet demand. Prestige projects such as the 1977 African cultural festival, FESTAC and a new capital city were initiated or pushed harder. Inflation accelerated and Nigeria's infrastructure was strained to the breaking point. For example, in 1975 over 100 ships loaded with cement for various building projects waited for months for unloading outside Lagos harbor. Agriculture was given lip service as the long term base of the economy but in practice was neglected. The window of economic opportunity that opened in the early 1970s was largely squandered.[37]

The oil price declines of the early 80s, and the roller coaster since, have made the Nigerian economy even harder to manage. Talks with the IMF (International Monetary Fund) on stabilizing matters were started and failed, partly under the pressure of unfavorable press reporting. Elements of offended nationalism and pride related to Nigeria's leading role in black Africa, a refusal to face the reality of economic disaster, and a stubborn refusal to devalue the national currency, the Naira; all played a part in aborting negotiations. Discussions in 1986 also failed to reach an agreement but starting late that year the President initiated a series of measures that could have been written by the IMF. They included devaluation of the currency (initially through an auction system) and a "Structural Adjustment Plan." The results over the next two years brought most of the misery associated with IMF adjustments but not so many of the benefits.[38]

Several times, fundamental questions about the nature of the Nigerian economic or political system have been given to commissions of "wise men." In 1987, both arenas were addressed by such a group, the *Political Bureau*. Its white paper noted that the society did not fit well into a Marxist analytic framework. For instance, the class structure was described as consisting of: traditional rulers, landed gentry, the industrial and commercial elites, the intellectual and military elites, the quasi-proletariat and workers, peasants, and the unemployed. Nonetheless, the Bureau recommended adoption of a socialist socio-economic system. The government rejected this, opting for the same general kind of economy as has existed since independence. This infuriated many intellectuals who say Nigeria's dependent capitalist economy is the root of its economic development problems and many of its political ones.[39]

In conclusion, my own rule of thumb evaluation of the state of the Nigerian economy at any given time depends on two indices: whether armed robbers are being publicly executed, and whether Murtala Muhammed airport in Lagos is unsafe for passengers and baggage. If both indices are affirmative, conditions are bad. If both are negative, things are in reasonably good shape. As of the time of writing (September 1990), and for several years previously, both were positive. What this suggests is that Nigeria's economy is at once overregulated and undercontrolled. It has enriched the few and impoverished the many. Attempts to satisfy aspirations have failed. Indicative of this problem is the politics surrounding the creation of new states. They are driven, in the main, by demands for a fairer spatial distribution of the national wealth. Each new state was allocated some projects and infrastructural improvements, particularly in the state capital. Given the underlying climate of suspicion, however, each area suspects that others have received more than they deserved. This is evidence of the decline in intrasocietal trust that followed the dashing of popular aspirations when post 1982 falling oil prices triggered economic decline. The natural question revolves about whom to blame. Among the many targets are Nigeria's elites.

Inter-Elite Politics

The importance of elites in a developing country can hardly be overestimated. This is partly because the size of the groups involved is small with considerable communication among them taking place. It is also because the social, political and economic structures are fragile. Each group may have the power to strangle development. At the least, substantial disagreement among them will hinder it.

In 1987, the Political Commission, charged with evaluating the state of the country's economic and political system and making recommendations for the future, identified two elite groups. They were the military and intellectual elite and the commercial and industrial elite.[40] The implied separation is itself interesting; no military-industrial complex here! In the following brief discussion, the components of each group are discussed separately followed by a summary.

As the group running the country for all but nine years since 1960, the military has received much attention.[41] A small professional force of about 8,000 left by the British grew to over 250,000 at the end of the civil war in 1970; since then it has been reduced to a current level of about 100,000. That has been a gingerly process, based on defusing potential disaffection, lack of discipline, and the dangers of unemployed men with military training. A number of military-civilian confrontations, and the rising incidence of armed robbery with actual or suspected involvement of ex-military, have kept civilian fear at a high pitch.[42]

The historic role of a military force is to defend a country's territory. Here the Nigerian army's major success occurred during the civil war. Conventional wisdom maintains that it has been less successful on other occasions. Although the country's territorial integrity has never been threatened, there have been numerous border incidents, particularly with Cameroon, but also with Chad. The response by Nigeria has been measured, constrained by the desire to avoid appearing a bully, but press comments have been less restrained.[43]

In practice, the military has run the country for most of its independence. Because of this involvement, the armed forces now reflect the internal tensions of Nigerian society. They make no pretence of acting as a purifying force—its stated role in the first coup in 1966. Internal tensions, in fact, preceded that date. The force at independence still had many British officers who were gradually repatriated or retired. The indigenous officers were dominantly from the south, and especially the east. Troops tended to be northerners. By as early as 1964, a quota system was started to install or rapidly promote northerners. This was at the expense, of course, of the easterners since there was no significant expansion of overall strength. The issue of ethnic quotas is a sensitive one, subject to much speculation. It is possible, though difficult, to get numbers by careful tracing. But for the purpose of this exposition the middle 60s ratios for new officer entrants are illustrative. These were: north 60 percent; east and west 15 percent each, and for the midwest 10 percent.[44]

The north now dominates the services, although there are always prominent positions for a few senior officers from the east and west. The import of ethnic origin on entrance and career prospects can be illustrated by an anecdote told me by a person involved. A young and idealistic northerner, a Christian as it happens, wanted to join the Air Force. He went before an initial selection committee, was encouraged, and he asked when the next tests were to be held. He was told, "the tests are for the others, you are in if you want to be." He declined the opportunity. But it is probable that his was not a common response, as the insightful report from James Brooke of the *New York Times* makes clear:

> Keeping officers happy involves allowing as many officers as possible a chance for power and personal enrichment. In late July, the President changed most of Nigeria's 22 state and territorial governors—the third such shake-up in three years. With the military in power here for 18 of the last 22 years, many Nigerians now believe that young men join the army seeking a sure route to political power. If the armed forces never tasted the goodies enjoyed by top Government officials, it would be possible to have a lasting civilian rule. . . ."[45]

Not many high ranking officers seem to leave office poor. Former President Obasanjo, for instance, is now one of the largest farmers in the western region. Farming is a popular retirement endeavor; in the context of Nigerian culture it conveys an impression of honesty to the naive and of ability to generate and use large amounts of money. Of course, the actual exercise of power presents unmatched opportunities. During the summer of 1989, rumors swept Lagos about the current President, Babangida. His wealth, set at $700 million in bank accounts, was said to make him the world's seventh richest leader. And it was alleged that his wife, Maryam, owned the largest and best boutique in Paris. Together they supposedly controlled the largest Swiss diamond/quartz watch factory. These rumors received sufficient currency to evoke a denial from the presidential palace. Given the President's brief time in office, they are unlikely to be true.[46]

While the military nominally controls government, policy making and implementation is in the hands of others. For most purposes, the government is run by the civil service, old system politicians, and assorted prominent individuals from such areas as the professions and the universities. The de facto rule by this combination of military and civilian elites has been considered normal for more than two decades; and the term "cimilitancy" has been proposed for it.[47]

Ethnic patronage is as rife in the bureaucracy as in the military, tempered somewhat by the necessity for technical competence in some posts. This manifests itself down to the lowest levels, as seen by frequent complaints in the press that "if you don't speak the right language to the clerk" you can't get service.[48] As in the army, the former domination of easterners in the civilian bureaucracy is now a memory, although they are still disproportionately represented. As more graduates start to pour from the newly established state universities (as well as the traditional "national" ones at Ibadan, Lagos, and Ife in the west, Nsukka in the east, and Zaria in the north), the competition for scarce places in the federal system will grow more intense. This will also be true at the state and local levels. For despite new talk about privatization and thinning down and cutting back emoluments, the civil service, whether postal or academic, is still often seen as a guarantee of stable salary and some perquisites, if not of munificent salaries. As such, it is likely to continue to be one of the arenas for playing out Nigeria's ethnic conflicts.

It has often been noted that Nigeria's press may be the freest in Africa. While that has not *always* been true, it is an accurate characterization of affairs for most of Nigeria's history. That, and the large number of publications, has made reporting a popular profession among graduates. Perhaps surprisingly, even when the press has been totally government controlled, it has been able to criticize official conduct. But this freedom does not extend to riskless comments about critical affairs of state, ethnic rivalry, or investigatory reporting of, say, the affairs of the Head of State or his family. As in other parts of Africa, reporters or editors may be called in to police headquarters for "discussions" extending over days or weeks. And as the letter bomb that took journalist Dele Giwa's life shortly after discussion with a senior security officer indicates, there are real dangers in being too inquisitive.[49]

Universities in today's Nigeria are a paradox. On one hand, they are seen by the governments as hotbeds of subversion. Students foment unrest over price rises, Christian versus Moslem groups fight, and the struggles move off campus. There is constant fulmination by students, and often faculty, against the wrongdoings of the military and the iniquitous structure of Nigeria's capitalist and "exploitive" society. There is not a year without at least one, usually several and sometimes all universities being closed, frequently for several months or more. The professoriat is demoralized. Among the reasons are salaries. One professor and former dean bitterly noted to me that his 1988 salary was the equivalent of $4,000. For those in fields where outside demand exists such as computer science, a university position is advantageous in obtaining housing. However, the bulk of one's earnings are made outside, with scant regard for students' needs. This is not unusual in Africa, nor indeed in other third world countries. But in Nigeria, this is a change from the 1970s; although like their counterparts elsewhere, Nigerian academics never feel their efforts are recompensed adequately.

The other side of the coin is that education is widely seen as the essential requisite for Nigerian development. One of the greatest prizes awarded a new state is a university, regardless of its sometimes nominal nature. And no national commission is complete without a goodly number of academic members. In Nigeria, the names of Bolaji Akinyemi, Babs Fafunwa, Ishaya Audu and others are as almost as well known as that of Fela Anikulapo-Kuti, the musician. Or Wole Soyinka, the Nobelist, who is also proudly a professor.[50]

The industrial and commercial elite are less in the public eye. In times past, this grouping encompassed leaders of the unions representing both the public and private sectors. It had great influence on government decisions. But after years of repression and unrest under the military, the industrial and commercial elite is no longer the power center it was during the petrobonanza of the seventies. Nevertheless, the industrial and commercial elite retains considerable influence. Its fall from societal "grace" means that businessmen, merchants and union leaders must operate behind the scenes. Ostentatious displays are avoided; unless of course, they can be portrayed as charitable activities. The attempt made in the early seventies to expand Nigerian control of business by an indigizenization decree (part of which was an officially mandated sale of 50 percent of businesses to Nigerian citizens) created a new and unanticipated class, Nigerians who profited from the windfall. But it has had little long term effect toward democratizing entrepreneurial activity. In addition, indigenous entrepreneurs have failed to end Nigerian dependency on the industrial north. Instead, they have fought for special privileges, notably in the award of lucrative import licenses. And in so doing, the industrial and commercial elite has increased the pervasive atmosphere of corruption and suspicion of ethnic favoritism.[51]

Response to Internal Threats

The correlation between intensifying internal conflict and the violent overthrow of governments has made Nigerian politicians ever vigilant toward the possibility of a coup d' etat. This does not mean they deal successfully with troubles. The first Republic's rulers failed to clamp down on corruption and ineptly tried their hand at electoral intimidation. The Gowon regime was lulled into complacency by the smoother than expected recovery after the Civil War. Tempted by the 1979 oil revenue bonanza, Shagàri and his advisors manipulated the electoral system to remain in power. They seem to have been surprised by the coup three months after their reelection. But one certainly cannot accuse the present regime or its predecessor of the least bit of complacency about internal threats.[52]

Each of the several kinds of threat response patterns identified by the editor has been used by Nigerian leaders in their efforts to manage internal threats. *Accommodation* has been a common reaction to serious problems. It has underpinned policies that ranged from negotiations and compromises by the military government to try to head off the Civil War in 1967, to the creation of new states when agitation threatened to become truly destabilizing. In the furor over the "joining" of the Official Islamic Conference several years ago, the accommodation was to unobtrusively withdraw from membership to observer status *sans* official announcement. In serious but less crisis ridden situations, the convening of a select committee of "wise men" to consider and recommend solutions remains common.

Deterrence through alliance dates back to the first republic with its alliance of northern and eastern political parties. The second republic also employed a similar alliance strategy. Thus the 1976 Constitutional Commission's popular recommendation that the winning Presidential candidate must receive at least a quarter of the vote in two-thirds of nineteen states (the number at that time). It enshrined regional coalition politics. The armed forces, too, operate a delicate ethnic balancing act with, for instance, a northern head balanced by a second in command from the east or west.

Preventive action through *state strengthening* activities is also common. The domestic analog of force projection is the creation and careful massaging of symbols identified with the goals of a strong, unified, and moral nation. The Head of State as the official embodiment of the nation receives almost excessive official adulation, by western standards. Other symbols such as the flag are made less of than in some democracies. But wherever possible, leaders make a strong attempt to identify Nigeria *as a state* that enshrines the perceived goals and ideals of the average citizen. Thus, the large expenditure in the oil boom days (1977) on the Black and African festival—later criticized for its extravagance. And in the international economic and political realm, Lagos allocated considerable sums to demonstrate Nigeria's importance in black Africa, or better yet, as a leader of the South in general.

Economic development, an essential component of state action, is assumed to enhance political stability and cohesion. The Nigerian style of economic development has included the following: a series of five year plans; the Nigerianization campaign intended to put the ownership of wealth in the hands of locals; the creation of parastatals; and, import substitution policies. They have been presented not only as accelerating development, but as increasing the stake of Nigerians in their own economic institutions. It remains unclear how the current turn towards privatization will be perceived given its departure from the socialist thrust of earlier policies.

Where necessary, threat is met by *counterthreat.* Counterthreat is most popular where the target is important enough to be annoying but not powerful enough to be truly threatening. Two military leaders, Muhammad Buhari (1983–1985) and the esteemed Murtala Muhammad (1975–1976), were especially unrestrained in acting against their critics; however, all governments have penalized their domestic foes. This has affected high ranking political figures after coups. As one might expect, the sanction may be death (as in January, 1966); or more frequently, exile or imprisonment for a few years. In one famous case, a "father" of independence, Chief Awolowo of the western Yorubas (leader of the moderately socialist Action Party), was jailed in the 1960s for a series of actions that displeased the government of the first republic. But since such actions, as in the Awolowo case, often lead to severe unrest, ranking politicians with substantial regional support are treated gingerly when they transgress or end up on the wrong side of a power struggle. Thus, a 1987 decree forbidding all former politicians from taking part in the runups to, and the election of 1992, has been implemented with great selectivity. The sometimes noisy professoriat is handled with almost equal respect.

Other segments of society are treated more harshly. The letter bomb that took the life of a crusading journalist, Dele Giwa, widely thought to have been delivered by a government carrier, is unusual. But journalists and their editors, print and electronic, are accustomed to a few days, weeks, or months of questioning about unwelcome stories. One outcome is a thriving weekly and monthly press in London with a heavy focus on Nigeria. Many publications are owned by Nigerians. They demonstrate far greater willingness to criticize than their domestic counterparts. Unions, after a heady dose of power during the seventies and in the second republic have been cowed by legal and other actions against them. Less organized groups like students have considerable reason to complain of police and even army brutality, although the nature of some of their own actions can make one pause before joining the criticism. The public has regularly been subject to casual brutality and frequent cases of soldiers running amok to revenge slights. While not part of official policy, these outbursts have generated a high level of fear.[53] An area of major concern, especially in the last several years, relates to participation in religious demonstrations and riots. Ringleaders are usually incarcerated. High levels of force are common, as with the 4,000 killed in the Kano riots of 1980. Nevertheless, as of late 1990 religious leaders had been treated with circumspection.

Perceptions of External Threats

Except during its Civil War, Nigeria has been relatively free from serious external threats to its integrity. The realization that no neighboring state or states can mount a credible threat contributes to the country's preoccupation with its internal problems. Broadly speaking, Nigeria's external relations have been conservatively handled. Exceptions include the time of "activism" (1975–1977), the first years of the second republic (1979–1981), and the period when Bolaji Akinyemi served as Foreign Minister. This does not include the continuous visceral reaction to the white racist regimes in southern Africa.

Nigerian involvement with its neighbors and with external powers has been harmonious only intermittently.[54] This becomes understandable, at least in part, if one reflects upon G. Obiozor's 1977 declaration that Nigeria's "position of leadership in Africa is inescapable." While made at the end of Nigeria's "activist" period, it is nevertheless representative of long held and widely shared feelings.[55] A brief review of troublesome incidents involving other nations is presented below, followed by analysis of responses to those that came to be viewed as threats to Nigerian regional leadership.

Experiences with Western Nations

While willing to give Nigeria its independence, the British were anxious to establish mutual defense arrangements. Ghana, which had distinction of being the first black African colony to achieve independence, was a radical state by the standards of the time and not amenable to such an agreement. So discussions were initiated with Nigerian leaders to allow basing rights and overflights. This proposed Anglo-Nigerian defence treaty was acceptable to the northern leadership and even the easterners. It died because of opposition from the mildly socialist Action Group, particularly its leader, Chief Awolowo. The bad feeling engendered lasted for years. It culminated in Awolowo's ouster, in 1963, as leader of the then Western-oriented state and later imprisonment. This was Nigeria's first coup.[56]

Britain has been involved in a number of other disputes with Nigeria. While eventually supporting the federal government during the Civil War, its long and close association with easterners made for susceptibility to Biafran pleas for support, or at least neutrality. After the peaceful overthrow of the Gowon regime in 1975, Britain offered the general a home at Warwick University. That was not a problem in Nigeria, but the refusal to hand him over to face charges of suspected involvement in the assassination of his successor in 1976 was. Similar refusal to return to Nigerian justice persons suspected of corruption and absconding with large sums of money during the second republic led to a bizarre attempted kidnapping attempt by Nigerian agents in London. It soured relations on both sides. More recently (1987) the initiation of visa requirements for Nigerians, Prime Minister Thatcher's response to an upsurge in illegal immigration, led to charges of racism and closure of the visa office in Lagos. British refusal to consider armed force to end Rhodesia's UDI (Unilateral Declaration of Independence) remained an increasing source of strain until Zimbabwe's independence. And a continual irritant in relationships has been British support for the racist South African regime.[57]

The official reactions of Nigeria to these problems, as opposed to comments on the streets and in the universities, has been moderated by the mutually beneficial economic ties between the two countries, especially since the post 1982 economic downturn in Nigeria. Nevertheless, when Nigeria was economically strong and Britain weak (in the late 1970s), Nigeria withdrew its sterling balances from London. The reason given by Lagos for this action was to pressure Westminster for a favorable settlement of the Rhodesian issue. Efforts to diversify financial and trade ties away from the former colonial power have continued.[58]

France, the other major European colonial power, has been an object of recurring suspicion; however the current desperate economic situation has led Nigeria to downplay persisting problems. The first major dispute between Paris and Lagos was over the former's all but official support of Biafra during the Nigerian Civil War. The assumption that France desires the dismemberment of Nigeria continued for many years. Other French policies reinforce Nigerian wariness. These include the presence of French bases in nearby countries, its involvement in Chad, Zaire and in coup attempts (pro and con) in former colonies over the years, its support of Cameroon in border disputes with Nigeria and its relations with South Africa. In the late 1980s, however, Lagos reversed itself. Instead of portraying France's presence in Africa as a worst case example of neocolonialism, French economic and aid policies were held up as models. However, despite the current warming of relations, it is probable that Paris continues to be regarded as the main external threat to Nigeria.[59]

The United States has been the object, like Britain, of a peculiar love-hate relationship. John F. Kennedy's presidency may have marked the high point in affection. Jimmy Carter, while seen as a friend, was also perceived as weak. Other administrations have had, at best, a neutral image. There is an official and popular perception that Nigeria can benefit economically from ties with the US. The Peace Corps and other aid projects have generally been appreciated. Then there is a fascination with black American culture that has increased over the years. The shared use of English is important in cultural and information interchanges.

Countering the positive are many negative images. Some relate to the pre-civil rights era status of Afro-Americans that Nigerians personally experienced as students in the United States. In the period since Nigeria's independence, negative images date from Patrice Lumumba's overthrow and death in the former Belgian Congo. This operation is widely perceived in Nigeria as having been masterminded by the CIA. As in Britain, Biafran propaganda in the U.S. was quite successful during the Civil War. U.S. support for Nigeria's integrity appeared lukewarm at that time. Reaction to Washington's policies in southern Africa has ranged from mildly hostile to frosty. Apart from the diplomatic niceties, Nigerians have viewed them as Europe-driven, mindlessly anti-Soviet, and racist. Responses to these irritants have ranged from expulsion of peace corps workers and closure of VOA radio transmitting and tracking stations to physical attacks on official U.S. diplomatic facilities, such as the United States Information Service offices.[60]

Problems with African Countries

Nigeria has had persistent problems with other African countries. While none of them are terribly serious, several have been internally embarrassing. Others have raised doubts about Nigeria's will and capacity to act as a regional hegemon. In general, the response in Lagos to regional problems has been low key. It reflects the official position that Nigeria is so dominant within West Africa that firm action would be viewed by its neighbors as bullying.[61]

As the first black African colonial possession to receive independence, Ghana saw itself as a regional model. It took an aggressive role in pushing for accelerating decolonization. Also, especially under its first President, Kwame Nkrumah, Ghana trumpeted socialist solutions to the problems of newly independent nations, especially West African ones. Despite the disparity in size and potential, Nigeria, in its first years of independence saw itself as threatened by Ghana. This reflected a fear on the part of Nigeria's conservative northern leaders over the attractiveness of socialism as espoused by Nkrumah. The reaction was perhaps not so foolish. The Action Party, dominant in Nigeria's western state and unrepresented in the national power structure, espoused similar ideas. In addition, as Nigeria and Ghana were former British possessions, labor traditionally surged across what became the international boundary between them. The direction varied, depending on which economy was prospering. The region in Nigeria most affected by these flows was the west, which this study has portrayed as the most disaffected.

Nigerian suspicion of Ghana's motives have permeated relations between the two since independence. It reached fever pitch in the early 1960s, with information that the latter had signed agreements with Zaire (the former Belgian Congo), a much bigger state physically, rich in natural resources, and a potential rival to Nigeria. At that time, Zaire was ruled by the previously mentioned Patrice Lumumba.[62] Subsequently, relations between Nigeria and Ghana remained strained but correct. More recently, tensions again increased, after the youthful and radical Flight Lieutenant Jerry Rawlings took over Ghana in a coup. Rawlings executed a number of conservatives from previous regimes, including former heads of state. Nigerian reaction to Rawlings has ranged from accommodation (through the sale of subsidized petroleum to a bankrupt Ghanaian economy) to confrontation (expressed by forced expulsions of illegal Ghanaian immigrants to their homeland).

Cameroon, to the east, has also presented problems. A former German colony it was split between a British West Cameroon and a French East Cameroon after the first World War. France granted its colony independence under the association agreements offered by the De Gaulle government. The British area presented a problem. There were conflicting sentiments: for independence; for association with the Francophone part of Cameroon; and for amalgamation with Nigeria. A nasty insurgency occurred in the west with spillovers into Nigeria. The eventual solution, decided in a plebiscite, was to have the northern part of the British Cameroons join Nigeria while the southern section associated with the former French territory. But the borders have been unsettled since. There is considerable smuggling, movement of people across the border, and disputes over fishing and oil-bearing areas offshore. The Cameroonians, supported by France, have pursued aggressive policies, particularly with respect to trespasses by Nigerian fishermen. Paris also encouraged Cameroonian backing for the Maitasane religious movement which caused the uprising in Kano during the early 1980s. Unlike the aggressive actions taken with respect to problems involving Ghana, official Lagos has been notably circumspect on its eastern border. However, some nationalistic Nigerian leaders have called for forcible solutions to this dispute. And media reporting of such problems as official harassment, beating and killing of Nigerians during the 1990 troubles in the Cameroon capital have been critical of official restraint.[63]

The situation vis a vis Chad, in several ways, bears similarities to that with Cameroon. There is a border dispute over the waters of Lake Chad, valuable for fishing to people on the border, and the Chadians have acted aggressively with little real reaction from Nigeria. But Chad is different. It has faced both internal and Libyan sponsored disruption, and received support from both France and the United States. Nigeria's response to the Chadian crisis of the late 1970s was to get heavily involved (on behalf of Chad) through an OAU (Organization for African Unity) sponsored expeditionary force. Lagos had convened a regional conference on the Chadian problem which drafted the 1980 Plan of Action, the basis for the expeditionary force. Unfortunately for Chad and Nigeria, the force proved a dismal failure. It was withdrawn. Subsequently, Lagos was reduced to issuing pious calls for negotiated solutions and to decrying French and Libyan involvement. More recently, as discussed earlier, Nigeria grudgingly supported French involvement. Assistance from Paris enabled Hissen Habre's troops to dislodge the Libyans from all but the Aozou Strip.[64]

In other areas close to home, persisting problems have fed Nigerian threat perceptions. Benin, a bankrupt Marxist state and former French colony, borders on the Nigerian west. Nigeria and Benin share ethnic groups. Historic smuggling among them, while disruptive and unstoppable, is bearable.[65] On the other hand, the late 1980s radical economic deterioration in Benin intensified fears that illegal migration would place unbearable strains on Nigeria's overtaxed infrastructure. Not only had declining petroleum revenue reduced Nigeria's ability to deliver services, capacity was stretched due to the absorption of Sahelian drought migrants from neighboring Niger. Economic subsidies from Lagos to Benin temporarily alleviated pressures for mass migration; however they remain cause for concern.

When attempting to cast its influence further afield, Nigeria has failed to resolve problems with countries as diverse as Liberia, Mali and Burkina-Fasso. In the first, as in their own state, Nigerian leaders could not prevent the murder by perpetrators of a military coup of the former ruler and his principal aids. In the second, Lagos' attempt to mediate a serious border dispute was blatantly disregarded, causing one commentator to lament that Nigeria's real "influence" in West Africa was close to zero.[66] As of this writing, Nigeria is coordinating an attempt by ECOWAS, which includes a combined intervention force, to resolve the continuing revolt in Liberia. With the Persian Gulf crisis driving petroleum prices higher, Nigeria is returning to solvency. Lagos appears in a better position to mediate this conflict than during its unsuccessful efforts in Chad.

Further afield, policy in the Southern Africa region does give Nigeria some cause for self congratulation, although only in Angola was its role significant. There, in 1975 and 1976, the Murtala Muhammad reforming regime successfully pressured for African and world recognition of the MPLA over the competing claims of UNITA and the FNLA. Also, Nigeria's refusal to countenance anything but a victory by the revolutionary forces was decisive in shaping the emergence of Zimbabwe as a black African state. Outcomes in both cases were critically affected by the temporary (as it proved) leverage gained by the mid-1970s flood of oil money. Not only did Zimbabwe and Angola reduce Nigerian influence after statehood was consolidated, they did not appear grateful for support during the struggle.[67] Finally, the magnitude of influence that Nigeria can exert on the rapidly evolving South African anomaly, even if higher oil prices persist throughout the 1990s, does not appear great.[68]

Responses to External Threats

As with its internal problems, Nigeria's reaction to perceptions of external threat has spanned the gamut of potential responses. In the cases of Britain, Cameroon, and France (not to mention the apparently dissimilar confrontation with the International Monetary Fund), Nigeria gave way to reality by accommodation.[69] With the Chadian situation, its preferred response was threat deterrence through alliance via the OAU. In the global arena, former Foreign Minister Akinyemi's espousal of a concert of Middle Powers (such as Brazil, India and Nigeria) demonstrated the attractiveness of deterrence through alliance as a strategy to stand against interference by the super and industrial powers. State strengthening through projection and development appeared when Nigeria used its oil weapon through subsidized provision to potential client states, by continued resource allocation to the ECOWAS (Economic Organization of West African States) and through attempts at mediation in Chad, Liberia and the Burkina-Mali and Senegal-Mauretania disputes.[70] Finally, counterthreat has been espoused and applied, albeit with circumscribed belligerence, in dealings with South Africa.

Conclusions

This chapter has emphasized the internal threat perceptions and strategic responses of Nigeria, as opposed to the more common treatment of external relations and regional alignments. But in Africa, as in much of the third world, domestic problems are the critical ones in shaping ability will to exercise regional influence. Timothy Shaw, a perceptive observer of the African scene, has noted in a recent book that "For the study of international relations in Africa to remain relevant to the continent's crisis and to comparative analyses it needs more than ever to treat 'economics' as 'high politics.'" I would add that in the Nigerian case the other domestic problem areas discussed above are at least as relevant.[71]

What can we say in conclusion about Nigeria as an aspiring regional hegemon? Observers divide into "optimists" and "realists." The former point to the existing disparities in population, industry and military power between Nigeria and its West African neighbors. They maintain that these advantages, coupled with reserves of gas and oil that will last for decades, give Nigeria a potential for self-sustained development that is unmatched in the region. When this potential is realized, and optimists view the structural dynamics of West African international relations as making fulfillment inevitable over the medium to long run, Nigeria will assume the role of regional hegemon.

The "realistic" assessment, in contrast, maintains that while Nigeria possesses the potential, the nature and level of internal fractioning forces makes the possibility of a cohesive and sustained external projection of power into West Africa over the next two decades at least improbable. A perhaps surprising test of this more pessimistic assessment is due in 1991. If Nigeria somehow succeeds in taking and publishing a census without its causing internal chaos and yet another coup, the optimist may have the last laugh.[72]

Notes

1. Quote from the *Times* of London, cited by Pauline Baker in her perceptive "A Giant Staggers: Nigeria as an Emerging Regional Power," in Bruce Arlinghaus, ed., *African Security Issues* (Boulder, CO: Praeger, 1986), p. 77.

2. See S. A. Akintoye, *Emerging African States* (Harlow: Longmans, 1976), ch. 12. Also, "A continental power has finally emerged in Africa," A. Bolaji Akinyemi, later Foreign Minister, in his chapter on the foreign policy of Murtala Muhammed and Olosegun Obasanjo in Oyeleye Oyediran, ed., *Nigerian Government and Politics Under Military Rule,* 1966–1979 (New York: St. Martin's Press, 1979), p. 168.

3. R. A. Akindele and C. Ate Bassey, "Nigeria's Foreign Policy, 1986–2000 A.D.: Background to and Reflections on the Views from Kuru," *Afrika Spectrum* 21(1986), pp. 363–370.

4. *West Africa* (5 November, 1987), p. 13.

5. "The trouble with Nigeria is Nigerians," *New Africa* (Jan., 1987), p. 23. Also Ad'Obe Obe "Trouble with 'The Nigerian' " *West Africa* (May 11, 1987), pp. 900–901.

6. In the sense that the peoples inside its borders did not, through agreement or conflict among themselves, create the state. Egypt, and Ethiopia before 1962, are exceptions. The idea is quite common among western observers, as in the statement that African countries are states but not nations in B. Arlinghaus and P. H. Baker, eds., *African Armies: Evolution and Capabilities* (Boulder: Westview Press, 1986), p. 3. This does not mean that there is no feeling of Nigerian nationalism now among its peoples. But the continued agitation for an "African"

language for Nigeria and the sensitivity of this topic is indicative. See, for instance, Festus E. Obiakor, "The Language Debate," *West Africa* (May 18, 1967), pp. 961–962. James S. Coleman, *Nigeria: Background to Nationalism* (Berkeley: University of California Press, 1965) provides an insightful account of the diversity within Nigeria and its likely impacts on political development.

7. See Sir Alan Burns, *A History of Nigeria* (London: Allen & Unwin, 5th ed., 1955). Also Walter Schwarz, *Nigeria* (London: Pall Mall, 1968).

8. An excellent survey emphasizing regional variation can be found in R. K. Udo, *Geographical Regions of Nigeria* (Berkeley: University of California Press, 1970). For a brief treatment see Harry Land, "Nigeria," in Colin Legum, ed., *Africa Handbook* (London: Penguin, 1969), pp. 303–324.

9. But Harry Land, in Colin Legum, ed., *Africa Handbook* (London: Penguin, 1969), p. 304 says "It is generally agreed the main ethnic divisions are approximately: Hausa-Fulani 14 million; Yoruba 13 million; Ibo 8 million."

10. See S. Egite Oyovbaire, *Federalism in Nigeria* (New York: St. Martin's Press, 1984). Also Land in Legum, ed., pp 307–312 for a cogent summary of these problems in the first republic.

11. Margery Perham, Lugard, 2 vols. (London: Collins, 1960), and Sir Alan Burns, *A History of Nigeria* (London: Allen & Unwin, 5th ed., 1955).

12. S. Egite Oyovbaire, pp. 28–58.

13. Land in Legum, ed., pp. 307–312.

14. Oyovbaire, pp. 90–100. Also see Robin Luckham, *The Nigerian Military. A Sociological Analysis of Authority and Revolt*, 1960–1967 (Cambridge: Cambridge University Press, 1971).

15. Oyovbaire, pp. 101–110.

16. See part one in Keith Panter-Brick, ed., *Soldiers and Oil: The Political Transformation of Nigeria* (Totowa, NJ: Frank Cass and Company, 1978).

17. One perspective on the 1975 coup can be found in Terisa Turner, "Commercial Capitalism and the 1975 Coup," in Panter-Brick, ed., pp. 166–200. Also see chapter 5 in Oyovbaire, pp. 118–161, and several chapters in Oyeleye Oyediran, ed., *Nigerian Government and Politics under Military Rule, 1966–1979* (New York: St. Martin's Press, 1979).

18. See E. Alex Gboyega, "The Making of the Nigerian Constitution," in Oyeleye Oyediran, ed., pp. 235–258 and S. Egite Oyovbaire, pp. 240–267.

19. By 1986, Shagari had been released from detention and a special panel inquiry led to a White Paper statement that his release was justified because "no evidence was led against him to warrant his trial for any offence known to law." But he was still banned from politics for life since "legal justice is not necessarily social justice." See *West Africa* (11 August, 1986), pp. 1665–1666.

20. Larry Diamond, "Nigeria Update," *Foreign Affairs* (Spring, 1986), pp. 326–336.

21. Diamond, p. 326.

22. *West Africa* (30 March, 1987), p. 549.

23. According to several Nigerian informants whose identities can not be disclosed.

24. The Uwaifo Panel reviewed over a thousand cases; *West Africa* (11 August, 1986), pp. 1665–1666.

25. This includes Babangida himself. *West Africa* in several issues in October, 1987 noted the extension of the banning to persons involved in all of the civilian regimes from the date of independence.

26. This was reported to me by a Nigerian friend who said it was arousing suspicion among all segments of Nigerians.

27. *Africa* 176 (April, 1986), p. 16 notes seven attempts to that date. The repercussions of a bizarre attempted coup in April, 1990 where a Christian officer "acting alone" took over a radio station in Lagos and broadcast a call for the overthrow of the government and the elimination of domination by northerners are still being played out at the time of writing.

28. Margery Perham, *Lugard*. Also see Anthony A. Akinola, "A Critique of Nigeria's Proposed Two-Party System," *The Journal of Modern African Studies*, 27 (1989), p. 113.

29. For a survey and analysis of federalism, see S. Egite Oyovbaire, *Federalism in Nigeria: A Study in the Development of the Nigerian State* (New York: St. Martin's Press, 1984). Agitation for statehood continues and the Political Bureau in 1987 had recommended six new ones rather than the two created. *West Africa* (5 October, 1987), p. 1953.

30. In the U.S., for the last several decades there have been suits filed, notably by large older cities, alleging undercounting. For 1990, suits have been filed to prohibit counting of illegal aliens on the grounds that this would distort both allocation of federal funds and voting power. The Census Bureau has agreed to do an extensive and expensive post-census survey to possibly rectify its initial counts.

31. S. A. Aluko, "How Many Nigerians: An Analysis of Nigeria's Census Problems, 1901–1963," *Journal of Modern African Studies* 3.3 (October, 1965), pp. 371–392. Also see R. K. Udo, "Population and Politics in Nigeria," in J. C. Caldwell and C. Okonjo, eds., *The Population of Tropical Africa* (London: Longmans, 1968). A detailed examination of problems affecting one region can be found in Thomas H. Eighmy's doctoral dissertation, *Modernization in a Regional Context: Pretheory and Practice in Western Nigeria* (Pennsylvania State University: Department of Geography, 1969).

32. I talked with a number of people involved in the planning, operating and processing of the census while in Nigeria during 1974 through 1976. The technical aspects seem to have been first class.

33. The Kano events in 1980 were too noteworthy to be ignored. So were the widespread disturbances in March, 1987 and later. The British newspaper, *The Guardian*, carried a thoughtful piece on both by Rufai Ibrahim, a Nigerian journalist from Jos, on 24 July, 1987 in their third world review. His article, titled "Behind Nigeria's Riots of Despair," sees religion as something interested persons can easily manipulate to aid their own agenda, whether "they" are Moslem, Christian or anyone interested in undermining the current status. He ascribes the basic cause to "the presence in Nigeria of a vast, easily excitable army of unemployed, desperate people." There were a number of reports in *West Africa*, with less controversial interpretations, over a period of several months. The President, Ibrahim Babangida, declared in a nationwide broadcast

I heard in Cameroon, that the riots were the equivalent of a civilian coup plot. The British Broadcasting Corporation's *Summary of World Broadcasts* reported the Muslim (ME/0573, 28 September, 1989) and Christian (ME/0662, 15 January, 1990) incidents. A very perceptive if brief analysis of the religious dimension in Nigeria's problems is found on pages 119–122 in Anthony A. Akintola, "A Critique of Nigeria's Proposed Two-Party System," *The Journal of Modern African Studies*, 27(1989), pp. 109–123.

34. Maxwell Nwagboso, "The religious dimension" *West Africa* (18 July, 1988), pp. 1294–1295 covers the religious problem in general as well as the OIC controversy.

35. For a good description of the traditional economy with a regional perspective, see R. K. Udo, *Geographical Regions of Nigeria* (Berkeley: University of California Press, 1970).

36. An interesting, and sometimes controversial, analysis of the economy can be found in I. William Zartman, ed., *The Political Economy of Nigeria* (New York: Praeger Publishers, 1983).

37. Of course, Nigeria is not that unusual in this regard. Mexico, Iran, and even Britain display similarities. One casualty of the oil boom has been agriculture. A February, 1988 government booklet noted that agriculture's share of gross domestic product had fallen from 56 percent between 1960–1969 to between 21 and 23 percent between 1981 and 1985 as reported in *West Africa* (4 July, 1988), p. 1199.

38. A nice, if perhaps somewhat optimistic, summary is given by James Brooke, "Ailing Nigeria Opens Its Economy," *New York Times* (August 15, 1988).

39. This point is made cogently by Michael Watts and Paul Lubeck, "The popular classes and the oil boom: a political economy of rural and urban poverty," in I. William Zartman, ed., *The Political Economy of Nigeria* (New York: Praeger Publishers, 1983), 105–144. Also see "Toward 1992," *West Africa* (3 August, 1987), pp. 1482–1483 where a select commission advocated a socialist economic system. And in his *The Nigerian Condition* (Enugu: Fourth Dimension, 1987), Victor Kalu states that a dependent capitalist economy is the bane of Nigeria's development efforts.

40. The Political Bureau White Paper, as reported in *West Africa* (3 August, 1987), pp. 1482–1483.

41. A sampling of books on the topic includes a study of the military before and for the first six years of independence by N. J. Miners, *The Nigerian Army 1956–1966* (London: Methuen, 1971), I. O. Oyeleye, ed., *Nigerian Government and Politics Under Military Rule, 1966–1979* (New York: St.Martin's Press, 1979), Keith Panter-Brick, ed., *Soldiers and Oil. The Political Transformation of Nigeria* (London: Frank Cass, 1978), and J. Bayo Adekson, *Nigeria in Search of a Stable Civil-Military System* (Boulder CO: Praeger, 1986).

42. The problems start at the top with political maneuverings among officers from field grade up, although lower ranks are sometimes involved. Rumors abound, such as ". . . certain officers dismissed, retired or even shot," *West Africa* (30 May, 1988), p. 987. Real or rumored slights by civilians against lower ranks, reacted to by responses ranging from beatings to arson to murder are staples in the Nigerian press.

43. A. Bolaji Akinyemi, later External Affairs Minister, wrote "From 1960 successive Nigerian governments have realized that the size of the country has been perceived as a threat by Nigeria's neighbors. The strategy adopted by Nigeria to neutralize this threat has been to give no cause for offence;" see Oyeleye Oyediran, ed., *Nigerian Government & Politics under Military Rule, 1966–1979* (New York: St. Martin's Press, 1979), p. 163.

44. For an account of the origin of these quotas, see N. J. Miners, *The Nigerian Army 1956–1966* (London: Methuen, 1971). In his book, *The Nigerian Revolution and the Biafran War* (Enugu: Fourth Dimension Publishing Co. Ltd., 1980), Major General Alexander A. Madiebo, former Commander of the Biafran Army, noted the concentration of major military installations in the north (p. 9) and the quotas indicated (p. 10). In a bitter comment on the military, he says "The situation today therefore, is that Black African armies are increasingly constituting the greatest threat to the governments they exist to protect. It is only the African politician who can put an end to military coups in Africa." (p. 386).

45. *New York Times* (11 August, 1988), p. 6.

46. *New York Times* (12 June, 1989), p. 4.

47. Victor Eke Kalu, *Cimilitancy: Socialist Implications* (Enugu: Fourth Dimension Publications, 1986).

48. This is not just a Nigerian phenomenon. Similar complaints are common in francophone and anglophone countries in Africa.

49. Larry Diamond, a perceptive scholar of Nigerian affairs, noted that "The assassination of Dele Giwa is a challenge to the press in Nigeria," *Africa Report* 32(January–February, 1987), pp. 40–42. One alternative is to report on Africa from abroad; there is, for instance, a flourishing magazine press in London focusing on Africa, especially Nigeria, supported by African money.

50. A number of colleagues have written me concerning the deterioration in conditions over the past several years.

51. See I. William Zartman, ed., *The Political Economy of Nigeria* (New York: Praeger Publishers, 1983).

52. There is some cynicism about reactions of successive governments, both civilian and military. A review of the book by A. Adebayo, *Power and Politics* (Ibadan: Spectrum, 1987) in *West Africa* (30 March, 1987), p. 620 notes a pattern of abuse of power and energy devoted to showmanship.

53. Larry Diamond, "Nigeria Update," *Foreign Affairs* (Spring, 1986), pp. 326–336 surveys abuses committed by the Buhari government, 1983–1985. Students have seen their universities closed many times; many Nigerians cannot remember when at least one university was not shut down for all or part of a year. The recent years of economic austerity have been especially stressful as students have taken it on themselves to express their displeasure with government policies, especially price rises. For instance, an item in *West Africa* (25 April, 1988), p. 727 notes that ten of the country's universities were closed after students had protested against rises in the price of fuel. Student deaths, unheard of until the 1970s, are now all too common. Sympathy demonstrations often result at other universities, resulting in their closure, too. Perhaps as a warning, such incidents are often reported in the press of other African countries as in "Fermeture de l'Universite de Lagos," *Cameroun Tribune* (29 April, 1987), p. 24.

54. See Timothy Shaw and Olajide Aluko, eds., *Nigerian Foreign Policy: Alternative Perceptions and Projections* (New York: St. Martin's Press, 1983).

55. *Lagos Times* (22 October, 1977).

56. Harry Land, "Nigeria," in Colin Legum, ed., *Africa Handbook* (London: Penguin, 1969), p. 309. N. J. Miner in his The Nigerian Army 1956–1966 notes that Awolowo was in a minority in arguing for a ceremonial army and no air force or navy (p. 63).

57. A recent cause of conflict was the introduction of a policy requiring visas for Nigerians wishing to visit Britain. Among the reactions was the closing of a visa office set up by the British to process applications; see *West Africa* (23 March, 1987). Yet by 1988, the then new External Affairs Minister, Major-General Ike Nwachukwu after holding bilateral talks with the British government noted "disagreement on the methodology of settling the South African dispute," but that was the only problem mentioned in an interview for *West Africa* (April 4, 1988) pp. 584–585. On the same page, another article noted that President Babangida had established British sympathy for Nigeria's economic needs and in turn did not let its position on South African sanctions stand in the way of rapprochement with the former colonial power. Warm relations were cemented by a 1989 visit to London according to a report in *West Africa* (15–21 May, 1989), p. 805.

58. But as the note above indicates, the current parlous economic situation dictates caution.

59. The suspicion does have a long history. The *Congressional Research* Service report 82-81F (27 April, 1982) cites comments by A. Bolaji Akinyemi resenting French involvement in African affairs, and a comment by Olosegun Obasanjo, former President of Nigeria, regarding Franco-Belgian intervention in Shaba Province, Zaire that "Paratroops are no more acceptable to us than gunboats." Akinyemi continued to criticize France, saying in 1981 that it was the "number one enemy of Africa," *West Africa* (1 February, 1988), p. 160. After he became External Affairs Minister, he complained about Chad's rate of arming, warning that relations between Nigeria and France could be affected; see *West Africa* (12 October, 1987), p. 2045. As with Britain, criticism has been muted with the economic crisis. The foreign minister in 1988 was quoted as saying "with former colonies of the French around Nigeria, it would be foolish not to consider the French factor in our foreign policy. As you also know they do a lot of trade and investment in Nigeria." *West Africa* (4 April, 1988), p. 595. And supposedly, *West Africa* (5–11 January, 1989), p. 937, Nigeria was seeking French assistance in its quest to become a nuclear power.

60. See Oyeleye Oyediran, ed., *Nigerian Government & Politics under Military Rule 1966–1979* (New York: St. Martin's Press, 1979), p. 131.

61. Akinyemi in Oyeleye Oyediran, ed., p. 163.

62. See *Africa* 176 (April, 1986), p. 36 on the supposed 1960 secret agreement between Ghana and the former Belgian Congo.

63. The importance of French support for Cameroon must be granted here. It was noted that there might be some fear of Nigeria on the part of Cameroon. For instance, in *West Africa* (1 February, 1988), p. 160 it was noted the France was intending to supply Cameroon with the Mirage F1.

64. See Timothy Shaw, "Nigeria Restrained: Foreign Policy under Changing Political and Petroleum Regimes," *Annals of the American Academy of Political and Social Science* 489 (January, 1987), p. 40–51.

65. Since January, 1983 there has been military cooperation and joint training with Benin. See IISS, *The Military Balance 1985–86* on this and the ECOWAS protocol on mutual assistance on defense matters.

66. See Segun Johnson, "Burkina-Mali War: Is Nigeria Still a Regional Power," *India Quarterly* (July–September, 1986) 3:294–308. He indicates that it was the Francophone states who mediated the problem.

67. In its current weakened economic state, Nigeria is reduced to verbal and diplomatic pressures, even on this key problem which it has seen as critical since independence. See Oyeleye Oyediran, ed., *Nigerian Government & Politics under Military Rule,* 1966–79 (New York: St. Martin's Press, 1979).

68. As with the disenchantment over the lack of support by other African states for its lead role in trying to resolve the Chad problem in 1980–1982.

69. See notes 57 and 59 above. As of the time of writing, in August of 1989, accommodation was still policy.

70. Perhaps in reaction to its dissatisfaction with its lack of influence in its neighborhood, Nigeria under former External Affairs Minister Bolaji Akinyemi called at the Lagos Forum on March 16–18, 1987 for a concert of medium powers. With a peculiar mix of neutral and Marxist states it, like his proposal for a "Black bomb" drew denunciations from fellow Nigerians as a waste of thought and time as reported in *West Africa* (4 April, 1988), p. 584.

71. Ralph I. Onwuka and Timothy Shaw, eds., *Africa in World Politics.* (London: MacMillan Press Ltd., 1989).

72. Grateful acknowledgement is due to the Rockefeller Foundation for support in Nigeria under grants RF-VF-94 and RF-VF-214, and for a Fulbright Fellowship in 1986–1987.

9

Patterns of Aspiring Hegemon Threat Perception and Strategic Response: Conclusions and Directions for Research

David J. Myers

This concluding chapter integrates elements from the overview framework into an interactive paradigm that draws upon information from seven hegemon-centered, subordinate state systems. To recapitulate, these are; the United States in the Circum-Caribbean, Israel in the Middle East, South Africa in Southern Africa, the People's Republic of China in Southeast Asia, India in South Asia, Brazil in South America, and Nigeria in West Africa. While additional subordinate state systems have been identified by others,[1] even some with an influential state desirous of playing a special regional role, the aforementioned seven, except for the dramatically fluid Eastern Europe and the North Atlantic, are unsurpassed in importance.

The overview essay drew upon international relations theory to identify the perspectives or categories with the greatest potential to provide variables for systematically abstracting and comparing the threat determination structures and processes involved in an aspiring hegemon's pursuit of regional goals. It repeated this search, seeking in the second instance to ascertain how aspiring hegemons build upon perceived threats when selecting among strategic responses. In each subordinate state system case study, overview concepts and insights organized analysis and explained aspiring regional hegemon behavior. Findings from these case studies form the basis for identifying the structures and reconceptualizing the process of regional hegemon threat perception and strategic response.

Reconceptualization will proceed in several phases. The first presents an overview of the threat perception and strategic response model as it emerges from the subordinate state system case studies. Subsequently, the focus is on describing and analyzing model components and action patterns. Components include: (1) the geopolitical environments (domestic, regional and global international); (2) policy maker role conceptions; (3) the filtering impact of lessons learned; (4) information perceived as threatening; and, (5) strategic responses. Discussion of each component aims at identifying and describing the most important action patterns as suggested by the case studies, and at assessing the reconceptualized paradigm's utility to organize information and predict behavior. A final concern involves briefly examining how the reconceptualized paradigm assists scholars to focus on fruitful research.

Schematic Overview

This schematic overview (see Figure 9.1) organizes data from the regional chapters. It introduces the principal components of our reconceptualized threat perception and strategic response model. Serving as a guide for what follows, the overview portrays the structures and processes by which aspiring regional hegemon elites arrive at: (1) the perception that a threat to their regional designs is coalescing, persisting or intensifying; and, (2) decide upon a strategic response. Unlike other paradigm components, strategic response takes place after threat perceptions have crystallized.

Figure 9.1 paints aspiring hegemon policy makers as concerned that activity in one of three arenas: (1) the domestic; (2) the regional; or (3) the global international, threatens their drive for special geopolitical influence. The patterned flow of action associated with the structure of these arenas, especially that of the second, holds the key to understanding threat perception crystallization. Determination of which geopolitical arena attributes are critical in threat perception crystallization depends heavily on the kinds and magnitude of influence aspiring hegemon policy makers see their state as possessing, or capable of achieving.

To repeat, this study's focus is on the threat perception and strategic response of seven important states as they pursued regional influence. Thus it is concerned only with those attributes of the domestic and global arenas which have a direct bearing on threat perception formation and strategic response selection in defense of regional designs. In most instances, the relevant dimensions of domestic and global environmental attributes can be grasped by examining them as they shape the views of each aspiring hegemon regarding what constitutes a regional international system's critical attributes.

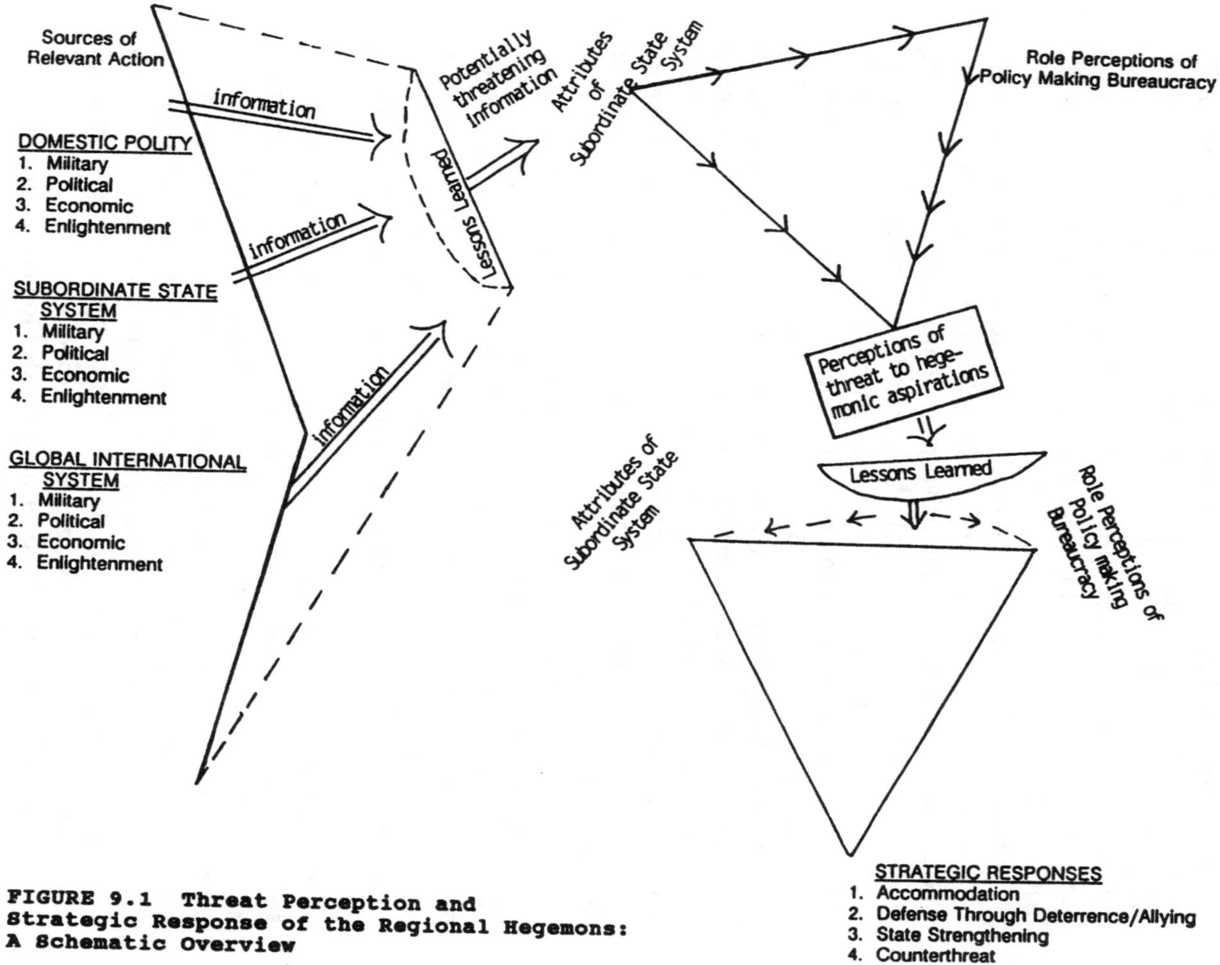

FIGURE 9.1 Threat Perception and Strategic Response of the Regional Hegemons: A Schematic Overview

Perception formation also involved the passing of data through predispositional filters. Figure 9.1 portrays predispositional filtering as critical in both the crystallization of threat perception and in the choice of a strategic response. The critical filtering lenses focused perceptions of the lessons that aspiring hegemon policy makers learned while in search of special regional status. Data suggests that aspiring regional hegemon policy makers subsequently processed this filtered information with a view toward what they envisioned as the subordinate state system's critical attributes.

Attention catching activity within the three arenas involved challenges to one or more of each aspiring hegemon's national role conceptions. These role conceptions, a pervasive part of national political culture, shaped perceptions of politically feasible policy alternatives. They reduced the likelihood that idiosyncratic variables would play a critical part in threat perception crystallization or in the selection of strategic responses. Ten national role perceptions shaped aspiring hegemon behavior. They were: regional leader/opponent; protector/patron of externals; combatant; mediator; regional pariah; international pariah; policeman; defender of the faith; liberator; and, regional economic engine.[2] Reduced to its most essential ingredients, therefore, the struggle for subordinate state influence consisted of two elements; national objectives to be achieved and the means for achieving them.[3]

Activity which hegemon policy makers perceived as threatening to their regional designs often involved a blending of challenges to the aforementioned national roles. This mix of challenges emanated from any combination of the three geopolitical arenas (domestic, regional and global). When viewed as part of a threatening brew, actions which in isolation would have been perceived as benign raised anxiety to critical levels.

In summary, crystallization of a perception of threat to subordinate state system aspirations, as well as the failure to crystallize, emerged as the consequence of aspiring hegemons having assessed filtered information in terms of regional attributes, and the roles they sought to play within the region. Once perceived, the threat (again, refer to Figure 9.1) was dealt with on the basis of the same considerations which initially led to recognition of the threat. This second interaction resulted in the selection of a strategic response or responses.

States aspiring to regional influence responded to perceptions of threat by choosing among four general options. They were: accommodation; defense through deterrence/allying; state strengthening; and, counter-threat. Patterns of response selection varied with circumstances, and from region to region. In choosing a response, perceptions of the role various policy implementing bureaucracies would play, and of their comparative capabilities, took on special significance.

Subordinate State System Attributes

For this volume's subordinate state systems, the introductory discussion of aspiring hegemon, bargainer, peripheral, and intrusive power captures important descriptive dimensions common to all. However, the individual chapters suggest modifications. First, the concept of bargainer needs additional work. Subtypes; for example, "primary bargainer" and "secondary bargainer," appear useful for understanding regions in which one bargainer state is stronger than any other, but weaker than the aspiring hegemon. Second, when an aspiring hegemon interacts with its neighbors, the more powerful normally attempts to secure recognition of its special status. In other words, for subordinate state systems in which one state possesses the potential to dominate, there is an element of structural determinism.

Twelve subordinate state system attributes important in the crystallization of hegemon threat perception and strategic response emerge from the regional case studies. Table 9.1 compares these attributes across subordinate state systems. The first attribute is the magnitude of dominance exercised by an aspiring regional hegemon. The possible responses are tracheotomized: (1) high, (2) medium and (3) low. Attribute one responses also encompass the dimensions of potential intrasystem dominance along which each aspiring hegemon's influence was strongest.

Most other Table 9.1 attributes, and the possible responses, are self explanatory. It merits pointing out, however, that "degree of subsystem autonomy" within the aspiring hegemon (attribute #10) is tracheotomized as follows: (1) high, (2) medium and (3) low. These options correspond to the commonly used categories descriptive of political regimes: democratic, authoritarian and totalitarian. Also, attribute #5 (nature of system organization) concerns the subordinate state subsystem, and not the political system of the aspiring hegemon. Here the response refers to the presence or absence of functional interstate associations within the subordinate state system. These associations may pivot on economic issues (the Argentine–Brazilian Common Market), military issues (the Inter-American Treaty of Reciprocal Defense) or political issues (The Organization of African Unity). Within the examined subordinate state systems there are also transnational organizations constructed around ideology (the Latin American Social Democratic International) and enlightenment (the Roman Catholic Church). Regional issues, however, are secondary; ideological and enlightenment based organizations emphasize the universal.

TABLE 9.1 Cross Regional Comparison of Subordinate State System Attributes

	Subordinate State System Attribute	U.S. in Circum-Caribbean	Israel in Middle East	South Africa in Southern Africa	Brazil in South America
1)	Extent of regional dominance exercised by the aspiring hegemon	High/multi-dimensional	low/military	moderate/ multidimen-sional	low/ economic
2)	Prevailing attitude toward aspiring hegemon's regional leadership	acceptance	rejection	extreme rejection	in formation
3)	Significant minority with alternative view of hegemon's leadership	yes/rejection	yes/sharing	no	yes/sharing
4)	Presence of "stand out" bargainer	Mexico	Egypt (Iraq aspires)	no	Argentina
5)	Nature of system organization	functional associations some hegemon coercion	hegemon/bar-bargainer functional organizations absent	hegemon/ bargainer functional organizations absent	functional associations low hegemon coercion
6)	Intraregional questioning of hegemon state's legitimacy	by militant marxists	some	yes	no

TABLE 9.1 (Continued)

	Subordinate State System Attribute	U.S. in Circum-Caribbean	Israel in Middle East	South Africa in Southern Africa	Brazil in South America
7)	Intensity of involvement in superpower rivalry	high	high	moderate	low
8)	External state aspires/has aspired to replace identified hegemon	no	no	no	United States
9)	Presence of system-reinforcing regional int. organization	yes	yes	no	yes
10)	Degree of subsystem autonomy within aspiring hegemon	high	high	medium (whites) low (others)	medium
11)	Extent of political legitimacy consolidation within hegemon	high	moderate	low (rising)	low
12)	Level of economic development	mixed	mixed	mixed	developing

(Continues)

TABLE 9.1 (Continued)

	Subordinate State System Attribute	India in South Asia	China in Southeast Asia	Nigeria in West Africa
1)	Extent of regional dominance exercised by the aspiring hegemon	low/military	low/diplomatic	low/diplomatic
2)	Prevailing attitude toward aspiring hegemon's regional leadership	marginal acceptance	in formation	in formation
3)	Significant minority with alternative view of hegemon's leadership	yes/rejection	yes/rejection	no
4)	Presence of "stand out" bargainer	Pakistan	Indonesia (Vietnam?)	no
5)	Nature of system organization	functional associations some hegemon coercion	functional organizations some hegemon coercion	functional organizations low hegemon coercion
6)	Intraregional questioning of hegemon state's legitimacy	no	some	some

TABLE 9.1 (Continued)

	Subordinate State System Attribute	India in South Asia	China in Southeast Asia	Nigeria in West Africa
7)	Intensity of involvement in superpower rivalry	low	moderate	low
8)	External state aspires/has aspired to replace identified hegemon	no	Japan	no
9)	Presence of system-reinforcing regional int. organization	yes	yes	yes
10)	Degree of subsystem autonomy within aspiring hegemon	high	low	medium
11)	Extent of political legitimacy consolidation within hegemon	moderate	high	low
12)	Level of economic development	developing	developing	developing

The second dimension of "nature of system organization" looks at the degree of coercion applied within the regional system by the aspiring hegemon. Again, the response is a trichotomy. "High" describes a situation in which the aspiring hegemon has dispatched troops in defense of its regional interests; and maintains a veto over essential military, political, and economic decisions within the bargainer states. "Some" suggests that on occasion the aspiring hegemon has used or threatened to use military force against one or more bargainer states. Aspiring hegemons applying "some" coercion also attempt, on a regular basis, to influence political, economic and defense decision making within the bargainer states. Aspiring hegemons projecting "low" levels of coercion over neighboring bargainers have not deployed troops against them during the twentieth century. Finally, it is significant that among aspiring regional hegemons, a "no coercion" response is conspicuous by its absence. For those arenas in which the coercion response is not classified (Southern Africa and the Middle East), the aspiring hegemon is viewed as a pariah by a significant group of bargainers. Here relations between the aspiring hegemon and those states perceiving it as a pariah are confrontational. At a minimum, the former seeks regional military hegemony. Military inferiority in relation to any alliance of bargainer states is viewed as potentially fatal.

Attribute Structure and the Operational Characteristics of Regional Systems

Table 9.1, viewed in light of the seven regional cases, suggests broad generalizations about the attribute structure of subordinate state systems with aspiring hegemons. These attributes shaped important operational characteristics of the regional systems within which hegemonic aspirations were pursued. The first characteristic concerns differences between the region in which the aspiring hegemon was also a superpower and those in which it was not. Circum-Caribbean bargainer states appeared more vulnerable to pressure from the United States than did bargainers in the other six regions to their aspiring hegemon. This is hardly surprising in view of Washington's immense military advantage. A second operational characteristic, common to all regions, also revolved about member state autonomy. Aspiring hegemons, when organizing a sphere of influence, sought to replicate the level of subsystem autonomy conceded to their domestic interest groups.

Third, while all bargainer states resisted claims to unique geopolitical spheres of influence, regions in which the aspiring hegemon's domestic political regime was widely perceived as illegitimate (the Middle East and Southern Africa) experienced special problems. They were characterized by high levels of terrorism and intrasystem violence. While terrorism sometimes was used by one bargainer state against another, its principal target was the pariah hegemon. Fourth, each of the seven examined regional international systems was viewed by aspiring hegemon policy makers, as well by their counterparts in bargainer and peripheral states, as a coherent and critical arena in which to pursue national interests. For five of the seven regional systems structure appeared stable, at least over the foreseeable future. The two exceptions were South America and Southeast Asia. In the former the United States clung to the Western Hemisphere myth that combined the Circum-Caribbean and South America into a single dependent sphere. In the latter Japan stood ready to displace China as the regionally dominant power. Bargainer states in both regions opposed integration into an orbit presided over by the alternative aspirant.

Bargainer state reaction to hegemonic pretensions also were reflected in the fifth operational characteristic. Here the pivotal concern was with perceptions of extraregional threats. Aspiring hegemons were most successful in gaining acceptance for their exercise of special regional influence where bargainer states perceived threats from the larger international environment as greater than any posed by the most regionally influential state's aspirations. Under these conditions, bargainer states found economic and technological dependence on the aspiring hegemon more palatable. Thus fear of Soviet military power, and anticipation that transferred United States technology would increase economic development, combined briefly during the early 1960s to soften Circum-Caribbean antagonism toward Washington's hegemony. This suggests that acceptance of regional leadership depends on three factors; bargainer state perceptions about the magnitude of hegemon power, the intentions of the hegemon, and extraregional threat.

Regional international organizations (attribute five of Table 9.1), were present in each of the seven subordinate state systems. Several operational characteristics revolved about this attribute. First, where the aspiring hegemon was viewed as a pariah, bargainer states formed regional organizations in order to increase their power and options for undermining the offending pariah. In the other geopolitical arenas, the aspiring hegemon usually participated in regional international organizations. Economic and political varieties were most common. Often, however, hegemon policy makers perceived the purposes and utility of regional organizations quite differently than their counterparts in bargainer and peripheral states. The former tended to look upon regional political and economic organizations as mechanisms for increasing the power they hoped to project from the region into the global arena. The latter viewed regional political organizations as mechanisms for constraining the aspiring hegemon's ability to act unilaterally inside of the subordinate state system.

Regional military organizations, not surprisingly, were less common than political and economic arrangements. The success of regional military organizations was directly related to the intensity of bargainer state fears that an extraregional power would use armed force against them. When bargainer states failed to detect a significant external threat, they became alarmed over even the existence of a regional military organization; it was perceived as inviting hegemon interference in their internal affairs. Developments in South Asia and Southeast Asia illustrated the importance of the relative intensity of perceived threats in creating support for regional military organizations. Neither region developed an effective international military organization because neighbors distrusted each other more than they feared any external threat.

Finally, the tenth Table 9.1 attribute focuses attention on an operational societal characteristic associated with competitiveness. Democratic hegemons experienced greater difficulties than their authoritarian counterparts in crafting a domestic consensus to pursue regional aspirations. Shifts toward greater democracy, such as those which occurred in South America during the late 1980s, subjected to public questioning the earlier authoritarian consensus on regional and other international goals. Relaxing control over civil society reduced the latitude of government to pursue regional policies that the public viewed as costly. On the other hand, mass opinion was often indifferent toward other regional and larger global issues. An important exception was when an external threat was perceived so intensively that a consensus coalesced behind some specific response.

Subsystem Attributes in Threat Perception Crystallization and Strategic Response

Subordinate state system chapters portray the dynamics of regional structure as influencing the crystallization of threat perception along two paths. The first is straightforward; attribute dynamics directly strengthen or weaken perceptions that a threat to the aspiring hegemon's regional interests is coalescing, continuing or intensifying. The second is more subtle. Here attribute dynamics contribute to shaping hegemon role conceptions; in turn, these conceptions, through the action scenarios they imply, influence policy makers' judgment that events do or do not constitute a threat to their regional interests. Also, as figure 9.1 portrays, the path by which attribute dynamics shape the strategic responses to threat perceptions is analogous to that along which threat perception crystallization proceeds. In other words, action flowing from the attribute dynamics within a geopolitical sphere of influence directly and indirectly (by impacting on role conception) shapes the choice of strategic response. This process is repeated when the aspiring hegemon selects a strategic response.

Attribute Dynamics and the Crystallization of Threat Perception

Our case studies suggest at least six ways in which subordinate state subsystem attributes directly shape aspiring hegemon perceptions about the existence and intensity of threats to its regional interests. First, superpower rivalry in a region over which one superpower sought special influence exacerbated perceptions of danger. When the external superpower inserted itself into regional affairs tensions became acute. All intrusions by the Soviet Union into the Caribbean Basin raised and sustained high levels of anxiety on the part of the United States. Even given the Cold War's winding down, Soviet support for Fidel Castro continued to poison relations between Moscow and Washington.

Second, when either the United States or the Soviet Union appeared to be gaining influence with bargainer states over which a non-superpower aspiring hegemon sought influence, that latter state felt threatened. Most such aspiring hegemons had struggled against the imperialism of at least one North Atlantic power, or Japan; a legacy of those struggles was distrust of all industrialized states. In addition, the presence of external power armed forces shaped threat perceptions. They raised levels of insecurity within the aspiring hegemon perceiving its special regional preserve to have been invaded. Insecurity predisposed aspiring hegemon policy makers to magnify the severity of all challenges.

Perceptions within a region that the aspiring hegemon was a pariah also shaped how regional events were viewed. Thus a fourth path whereby subsystem attributes directly influenced threat perception crystallization emanates from the pariah state syndrome. As Albright and Irwin documented, this syndrome inclined the state desiring special regional influence toward viewing any organization of its neighbors as a potential threat. Conversely, aspiring regional hegemon policy makers perceived little or no threat from cooperative activities among bargainer states whose leaders shared their values, viewed them as friends, and did not challenge their domestic regime.

The fifth action pattern shaping threat perception derives from the level of aspiring hegemon regional dominance. Hegemon elites viewed declines in influence over their subordinate state system with apprehension. In subsystems where influence was high (for example; the Caribbean Basin), merely maintaining the status quo proved difficult.

Influence always seemed to be eroding, although as Atkins discussed, the United States possessed usable power capable of reversing negative developments. By and large, however, high influence situations appear predisposed to generate information viewed by aspiring hegemons as threatening.

Threatening information also crystallized inside of subordinate state systems in which the aspiring hegemon's influence was more modest. South America, South Asia, West Africa, and Southeast Asia were cases in point. In these regions there was an endemic fear of falling behind in the race for economic and technological advancement. Lower hegemon growth rates intensified hegemon insecurity when they involved heavy industry, or suggested decline in the aspirant's economic position in relation to an external state with demonstrated interest in a sustained regional presence.

The presence of a "primary challenger" within any region proved a final structural condition that heightened aspiring hegemons' threat perceptions. Aspiring hegemons were especially suspicious of primary challenger activity directed toward the creation, enhancement or participation in regional international organizations that excluded them. These activities were viewed as evidence of the primary challenger's intention to dilute the aspiring hegemon's regional influence. India's insecurity over Pakistan's involvement in CENTO illustrated this concern, as did Brasilia's suspicions in the 1970s over Argentine resistance to Brazilian inclusion in a Plata River economic community.

Attributes and the Selection of Strategic Responses

In their selection of strategic responses to regional threats, aspiring hegemons confirmed that in fact they did favor the policies and instruments in which they possessed the greatest comparative advantage. Data from the seven regional cases also revealed important, unanticipated paths along which the dynamics of regional attributes shaped the responses of aspiring hegemons to threat perceptions.

First, the breath and depth of hegemon dominance within the subordinate state system influenced the choice of strategic response. This is illustrated by comparing situations of dominance with ones in which special influence more accurately described the aspiring hegemon's regional status. In the later, aspiring hegemons, upon perceiving a threat to be increasing in the short or medium term, gravitated toward the response of deterrence by allying. Thus Chang reported that China reacted to perceptions of heightened threat from the Soviet Union in Southeast Asia by switching from opposition to cooperation with the ASEAN grouping. Also, threatened aspiring hegemons complemented deterrence by allying with deterrence through defense. Where the aspirant enjoyed great power advantages, it tended to act unilaterally. For example, the United States snuffed out numerous Caribbean Basin revolutions that threatened its regional hegemony, and India acted analogously in the Maldives.

In all seven cases, deterrence through defense centered around resource reconfiguration, most often involving armed force. Thus Albright portrayed South Africa as reorganizing its military to cope with the changing strategies of hostile neighbors, and Brazil redeployed its army following Argentina's use of armed force in the Malvinas Islands dispute. In both situations, the aspiring hegemon's intent was to redress a potential deterioration in the regional balance and accompanying perceptions of increasing danger.

Aspiring hegemons also opted for deterrence through defense and allying when viewing their advantage over bargainer states as inadequate to exercise the influence desired; and, when perceiving this inadequacy as a long term problem, However, especially in regions of the developing world, state strengthening was the more common response.

The case studies documented the presence in most subordinate state systems of a diversity of views in regard to the aspiring hegemon's leadership aspirations; however, a "prevailing attitude" also emerged. *The dimensions of this "attitude" emerged as a second subordinate system attribute (Table 9.1) that influenced the selection of strategic responses,* especially when the aspiring hegemon was viewed as a pariah. The deterrence through alliance response, at least within the region over which the aspirant sought special influence, was not available to aspiring hegemons which bargainer states perceived as pariahs. Thus when alliance was attempted, it was with external powers; for example, Israel with the United States and with South Africa. Also, pariah hegemon policy makers, in a reflection of their siege mentality, appeared skeptical about the capability to deter of a response built around reconfiguring resources alone.

Pariah hegemons, again influenced by perceptions of bargainer state hostility, found accommodation a strategy of limited utility. However, Irwin's analysis of Israel in the Middle East profiled Jerusalem's efforts to experiment with accommodation toward Egypt following the Camp David Accords. Here differences between Middle East and South Africa proved significant. In the Southern Africa subordinate state system no bargainer state stood in relation to Pretoria in a manner analogous to the position Cairo occupied vis-a-vi Jerusalem. This difference underscored that variations in the intensity of hostility toward an aspiring hegemon can expand or reduce the pariah's maneuvering space. However, the two pariah hegemons feared that as soon as the regional balance of power turned against them, accommodation on the part of an even mildly hostility bargainer would give way to threatening behavior. Not only would the newly disadvantaged pariah hegemon's role as a major regional actor be threatened, but the state organization on which the power of its elite rested might come under attack.

South Africa and Israel, also employed counterthreat as a strategic response to their neighbor's threatening behavior. In so doing, despite a willingness to wield economic counterthreats, they usually ended by emphasizing the military dimension. Finally, Irwin and Albright demonstrated that pariahs with hegemonic needs or aspirations looked to state strengthening for the provision of long term security within the immediate geopolitical arena.

In some subordinate state systems, attitudes toward the aspiring hegemon have yet to crystallize. Attitudes remained fluid in South America, West Africa, and to a lesser extent in Southeast Asia. While bargainers in these regions displayed the expected insecurities of lesser states when confronted with sphere of influence aspirations, opportunities remained for the relevant aspiring hegemon to emerge as a champion of regional interests. In this context, the weakness of all third world states increased the attractiveness of allying as a strategy for creating leverage in bargaining with advanced industrialized states

Degree of political openness within the region's leading state is a third attribute influencing that state's selection of strategic responses. Democracies, as often noted, have greater difficulties in maintaining and modifying their alliance policies than authoritarian or totalitarian regimes. Mass public opinion is more important in democracies and it resists rapid changes in how national interest is defined. Chang confirmed this in his discussion of Washington's rapprochement with mainland China. After having sold the American public on the desirability of assisting with Beijing's modernization, leaders in the United States found it difficult to abandon this policy, even taking into account their anger over the crushing of student dissidence at Tiananmen Square in 1989. In most cases, however, democracies experienced difficulties in allying with states or regimes engaging in behavior seen as antithetical to their prevailing morays. Thus Atkins described how the United States government found it almost impossible to support military dictatorship in Guatemala despite Washington's interest in smothering a peasant insurgency which, if successful, would have increased Cuban and Soviet influence in Central America. President Reagan became free to assist the Guatemalan government only after the open election of a Christian Democratic president.

Democratic leaders are at a disadvantage when using armed force for political ends. In order to gain mass support for military deployment, they must so exaggerate the threat and venality of the offending state that when force is employed the only satisfactory outcome (from the perspective of the masses) is total victory. The costs of total victory, however, may be unacceptable. In light of this dilemma, several aspiring hegemons attempted clandestinely to implement regional policies that lacked broad support. But it proved impossible to keep these efforts secret; and discovery paralyzed the aspirant's capability to continue implementing the discordant policy. Atkins' analysis of President Reagan's Nicaraguan adventure illustrates this problem. That Nicaragua's Sandinista government lost presidential elections in February 1990 in no way diminishes the difficulties faced by democratic aspiring hegemons when attempting to implement an unpopular regional policy.

Intensity of intraregional superpower rivalry is the fourth attribute impinging on the selection of strategic responses. In no region was this rivalry more intense than in the Middle East. Irwin described an arena in which Israel's pariah status, Egypt and Iraq's capability to lead, and the volatility of Arab state political regimes invited superpower intrusion (especially in view of global energy needs). Not surprisingly, deterrence by allying became a strategy favored by Israel and her neighbors. It was commonly expressed in a search for armaments and technology from the United States, the Soviet Union and other industrial countries. Tensions between clients armed by the United States and the Soviet Union gave rise to armed conflict, and the potential for direct superpower confrontation intensified danger.

South America, West Africa and South Asia (apart from the Afghanistan adventure), have been geopolitical arenas of secondary importance for the United States and the Soviet Union. Brazilians, Nigerians and Indians preferred to remain apart from superpower competition. They assigned highest priority to those dimensions of state strengthening that lead to increased regional influence and upward international mobility. Nigerian, Indian, and Brazilian leaders also sought good relations with regional bargainer states; defense through deterrence and counterthreat were used sparingly. They reserved these responses for situations in which bargainer states appeared to be intent on undermining an aspirant's regional influence. Also, in the quest for advanced technology with state strengthening ramifications, India, Brazil and Nigeria used a variant of defense through allying; attempting to play one superpower off against the other. Planning for the contingency of superpower military intrusion into South Asia, South America and West Africa was a final concern that evoked this response. Each regional power, when faced with intrusion by one superpower, stood ready to call upon the other for assistance.

From the perspective of superpower rivalry, the Caribbean Basin displayed some unique attributes. Washington's overwhelming naval, ground and air power guaranteed that no grouping of Basin states could deny the United States access to the two Basin minerals—petroleum and bauxite—which it viewed as critical. Also, state strengthening measures taken by Washington, all of which inevitably affected its capability to influence Circum-Caribbean events, were implemented largely in response to military challenges from the Soviet Union or economic competition from other OECD countries. Here, as in other dimensions of Basin policy, Washington's behavior appeared as a by-product of policies pursued in other geopolitical arenas.

Availability of a viable alternative hegemon is the fifth condition influencing the strategic response to perceptions of threat. Chang and Myers describe Southeast Asia and South America as subordinate state systems in which an external but influential power stands ready to alter the dominant pattern of regional international politics. Military defeat in 1945 prevented Japan from gaining political domination over Southeast Asia. However, Tokyo's resurrected economy, when viewed in the context of Chinese stagnation and relative United States decline, opens the possibility that Japan might achieve by economic means what it failed to gain by armed force. Japan's economic strength continually constrains Chinese efforts to exercise special regional influence. Nevertheless, Beijing's potential to shape regional events should not be underestimated. Its Vietnamese intrusion and role in Cambodia demonstrated that China could, and would, act.

South America and the Caribbean Basin long have been viewed in Washington as a single United States-dominated region: Latin America. In practice United States influence never has been as pervasive in the former as in the latter. In the wake of post-Vietnam retrenchment, disparities between United States ability to act in these two parts of the Western Hemisphere widened. The Caribbean Basin was Washington's focus during the 1980s. Insurgency, trade, economic development and Soviet efforts to gain new client states in the Basin occupied successive administrations. Nevertheless, Brazil continues to perceive a threat in the perception of many Washington policy makers that South America remains part of their Latin American sphere.

Sixth, each aspiring hegemon's economic and technological sophistication shaped its strategic responses. Relative economic sophistication within the subordinate state system, and in comparison with external powers, had special relevance. Threat perceptions deriving from economic inferiority were associated positively with accommodation as the strategy of choice. This was especially true when an upwardly mobile third world aspiring hegemon calculated that its economic inferiority was being overcome by comparatively rapid rates of growth. However, only in Brazil (during the short-lived economic miracle) did a case study portray economic factors as overshadowing military and political calculations in the selection of strategic accommodation. Paranjpe and Thomas found some economic considerations behind India's selection of accommodation in South Asia; however, they appeared secondary.

Finally, behavior in the seven regional systems confirmed *comparative technological sophistication (especially in defense and related industries), as a requisite for projecting subordinate state system influence.*[4] Technological advantage by itself, however, proved only marginally able to undergird projection. In the Caribbean Basin it facilitated employment of counterthreat as a United states response; but Washington enjoyed a multifaceted advantage throughout the region. Counterthreat also was important in the strategies of the aspiring pariah hegemons. However, the middle level of technological sophistication achieved by them, as well as the relatively small size of their technological establishments, limited capability to sustain counterthreat and other responses. Third world aspiring hegemons experienced even more severe limitations, although in their regions attainment of relative technological superiority might have been expected to bestow substantial capabilities for influencing underdeveloped neighbors. However, Chang documented how China failed in its efforts to influence Vietnam following the withdrawal of the United States. Hanoi's success in stalemating Beijing illustrated the utility of alliance strategies for bargainer states determined to resist the influence of an aspirant possessing only a marginal advantage in technological sophistication.

To summarize, in all seven subordinate state systems activities were observed along the six attribute dimensions that shaped strategic responses. The most critical response patterns derived from the breath and depth of influence exercised by the region's most powerful state. They confirmed a distinctiveness among responses for the single region with a superpower hegemon; the two dominated by aspiring hegemon pariahs, and the four in which the aspiring hegemon was an upwardly mobile third world state. Differences in degree of political openness, intensity of superpower penetration, and availability of a viable alternative hegemon were significant for the selection of strategic responses. However, these attribute dimensions proved less powerful than breath and depth of hegemon domination. A sixth dimension, aspiring hegemon economic and technological sophistication, became more important in the wake of accommodation between the United States and the Soviet Union. Finally, as suggested earlier, subordinate state system attributes also proved to be a source of foreign policy role perceptions. Attention now turns to this relationship.

Role Perceptions

The overview chapter drew attention to international relations theorizing which maintains that in many situations foreign policy makers operate as "guardians" of one or more national role conceptions. These national role conceptions, as they become a more pervasive part of the political culture of a nation, shape perceptions of politically feasible policy alternatives and reduce the likelihood that idiosyncratic variables will play a critical part in decision making. Assumptions of the centrality of role perceptions in policy making were supported by the regional cases. Ten national role perceptions emerged as shaping the efforts of aspiring hegemons to exercise subordinate state system influence: (1) regional leader/opponent; (2) protector/patron of externals; (3) combatant; (4) mediator; (5) regional pariah; (6) international pariah; (7) policeman; (8) defender of the faith; (9) liberator; (10) regional economic engine.

Roles and Aspiring Hegemons

The above roles are variations of those formulated within the Ohio State University CREON project.[5] The first, regional leader/opponent, was common to all aspiring regional hegemons. States with this self image enthusiastically acted out the role of subordinate state system caretaker. They also opposed others within the region who challenged their special status. The second role, protector/patron of externals, revolved about whether aspiring regional hegemon policy makers saw their state as having a special and significant role to play in the larger international system. Multifaceted opportunities arose in the global arena for acting out diverse roles perceived as "significant." Those favored by aspiring regional hegemons tended to involve: (1) seeking special influence in a second geopolitical region; (2) protecting nationals ("tribe" members) residing outside the region; and, (3) supporting external organizations sharing the regional influential's ideological or religious beliefs.

The third role, regional combatant, focused on whether the aspiring hegemon recently had deployed, and remained willing to use, armed force inside of the subordinate state system. Here the aspiring hegemon targeted military assets on regional actors whose activities were undermining its regional influence. Fourth, the mediator role involved a commitment by the aspiring hegemon to play a central role in peaceably settling disputes among the region's bargainer and peripheral dependent states. On occasion acting out this role encompassed efforts to establish and legitimate regional international procedures for mediating conflicts within the subordinate state system.

The role of pariah derived from perceptions that the aspiring hegemon state, or its political regime, was illegitimate. Pariah aspirants, as suggested earlier, found themselves isolated; and isolation created a siege mentality. Perceptions of pariah illegitimacy, a constant feature within regions over which an outcast state sought influence, sometimes spilled over into the larger international community.

In the seventh role, policeman, the aspiring hegemon stood ready to provide military assistance to bargainer and peripheral dependent state regimes that faced an overt and active military threat from within their own society. Regional hegemons inclined toward assuming the policeman role when insurgency within a neighboring bargainer state appeared to have been initiated and nurtured by extraregional forces.

The eighth aspiring hegemon role, defender of the faith, embodied an expectation that aspiring hegemon policy makers would interpret and comment upon affairs within the subordinate state system in terms of an ideology on which their legitimacy rested. Playing out this defender of the faith role inclined policy makers to dichotomize neighboring states into ones governed by followers of "the ideology," and others who rejected or interpreted it for their own ends. As suggested in the overview chapter, pressure for conversion crept into scenarios that gave importance to the role of defender of the faith.

The drive to convert also found expression in the adoption of an additional role, that of liberator. When fulfilling liberator role expectations, the aspiring hegemon stood ready to provide military and propaganda support for organized revolutionary or guerrilla forces in other regional states. Bargainers whose regime legitimacy rested on an ideology which challenged that used to legitimate aspiring hegemon elites were the most likely to experience pressures associated with an aspiring hegemon's adoption of the liberator role.

The final role, regional economic engine, derived from perceptions within the aspiring hegemon that it had a special duty or calling to assist with the economic development of other states in the region. Often expressed as a commitment to improving the economic well being of the poor, especially in regions where developing countries predominated, aspiring hegemon elites appeared most enthusiastic about fulfilling this commitment when they viewed their interest as being served by anticipated quality of life improvements. A variation of the regional economic engine role scenario occurred when the aspiring hegemon was locked in global competition with a state possessing equal or greater power than itself. Here success in the role of regional economic engine demonstrated the aspiring hegemon's multidimensional capacity and upward international mobility. Economic success appeared to facilitate upward mobility regardless of whether the regional bargainers being "pulled along" had enlisted as the "engine's" allies in the more encompassing geopolitical competition.

Appearance in Hegemon-Centered Subordinate State Systems

Table 9.2 compares the frequency of aspiring hegemon use of the aforementioned roles in the seven international regions.

The roles in Table 9.2, except for that of "patron/protector of externals," entail special involvement with the bargainer and peripheral states of the regional international system over which special influence is desired. Classifications of "high," "low," and "n.p." (no prominence) derive from comparisons of the importance given to each role in the regional chapters.[6] Not surprisingly, the United States received the largest number of "high" and the smallest number of "n.p." designations. More than other aspirants, this superpower hegemon sought to alter bargaining state behavior. Nigeria, Brazil and India, in contrast, frequently received "n.p." and "low" designations. They may have aspired to imitate Washington, however in the short run they appeared resigned to their smaller capacity to shape regional events. Israel, China and South Africa fell in a middle range. However, all seven aspirants appeared determined to exercise the role of "regional leader" and opponent of those challenging their designs. Had this been otherwise, it would have mandated a reevaluation of whether the hypothesized regional influential not receiving a "high" ranking could be viewed usefully as an aspiring hegemon.

The pariah status of South Africa, and to a lesser extent Israel, differentiates them from other leading regional states. Their aspirations to achieve and sustain a capability to exert special influence appeared largely defensive. This was because within the Middle East and Southern Africa the lack of legitimacy accorded to the domestic political regimes of Israel and South Africa caused their policy makers to fear that being perceived as weak was to invite an armed attack. Also, as suggested earlier, Israeli and South African feared that even the appearance of growing weaker encouraged hostile neighbors to press for changes in dimensions of their domestic political regimes which they viewed as critical to their national survival.

Table 9.2 also profiles "combatant" as an important role assumed by states desirous of exercising subordinate state system leadership. Concern that the aspiring regional hegemon would flex its military muscles was most pervasive within the region with a superpower hegemon. Events since the dawn of the atomic age suggested that other states, including the superpowers, would hesitate to challenge a nuclear power when it employed military force within a region it viewed as its sphere of influence. In addition, the balance of terror made it even more unlikely that one superpower would risk engaging the military forces of the other.

Only Brazil received a "n.p." classification in relation to the role of combatant. This reflects the *Pax Americana* imposed on South America

TABLE 9.2 Cross Regional Comparison of Role Use by Aspiring Hegemon Within Seven Regional International Systems

Role	U.S. in Circum-Caribbean	Israel in Middle East	South Africa in Southern Africa	Brazil in South America	India in South Asia	China in Southeast Asia	Nigeria in West Africa
Protector/Patron of Externals	high	high	n.p.*	n.p.*	n.p.*	low	n.p.*
Regional Leader/Opponent	high	high	high	high	high	high	high
Combatant	high	high	low	n.p.*	medium	medium	low
Mediator	high	n.p.*	n.p.*	low	medium	medium	medium
Regional Pariah	n.p.*	medium	medium	n.p.*	n.p.*	n.p.*	n.p.*
International Pariah	n.p.*	low	low	n.p.*	n.p.*	n.p.*	n.p.*
Policeman	high	n.p.*	n.p.*	medium	low	low	low
Defender of the Faith	high	n.p.*	low	low	low	medium	low
Liberator	medium	low	low	low	low	medium	low
Regional Economic Engine	high	n.p.*	medium	medium	medium	low	low

*no prominence in the region

by Washington during most of the twentieth century. With the decline in United States capacity to influence South America, however, the regional international tensions which spawned conflicts during the nineteenth century could again, in the twenty first, take the form of armed combat.

Finally, within each subordinate state system there were at least some occasions on which the aspiring hegemons attempted to act as a regional economic engine. Here capacity appeared critical. Thus the United States, in keeping with its relatively great economic power, obtained a classification of "high." References to the regional economic engine role in descriptions of Brazil, India and South Africa fell into the "medium" range. Israel, Nigeria and China were less aggressive. Lack of capability explains the "low" ranking for China and Nigeria (although throughout the 1970s petrobonanza, when Nigeria's capacity was greater; Lagos' behavior fell in the "high" range). The Israeli situation was different. Jerusalem's classification in regard to the role of regional economic engine reflected the unwillingness of her Arab neighbors to cooperate with a pariah. Nevertheless, neither Israel, nor any other aspiring regional hegemon, received a "n.p." classification in regard to the role of regional economic engine. This confirms that all aspiring hegemon policy makers believe that some economic power projection capability is necessary if their regional leadership pretensions are to be taken seriously.

Subordinate State System Attributes and Elite Role Perceptions

Our framework for comparing subordinate state systems implies that decisions to emphasize or downplay roles with utility for the pursuit of regional influence are driven by geopolitical considerations. Earlier analysis confirmed that the geopolitical structure of a subordinate state system[7] impacts on policy making directly, by constraining or facilitating the aspiring hegemon's capacity to act. Not discussed was the Figure 9.1 hypothesis portraying geopolitical structure as indirectly shaping regional international relations by its impact on aspiring hegemon role perceptions and the policy goals they imply. In this context policy goals specify what states aspiring to special regional influence hope to accomplish within "their" subordinate state system.

The greater power and influence of aspiring regional hegemons provided a foundation for regional leadership; on occasion it crystallized into hegemony. Keeping this in mind, analysis returns to the seven subordinate state system attribute clusters that shaped role selection by the aspiring hegemons. To review, they were: capacity to exercise hegemony; prevailing regional attitudes toward hegemonic pretensions;

the magnitude of structural challenges to hegemony; the region's susceptibility to external efforts that might restructure the region; the nature of the aspiring hegemon's domestic regime; and, the hegemons relative economic power and technological sophistication.

The first cluster, capacity to exercise regional influence, revolved about the aspiring hegemon's relative political and economic power, including its capacity to dominate regional international organizations (where they existed). Within the most influential state in each region, great importance was attached to conserving privileged status. Aspiring hegemons also seized most opportunities (diplomatic, military and economic), which strengthened their regional leadership. Without exception, the regional leader role was viewed as feasible and desirable.

Aspiring hegemons attached varying degrees of importance to their larger global interests. For India, Israel and South Africa, no other foreign policy interest surpassed that of preserving and increasing capacity to influence within their special regional spheres. Brazil viewed South American and other foreign interests as of roughly the same magnitude. On the other hand, Beijing's relations with Moscow received a higher priority than achieving hegemony in Southeast Asia; similarly, Nigeria attached greater practical importance to economic relations with the OECD countries than to exercising West African regional influence. For the United States, as discussed earlier, Circum-Caribbean hegemony remained secondary to preventing the Soviet Union from dominating Western Europe.

Regional international influence, even when perceived by an aspiring regional hegemon as a secondary foreign policy interest, was never considered unimportant. When threatened, aspiring hegemons pursued it with redoubled vigor. Also, based on the assumption that their influence was greatest in these special geopolitical spheres, regional powers preferred resolving local disputes in institutions specially crafted to service the region. Only if regional institutions produced unsatisfactory results were subordinate state system problems willingly taken by the aspiring hegemon to a global forum, such as the United Nations.

A second grouping of subordinate state system attributes influencing role perception fell under the general heading of attitude toward hegemonic pretensions. They included: (1) nature and existence of a prevailing attitude among bargainers toward the state aspiring to influence (this encompasses the special case of the pariah state syndrome); and, (2) the strength of a significant minority view toward the aspiring hegemon's exercise of special regional influence.

Results summarized in Table 9.1 suggest that hegemonic aspirations generate opposition within the subordinate state system over which influence is sought. Only in two regions (South Asia and the Caribbean

Basin), was there even momentary acceptance of aspiring hegemon leadership by a majority of bargainer states. Significant elements never reconciled themselves to the exercise of special influence; and recently they have become stronger. In the Middle Eastern bargainers vehemently rejected Israel's aspirations for special influence, although a minority view existed in Egypt (since the time of Anwar Sadat). Egypt's preferred alternative involved a sharing of special regional influence and responsibilities between Cairo and Jerusalem. Iraq challenged Egypt's portrayal of itself as the leading Arab state and remained hostile to Israel. Other Arab bargainer states ruled out accommodation with the Jewish state as long as the Palestinian issue remained unresolved.

In South America, South East Asia, and West Africa, aspiring hegemon capability to dominate neighboring bargainers was far less. Nevertheless, when Brazil, China and Nigeria attempted to lead, bargainer state fears frustrated their efforts. Deadlock revealed that structural tensions often undermined the subordinate state system's capacity to act as a cohesive force within the broader global arena.

The third and fourth subordinate state system characteristic influencing role selection revolved about the presence of a stand out bargainer and the likelihood of external, especially superpower, involvement. These two attributes profiled the magnitude of structural challenge to the aspiring hegemon's regional position. Table 9.1 revealed that in four geopolitical arenas (the Circum-Caribbean, South America, the Middle East and South Asia), an especially influential bargainer (Mexico, Argentina, Egypt and Pakistan) challenged the hegemonic aspirations of the most powerful state. In these four, aspiring hegemon elites assigned a high priority to conserving and expanding their regional advantage over the primary challenger. Such efforts, however, facilitated intrusion into the region by external states, especially the superpowers. Individual chapters chronicled several instances of important bargainer states inviting an external power into their region. Invitations usually were intended to counter an aspiring hegemon whose behavior appeared threatening. Pakistan's use of the United States to counter Indian power is perhaps the classic case.

When an aspiring hegemon decided that a regional bargainer was encouraging intervention by an external state, it inclined to the role of regional protector from external interference. This appeared especially true when both the aspirant and the external power being "invited," were superpowers, as in the case of the 1962 Cuban missile crisis. In addition, fear that an external state might alter the regional balance of power sometimes led to adoption of the regional combatant role, as in Washington's 1965 Dominican Republic intervention. To take on the role of regional protector against outside influence, however, an aspiring hegemon did not have to be a superpower. During the Canal war of 1969-71, Israel continually sought to convince Egypt that dependence on the Soviet Union was futile. Finally, when the combatant role was not feasible, the role of liberator (for example, Brazilian support for opponents of Bolivia's leftist Torres government in the early 1970s) was substituted.

A fifth system attribute bearing on aspiring hegemon role selection was highly specific, reflecting the region's vulnerability to efforts by an external power to assume the role of regional leader. Of course all subordinate state systems were subject to outside influence. Two (Southeast Asia and South America), faced an external power with interest in recasting the regional international system as its own sphere. Their designs intensified levels of anxiety among policy makers in the state already perceiving the geopolitical arena as its sphere of influence. Response involved assuming the mantle of defender of the regional status quo; often this defense became cloaked in ideological baggage. Finally, there was the possibility that the threatened hegemon might adopt the role of regional combatant.

From 1890s until its military defeat in 1945, Japan attempted to organize an East Asian sphere from which the Western powers would be expelled and China transformed into a weak and servile neighbor. Similarly, between the second and eighth decades of the twentieth century, the United States behaved as if South America belonged to the more encompassing Western Hemisphere region over which it sought hegemony. Chang and Myers documented that policy makers in China and Brazil had long memories. Beijing and Brasilia continually scrutinized foreign policy from Washington and Tokyo for evidence that earlier American and Japanese hegemonic ambitions persisted.

Sixth, two other Table 9.1 structural attributes (descriptions of the aspiring hegemon's domestic regime) also influenced role perception. They were: (1) strength of domestic political legitimacy; and, (2) degree of subsystem autonomy. Precarious regime legitimacy, especially when government operated in an authoritarian mode, increased the aspiring hegemon's inclination to adopt a defender of the faith role in relation to whatever "political faith" its ruling elites were attempting to institutionalize. Thus between the late 1960s and the middle 1980s, Brazil's conservative officer corps offered assistance to neighboring militaries whom they viewed as struggling against domestic leftists.

Democratic as well as authoritarian hegemons sought to increase the number of regional bargainer states with political systems that resembled their own. However, differences existed in the vigor with which the two kinds of governments plotted to clone their own state organization in that of their neighbors. Aspiring regional hegemons conceding significant space to diverse domestic groups (democracies) were more willing, unless faced by a threatening intrusion from a powerful external power, to tolerate diversity among the domestic political regimes of their neighbors. Democracies also appeared more accepting of a "loose," in contrast to a "tight," coordination within their sphere of interest. Acceptance of domestic political diversity, and of a loosely organized regional international system, were negatively associated with adoption of the combatant, policeman and liberator roles. Finally, elites advocating a messianic ideology were present in democratic as well as authoritarian aspiring hegemons. In both they tended toward intolerance. Intrasystemic intolerance was intensified when neighboring states were organized around norms that the messianic ideology portrayed as evil.

Relative strength and size of the aspiring hegemon's economy is a final subordinate state system attribute influencing the choice of political role. The greater an aspiring hegemon's economic advantage over its neighbors, the more likely it was to weave assertive economic policies into its regional leadership strategy. Also, when contrasted with the pursuit of military and political advantage, aspiring regional hegemons encountered less opposition when they emphasized economic leadership.

Visions of increasing economic influence appeared to have strengthened perceptions among hegemon policy makers that an ever greater number and variety of regional issues were relevant to them.[8] It was a short step from heightened awareness to the formulation and implementation of policies designed to consolidate and increase regional influence. Also, technological dominance appeared to strengthen policy maker perceptions that they must shape the regional environment. In conjunction with messianic ideology, technological dominance intensified the imperative of spreading aspiring hegemon values throughout the region.

To summarize, the seven subordinate state system characteristics or attribute clusters described above indirectly influenced the crystallization of threat perception through their impact on the selection of roles by aspiring hegemon's policy makers. These roles, to repeat, were: (1) protector/patron of externals, (2) regional leader, (3) combatant, (4) mediator, (5) regional pariah, (6) international pariah, (7) policeman, (8) defender of the faith, (9) liberator, and (10) regional economic engine. Adoption of any role locked policy makers into its associated action scripts. The viability of action scripts was largely a product of subordinate state system structure. Thus awareness of structure increased the probability that certain roles would be adopted and others rejected. Aspiring regional hegemons were unlikely to adopt roles with action scripts that, in light of regional structure and dynamics, stood little chance of adding to their capability to exercise influence.

Finally, role selection and implementation depended heavily on the content of the information aspiring hegemon policy makers received, as well as on the perceptual filters through which it passed. Attention now shifts to filtering. Specifically, the focus will be on how aspiring hegemon elites used the lessons they learned in their exercise of regional influence to filter current information about events within the regional international system over which they desired special influence.

The Filtering of Past Experience

Filtering emerged from the case studies as a process in which experience predisposed aspiring hegemon policy makers in their assessment of whether actions (or events) were threatening to their regional aspirations. The structure of predispositions was multifaceted. For example, it sometimes inclined aspiring hegemon policy makers in one region to view efforts by a bargainer state to alter the domestic political life of its neighbors as highly threatening. In another region, predispositional filtering could have the opposite effect. This held for how policy makers perceived such critical developments as shifts in the balance of power between regional bargainer states and intensified relations between regional actors and those in the larger international environment.

Once actions came to be viewed as threatening to the exercise of regional influence, this perception was highly resistant to change. Linkages between interpretations of filtered information and choices among alternative strategic responses also proved long lasting. Policies that earlier succeeded in defusing dangerous situations usually were favored over untried alternatives. Failed policies seldom received a second hearing.

Memories of past events with significant filtering power fell into four categories: military, diplomatic, economic and cultural/ideological. Table 9.3 summarizes findings from the regional chapters for these categories. It employs the concepts of "emphasis" and "utility" in exploring the filtering impact of memories on threat perception crystallization and strategic response selection. "Emphasis" assesses the relative attention given by aspiring hegemon elites, in exercising regional influence, to each of the aforementioned categories. "Utility" encompasses the perceived effectiveness (by the aspiring regional hegemon) of the category in achieving desired outcomes.

Military Lessons Learned

The filtering impact of military experience in efforts to exercise special regional leadership varied. For none of the contemporary regional powers was the lessons learned from employing military power ones that placed

TABLE 9.3 The Filtering Impact of Lessons Learned in the Exercise of Regional Influence with Bargainer States

Area in Which Lesson Was "Learned" (by Hegemon) Concerning the Exercise of Regional Influence	U.S. within Caribbean Basin		Israel in Middle East		Brazil in South America		India in South Asia	
	emphasis	utility	emphasis	utility	emphasis	utility	emphasis	utility
Military Force (on bargainers)	medium	positive	high	positive	low	positive	medium	unclear
Diplomacy	high	positive	medium	medium	high	positive	high	positive
Economic Instruments	medium	unclear	low	unclear	medium	positive	medium	positive
Cultural/Ideological	medium	unclear	low	negative	low	unclear	low	unclear

Area in Which Lesson Was "Learned" (by Hegemon) Concerning the Exercise of Regional Influence	South Africa in Southern Africa		China in West Africa		Nigeria in West Africa	
	emphasis	utility	emphasis	utility	emphasis	utility
Military Force (on bargainers)	high	positive	medium	unclear	low	negative
Diplomacy	medium	unclear	high	unclear	high	low
Economic Instruments	medium	positive	medium	unclear	medium	positive
Cultural/Ideological	low	negative	low	unclear	medium	unclear

an absolute prohibition on its use. No post 1945 resort to armed force in exercising regional influence resulted in a traumatic defeat of the magnitude experienced in World War II, by Germany, Italy and Japan. Thus, for the seven aspiring regional hegemons, military force appeared as a dangerous but potentially useful option. Its employment in the exercise of subordinate state system influence was seen as acceptable under given calculations of cost and benefit.

Two critical lessons learned since the end of World War II made aspiring regional hegemons view the use of military force as highly risky. In the first place, on numerous occasions initiating violence altered the cost-benefit ratio of its employment. Actions which initially appeared strongly beneficial might have consequences that were unanticipated and unfavorable. The most notable example was in the Caribbean Basin, following the failure of President Kennedy's invasion of Cuba at the Bay of Pigs. Castro's victory convinced Moscow that his regime was viable. Subsequent Soviet assistance to Cuba and other Communist insurgencies dramatically increased the costs of exercising Circum-Caribbean hegemony to the United States.

The second critical lesson involved public opinion's increasing influence on policy making. Since the 1960s, public opinion has complicated the use of military force, even within highly regimented states such as the People's Republic of China. The constraints are even more pronounced inside of democratic aspirants. For example, divisive debate over India's dispatch of troops to Siri Lanka, for the purpose of breaking the Tamil insurgency, played a significant role in Prime Minister Rajiv Ghandi's defeat at the polls. This suggests that only if the cost is minimal, and success highly probable (as with the United States in its 1990 invasion of Panama), can governments ignore domestic critics when projecting military power abroad. In other words, since the 1960s, protracted military adventures to exercise regional dominance have generated internal conflicts that undermined, usually fatally, the ability of government to accomplish its intended purposes.

Diplomatic Lessons Learned

The filtering impact of lessons learned about the capacity of diplomacy to advance regional aspirations confirmed that to influence effectively diplomacy must command multifaceted resources. The most useful of these were military force, economic power and ideological attraction. By definition aspiring hegemons possessed more of one or all of the aforementioned than did bargainer or peripheral states. Skillful diplomacy amplified the hegemon's advantages when responding to threat perceptions. However, it could not create resources.

Five of the seven aspiring hegemons treated diplomacy as the most important activity in advancing their regional aspirations. Only for Israel in the Middle East, and for South Africa in Southern Africa, was diplomacy secondary. As pointed out on numerous occasions, most states in these regions either denied the right of Israel and South Africa to exist or viewed their ruling elites as illegitimate. Thus intense hostility on the part of regional bargainers forced Israel and South Africa to give highest priority to the military instrument. Nevertheless, Irwin and Albright noted that Israel and South Africa remained hopeful that they could alter the balance between armed force and other instruments when pursuing regional policies.

United States preference for diplomacy to exercise Caribbean Basin influence was unique in that Washington assigned low priority to a geopolitical region that it sought to dominate. Viewed as a necessary preserve from which to pursue more important global interests, the United States desired to keep the Circum-Caribbean tranquil. Bargain basement hegemony was the order of the day. Correspondingly, policy makers supported almost any Caribbean leader who would keep things quiet; and the United States became allied with the status quo. The appearance of hostile regimes in Cuba, Nicaragua and Grenada during the Cold War, however, taught the United States that benign neglect eroded Circum-Caribbean hegemony. This strengthened Washington's predisposition to oppose Marxist-Leninist regimes and search for moderate alternatives to intransigent traditionalists. Nevertheless, when diplomacy failed the United States employed force against recalcitrant elements it considered hostile.

Military threat was not a central component of Brazil's South American diplomacy, or of Nigerian relations with its West African neighbors. On the Brazilian side, one important lesson learned concerned the tangible benefits to be derived from a professional foreign service. Brazil's foreign service, the Itamaraty, outmaneuvered rival Hispanic American diplomats while acquiring important border territories for Brazil during the early twentieth century. Brasilia's diplomatic competence and strategy remained without peer in South America. Over the past decades it prevented the Andean Pact from evolving into an anti-Brazilian alliance, gained acceptance for an embryonic Amazon Development Pact, and engineered rapprochement with Argentina.

Nigeria initiated numerous diplomatic efforts to build its influence throughout West Africa during the halcyon days of high petroleum prices. Aside from increased prestige and raising Nigeria's profile, however, Lagos gained little that was tangible. In addition, the Nigerian foreign service failed to institutionalize the capabilities that would have allowed Nigeria to take advantage of the inroads made between 1973 and 1983. Thus, when plummeting petroleum prices reduced the Nigerian state's capabilities, most initiatives toward exercising influence throughout West Africa were abandoned.

Finally, the importance India attached to South Asia resembles that which China assigned to Southeast Asia; the regional aspirations of both fell midway within the hierarchy of their foreign policy concerns. Indian and Chinese policy makers viewed South Asia and Southeast Asia as more important than the Circum-Caribbean appeared in Washington. On the other hand, South Asia and Southeast Asia were of less concern to New Delhi and Beijing than was South America to Brazil.

Economic Lessons Learned

Economic instruments were the third dimension along which the exercise of influence filtered perceptions about the kinds of activities that facilitated acquiring and maintaining subordinate state system influence. Among the cases examined, Washington placed the most emphasis on economic measures in its designs to influence the Circum-Caribbean. However, these efforts failed to produce the clearly positive balance that the Marshall Plan yielded after World War II in Western Europe. Consequently, the United States grew more cautious in its use of economic means to influence other states, especially in the developing world.

In its Middle Eastern strategy, Israel gave less emphasis to the economic dimension than did any other aspiring hegemon. Irwin suggested that this was because maintaining a high level of military preparedness strained Jerusalem's limited economic capacity. In addition, Israeli leaders were pessimistic about the ability of economic instruments to further their regional goals as long as other Middle Eastern states treated their state as a pariah.

Brazil, India and South Africa saw economic strategies differently. They considered them useful in projecting regional influence; although less so than diplomacy, and on occasion military force. In general, these three viewed economic initiatives as having strengthened their leadership position. Each boasted by far the largest and most sophisticated economy within its subordinate state system.

Despite concerns about imperial designs, South American, South Asian and Southern African bargainer states, at least in the short run, opted for the economic benefits of cooperation with the aspiring regional hegemon. This decision was especially poignant in the Southern Africa region. As long as Pretoria clings to apartheid, Southern African bargainer states, portray their powerful neighbor as a pariah. Nevertheless, even while expressing distaste for racial segregation inside of South Africa, regional bargainer states cultivated economically beneficial relations. In this context, it is revealing that the magnitude of South Africa's economic power, in comparison with black African states in the region, was greater than that of Israel in relation to its Arab neighbors.

The remaining aspiring regional hegemons, China and Nigeria, attached a middle level of importance to economics in responding to threat perceptions. Both were apprehensive over with the disappointing results of their development programs. They approached the 1990s with serious constraints on their ability to wield economic instruments. Plummeting petroleum prices after 1982 prices forced Nigeria to all but abandon technical assistance for West Africa. China's economy, derailed by domestic turmoil in the 1960s and 1970s, recovered during 1980s. However, Japan's emergence as an economic superpower dwarfed China ability to employ economic incentives in pursuit of regional objectives.

To summarize, it appears that clearly positive balances from the exercise of regional economic strategies depend on the aspiring hegemon enjoying multidimensional qualitative and quantitative superiority over the economies of regional bargainer states. While this appeared as a necessary condition, it was not sufficient. Other conditions facilitating a clearly positive balance included a desire for hegemon economic resources by bargainer states and hegemon sensitivity to bargainer state fears of economic imperialism.

Ideological and Cultural Lessons Learned

In the quest for regional influence, no aspiring hegemon relied primarily on ideological or cultural strategies. Nevertheless, these strategies were regularly used by the United States in the Circum-Caribbean and by both superpowers when they challenged a resident aspiring hegemon. The superpowers were the only major players organized around legitimating myths (liberal democracy and communism) of potentially universal appeal. However, both found cultural and ideological strategies of limited utility in the exercise of geopolitical influence. Correspondingly, the Soviet Union and the United States, while not openly abandoning their contention that communism and liberal democracy were inevitable and desirable, became more tolerant of cultural and ideological diversity. The "lesson learned" suggested that overt efforts to proselytize were counterproductive. Nationalism, and religious fundamentalism, on the other hand, enjoyed growing popularity as mobilizing mechanisms available to bargainer states in their resistance to aspiring hegemon designs.

The Receipt of Information Perceived as Threatening

The above analysis portrayed threat perception crystallization among hegemon foreign policy makers as a process in which the designation of information as "threatening" occurred after its passage through lessons learned filtering. Designation derived from an assessment, in light of the subordinate state system's attributes, that newly reported events made the aspiring hegemon less capable of playing the regional role envisioned for it by its leaders. Filtering was a three-stage process. During the first, a decision was made as to whether the information being received revealed the existence of a threat to the aspiring hegemon's regional position or designs. When no threat was perceived, the information was discarded. If policy makers detected a threat, they analyzed the information to determine whether the threat was primarily military, diplomatic, economic, or ideological. Finally, policy makers assessed threat intensity.

Attention turns to the information that aspiring hegemon leaders viewed as threatening to their regional aspirations. The focus is on three kinds of threatening information: military, diplomatic and economic. Ideological information receives cursory attention. Except in cases involving Muslim fundamentalism, aspiring hegemons viewed the threatening potential of ideology as low and declining. Examination of threatening information also focuses attention on the three arenas of origin: domestic politics within each aspiring hegemon; the subordinate state system over which each sought special influence; and the larger international environment. Substantive threats emanating from the three arenas are analyzed.

The lens for detecting threatening information, as profiled in Table 9.4, differs in each arena. Threatening information from the domestic arena is trichotomized (high, medium low), in accord with the perceptions of intensity held by aspiring hegemon policy makers. The presence of information viewed as threatening, and originating in the regional international system, is noted by a simple yes/no dichotomy. Finally, the global arena is assessed. Here concern begins when aspiring hegemon policy makers discover capabilities and aspirations that they perceive as potentially destructive of their regional influence. Concern gives way to perception of threat when they detect policy making intended to fulfill those aspirations.

Militarily Threatening Information

Aspiring regional hegemon policy makers viewed each arena (domestic, regional and global) as a potential source of military threat. Militarily threatening information conveyed that in one of these arenas a critical threshold was being approached, or passed. Beyond this threshold the decay of civil society, or deterioration in the balance of military forces, would undermine the aspiring hegemon's capability to project power

TABLE 9.4 Cross Regional Comparison of Militarily Threatening Information

Information	U.S. in Circum-Carib-bean	Israel in Middle East	South Africa in Southern Africa	Brazil in South America
From Within the Aspiring Hegemon				
violent demonstrations	medium	high	high	high
insurgency	low	high	high	medium
regional revolt	low	high	high	low
From Within the Region				
bargainer state building up conventional arms capability	yes	yes/thrtng	yes/thrtng	yes/thrtng
bargainer state seeking/updating nuclear weapons capability	no	yes/thrtng	no	??/thrtng
bargainer state developing/improving indigenous arms industry	no	yes/thrtng	no	yes/non-thrt
From Global Arena				
external conventional military forces targeted on territory of aspiring regional hegemon	yes	yes	no	no
external nuclear military forces targeted on territory of aspiring regional hegemon	yes	yes	no	no
external power military force based inside subordinate state system	no	yes	yes	yes
external power has mounted combat operations inside subordinate state system since 1945	no	yes	yes	yes

TABLE 9.4 (Continued)

Information	India in South Asia	China in Southeast Asia	Nigeria in West Africa
From Within the Aspiring Hegemon			
violent demonstrations	medium	high	high
insurgency	medium	medium	medium
regional revolt	medium	medium	high
From Within the Region			
bargainer state building up conventional arms capability	yes/thrtng	yes/thrtng	no
bargainer state seeking/updating nuclear weapons capability	yes/thrtng	no	no
bargainer state developing/improving indigenous arms industry	yes/thrtng	yes/thrtng	no
From Global Arena			
external conventional military forces targeted on territory of aspiring regional hegemon	yes	yes	no
external nuclear military forces targeted on territory of aspiring regional hegemon	yes	yes	no
external power military force based inside subordinate state system	yes	yes	yes
external power has mounted combat operations inside subordinate state system since 1945	yes	yes	yes

regionally. Three domestic political events were seen as undermining power projection capability; rioting, insurgency, and revolt. At the regional level, four kinds of militarily threatening information were common. The first derived from evidence that a bargainer state, in relation to the aspiring hegemon, was improving its conventional arms capability. Also viewed as threatening were bargainer state efforts to acquire or modernize nuclear arms; or to develop an indigenous arms production capability. Fourth, perception of threat crystallized when hegemon policy makers came to believe that their neighbors were attempting to undermine the morale of their armed forces.

Finally, regional powers considered four kinds of military information originating in the global arena as potentially threatening. They felt threatened when an external state targeted its conventional and/or nuclear forces on their national territory, and by an extraregional state's retention or acquisition of regional military bases. Threat perceptions were magnified when the "offending" external power or powers had mounted combat operations inside the subordinate state system within the memory of aspiring hegemon leaders.

Two conditions identified in the case studies increased the probability of an aspiring hegemon's own domestic political processes generating information that would be viewed as potentially militarily threatening to their regional aspirations. The first revolved about perceptions that the aspiring hegemon's political regime was illegitimate. Legitimacy tensions forced aspiring hegemon leaders to remain on alert, holding back military resources to deal with possible violent demonstrations, insurgencies or revolts. The potential of these events to destabilize the aspiring hegemon's political regime increased if neighboring governments viewed those challenging the regime sympathetically. This problem was most pronounced in the Middle East and in Southern Africa, regional international systems with pariah hegemons. India faced an analogous problems with the Sikhs (and, to a lesser extent with the Tamils). Even the United States was forced to take into account the frustrations of its growing Hispanic population when dealing with the Caribbean Basin. However, the military threat potential of information emanating from dissident nationalities within India and the United States appeared less alarming than what was being received from Israel's Arab population or from South African blacks.

The second internal condition with a potential to generate militarily threatening information was the failure of an aspiring hegemon to have consolidated internal regime legitimacy among its core population (as opposed to national minorities). Aspiring hegemons in the Third World suffered from this condition more often than others. It crippled Brazilian, Nigerian and Chinese aspirations for long periods, although its impact on India has been marginal since the violence that accompanied Pakistani independence. Finally, the United States, despite sporadic internal violence protesting its armed involvement in the third world, generated the lowest overall level of domestic information viewed by its foreign policy makers as militarily threatening.

All aspiring regional hegemons, with the possible exception of Nigeria, were confronted with improvements in the conventional armed forces of their neighbors. Only in the Caribbean Basin did the United States fail to view this as potentially threatening, although even here Soviet military assistance to Cuba crystallized concerns. In the Middle East, South Asia, Southern Africa and South America, aspiring hegemon policy makers were especially unhappy with increases in their neighbors' military capabilities. Buildup, however, was seldom perceived as a prelude to attack; rather, hegemon policy makers saw its unfavorable potential in the reduced regional influence it implied.

Aspiring hegemons viewed success by bargainer states in creating their own arms industry as threatening. Israel was especially apprehensive when hostile Arab governments undertook development of such sophisticated armaments as chemical and biological weapons. Of course all aspiring hegemons perceived an intense challenge when bargainer states pursued research on nuclear arms. The overwhelming destructive power of nuclear weapons restricted the circumstances under which aspiring hegemons could use military superiority to influence events within the subordinate state system.

The global arena, between 1945 and 1970, acted differently as a source of militarily threatening information for the United States than for the six aspiring hegemons that were not superpowers. Only Washington possessed armed forces capable of intervention in each of the regional arenas. The often-cited trauma of Vietnam, however, demonstrated that if exercising this capability involved the shedding of American blood it could not be sustained for long periods. Thus the difficulties and costs of armed intervention in the third world constrained United States military options, although they remained greater than those available to less powerful aspiring hegemons.

Politically Threatening Information

Subordinate state system descriptions also traced the information from which political threat perceptions coalesced to arenas that were domestic, regional and global. Information from the first was viewed as politically threatening by hegemon policy makers when it conveyed that a threshold was being approached, or had been passed, beyond which strains in civil society diminished regional power projection capability. Three domestic political conditions undermined this capability: precariously low levels of state legitimacy; incomplete regime consolidation; and, significant opposition to the regional policy itself.

The regional international system gave rise to five kinds of political information with a potential to constrain hegemonic aspirations. The first two were geopolitical: persistence or emergence of conflicting territorial claims with a neighbor, and crystallization of an alliance among bargainer states or between a bargainer state and an external power. Two more (ideological clash and persisting ethnic or racial hostility between a bargainer state and the hegemon) revolved about value clash. Significant or intensifying legitimacy problems within a bargainer state, the final condition, was potentially threatening because accompanying instability often gave rise to unpredictable effects on foreign policy, and because internal violence easily could spill beyond the unstable state's frontiers.

Finally, the global arena generated three kinds of political information that regional aspirants found threatening. First, as with unstable states inside their sphere of influence, aspiring hegemons became anxious when a state bordering on the sphere experienced significant and intensifying legitimacy problems. Second, an increasing probability that some global international organization (for example, the United Nations) might intrude into the aspirant's region raised concerns. Finally, persisting or intensifying hostility in the global arena toward an aspiring regional hegemon, or its political regime, intensified hegemon elite insecurity.

Table 9.5 reveals that the threat potential of domestic political information from within the seven aspirants varied greatly. It was highest in South Africa and Israel, where large numbers (of blacks in the former and of Arabs in the latter) viewed both the state and political regime as illegitimate.

On the other hand, South African whites and Israeli Jews were passionately committed to the status quo. This increased tension, with hostility and support clashing to inflame passions. In the United States, India and Nigeria mediumly discordant or "mixed" political signals from domestic interests constrained capability to project power throughout the chosen geopolitical arena. "Mixed" signals, however, permitted significant latitude.

Persistently precarious regime legitimacy was less ambiguous. It set in motion declines in regional influence. Brazil suffered the most. Post 1985 civilian politicians, preoccupied with implementing and gaining acceptance for a new constitution, devoted less attention to regional matters than their military predecessors. In China, despite apparent conformity following the brutal response at Tiananmen Square, analogous

TABLE 9.5 Cross Regional Comparison of Politically Threatening Information

Information	U.S. in Circum-Caribbean	Israel in Middle East	South Africa in Southern Africa	Brazil in South America
From Within the Aspiring Hegemon				
precariousness of state's legitimacy	low	medium	medium	low
precariousness of regime's legitimacy	low	high	high	medium
level of opposition to regional foreign policy	medium	high	high	low
From Within the Region				
persistence of conflicting territorial claims	yes	yes	yes	yes
persistence/intensification of ideological clash	yes	yes	no	yes
persistence/growth of legitimacy problems within bargainer states	yes	yes	yes	yes
bargainer/external power cooperation more probable	yes	yes	yes	yes
persistence/growth of ethnic hostility between the bargainer state(s) and hegemon	no	yes	yes	no
From Global Arena				
persisting or increasing legitimacy problems in states bordering on subordinate state system	yes	yes	yes	yes
global organization is dealing/has dealt with political problems inside region	yes	yes	yes	no
significant hostility toward the region's aspiring hegemon	yes	yes	yes	no

(Continues)

TABLE 9.5 (Continued)

Information	India in South Asia	China in Southeast Asia	Nigeria in West Africa
From Within the Aspiring Hegemon			
precariousness of state's legitimacy	low	low	medium
precariousness of regime's legitimacy	medium	medium	medium
level of opposition to regional foreign policy	medium	low	medium
From Within the Region			
persistence of conflicting territorial claims	yes	yes	yes
persistence/intensification of ideological clash	yes	yes	no
persistence/growth of legitimacy problems within bargainer states	yes	yes	yes
bargainer/external power cooperation more probable	yes	yes	yes
persistence/growth of ethnic hostility between the bargainer state(s) and hegemon	yes	yes	yes
From Global Arena			
persisting or increasing legitimacy problems in states bordering on subordinate state system	yes	yes	yes
global organization is dealing/has dealt with political problems inside region	no	no	yes
significant hostility toward the region's aspiring hegemon	no	no	no

disagreement over political rules of the game focused policy making on the domestic arena.

Information confirming international (although subordinate state system bounded) threats to aspiring hegemon designs circulated in each of the seven regions. It was especially prevalent in the third or "Southern" world. Patterns of interaction in these regions had only recently crystallized, or were in the process of crystallizing. The force projection capabilities of these aspirants was greatly inferior to those of the United States, which as discussed earlier, had declined. This led to speculation that, setting aside the nuclear weapons dimension, it had become prohibitively costly for aspiring hegemons to pursue regional policies whose feasibility rested on military power alone. Correspondingly, bargainer states appeared less fearful of powerful neighbors and more inclined to assert their autonomy. Whether fallout from the 1990 Persian Gulf crisis will weaken this trend remains an open question.

Finally, from the global arena, each aspiring hegemon received information that some state(s) bordering on its regional sphere of influence was (were) experiencing significant legitimacy problems. Thus the precariousness of regime legitimacy throughout South America was viewed as serious by the United States; reduced governmental authority in states such as Colombia and Peru created almost insurmountable problems for Washington's domestic war on drugs. In China, on the other hand, instability in Burma seemed only tangentially threatening as a Southeast Asian regional problem. However, this did not mean that China, or any other aspiring hegemon, looked with indifference when a regime legitimacy crises exploded on the periphery of its desired sphere of influence.

Significant variation existed in how threatened aspiring hegemons felt over the possibility that a global organization might intrude into their sphere of interest, and over perceptions of continuing international hostility toward them. In two regions (Southeast Asia and South America) the aspiring hegemon was not unduly concerned. China and Brazil welcomed a limited presence by global international organizations as a means of constraining the penetrative impulses of the United States and the Soviet Union. Within the Circum-Caribbean, Middle East, and Southern Africa, in contrast, the aspiring hegemon perceived information about contemplated intervention by a global international organization (especially the United Nations), as undermining its regional prerogatives. On the other hand, the increased costs of sealing off "special" regions oriented hegemon policy makers toward accommodating the bargainer states.

The final kind of political information from the global arena with the potential to threaten regional aspirations, confirmation of widespread hostility toward the aspiring state, predominated in descriptions of three aspiring hegemons. Those with overall negative images were the United States, Israel and South Africa. The first was a superpower; neighbors of the others viewed them as creatures of Western imperialism. Aspirants evoking little global hostility (Brazil, India, China and Nigeria) were third world states. They themselves had experienced European and North American colonialism. In addition, they possessed little capacity to project power outside of the region over which they sought special influence.

Economically Threatening Information

In the economic sphere, as with the military and political, domestic, regional and global arenas each produced distinctive information that could be viewed as threatening. Threats from the domestic arena conveyed that a threshold was being approached, or had been passed, beyond which strains in the hegemon's economy undermined capability to exercise regional influence. Here two conditions appeared especially threatening: persistently high levels of unemployment and low levels of economic growth. Regional capabilities experienced additional erosion when these conditions were accompanied by high rates of population increase. Within the regional arena two kinds of economic information also appeared ominous for hegemonic aspirations. The first signaled whether the aspiring hegemon's economy was declining in relation to regional bargainer states, and the magnitude of influence that it retained within the region. The second revolved about bargainer state economic health. When a neighbor's economy experienced the destabilizing mixture of high unemployment, low economic growth, and explosive rates of population increase, aspiring hegemon policy makers became concerned.

Moving beyond region, the global arena generated three strands of economic information seen as potentially threatening. First, hegemon elite insecurity grew when the relative size of their state's GDP declined. Also alarming was evidence that economic dependence for critical raw materials or industrial products on a single extraregional state or cartel was increasing. Finally, anxiety intensified when the hegemon's economy experienced difficulties in developing or assimilating new technologies. Inability to innovate or incorporate innovation raised the specter of declining capacity to resist intrusion by unwanted but sophisticated outsiders. In earlier times, these anxieties often led to foreign military adventures; history abounds with leaders who urged military action against a rapidly developing rival. The late twentieth-century balance of terror, while not ruling out this option completely, magnified the dangers of implementing it. Most often perceptions of dependency and decline forced aspiring hegemons to focus on domestic economic growth and reactivation.

Table 9.6 reveals that threat perceptions derived from information about the domestic economy of aspiring hegemons varied greatly. Its content appeared most ominous for Brazilians and Nigerians. Plagued by persisting unemployment and inflation, Brazilian and Nigerian economic development failed to keep pace with population growth. China found itself in a milder version of the same predicament. Indian economic development barely exceeded population growth; and the large number of unemployed remained a debilitating legacy. The domestic economy of South Africa also generated threatening information, although as in so much else, perceptions of danger derived from differences between the life-styles and treatment accorded to blacks and whites. The more numerous and rapidly reproducing blacks, despite some improvement in the quality of their lives, appeared ever more threatening to the ruling Afrikaner minority. On a smaller scale, Israel faced the same problem with its Arab population.

The United States, alone among the aspiring regional hegemons, enjoyed consistently low levels of unemployment, and an economy that kept pace with population growth. It boasted a large and sophisticated industrial plant that dwarfed that of its southern neighbors. Still United States economic dominance in the Circum-Caribbean declined between 1955 and 1990. Growing Japanese and European industrial might was a challenge; in the long term it threatened to undercut the economic foundations of United States capability to influence Caribbean Basin states. This was an artifact of the successes that Japan and West Germany enjoyed in their global economic competition with the United States during the 1980s. Another measure of this success was the massive deficit Washington experienced in bilateral trade with Tokyo and Bonn. The new constraints on Washington's ability to pursue regional and other interests were revealed in the compromises to which President Bush agreed at the July 1990 economic summit.[9]

The smaller and less sophisticated industrial and technological establishments of the other six aspiring hegemons constrained them from economically influencing their selected geopolitical arena to the extent that the United States dominated the Caribbean Basin. However, India and South Africa played important economic roles throughout South Asia and Southern Africa. Both also perceived some threat in the chronic economic difficulties experienced by several states bordering on these subordinate state systems. In general, South Africa's regional economic influence was greater; and during the 1970s and 1980s it increased. In addition, India benefitted from a favorable trend in South Asia, although on a more modest scale. Pretoria and New Delhi experienced few difficulties in digesting technological innovations from North America, Europe and Japan; both avoided losing ground. Nevertheless, Indian

TABLE 9.6 Cross Regional Comparison of Threatening Economic Information

Information	U.S. in Circum-Caribbean	Israel in Middle East	South Africa in Southern Africa	Brazil in South America
From Within the Aspiring Hegemon				
level of unemployment	low	low	low	high
rate of economic growth/population growth	medium/low	medium/low*	medium/high (black)	medium/high
From Within the Region				
hegemon's economic position declining with region (magnitude of influence)	yes(dominant)	no(marginal)	no(significant)	no(marginal)
persisting/growing economic instability in the domestic economies of bargainer states	yes	yes	yes	yes
From Global Arena				
hegemon GDP as % of global GDP declining	yes	yes	yes	yes
hegemon economic dependence on small number of extraregional states/cartels increasing	yes	yes	yes	no
hegemon economy with difficulty assimilating new technology or incorporating innovation	no	no	no	yes

TABLE 9.6 (Continued)

Information	India in South Asia	China in Southeast Asia	Nigeria in West Africa
From Within the Aspiring Hegemon			
level of unemployment	medium	medium	high
rate of economic growth/population growth	medium/high	medium/medium	low/high
From Within the Region			
hegemon's economic position declining with region (magnitude of influence)	no(significant)	no(marginal)	no(marginal)
persisting/growing economic instability in the domestic economies of bargainer states	yes	no	yes
From Global Arena			
hegemon GDP as % of global GDP declining	no	yes	yes
hegemon economic dependence on small number of extraregional states/cartels increasing	no	no	yes
hegemon economy with difficulty assimilating new technology or incorporating innovation	mixed	yes	yes

*growth rate for the Arab population is high

elites viewed the large absolute gap between the size and sophistication of India's economy and that of the OECD countries as threatening to its regional aspirations. The analogous gap for South Africa's economy caused less concern in Pretoria; not only was South Africa more technologically sophisticated, but white South Africans assumed that many multinational businesses, despite their public positions, were favorably disposed toward them.

Israel, Brazil and China were not central to economic life in the region each hoped to make its sphere of influence. Of the three, Israel's economy was the most sophisticated in comparison with that of its neighbors; but Jerusalem's status as a pariah crippled its potential to act as a regional engine of growth. It also forced Israel to produce many goods whose primary purpose was to defend the Jewish state. Brazil, in contrast, used its weapons production capability to enhance its regional and global influence. But the other dimensions of Brazil's large industrial plant provided only minimal support for efforts to influence South America. Protectionism led to technological obsolescence and poverty undercut growth potential. Brasilia hoped that development of a Southern Cone common market would lessen these constraints. However, massive indebtedness and Spanish South America's lack of hard currency to purchase foreign goods suggested that it would be difficult for Brazil to reduce dependence on exports to the OECD countries.

The People's Republic of China also dealt from weakness when relying upon economic strategies to support regional aspirations. While not weighted down by massive indebtedness, the Chinese economy, like its Brazilian counterpart, was depressed by massive poverty. China traded her most valuable exports for products and technology absolutely essential to economic development. The countries of Southeast Asia produced few of these essentials. Reliance on economic aid to gain regional influence was out of the question in all but the most threatening situations. However, China's economic influence in Southeast Asia was greater than Nigeria's presence in West Africa.

In summary, while the regional economic influence of the seven aspiring hegemons varied greatly, in no instance was economic pressure by itself decisive enough to force significant behavior modifications on bargainer states. Thus the United States had its greatest impact on the economies of Caribbean Basin states when it was able to integrate economic, political and military pressure. The power advantage of regionally influential states that were not superpowers lacked this multidimensionality. Finally, declining economic influence by itself, unless dramatic, was perceived as only mildly threatening. Low domestic economic growth rates, in contrast, were viewed with alarm. A stagnating economy made improvement in living standards impossible; and, in the case of aspirants with rapidly expanding populations, signaled declines in living conditions that already were considered unacceptable. When policy makers calculated that increased regional economic influence might alleviate domestic economic difficulties, they turned outward. Exploration of these and other responses is the next task of this analysis.

Strategic Responses

Our concern, as stated earlier, is not with all international challenges; rather, it focuses on responses to perceptions of medium and long term threat to regional interests. This excludes options for dealing with such immediate contingencies as armed attack and demands for surrender. Strategic response, to a greater extent than threat perception crystallization, forced policy makers to examine the comparative capabilities of their state to act. In choosing a strategic response, therefore, the roles that involved bureaucracies were believed capable of playing acquired special significance.

Aspiring hegemon responses to regional strategic threats revolved about four options. Three; accommodation, defense through deterrence/allying, and counterthreat; employed the resources a state possessed at the time of response selection. The fourth, state strengthening, sought to create new capabilities. Pursued when a strategic threat appeared likely to persist indefinitely, state strengthening emphasized increasing state power along three dimensions; the political, the economic, and the military.

Within the seven regions, there were variations over time in the frequency of appearance and importance assigned to each strategic response. Whether the domestic, regional or global arena (or some combination) appeared as the primary source of a threat shaped the differing patterns of strategic response. Aspiring hegemons sometimes concentrated on a single strategic response; more often they crafted a strategic mix.

Patterns of Strategic Responses

The extent of reliance that individual aspiring regional hegemons placed on alternative strategic responses is summarized in Table 9.7. Total aspiring hegemon reliance on all strategies in each arena (domestic, regional, and global) is assumed to be 100 percent. In selecting among these responses, aspiring hegemon policy makers gave a relative weighting to each response. (The domestic arena excluded the defense through deterrence/allying option because it was absent in the accounts of individual regions). When a strategic response received 35 percent or

TABLE 9.7 Cross Regional Comparison of Strategic Responses (Extent of Reliance)

Information	U.S. in Circum-Caribbean	Israel in Middle East	South Africa in Southern Africa	Brazil in South America	India in South Asia	China in Southeast Asia	Nigeria in West Africa
From Within the Aspiring Hegemon							
accommodation	moderate	low	low	moderate	moderate	moderate	moderate
state strengthening	moderate	heavy	heavy	heavy	heavy	heavy	heavy
counterthreat	moderate	heavy	heavy	moderate	moderate	moderate	moderate
From Within the Region							
accommodation	moderate	low	low	moderate	moderate	moderate	moderate
defense through deterrence/allying	heavy	heavy	heavy	moderate	moderate	moderate	moderate
state strengthening	moderate	moderate	moderate	heavy	heavy	heavy	heavy
counterthreat	heavy	heavy	heavy	low	moderate	moderate	low
From Global Arena							
accommodation	low	moderate	moderate	heavy	moderate	moderate	heavy
defense through deterrence/allying	heavy	heavy	heavy	moderate	heavy	heavy	low
state strengthening	moderate	heavy	heavy	heavy	heavy	heavy	heavy
counterthreat	moderate	moderate	moderate	low	moderate	moderate	low

more of the total arena emphasis, the level of reliance upon it was considered "heavy." A reliance level of between 15 and 34 percent was "moderate;" and a "low" level of response indicated that policy makers placed less than 15 percent of total arena reliance on the response.[10]

Strategic response selection patterns in the domestic arena again confirmed similarities within each of the three categories of aspiring regional hegemons: the superpower; the pariahs; and the third world states. The United States government, in responding to domestic threats against its Circum-Caribbean policies, placed roughly equal (moderate) reliance on the three available strategic responses. The Reagan presidency was especially notable for experimenting with counterthreat. This choice flowed from frustration over domestic opposition to support for its El Salvador client whose government remained cavalier toward human rights, and over orchestration of "clandestine" intervention in the domestic affairs of Sandinista Nicaragua. However, mild sanctions proved ineffective; and the successor Bush administration, with the significant exception of the Panama invasion, shifted toward accommodation. This reversal underscored the growing importance of public opinion.

Israel and South Africa assigned similar priorities among the possible strategic responses to threats of domestic origin. Both calculated the threat potential from the three common military contingencies originating inside the country (violent demonstrations, insurgency, and regional revolt) to be high. Israeli and South African leaders placed heavy reliance on the strategic responses of state strengthening and counterthreat. Emphasis on the former reflected fears that any weakening of pariah hegemon comparative regional advantage invited hostile moves by neighboring bargainer states. Heavy reliance on counterthreat revealed determination not to compromise with alienated dissidents, especially those belonging to racial or ethnic groups which viewed political order within the aspiring hegemon as illegitimate. Finally, South Africa and Israel opted for medium reliance on accommodation, although the former increasingly emphasized this strategy after 1989. Israel, in contrast, only pursued accommodation tangentially in dealings with the Palestinians.

Third world aspiring hegemons also resembled each other in their choices of strategic responses to threats of domestic origin. Brazil, China, India and Nigeria, while employing accommodation and counterthreat on occasion, relied heavily on state strengthening. This reflected their determination to overcome the weakness of the political institutions from which their forbearers dealt with Europeans and North Americans. When the Cold War had been most intense, the Brazilian, Chinese, Indian and Nigerian states proved fragile platforms from which to resist the United States and the Soviet Union. The superpowers, and foreigners in general, achieved important successes in compromising the loyalties of Brazilians, Chinese, Indians and Nigerians. Thus state strengthening came to include increasing the capabilities of governing elites to control their own citizens. A stable legitimate domestic order strengthened the aspiring hegemon's ability to exercise regional leadership.

A shifting of attention to the regional arena again finds the two pariah hegemons with similar response patterns. Both viewed deterrence through defense and allying, as well as counterthreat, as obvious and necessary. Here it is instructive to recall that Israel and South Africa shared perceptions of significant military threats being directed against them, not to mention that both felt themselves subject to the highest possible level of political threat from their neighbors. Thus Jerusalem and Pretoria selected strategies for dealing with implacable protagonists, not for allies or partners. Their choice is additional evidence of pariah hegemon siege mentality, with its assumption that accommodation will be seen as weakness. Weakness, in this context, was perceived as inciting hostile neighbors to violence.

The moderate reliance Israel and South Africa placed on state strengthening reflected perceptions of the regional power balance. At least in their regional spheres, Jerusalem and Pretoria viewed themselves as politically and economically stronger than their enemies. They saw crash efforts at economic and political development as yielding only marginal increments in security, especially when compared to allying with powerful external states or organizing optimally the advantages they already possessed.

In responding to threats from the regional arena, third world aspiring hegemons also resembled each other. Brazil, India, China, and Nigeria placed heavy reliance on state strengthening. This reflected an important lesson that they had learned from their dealings with the superpowers; weakness invites exploitation. Third world hegemons calculated that the acquisition of multidimensional capabilities, especially technological sophistication, was a prerequisite for successfully influencing their neighbors on a sustained basis. Accommodation and defense through deterrence and allying, while never discarded, were less valued. Finally, given the global weaknesses of third world hegemons, counterthreat was perceived by them as an option of last resort or desperation.

Responses to threats from the global arena found the United States, when defending its position in the Circum-Caribbean, to be relying heavily on military capabilities. In addition, coordinating bargainer state political and economic policies was important. Multidimensional advantages provided incentives for falling into line that bargainer states found hard to resist. Washington's capabilities also were expressed in the sanctions implicit in counterthreat. Perhaps because its culture glorified a frontier style of coercive leadership, the United States appeared to lack enthusiasm for the accommodation strategy.

Pariah hegemons, in their responses to threats from the global arena, were more inclined to experiment with accommodation than the United States. This reflected the need for extraregional support to off-balance their neighbors' hostility. Security for Israel and South Africa, far more than for the United States, depended on the backing and approval of influential external states. Thus, when pariah policy makers decided that global trends were weakening their regional position, they embraced defense through allying with extraregional powers. Finally, pariah hegemons became apprehensive when external states provided technological assistance to their neighbors. Always on guard against any increase in the relative economic capability of other regional states, they especially feared the transfer of military technology.

Brazil, Nigeria, China and India exhibited similarities and differences when responding to threats from the global arena to their regional aspirations. For reasons discussed earlier, all four placed heavy reliance on state strengthening. Despite enjoying local power advantages, failure by any of the four to add new capabilities consigned it to being an "aspirant" with special regional status, rather than the guardian over a geopolitical sphere of influence. Brazil and Nigeria, in contrast to China and India, placed heavy reliance on accommodation. This reflected the greater absolute power of the Asian states, and the higher vulnerability of Brazil and Nigeria to influences outside of their own subordinate state system.

China and India, when faced with threats to their regional position from the larger international system, also relied heavily on defense through deterrence and allying. Upon confronting the same situation, Brazil gave only moderate importance to this option. In contrast, Nigeria's reliance on defense through deterrence and allying was low. Again the explanation would seem to reside in India and China's greater capability to mobilize resources which would give global powers pause when considering regional intervention. Brazil, despite its growing economy and sophisticated arms industry, was handicapped by geography. It sought special influence within a region that many in the United States viewed as part of their Latin American sphere. Thus attempts by Brasilia to exercise special influence in South America ran a high risk of activating opposition from Washington. Finally, underdevelopment, fragile national unity, and a petroleum dependent economy made it almost impossible for Nigeria to oppose intrusions into West Africa by powerful outsiders.

No third world hegemon placed heavy reliance on counterthreat as a response to threats emanating from the larger international environment. China and India, despite their standing among third world hegemons, remained vulnerable and underdeveloped. They feared that counterthreat, particularly against an OECD country, invited economic, and possibly military, retaliation. Brazil (concerned about confronting a superpower) and Nigeria (fearful for its continuation as a unified state) preferred to avoid counterthreat altogether.

To summarize, similarities and differences in strategic response selection mirrored the strengths and weakness of the seven aspiring hegemons. Three broad patterns of strategic responses emerged: the first associated with the superpower; the second with pariah states; and, the third with regional influentials in the third world. Each kind of aspiring hegemon possessed analogous resources with which to pursue and consolidate subordinate state system influence. Aspirants behaved in ways that played to their comparative advantage. States with similar strengths and weaknesses favored similar strategic responses. This suggests that when pursuing special regional influence, structural dynamics may be at least as important in assigning priorities among alternative strategic responses as threat content.

Hegemonic Aspirations, Regional International Systems: Concluding Comments

The basic premise of this volume affirmed the growing importance of subordinate state systems, and efforts by influential states to acquire special prerogatives within restricted geopolitical arenas. Specifically, the focus was on how states desiring special regional influence perceived threats to their designs; and, on how they responded to these perceptions. Not only is this topic one of primary importance for foreign policy makers and international relations theorists, its significance is increasing. The insights of this volume serve as starting points for better understanding and more systematically analyzing regional international politics. In closing, therefore, this chapter identifies and discuss briefly the most important of these starting points.

The data suggest four directions for future research as likely to provide fruitful insights into the structure and dynamics of regional international systems. They are: distillation of the critical dynamics identified in this conclusion into a simpler model; analysis of interaction between the role of hegemon and the other roles that regionally influential states have internalized; analysis of the threat perceptions and strategic responses of bargainer states; and, identification of the threat perceptions and strategic responses within regions that lack an aspiring hegemonic, and their comparison with the perceptions and responses of regions profiled in this volume.

The structures and processes that have been identified are multifaceted and complex. They begin with basic similarities ranging from the blocking out and passing of information by "lessons learned" filtering to the impact that "kind" and "intensity" of perceived threat exerts on strategic response selection. Important differences also appeared. One grouping revolved about variations between systems having a superpower hegemon, a pariah hegemon, and a third world aspiring hegemon. Another focused on systems in which an outside power was attempting to displace the current regional influential. In addition, changes occurred over time; although, beginning in the middle 1960s, all subordinate state systems became more autonomous.

The structures and processes of regional hegemon threat perception and strategic response remain to be distilled into an integrative theory. To create good theory, two requirements must be satisfied: conceptualization should describe accurately a large class of observations on the basis of a paradigm that contains a few arbitrary elements; and, this model should make definite predictions about the results of future observations. Thus the first additional research task is to integrate this volume's findings and insights with other work on regional powers. The few "essential but arbitrary" elements of such a synthesis must be crafted with an eye to making accurate predictions about how aspiring hegemons perceive and respond to threats to their position within regional international systems.

The second and third directions suggested for future research would further illuminate the struggle for special regional influence. The second is close to what Walker and Holsti have labeled role location. Here the focus is on examining how regionally influential states assign a preference to the hegemon role among the many role possibilities. In addition to enriching role theory, this research would illuminate differences in how superpower hegemons, pariah hegemons, and developing area aspirants perceive and respond to threat. The third direction for future research describes and analyzes the threat perceptions and strategic responses of bargainer states when they are subjected to pressures from aspiring regional hegemons. Focusing of bargainer state threat perception and response is the other side of the coin from this study's principal concern. Along with suggested research on aspiring hegemon role selection, it promises to advance the construction of a comprehensive theory of state behavior within international regions.

The final focus for suggested research would examine subordinate state systems which lack a state capable of aspiring to regional hegemony. Almost no work has been done on them; as with regions that revolve about a state seeking to exercise special geopolitical influence, they are of growing importance.

Notes

1. Kenneth Waltz, *Theory of International Politics*, (Reading, MA: Lexington, 1979), pp. 118–119.

2. "Appendix 1, Properties of National Role Conceptions and Their Sources" in Stephen G. Walker, ed., *Role Theory and Foreign Policy Analysis*, (Durham: Duke University Press, 1987), pp. 265–266. Role issues or substantive problem areas are defined as follows: (1) *Territorial/defense*. The nation maintains, defends, or expands its own or its collaborator's territorial integrity or security, or inhibits that of his competitors; (2) *Ideological*. The nation defends, promotes, or inhibits a value system or way of life (Examples: communism, capitalism, socialism, democracy); (3) *Political/diplomatic*. The nation affects the positions or relationships between states—for example, a decision maker identifies his nation's relationships with other states as nonalignment, peaceful coexistence, or a mediator between states; (4) *Universal values*. The nation promotes a situation of peace, racial harmony, justice, etc.; and (5) *Economic*. The nation maintains or expands its own or another's economic resources or industrial development.

3. C.V. Crabb Jr., *American Foreign Policy in a Nuclear Age*, (New York: Harper and Row, 1972), p. 1.

4. Compare Manuel Castells, "High Technology, World Development and Structural Transformation: The Trends and the Debate," in Toivo Miljan, ed., *The Political Economy of North-South Relations*, (Peterborough, Canada: Broadview Press, 1987), pp. 11–38.

5. "Appendix 4, Descriptions for Roles Associated with Selected Core Political System Beliefs in the CREON Regime Orientations" in Walker, ed., *Role Theory and Foreign Policy Analysis*, pp. 282–289.

6. Content analysis of the individual chapters by the editor.

7. Also see M.A. East and C.F. Hermann, eds., *Why Nations Act: Theoretical Perspective for Comparative Foreign Policy Studies*, (Beverly Hills, CA: Sage, 1978), pp. 122–124.

8. Rodney W. Jones and Steven Hildreth, eds., *Emerging Powers: Defense and Security in the Third World*, (Westport, CT: Praeger/Greenwood Press, 1986), pp. 403–409, also documents this relationship.

9. The text of the summit's political declaration appears in the *New York Times*, July 11, 1990.

10. These classifications reflect the collective judgment of the individual contributors and the editor.

Selected Bibliography

This bibliography includes some items referred to in the notes as well as additional sources that would be useful for a further study of aspiring hegemon threat perception and strategic response. It is divided into eight parts: The first section includes works of conceptual and theoretical interest, and the other seven sections correspond to the chapters on subordinate state systems.

Works of Conceptual Interest

Ayoob, Mohammed, ed. *Regional Security in the Third World.* Boulder: Westview, 1986.

Baker Fox, Annette. *Politics of Attraction: Four Middle Powers and the United States.* New York: Columbia University Press, 1977.

Cantori, Louis J. and Steven Spiegel. "The International Politics of Regions," *Polity,* Vol. 2, No. 4 (1970), pp. 397–425.

Cohen. *Threat Perception in International Crisis.* Seattle: University of Washington Press, 1979.

Cottam, Marta L. *Foreign Policy Decision Making: The Influence of Cognition.* Boulder: Westview, 1986.

Falk, Richard A. and Saul H. Medlovitz. *Regional Politics and World Order.* San Francisco: W.H. Freedman and Co., 1973.

Jones, Rodney W. and Steven A. Hildreth, eds. *Emerging Powers: Defense and Security in the Third World.* New York: Praeger, 1986.

Keal, Paul. "Contemporary Understanding About Spheres of Influence," *Review of International Studies,* Vol. 9, No. 3 (1983), pp. 153–72.

Masters, Roger D. "A Multi-bloc Model of the International System," *American Political Science Review,* Vol. 55, No. 4 (December 1961), pp. 782–794.

Rosecrance, Richard N. "Reward, Punishment, and Interdependence," *Journal of Conflict Resolution,* Vol. 25, No. 1 (1981), pp. 31–46.

Spiegel, Steven. *Dominance and Diversity: The International Hierarchy.* Boston: Little, Brown & Co., 1972.

Thompson, William R. "The Regional Subsystem," *International Studies Quarterly,* Vol. 17 (March 1973), pp. 89–117.

Tow, William T. *Subregional Security Cooperation in the Third World.* Boulder: Lynne Rienner, 1990.

Triska, Jan F. "Dominant Powers and Their Dependencies," *Kosmas,* Vol.3, No. 1 (1985), pp. 11–24.

Wagner, R. Harrison. "Deterrence and Bargaining," *Journal of Conflict Resolution*, Vol. 26 (1982), pp. 329–357.

Walker, Stephen G. ed. *Role Theory and Foreign Policy Analysis*. Durham: Duke University Press, 1987.

Yalem, Ronald. *Regional Subsystems and World Politics*. Tucson: University of Arizona, 1970.

Zimmerman, William. "Hierarchical Regional Systems and the Politics of System Boundaries," *International Organization*, Vol. 26, No. 1 (1972), pp. 18–36.

The United States and the Caribbean Basin

Atkins, G. Pope. *Latin America in the International Political System*. Boulder: Westview, 1989.

Child, John. *Unequal Alliance: The Inter-American Military System, 1938–1978*. Boulder: Westview 1980.

Craig, Richard B. "Domestic Implications of Illicit Colombian Drug Production and Trafficking," *Journal of International Studies and World Affairs*, Vol. 23 (August 1983), pp. 325–350.

Etheredge, Lloyd S. *Can Governments Learn? American Foreign Policy and Central American Revolutions*. New York: Pergamon, 1985.

Erisman, H. Michael. *Cuba's International Relations: The Anatomy of a Nationalistic Foreign Policy*. Boulder: Westview, 1985.

Falcoff, Mark and Robert Royal, eds. *The Continuing Crisis: U.S. Policy in Central America and the Caribbean*. Washington, D.C.: The Ethics and Public Policy Center 1987.

Kaufman, Edy. *The Superpowers and their Spheres of Influence: The United States and the Soviet Union in Eastern Europe and Latin America*. London: Croom-Helm, 1976.

Kirkpatrick, Jeane. "Dictatorships and Double Standards," *Commentary*, (November 1979), 34–45.

Larkin, Bruce D. *Vital Interests: The Soviet Issue in U.S. Central American Policy*. Boulder: Lynne Reinner, 1988.

Langley, Lester. *Struggle for the American Mediterranean: United States-European Rivalry in the Gulf-Caribbean, 1776–1904*. Athens: University of Georgia Press, 1976.

Langley, Lester. *The United States and The Caribbean in the Twentieth Century*, 4th ed. Athens: University of Georgia Press, 1989.

Marshall, Jonathan, et al. *The Iran-Contra Connection: Secret Teams and Covert Operations in the Reagan Era*. Boston: South End, 1987.

Martz, John D. ed. *United States Policy in Latin America: A Quarter Century of Crisis and Challenge, 1961–1986*. Lincoln: University of Nebraska, 1988.

Myers, David J. *Venezuela's Pursuit of Caribbean Basin Interests: Implications for United States National Security*. Santa Monica: Rand R-2994-AF, 1985.

Padelford, Edward A. "Caribbean Security and U.S. Political Military Pressure," *Strategic Review*, Vol. 14 (Fall 1986), pp. 54–62.

Pastor, Robert A. *Condemned to Repetition: The United States and Nicaragua.* Princeton: Princeton, 1988.
Roett, Riordan, ed. *Mexico's External Relations in the 1990s.* Boulder: Lynne Reinner, 1990.
Serbin, Andres. *Caribbean Geopolitics: Toward Security Through Peace, tr. Sabet Ramirez.* Boulder: Lynne Reinner, 1990.
Watson, Bruce W. and Peter G. Tsouras, eds. *Operation Just Cause: The U.S. Intervention in Panama.* Boulder: Westview, 1990.
Wiarda, Howard. *Latin America at the Crossroads: Debt and Development Strategies for the 1990s.* Boulder: Westview 1986.

Israel: An Aspiring Hegemon

Al-Mshat, Abdul-Monem. "The Egyptian-Israeli Settlement," *Journal of Arab Affairs,* Vol. 5 (Spring 1986), pp. 81–110.
Bossiouni, M. Chief. "Reflections on the Arab-Israeli Peace Process and its Future Prospects," *American-Arab Affairs* (Summer 1987), pp. 47–63.
Brecher, Michael. *The Foreign Policy System of Israel: Setting, Images, Process.* New Haven: Yale, 1972.
Cohen, Saul. *The Geopolitics of Israel's Border Question.* Jaffee Center for Strategic Studies, Study No. 7. Boulder: Westview Press, 1986.
Eban, Abba. *An Autobiography.* New York: Random House, 1977.
Harkabi, Yohoshafat. *Israel's Fateful Hour.* New York: Harper & Row, 1986.
Rabinovich, Itamar and Jehuda Reinharz, eds. *Israel in the Middle East.* New York: Oxford University Press, 1984.
Freedman, Robert O., ed. *Israel in the Begin Era.* New York: Praeger, 1982.
Hasan Al-Naqeeb, Khaldoun. *Society and State in the Arab Gulf Peninsula: A Different Perspective.* London: Routledge, 1991.
Klinghoffer, Arthur Jay. "Soviet-Israeli Relations and a Middle East Peace Settlement," *Crossroads,* Vol. 23 (1987), pp. 1–13.
Lanir, Zvi, ed. *Israeli Security Planning in the 1980s.* Jaffee Center for Strategic Studies. New York: Praeger, 1984.
Lewis, Samuel W. "Israeli Political Reality and the Search for Middle East Peace," *SAIS Review,* Vol. 7 (Winter/Spring 1987), pp. 67–80.
Peretz, Don. *Intifada: The Palestinian Uprising.* Boulder: Westview, 1990.
Peri, Yoram. *Between Battles and Ballots, Israeli Military in Politics.* Cambridge: Cambridge University Press, 1983.
Quandt, William B., Fuad Jabber, Ann Mosely Lesch. *The Politics of Palestinian Nationalism.* Berkeley: University of California Press, 1973.
Reich, Bernard, ed. *The Powers in the Middle East, the Ultimate Strategic Arena.* New York: Praeger, 1987.
Rabinovich, Itamar. *The War for Lebanon, 1970–1983.* Ithaca: Cornell, 1984.
Safram, Nadav. *Israel: The Embattled Ally.* Cambridge: Harvard, 1978.
Smooha, Sammy. *Israel, Pluralism and Conflict.* Berkeley: California, 1978.
Yaniv, Avner. *Dilemmas of Security, Politics Strategy and the Israeli Experience in Lebanon.* New York: Oxford, 1987.

South Africa in Southern Africa

Berger, Peter L. and Bobby Godsell, eds. *A Future South Africa: Visions, Strategies and Realities.* Boulder: Westview, 1989.

Bissell, Richard E. and Chester A. Crocker, eds. *South Africa into the 1980s.* Boulder: Westview, 1979.

Bryant, Coralie, ed. *Poverty, Policy, and Food Security in Southern Africa.* Boulder: Lynne Reinner, 1988.

Chen, Stephen. *Exporting Apartheid: Foreign Policies in Southern Africa 1978–1988.* New York: St. Martins, 1990.

Collins, Peter, ed. *Thinking About South Africa.* New York: St Martins, 1990.

Davies, Robert and Dan O'Meara. "Total Strategy in Southern Africa: An Analysis of South African Regional Policy since 1978," *Journal of Southern African Studies,* Vol. 11, No. 2 (April 1985), pp. 183–211.

February, Vernon A. *The Afrikaners of South Africa.* London: Kegan Paul International, 1990.

Grundy, Kenneth W. *Confrontation and Accommodation in Southern Africa: The Limits of Independence.* Berkeley: University of California Press, 1973.

Harrison, David. *The White Tribe of Africa: South Africa in Perspective.* Berkeley: University of California, 1981.

Jaster, Robert S. *South Africa and Its Neighbours: The Dynamics of Regional Conflict,* Adelphi Papers No. 209. London: International Institute for Strategic Studies, Summer 1986.

Karis, Thomas. "Revolution in the Making: Black Politics in South Africa," *Foreign Affairs,* Vol. 62, No. 2 (Winter 1983-84), pp. 378–406.

Keller, Edmond J. and Louis A. Picard. *South Africa in Southern Africa: Domestic Change and International Conflict.* Boulder: Lynne Reinner, 1989.

Khan, Haider Ali. *The Political Economy of Sanctions Against Aparteid.* Boulder: Lynne Reinner, 1989.

Msabaha, Ibrahim S.R. and Timothy Shaw, eds. *Confrontation and Liberation in Southern Africa: Regional Directions After the Nkomati Accord.* Boulder: Westview, 1987.

Mungazi, Dickson, A. *Struggle For Social Change in Southern Africa: Visions of Liberty.* New York: Crane Russak, 1989.

Nolutshungu, Sam C. *South Africa in Africa: A Study in Ideology and Foreign Policy.* New York: Africana, 1975.

Simon, Alan. "Rhodesian Immigrants in South Africa: Government Media and a Lesson for South Africa," *Africa Affairs* (U.K.), Vol. 87, No. 346 (January 1988), pp. 53–68.

Spence, Jack E. *The Strategic Significance of Southern Africa.* London: Royal United Services Institution, 1970.

St. Jorre, John de. "South Africa Embattled," *Foreign Affairs,* Vol. 65, No. 3 (1986), pp. 538–563.

Thompson, Leonard. *The Political Mythology of Apartheid.* New Haven: Yale University Press, 1985.

Van de Merwe, Hendrink W., and Meyer Gabi. "Negotiation and Mediation in S. Africa in Perspective," *South African International Quatery* (S.Africa), Vol. 18, No. 2 (Oct 87), pp. 79–92.

India and South Asia

Ayoob, Mohammed. "India in South Asia: The Quest for Regional Predominance," *World Policy Journal*, Vol. 17, No. 1. (Winter 1989–90), pp. 107–134.

Khan, Asgar. *The First Round: Indo-Pakistan War 1965.* Sahibabad: Vikas Publishing House, 1979.

Kodikara, Shelton U. *South Asian Strategic Issues: Sri Lankan Perspectives.* Newbury Park: Sage, 1990.

Kukreja, Veena. "Parliamentary Democracy in South Asia: A Regional Comparative Perspective," *India Quarterly* (India), Vol. 2 (Ap-Ju, 86), pp. 167–176.

Levi, Werner. *The Challenge of World Politics in South and South East Asia.* New Jersey: Prentice Hall, 1968.

Mahmoodi, Elahi. "From Confrontation to Cooperation: Emerging Regionalism in South Asia," *Asian Profile*, Vol. 14 (December 1986), pp. 541–56.

Paranjpe, Shrikant. *India and South Asia Since 1971.* New Delhi: Radiant Publishers, 1985.

Phadnis, Urmila. *Ethnicity and Nation Building in South Asia.* Newbury Park: Sage, 1990.

Prasad, Biseshwar. *Our Foreign Policy Legacy: A Study of British Indian Foreign Policy.* New Delhi: Peoples Publishing House, 1965.

Sisson, Richard and Leo E. Rose. *War and Succession: India, Pakistan and the Creation of Bangladesh.* Berkeley and Los Angeles: University of California, 1990.

Spencer, Jonathan. *Sri Lanka: History and the Roots of Conflict.* London: Routhledge, 1990.

Syed, Anwar Hussein. *China and Pakistan: Diplomacy of an Entent Cordiale.* Amherst: University of Massachusetts Press, 1974.

Thomas, Raju G.C. "The Afghanistan Crisis and South Asian Security," *Journal of Strategic Studies*, Vol. 4 (December 1981), pp. 415–434.

Thomas, Raju G.C. *Indian Security Policy.* Princeton: Princeton University, 1986.

Waqif, Arif A. *South Asian Cooperation In Industry, Energy, and Technology.* Newbury Park: Sage, 1988.

Wignaraja, Ponna, ed. *The Challenge in South Asia: Development, Democracy and Regional Cooperation.* Newbury Park: Sage 1989.

China and Southeast Asia

Duiker, William J. *China and Vietnam: The Roots of Conflict.* Berkeley: California: 1986.

Fifeld, Russell. *Americans in Southeast Asia: The Roots of Commitment.* New York: Thomas Y. Crowell, 1973.

Gunn, Geoffrey. "Indonesian-Chinese Relations," *Asian Pacific Review* (Australian), Vol.5 (Summer 87), pp. 17–33.

Israeli, Raphael. "Living in China's Shadow," *Orbis*, Vol. 31, No. 3 (Fall 87), pp. 339–350.

Kiernan, Ben and Chantou Boua, eds. *Peasants and Politics in Kampuchea, 1942–1981*. London: Zed, 1982.

Leifer, Michael. *ASEAN and the Security of South-East Asia*. London: Routledge, 1989.

Lo, Chi-Kin. *China's Policy Toward Territorial Disputes: The Case of the South China Sea Islands*. London: Routledge: 1989.

Nelson, Harvey W. *Power and Insecurity: Beijing, Moscow, and Washington, 1949–1988*. Boulder: Lynne Reinner, 1989.

Silverstein, J., ed. *Southeast Asia in World War II*. New Haven: Yale University 1966.

Pike, Douglas. *Vietnam and the Soviet Union: Anatomy of an Alliance*. Boulder: Westview, 1987.

Purcell, Victor. *The Chinese in Southeast Asia*. London: Oxford, 1965.

Suryadanita, Leo. *China and the ASEAN States: The Ethnic Chinese Dimension*. Singapore: Singapore University, 1982.

Tajima, Takashi. *China and South-East Asia: Strategic Interests and Policy Perspectives*. London: Adalphi Papers, Winter 1981), No. 172.

Tanham, George. *Military Basing & U.S.-Soviet Military Balance in Southeast Asia: A Vietnam Legacy*. Bristol: Crane Russak, 1989.

Thien, Ton That. *The Foreign Politics of the Communist Party of Vietnam*. Bristol: Crane Russak, 1989.

Tilman, Robert O. *Southeast Asia and the Enemy Beyond: ASEAN Perceptions of External Threats*. Boulder: Westview, 1987.

Vickery, Michael. *Cambodia 1975–1982*. Boston: South End, 1984.

Wong, John. *The Political Economy of China's Changing Relations with Southeast Asia*. London: McMillan, 1984.

Zasloff, Joseph J. and Leonard Unger. *Laos: Beyond the Revolution*. New York: St. Martins, 1990.

Brazil: The Quest for South American Leadership

Atkins, G. Pope, ed. *South America into the 1990s: Evolving International Relationships in a New Era*. Boulder: Westview, 1989.

Baily, Samuel L. *The United States and the Development of South America, 1945–1975* New York: New Viewpoints, 1976.

Bond, Robert D. "Venezuela, Brazil and the Amazon Basin," *Orbis* (Fall 1978), pp. 635–650.

Braveboy-Wagner, Jacqueline Anne. *The Venezuelan-Guyana Border Dispute: Britain's Colonial Legacy in Latin America*. Boulder: Westview, 1984.

Child, Jack. *Geopolitics and Conflict in South America: Quarrels Among Neighbors*. New York: Praeger, 1984.

Franko-Jones, Patrice. *The Brazilian Defense Industry: A Case Study of Public-Private Collaboration.* Boulder: Westview, 1991.
Kearns, Kevin C. "The Andean Common Market," *Journal of Inter- American Studies and World Affairs,* Vol. 14 (May 1972), pp. 225–249.
Kelley Philip and Jack Child. *Geopolitics of the Southern Cone and Antarctica.* Boulder: Lynne Reinner, 1988.
Levin, Peter. "The Development Program of the Rio de la Plata Basin," *Journal of Developing Areas,* No. 6 (July 1972), pp. 493–522.
Lisansky, Judith. *Migrants to Amazonia: Spontaneous Colonization in the Brazilian Frontier.* Boulder: Westview, 1989.
Morris, Michael, ed. *Great Power Relations in Argentina, Chile and Antarctica.* London: St. Martins, 1990.
Myers, David J. "Brazil: Reluctant Pursuit of the Nuclear Option," *Orbis* (Winter 1984), pp. 881–911.
Porzecanski, Arturo. *Uruguay's Tupamaros.* New York: Praeger, 1973.
Roett, Riordan. "Democracy and Debt in South America: A Continent's Dilemma," *Foreign Affairs,* Vol. 62 (1984), pp. 695–720.
Schneider, Ronald M. *Brazil: Foreign Policy of a Future World Power.* Boulder: Westview, 1976.
Selcher, Wayne A., ed. *Brazil in the International System: The Rise of a Middle Power.* Boulder: Westview, 1981.
Ware, David. "The Amazon Treaty: A Turning Point in Latin American Cooperation?" *Texas International Law Journal,* Vol. 15 (Winter 1980), pp. 117–137.
Wesson, Robert, ed. *The United States and Brazil: Limits of Influence.* New York: Praeger, 1981.

Nigeria in West Africa

Adebayo A., *Power and Politics.* Ibadan: Spectrum, 1987.
Adekson, J. Bayo. *Nigeria in Search of a Stable Civil-Military System.* New York: Praeger, 1986.
Akindele, R. A. and C. Ate Bassey. "Nigeria's Foreign Policy, 1986–2000 A.D.: Background to and Reflections on the Views from Kuru," *Afrika Spectrum,* Vol. 21 (1986), pp. 363–370.
Akinola, Anthony A., "A Critique of Nigeria's Proposed Two-Party System," *The Journal of Modern African Studies,* Vol. 27 (1989), pp. 109–123.
Aluko, S. A., "How Many Nigerians: An Analysis of Nigeria's Census Problems, 1901–1963," *Journal of Modern African Studies,* Vol. 3 (October, 1965), pp. 371–392.
Arlinghaus, B. and P. H. Baker, eds. *African Armies: Evolution and Capabilities.* Boulder: Westview, 1986.
Baker, Pauline. "A Giant Staggers: Nigeria as an Emerging Regional Power," in Bruce Arlinghaus, ed., *African Security Issues.* New York: Praeger, 1986.
Burns, Sir Alan. *A History of Nigeria.* London: Allen & Unwin, 5th ed., 1955.
Diamond, Larry, "Nigeria Update," *Foreign Affairs* (Spring, 1986), pp. 326–336.

Johnson, Segun. "Burkina-Mali War: Is Nigeria Still a Regional Power," *India Quarterly*, Vol. 3 (July–September, 1986), pp. 294–308.

Kalu, Victor Eke. *Cimilitancy: Socialist Implications*. Enugu: Fourth Dimension Publications, 1986.

Kalu, Victor. *The Nigerian Condition*. Enugu: Fourth Dimension, 1987.

Mills, William F. S. *Elections in Nigeria: A Grassroots Perspective*. Boulder: Lynne Rienner, 1987.

Onwuka, Ralph I. and Timothy Shaw, eds. *Africa in World Politics*. London: MacMillan Press Ltd., 1989.

Oyediran Oyeleye, ed. *Nigerian Government & Politics Under Military Rule, 1966–1979*. New York: St. Martin's, 1979.

Oyovbaire, S. Egite. *Federalism in Nigeria: A Study in the Development of the Nigerian State*. New York: St. Martin's, 1984.

Panter-Brick, Keith, ed. *Soldiers and Oil: The Political Transformation of Nigeria*. Totowa, NJ: Frank Cass and Company, 1978.

Shaw, Timothy, "Nigeria Restrained: Foreign Policy Under Changing Political and Petroleum Regimes," *Annals of the American Academy of Political and Social Science*, No. 489 (January, 1987), pp. 40–51.

Shaw, Timothy and Olajide Aluko, eds. *Nigerian Foreign Policy: Alternative Perceptions and Projections*. New York: St. Martin's 1983.

Udo, R.K. *Geographical Regions of Nigeria*. Berkeley: University of California, 1970.

Zartman, I. William, ed. *The Political Economy of Nigeria*. New York: Praeger, 1983.

About the Editor and Contributors

David E. Albright is currently Professor of National Security Affairs at the Air War College, Maxwell Air Force Base, Alabama. Previously, he worked for more than a decade at the journal *Problems of Communism,* serving first as associate editor and later as senior text editor. He has also been a research associate at the Council on Foreign Relations in New York City and has traveled extensively throughout the developing areas. Dr. Albright has written numerous articles and book chapters on Soviet influence on the third world, especially Africa. Among his best known books on this topic are *Communism in Africa* and *The USSR and sub-Saharan Africa in the 1980s.*

G. Pope Atkins is Professor of Political Science at the United States Naval Academy. He has lived and worked in Argentina and Ecuador and has been a visiting scholar at the Brookings Institution, the Institute of Latin American Studies at the University of London, the Fondo para Avance de las Ciencias Sociales in Santo Domingo, and the international relations department at the London School of Economics and Political Science. He also has been a senior associate at the Center for Strategic and International Studies in Washington, D.C. Dr. Atkins has written extensively on Latin American international and comparative politics, including two books on the Dominican Republic.

Parris H. Chang is Professor of Political Science and Director of the Center for East Asian Studies at Penn State University. A native of Taiwan, he has lectured and undertaken research in the People's Republic of China and Japan. He has been a visiting Professor of Foreign Studies at Tokyo University. In addition, he has been a special advisor to President Bush and a consultant to the Department of State. Dr. Chang has written extensively on Chinese and South East Asian international and comparative politics, including two books on China.

Zhiduan Deng is a native of Canton, China. He received his Ph.D. in political science from Penn State University in May 1990. Dr. Deng, a Fulbright scholar, was awarded a B.A. from Shanghai's Fudan University and a M.A. from George Washington University.

Zachary T. Irwin is Associate Professor of Political Science at Penn State University-Erie, The Behrend College. He has traveled, lectured and undertaken research in the Middle East and Eastern Europe. Professor Irwin has published on the Middle East and communist political systems. He recently coauthored, the Prentice Hall text, *Introduction to Political Science.*

David J. Myers is Associate Professor of Political Science at Penn State University. He has traveled extensively throughout South America, the Caribbean Basin and Western Europe. Dr. Myers has been a visiting professor at the Central University of Venezuela, the Instituto de Estudios Superiores de Administracion (Caracas, Venezuela), and the U.S. Military Academy at West Point. He has published numerous articles and book chapters on Venezuelan politics, Latin American international relations and comparative urban politics; he is also the author of two books and the coeditor of another.

Shrikant Paranjpe is Reader in the Department of Defense and Strategic Studies, University of Poona, Pune, India. He has traveled extensively in the United States and South Asia. During 1984/85 he was a visiting Fulbright Research Fellow at the George Washington University in Washington, D.C. Dr. Paranjpe has published on Indian politics in journals in India and Western Europe; he is also the author of two books dealing with South Asian international relations.

Raju G.C. Thomas is Professor and Head of the Department of Political Science at Marquette University. A native of India, he has traveled extensively throughout South Asia, Western Europe, and North America. Dr. Thomas has been a visiting research scholar at the Center for International Studies at the Massachusetts Institute of Technology and the Center for International and Strategic Affairs at UCLA. He has published numerous book chapters and articles on international relations, Indian security policy and nuclear energy. Dr. Thomas authored two books on these subjects, and edited two others.

Anthony V. Williams is Associate Professor of Geography at Penn State University. A native of England, he has lived in and traveled extensively throughout tropical Africa and Western Europe. During 1988/89 he held a Fulbright Research fellowship in Cameroon; during 1989/90 he was a visiting fellow in the Subfaculty of Human Geography at the University of Amsterdam, Netherlands. He has published numerous articles and book chapters on African geopolitics and the uses of computers for geography research.

Index

www.ingramcontent.com/pod-product-compliance
Lightning Source LLC
LaVergne TN
LVHW011107300926
849160LV00008B/302
9780367300920